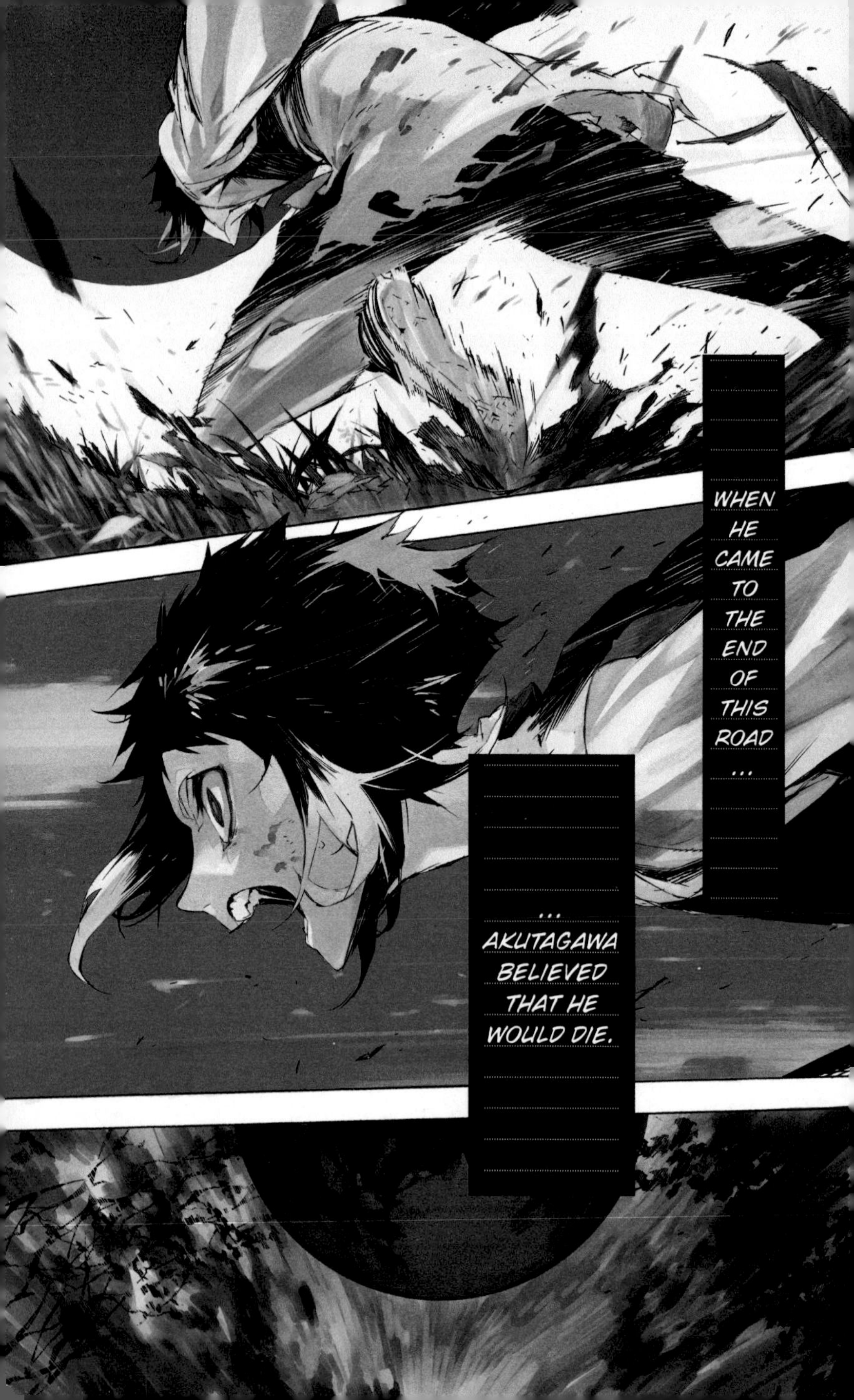
WHEN HE CAME TO THE END OF THIS ROAD...
...AKUTAGAWA BELIEVED THAT HE WOULD DIE.

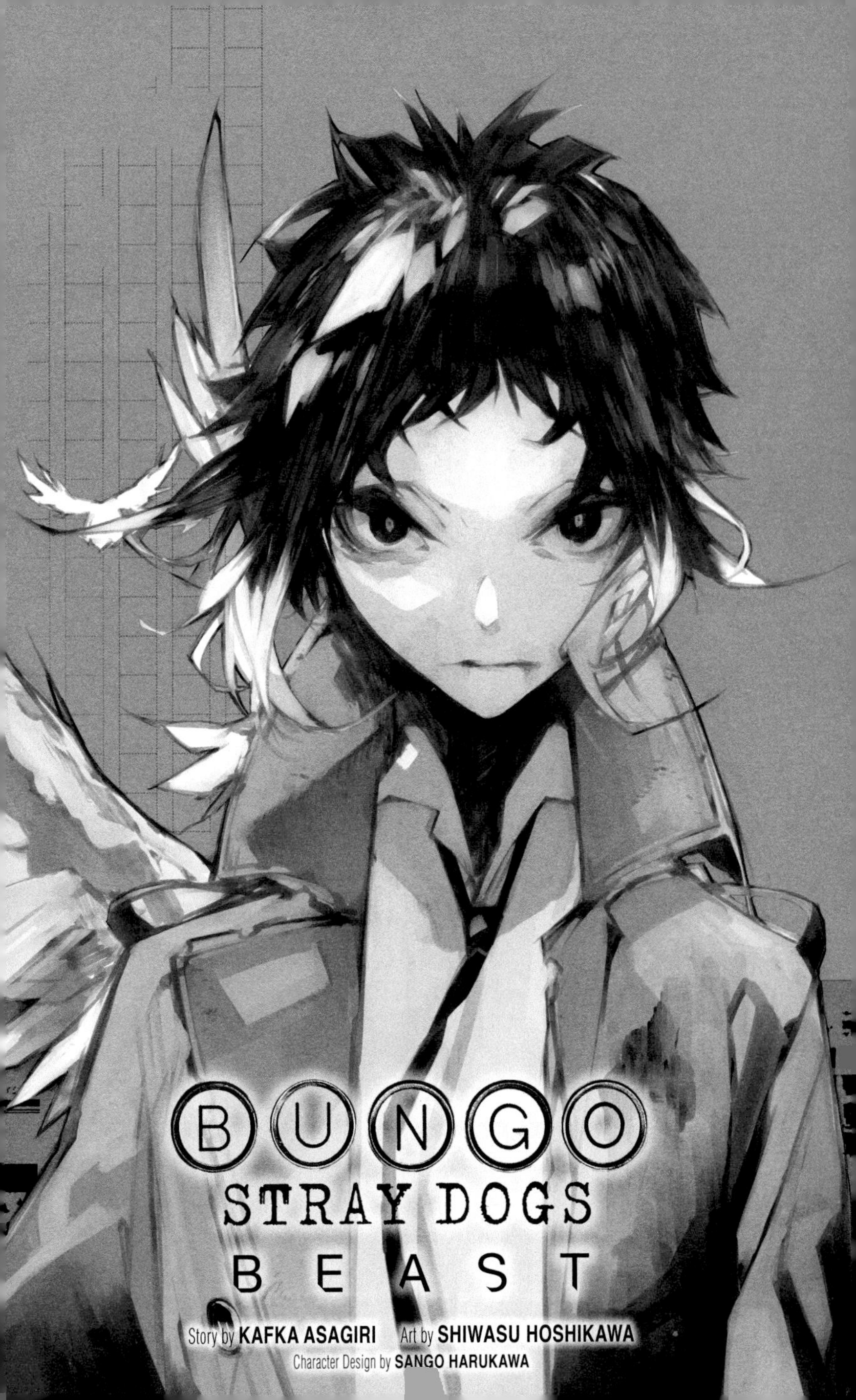
BUNGO
STRAY DOGS
BEAST
Story by KAFKA ASAGIRI
Art by SHIWASU HOSHIKAWA
Character Design by SANGO HARUKAWA

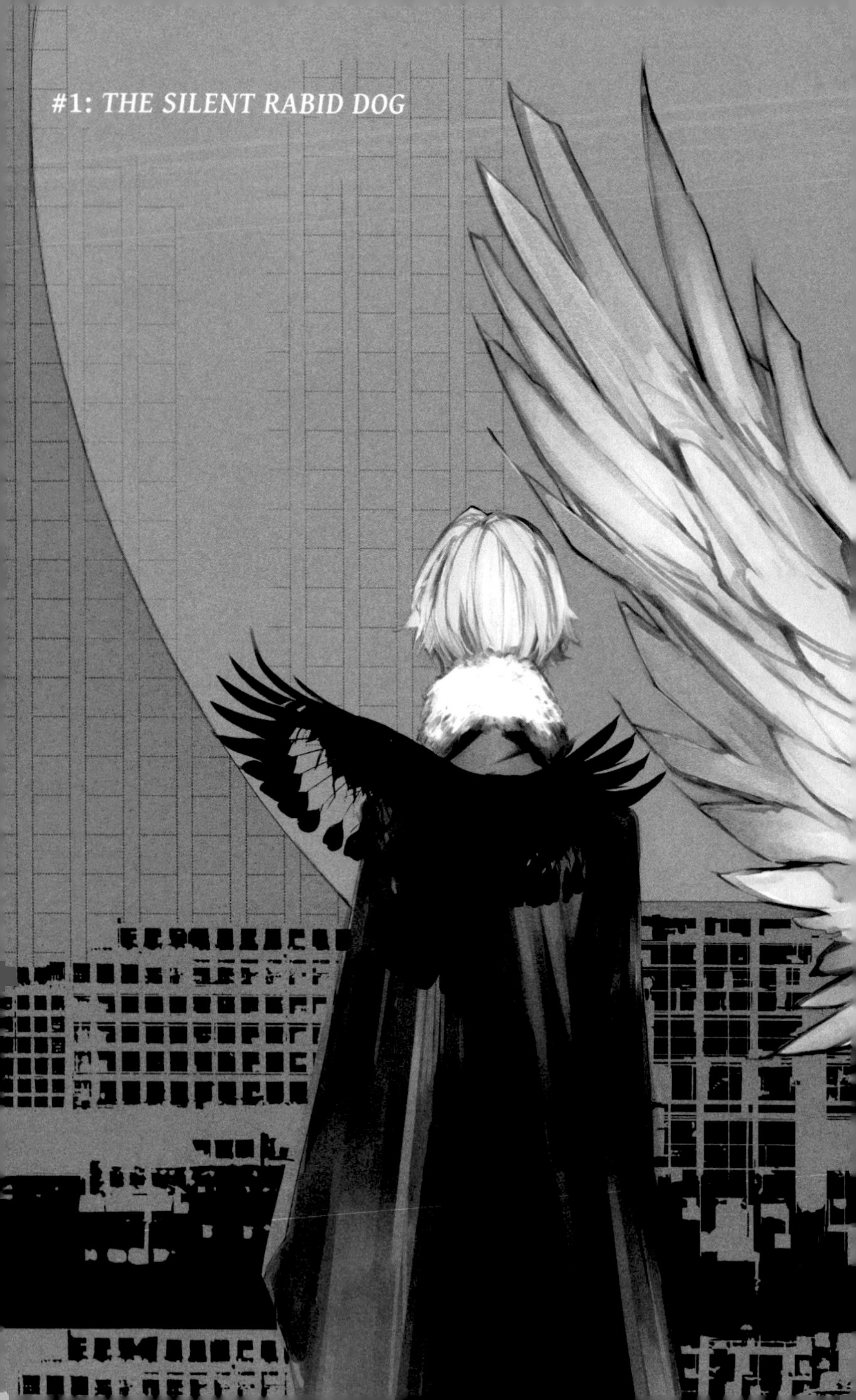
#1: THE SILENT RABID DOG

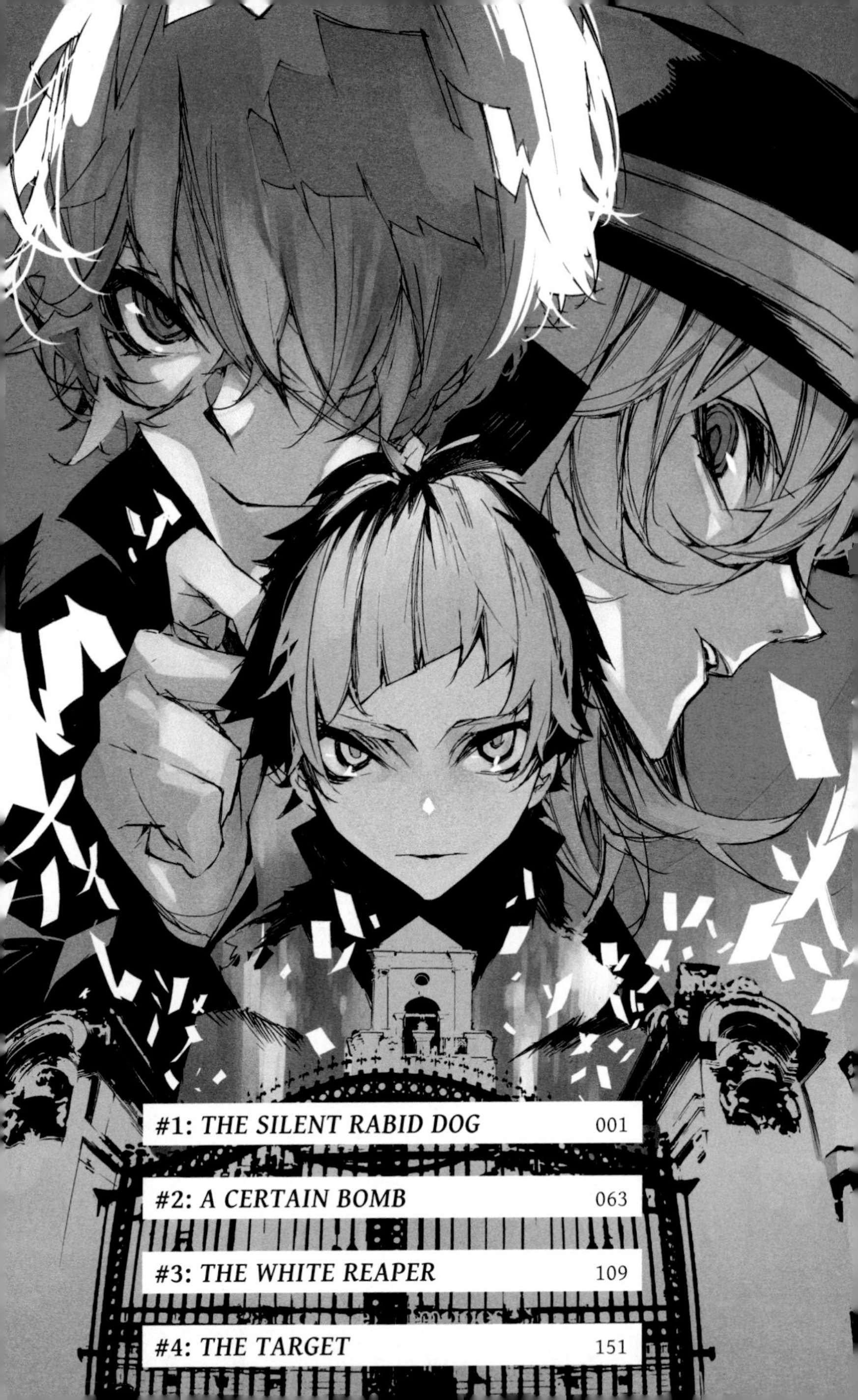

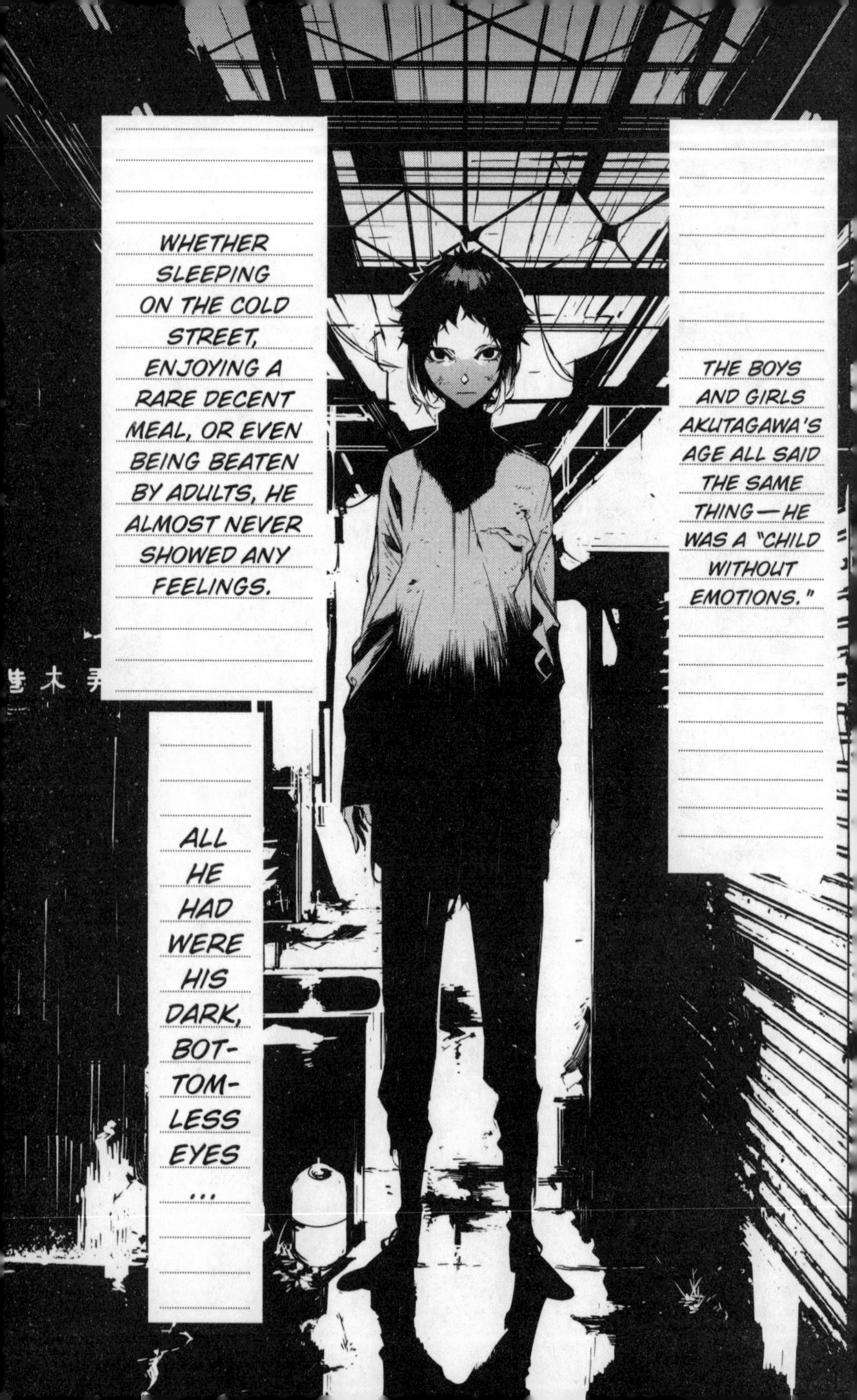
THE BOYS AND GIRLS AKUTAGAWA'S AGE ALL SAID THE SAME THING—HE WAS A "CHILD WITHOUT EMOTIONS."
WHETHER SLEEPING ON THE COLD STREET, ENJOYING A RARE DECENT MEAL, OR EVEN BEING BEATEN BY ADULTS, HE ALMOST NEVER SHOWED ANY FEELINGS.
ALL HE HAD WERE HIS DARK, BOT-TOM-LESS EYES...

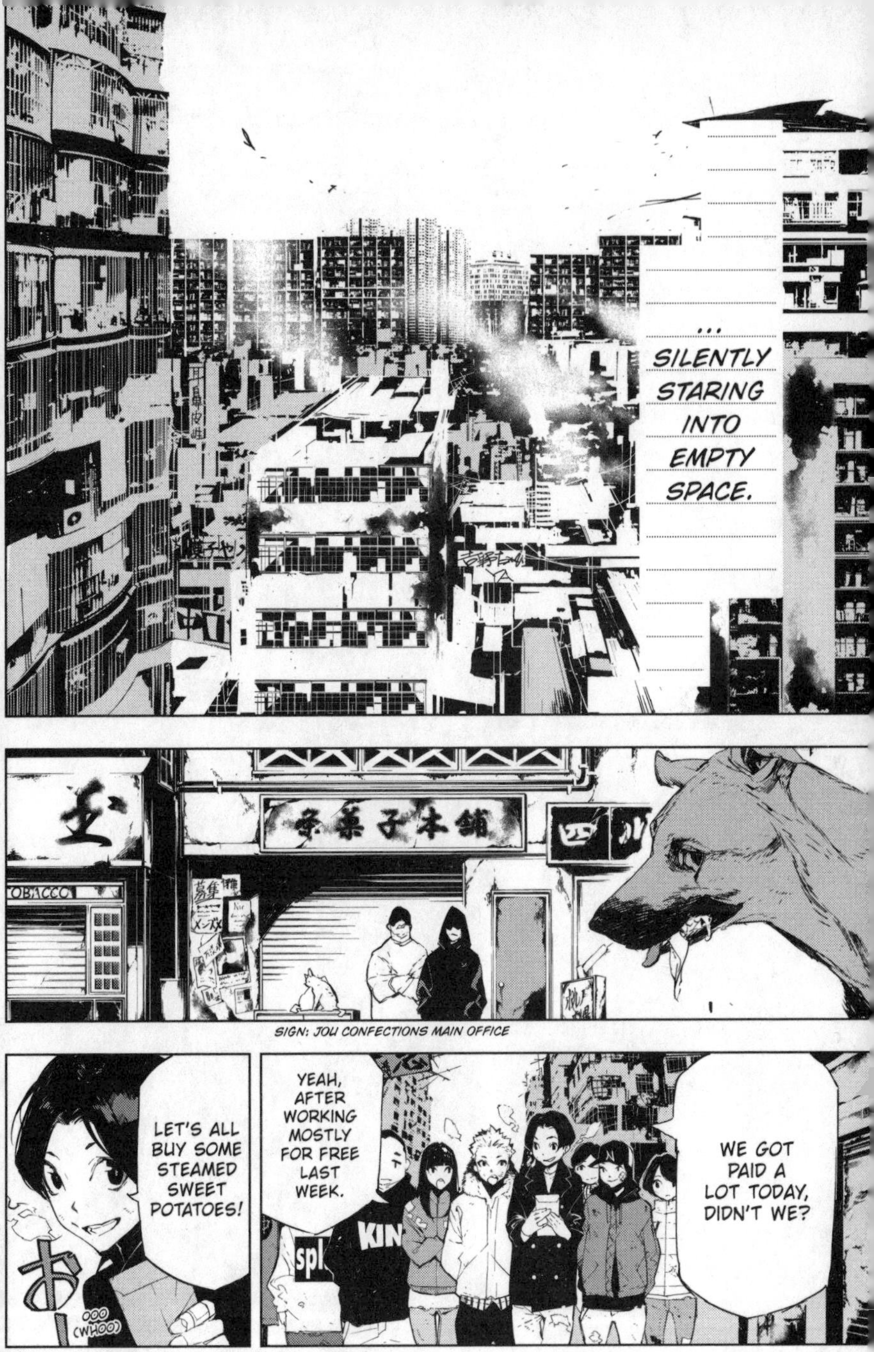
... SILENTLY STARING INTO EMPTY SPACE.
SIGN: JOU CONFECTIONS MAIN OFFICE
WE GOT PAID A LOT TODAY, DIDN'T WE?
YEAH, AFTER WORKING MOSTLY FOR FREE LAST WEEK.
LET'S ALL BUY SOME STEAMED SWEET POTATOES!
OOO (WHOO)

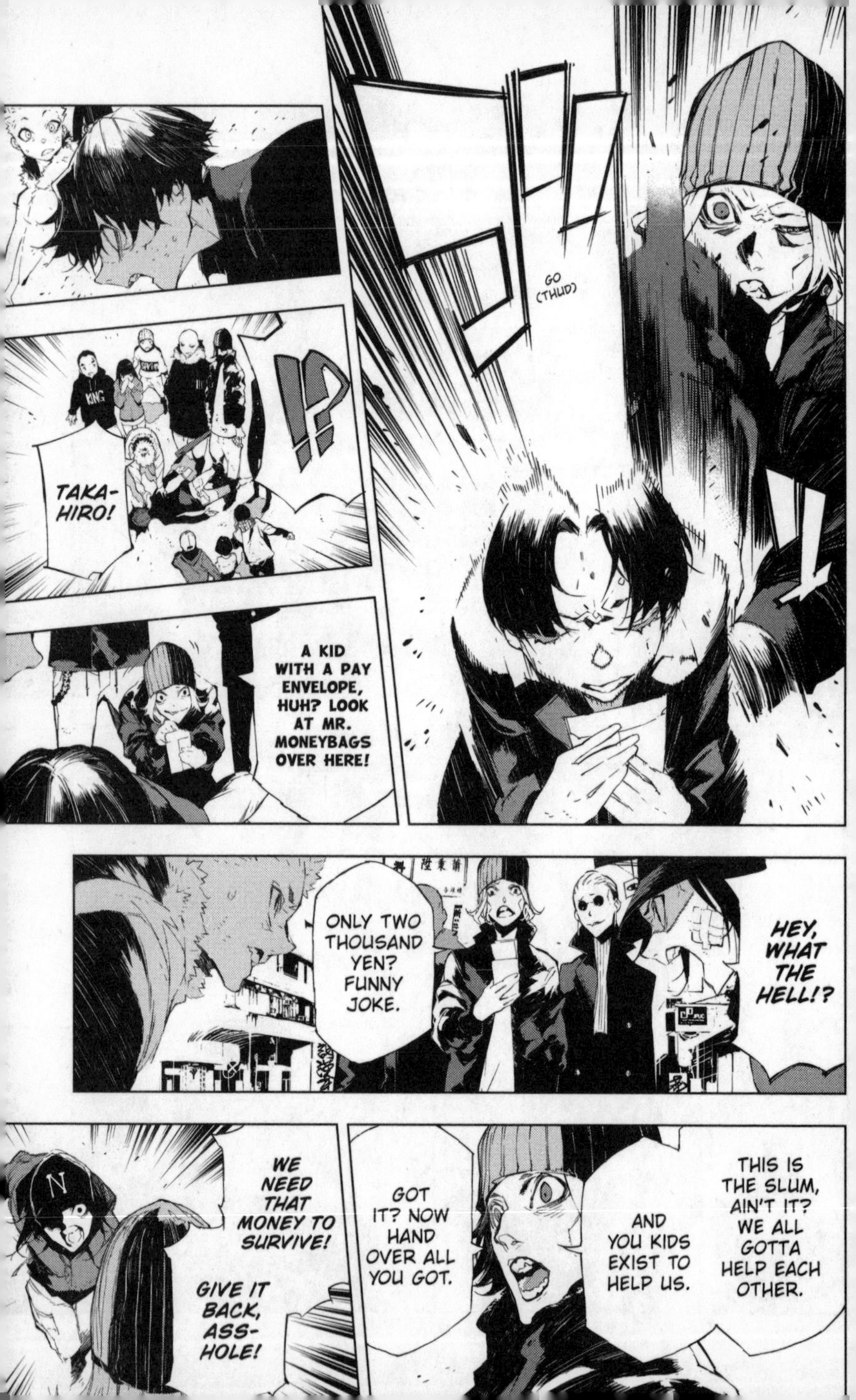
GO (THUD)
!?
TAKA-HIRO!
A KID WITH A PAY ENVELOPE, HUH? LOOK AT MR. MONEYBAGS OVER HERE!
HEY, WHAT THE HELL!?
ONLY TWO THOUSAND YEN? FUNNY JOKE.
THIS IS THE SLUM, AIN'T IT? WE ALL GOTTA HELP EACH OTHER.
AND YOU KIDS EXIST TO HELP US.
GOT IT? NOW HAND OVER ALL YOU GOT.
WE NEED THAT MONEY TO SURVIVE!
GIVE IT BACK, ASS-HOLE!

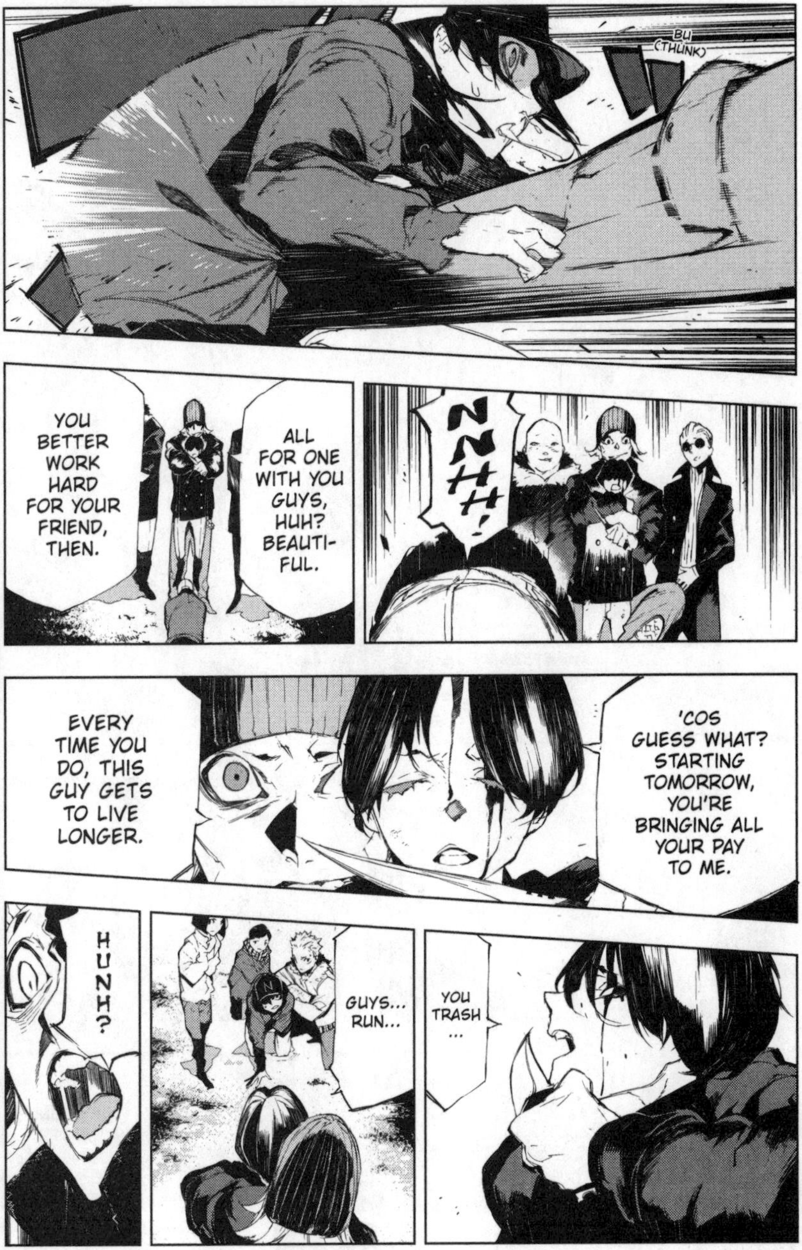
BU
(THUNK)
NNHH!
ALL FOR ONE WITH YOU GUYS, HUH? BEAUTIFUL.
YOU BETTER WORK HARD FOR YOUR FRIEND, THEN.
'COS GUESS WHAT? STARTING TOMORROW, YOU'RE BRINGING ALL YOUR PAY TO ME.
EVERY TIME YOU DO, THIS GUY GETS TO LIVE LONGER.
YOU TRASH ...
GUYS... RUN...
HUNH?

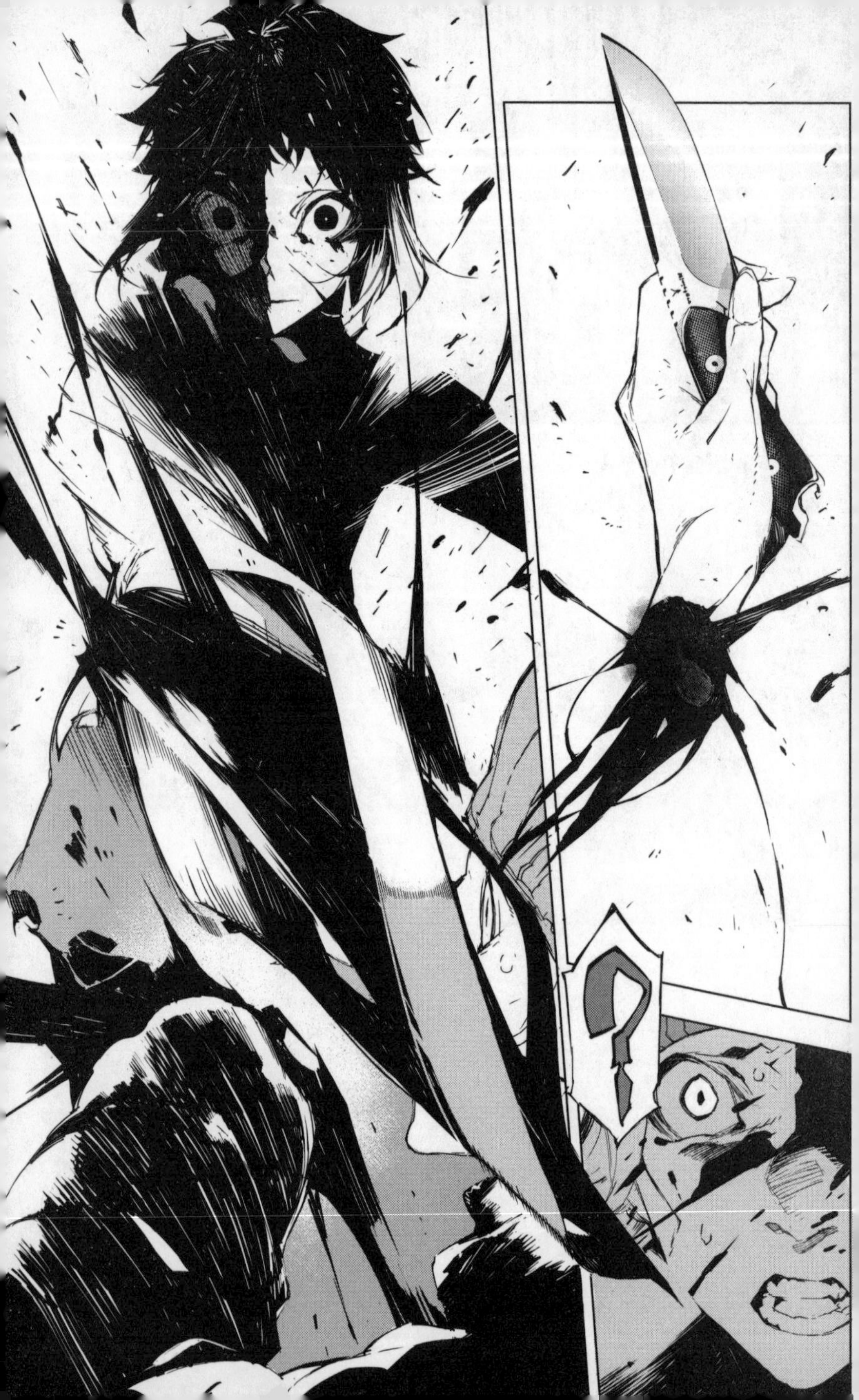

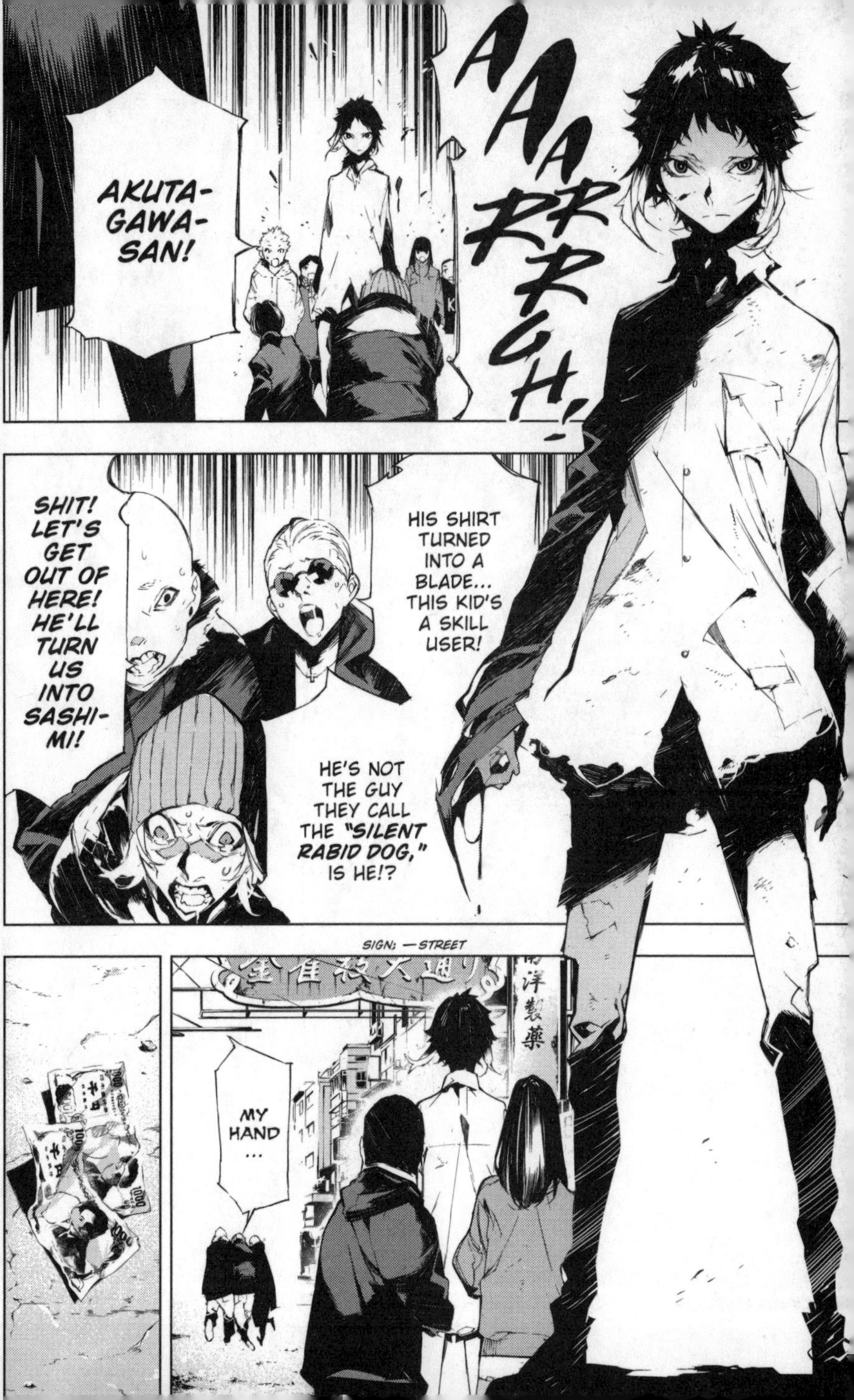
AAARRRGH!
AKUTA-GAWA-SAN!
HIS SHIRT TURNED INTO A BLADE... THIS KID'S A SKILL USER!
HE'S NOT THE GUY THEY CALL THE "SILENT RABID DOG," IS HE!?
SHIT! LET'S GET OUT OF HERE! HE'LL TURN US INTO SASHIMI!
SIGN: —STREET
MY HAND ...

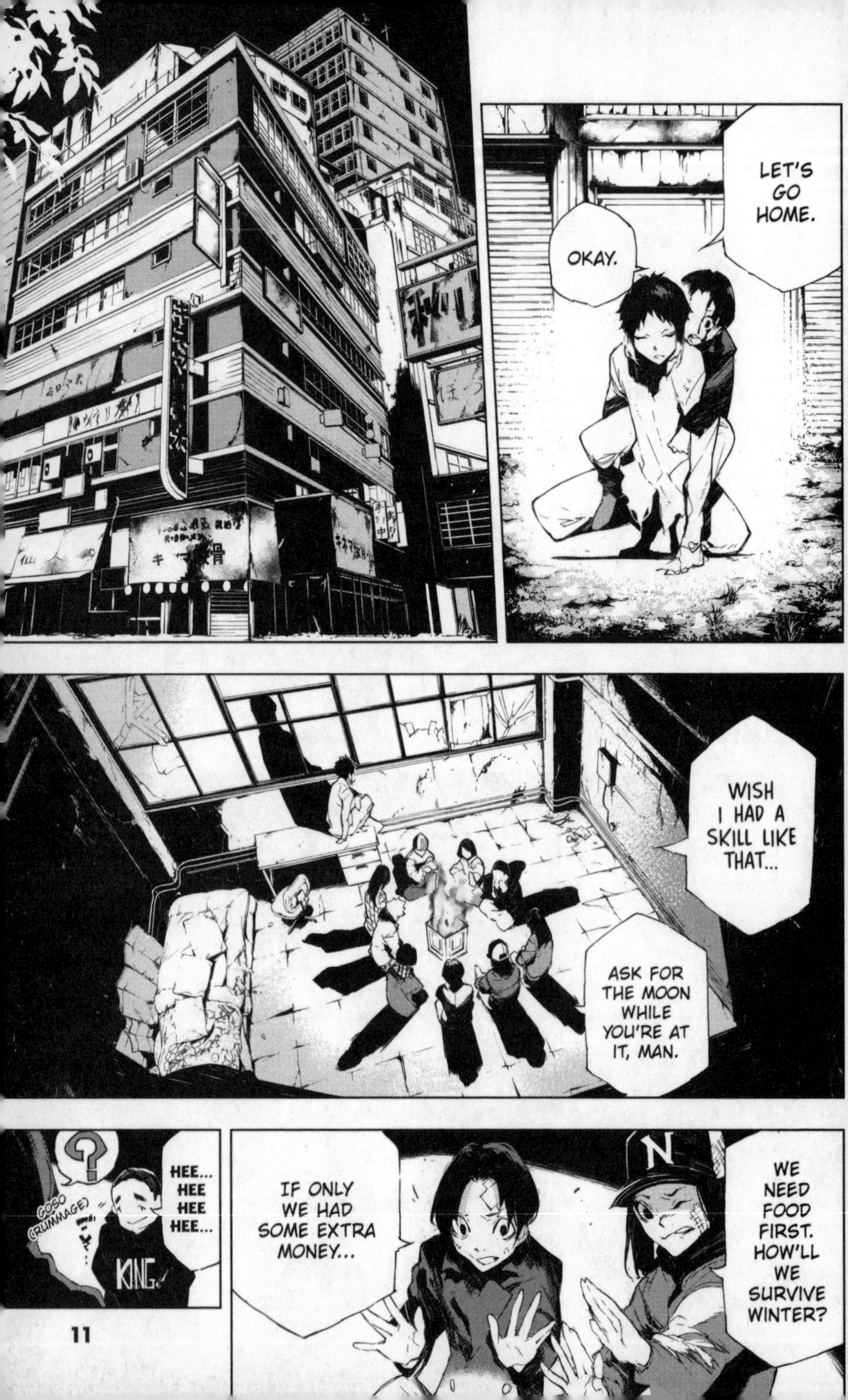
LET'S GO HOME.
OKAY.
WISH I HAD A SKILL LIKE THAT...
ASK FOR THE MOON WHILE YOU'RE AT IT, MAN.
WE NEED FOOD FIRST. HOW'LL WE SURVIVE WINTER?
IF ONLY WE HAD SOME EXTRA MONEY...
HEE... HEE HEE HEE...
GOSO (RUMMAGE)
?
KING

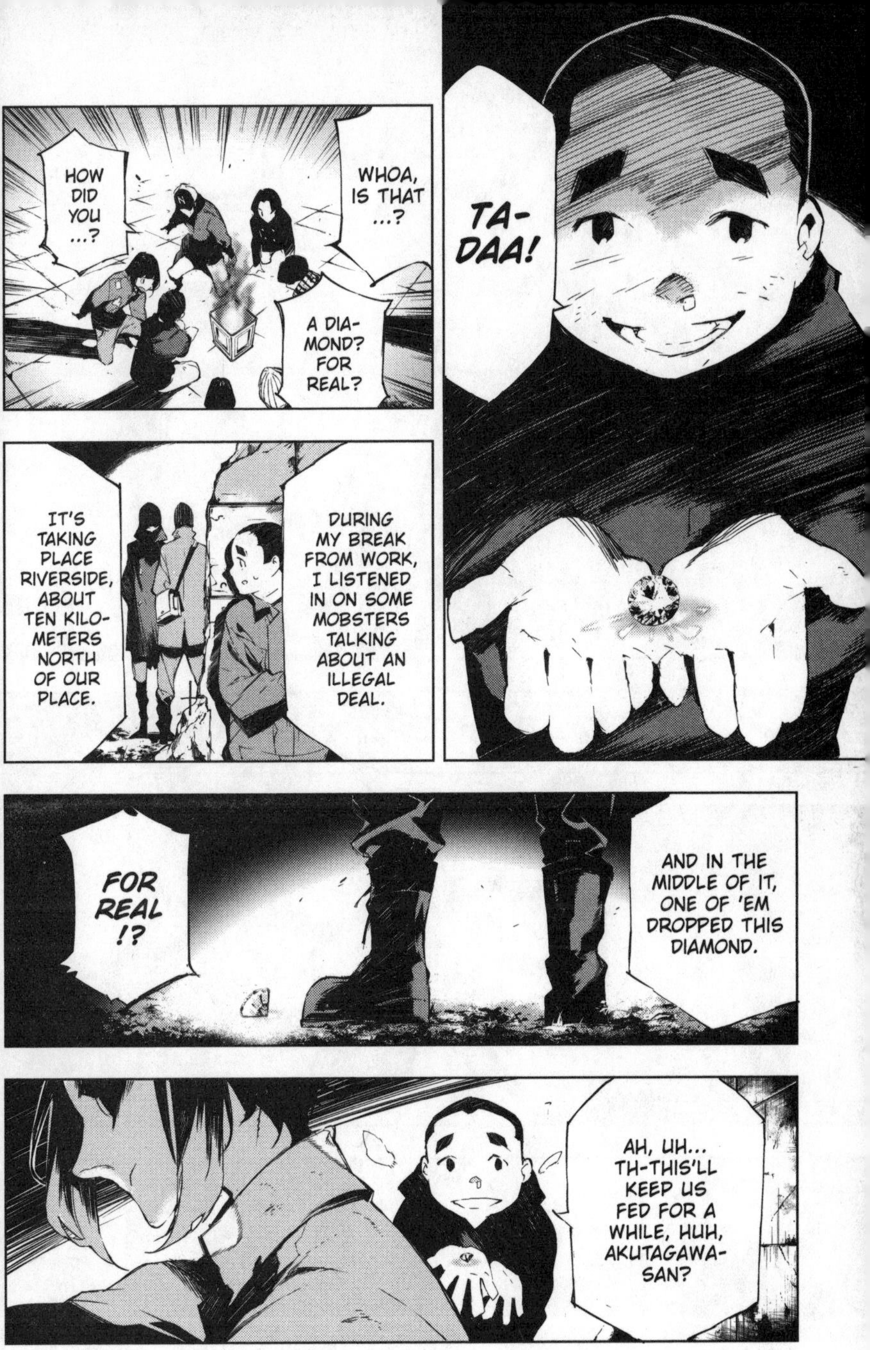
TA-DAA!
WHOA, IS THAT ...?
A DIA-MOND? FOR REAL?
HOW DID YOU ...?
DURING MY BREAK FROM WORK, I LISTENED IN ON SOME MOBSTERS TALKING ABOUT AN ILLEGAL DEAL.
IT'S TAKING PLACE RIVERSIDE, ABOUT TEN KILO-METERS NORTH OF OUR PLACE.
AND IN THE MIDDLE OF IT, ONE OF 'EM DROPPED THIS DIAMOND.
FOR REAL!?
AH, UH... TH-THIS'LL KEEP US FED FOR A WHILE, HUH, AKUTAGAWA-SAN?

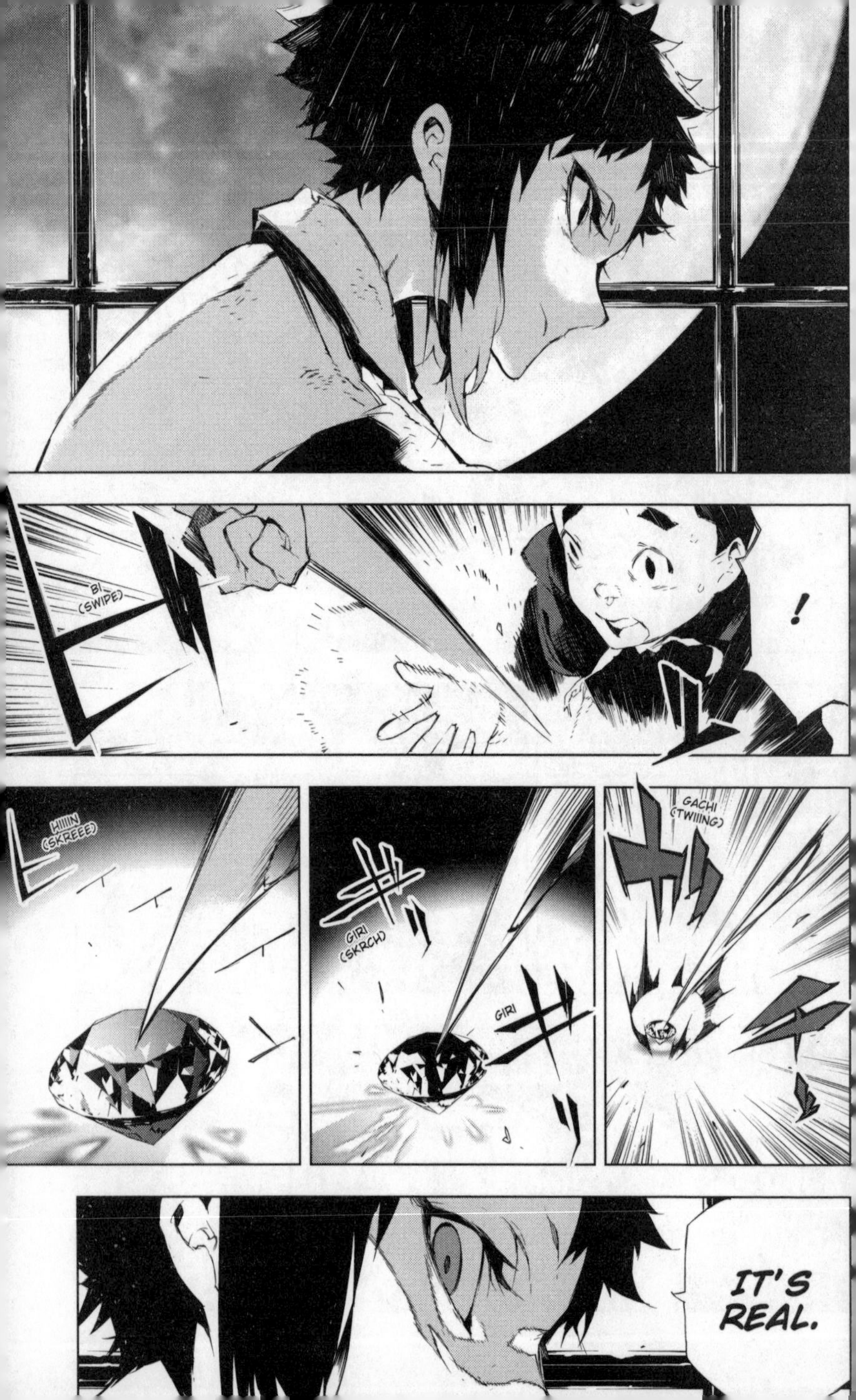
BI (SWIPE)
!
GACHI (TWIIING)
GIRI (SKRCH)
GIRI
HIIIN (SKREEE)
IT'S REAL.

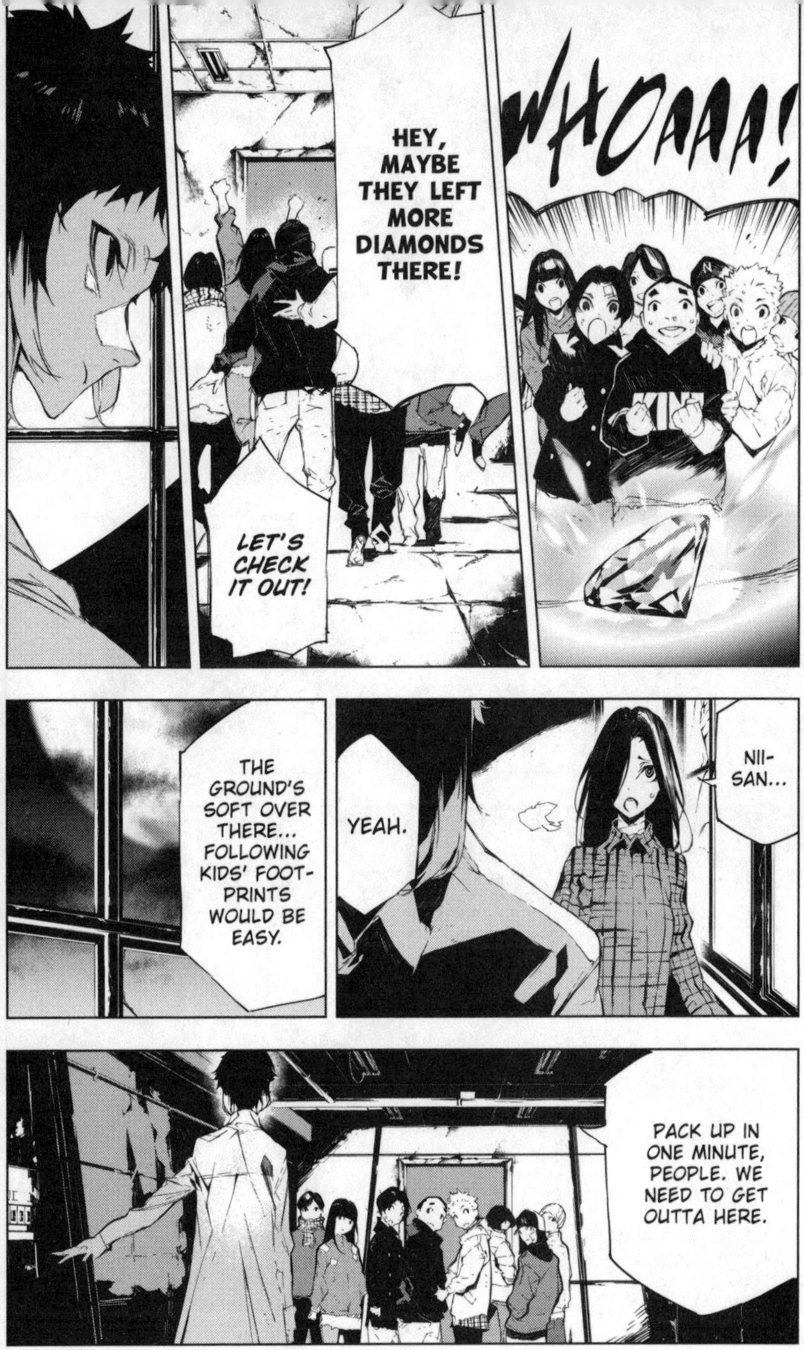
WHOAAA!
HEY, MAYBE THEY LEFT MORE DIAMONDS THERE!
LET'S CHECK IT OUT!
NII-SAN...
YEAH.
THE GROUND'S SOFT OVER THERE... FOLLOWING KIDS' FOOT-PRINTS WOULD BE EASY.
PACK UP IN ONE MINUTE, PEOPLE. WE NEED TO GET OUTTA HERE.

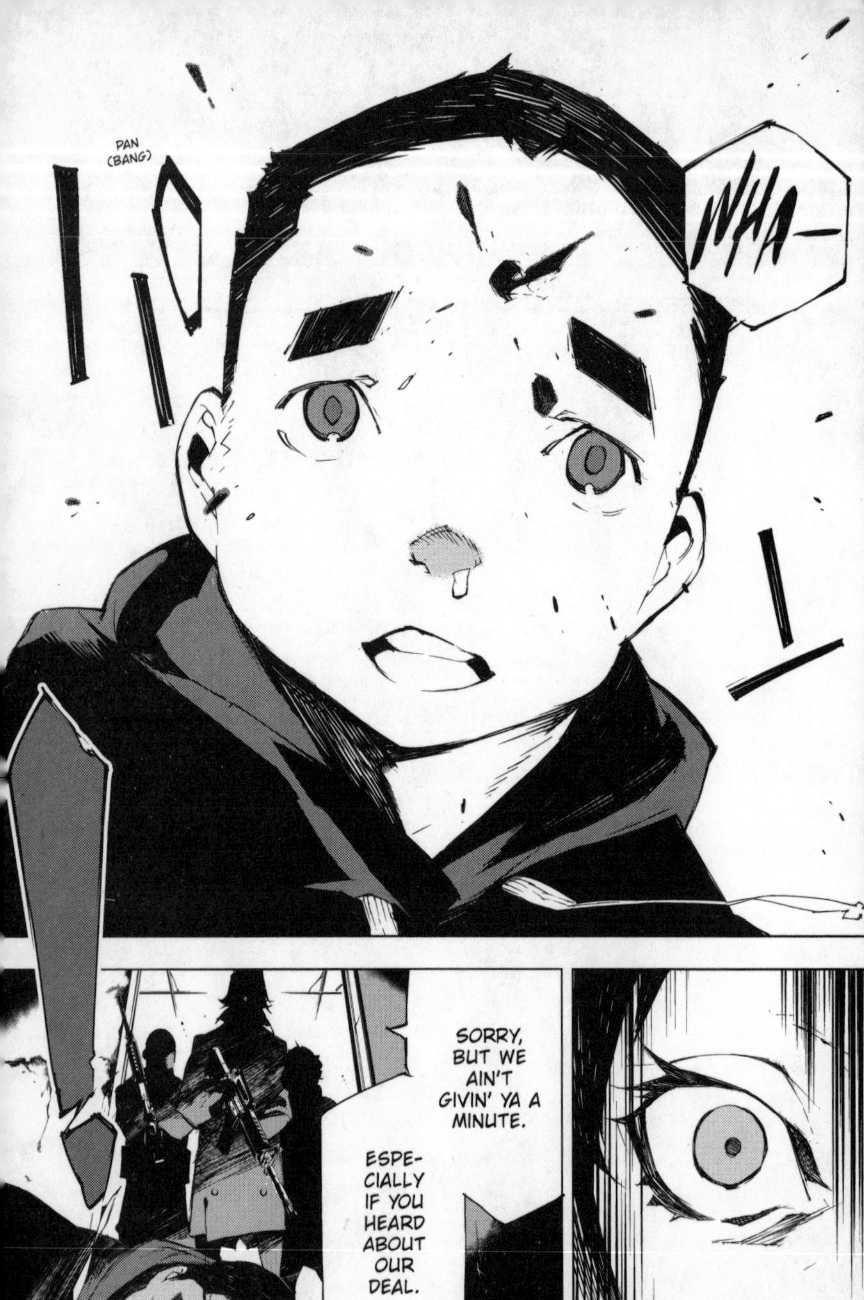
WHA—
PAN (BANG)
SORRY, BUT WE AIN'T GIVIN' YA A MINUTE.
ESPE-CIALLY IF YOU HEARD ABOUT OUR DEAL.

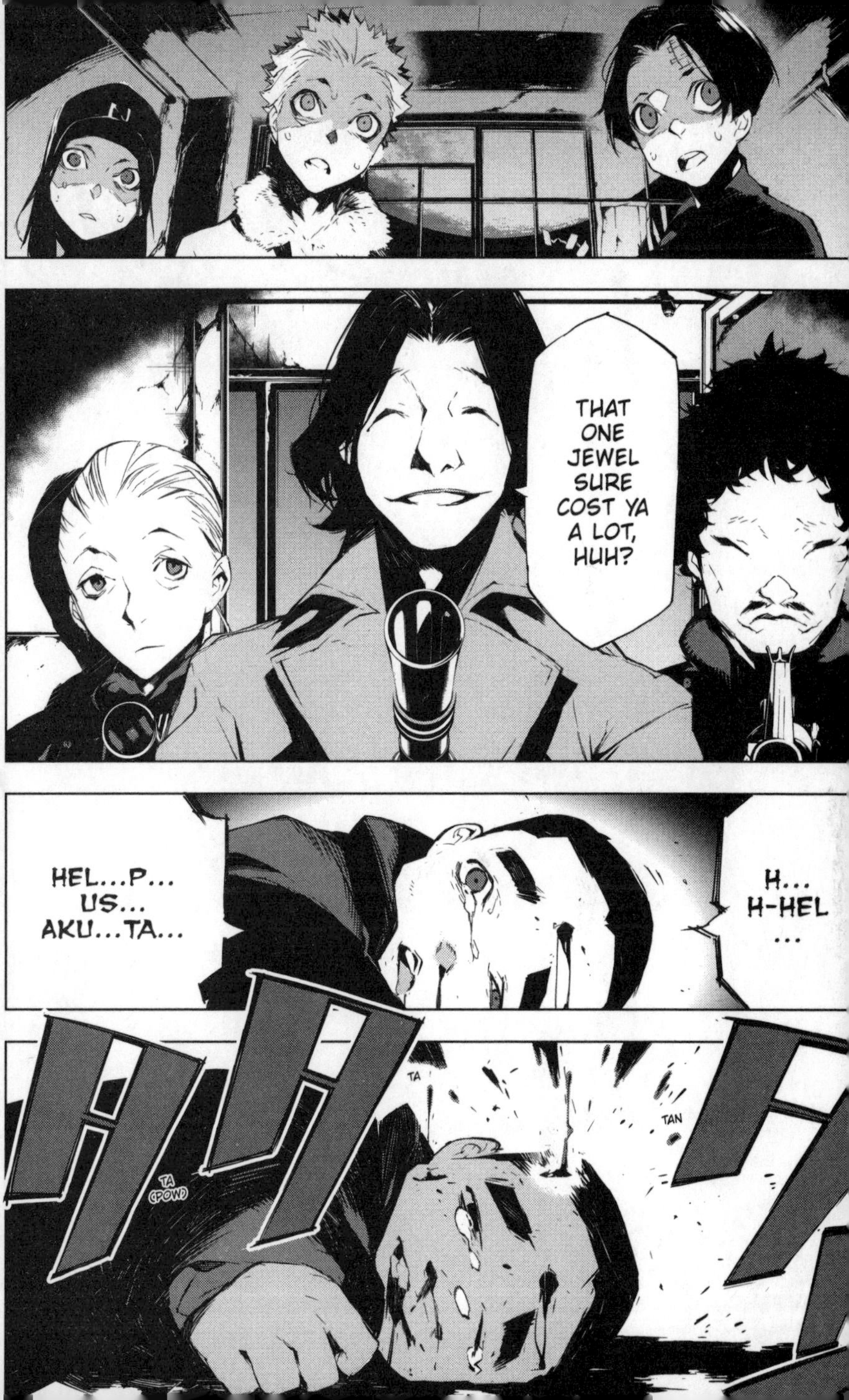
THAT ONE JEWEL SURE COST YA A LOT, HUH?
H... H-HEL ...
HEL...P... US... AKU...TA...
TAN
TA
TA (POW)

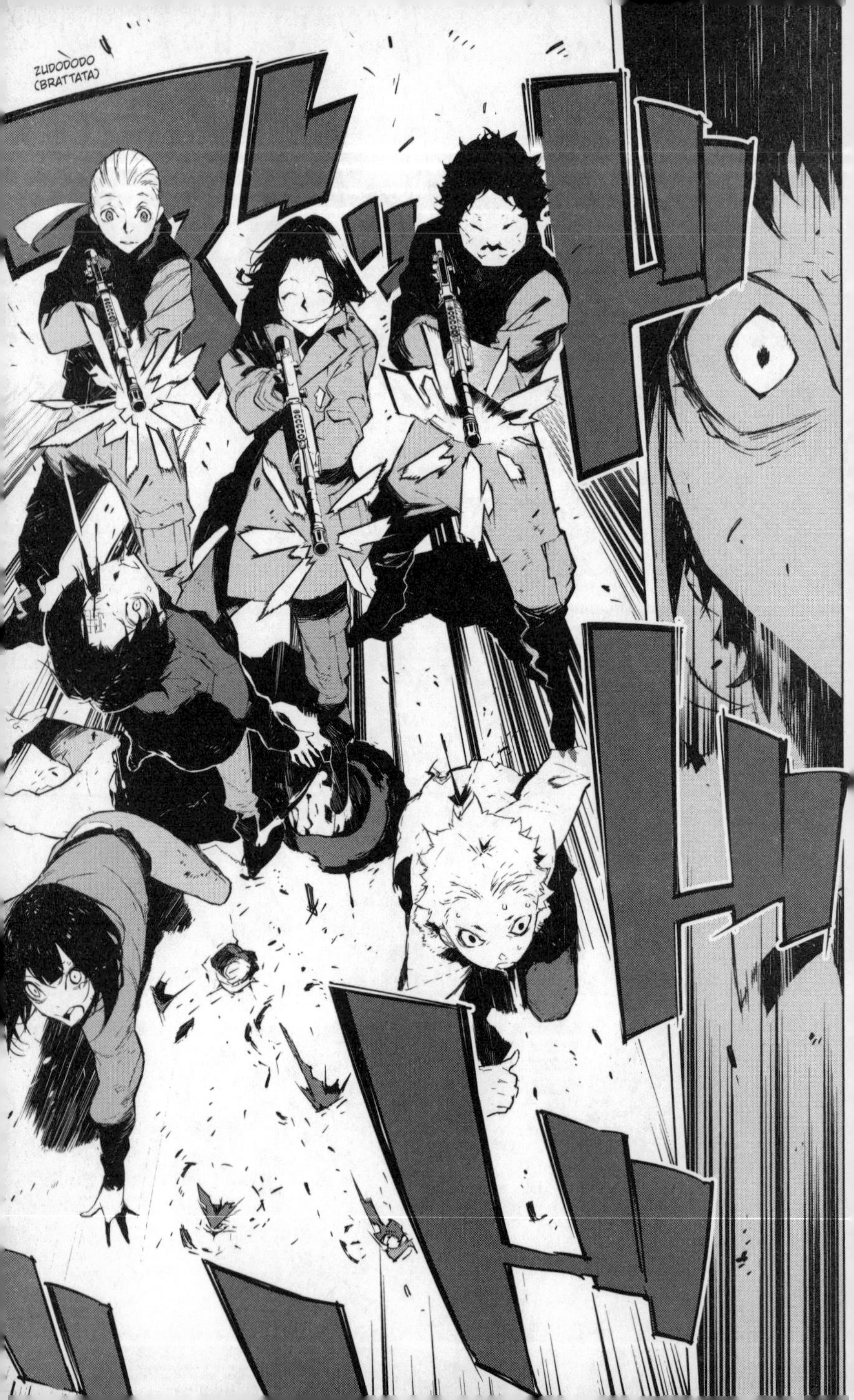
ZUDODODO
(BRATTATA)

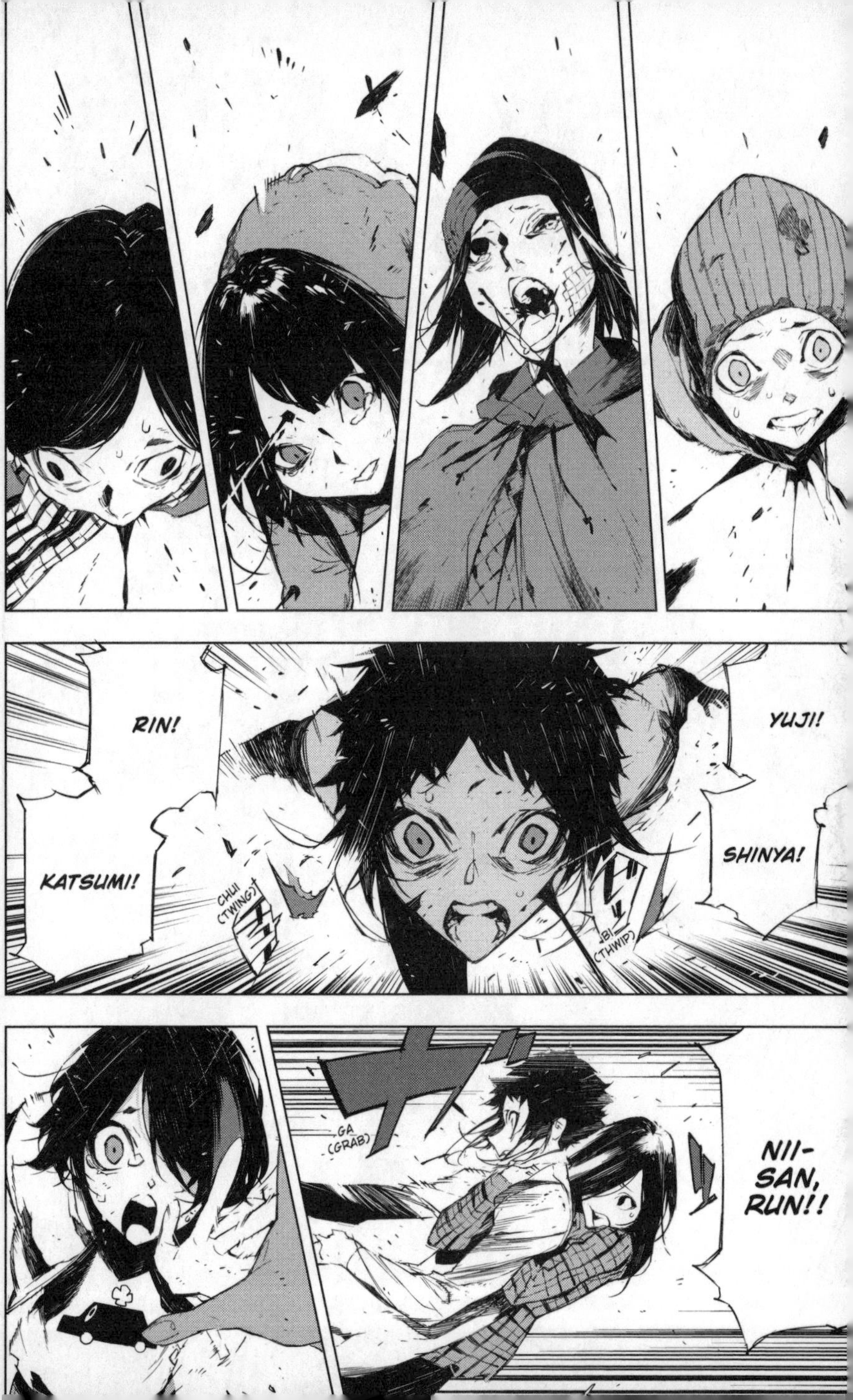
YUJI!
SHINYA!
BI (THWIP)
CHUI (TWING)
RIN!
KATSUMI!
NII-SAN, RUN!!
GA (GRAB)

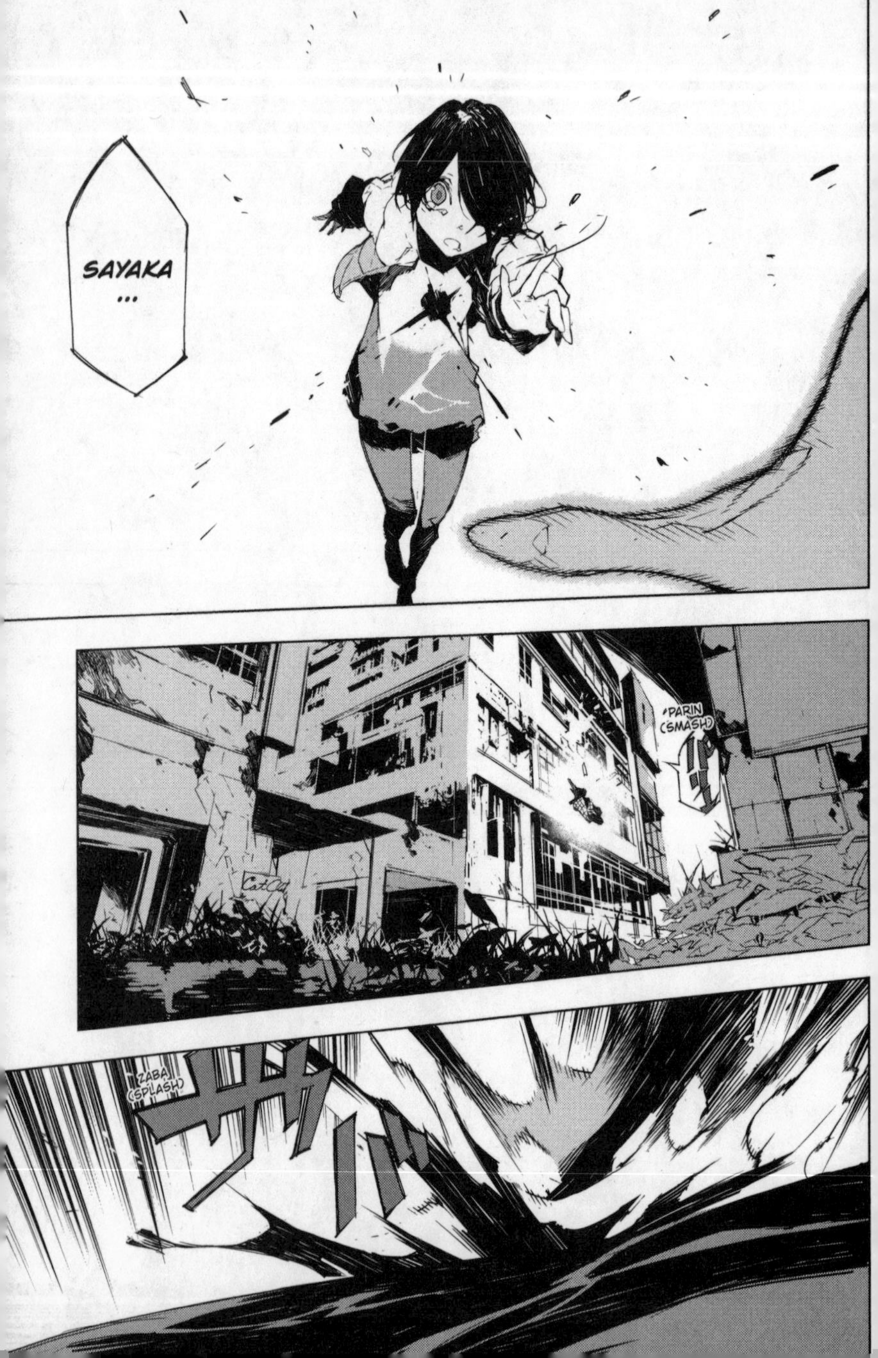
SAYAKA ...
PARIN (SMASH)
ZABA (SPLASH)

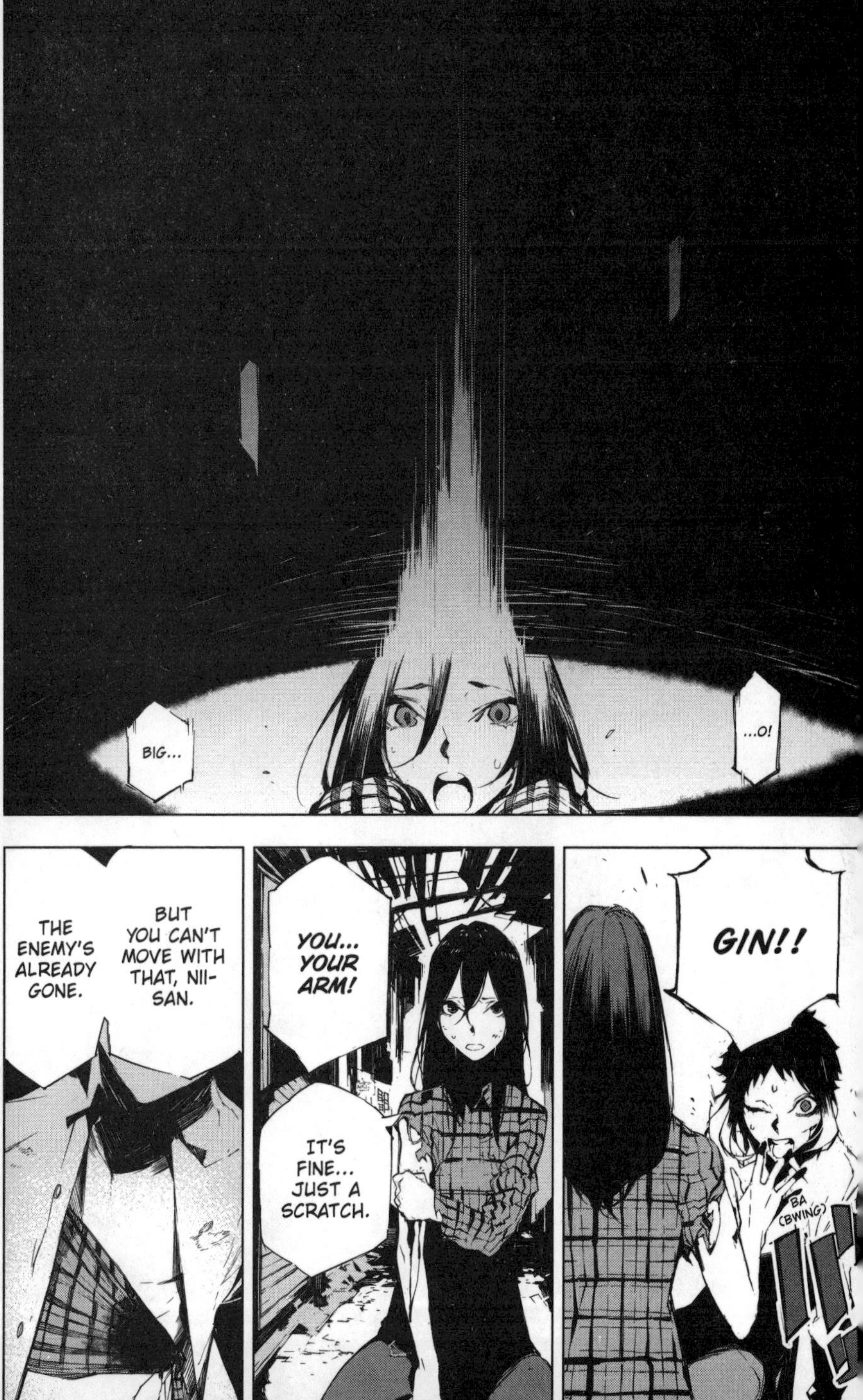
...O!
BIG...
GIN!!
BA (BWING)
YOU... YOUR ARM!
IT'S FINE... JUST A SCRATCH.
BUT YOU CAN'T MOVE WITH THAT, NII-SAN.
THE ENEMY'S ALREADY GONE.

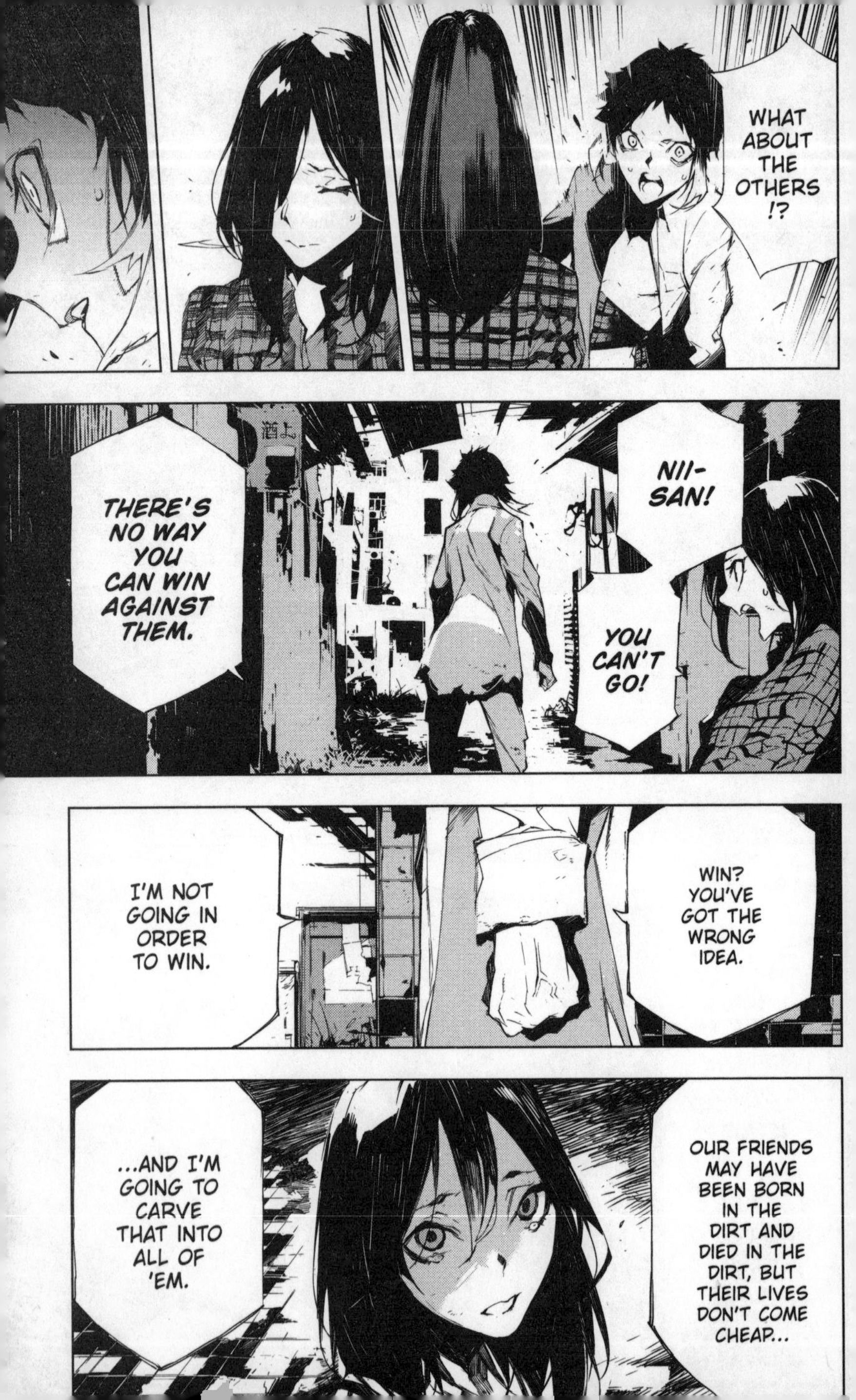
WHAT ABOUT THE OTHERS !?
NII-SAN!
YOU CAN'T GO!
THERE'S NO WAY YOU CAN WIN AGAINST THEM.
WIN? YOU'VE GOT THE WRONG IDEA.
I'M NOT GOING IN ORDER TO WIN.
OUR FRIENDS MAY HAVE BEEN BORN IN THE DIRT AND DIED IN THE DIRT, BUT THEIR LIVES DON'T COME CHEAP...
...AND I'M GOING TO CARVE THAT INTO ALL OF 'EM.

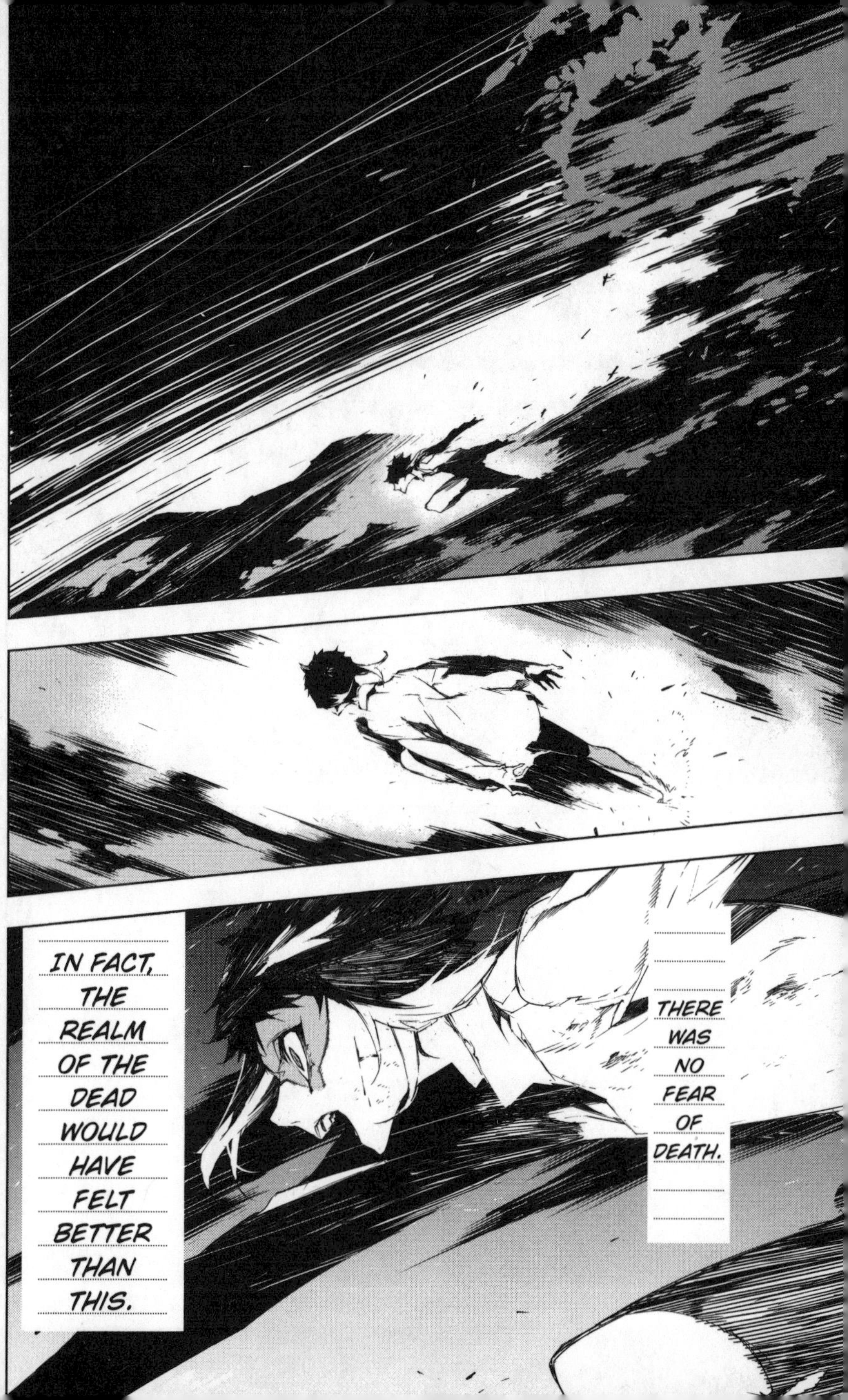
THERE WAS NO FEAR OF DEATH.
IN FACT, THE REALM OF THE DEAD WOULD HAVE FELT BETTER THAN THIS.

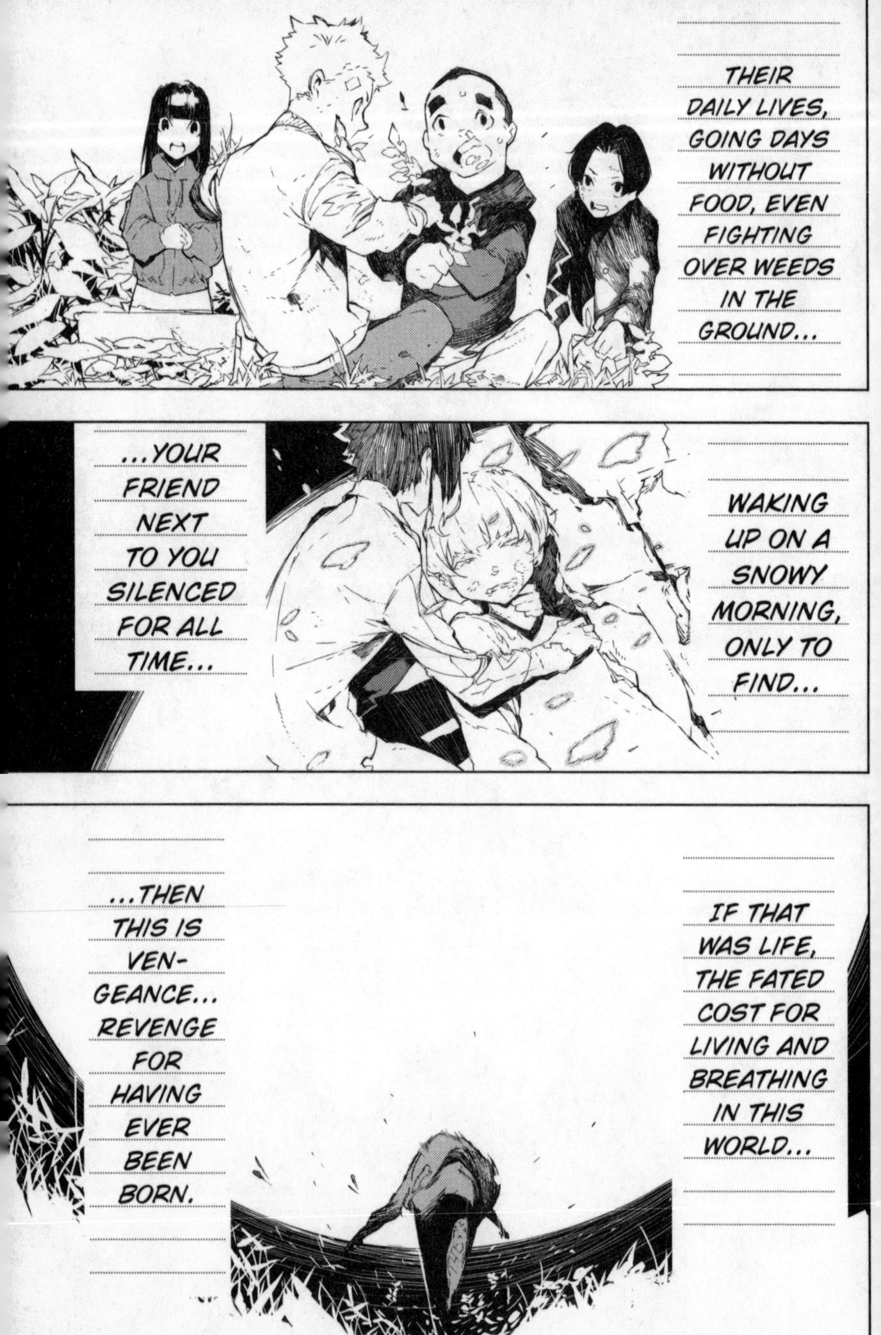
THEIR DAILY LIVES, GOING DAYS WITHOUT FOOD, EVEN FIGHTING OVER WEEDS IN THE GROUND...
WAKING UP ON A SNOWY MORNING, ONLY TO FIND...
...YOUR FRIEND NEXT TO YOU SILENCED FOR ALL TIME...
IF THAT WAS LIFE, THE FATED COST FOR LIVING AND BREATHING IN THIS WORLD...
...THEN THIS IS VEN-GEANCE... REVENGE FOR HAVING EVER BEEN BORN.

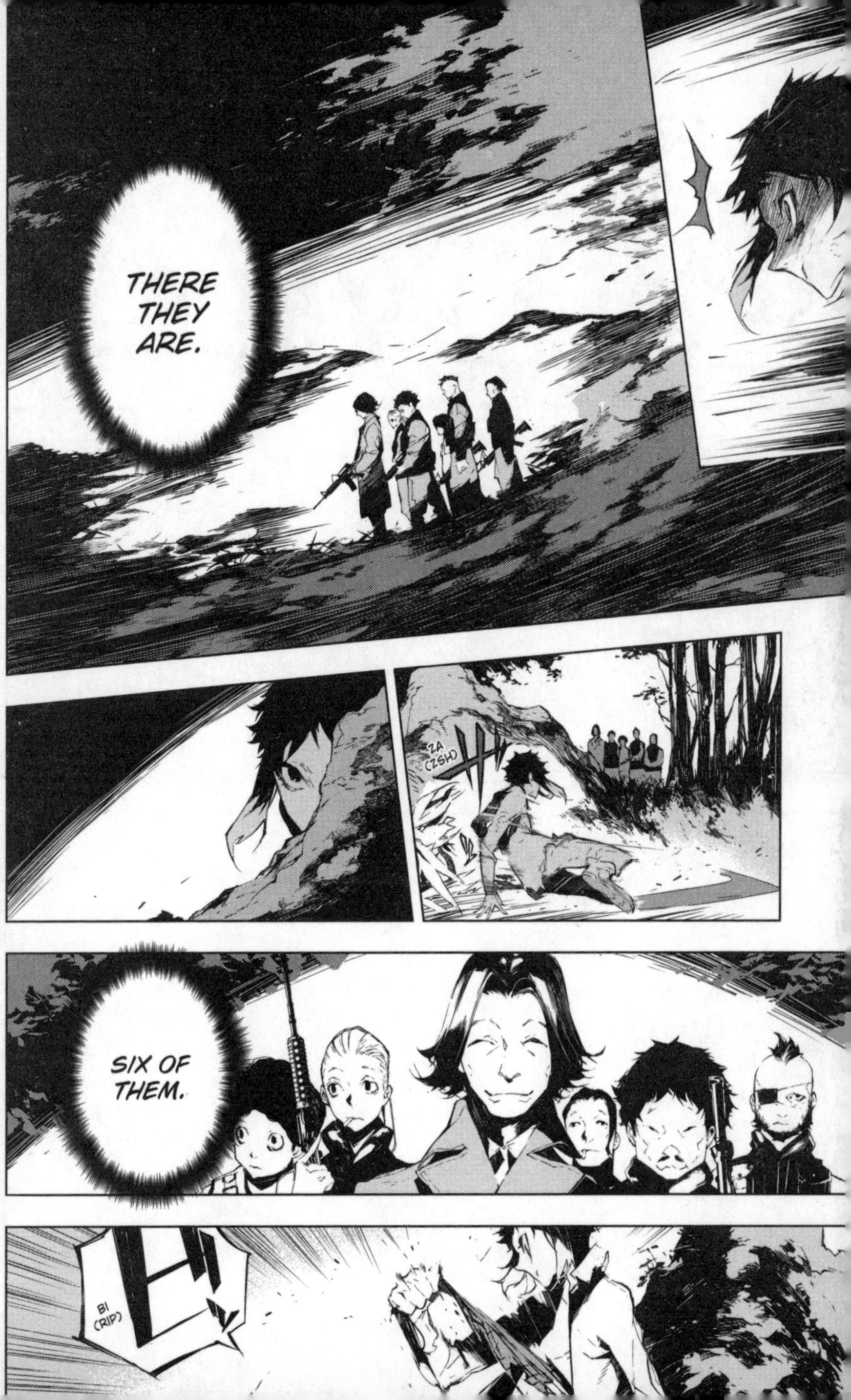
THERE THEY ARE.
ZA (ZSH)
SIX OF THEM.
BI (RIP)

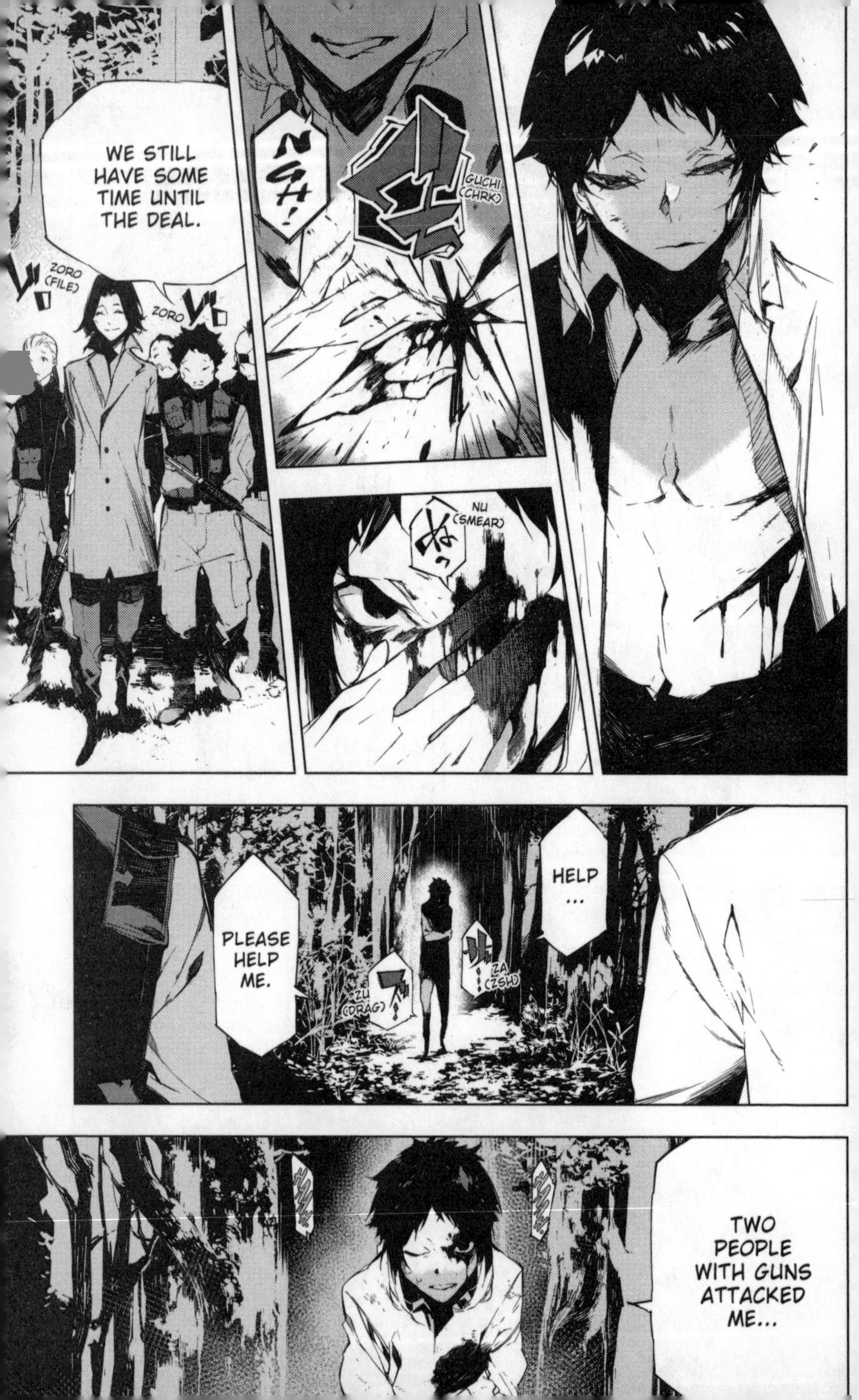
NGH!
GUCHI (CHRK)
NU (SMEAR)
WE STILL HAVE SOME TIME UNTIL THE DEAL.
ZORO (FILE)
ZORO
HELP ...
ZA (ZSHH)
ZU (DRAG)
PLEASE HELP ME.
TWO PEOPLE WITH GUNS ATTACKED ME...

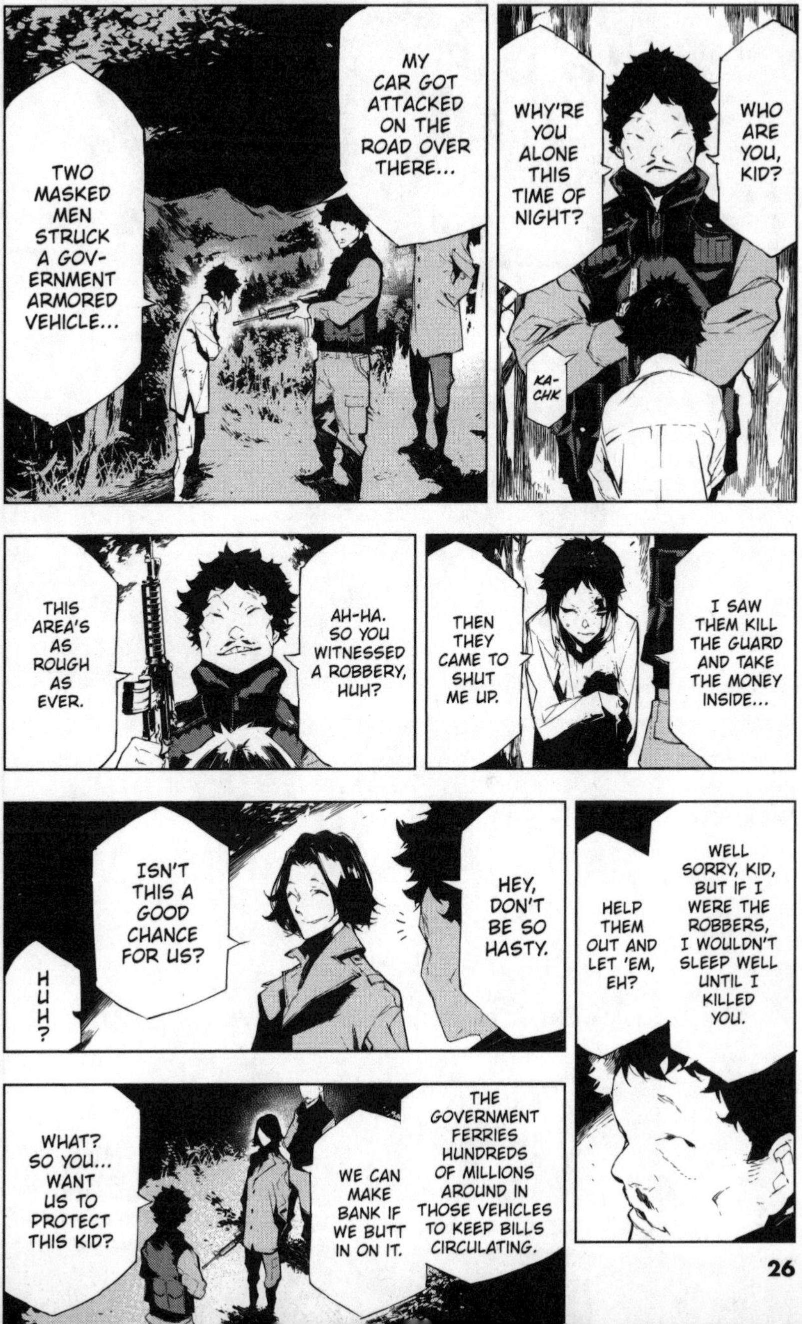
WHO ARE YOU, KID?
WHY'RE YOU ALONE THIS TIME OF NIGHT?
KA-CHK
MY CAR GOT ATTACKED ON THE ROAD OVER THERE...
TWO MASKED MEN STRUCK A GOVERNMENT ARMORED VEHICLE...
I SAW THEM KILL THE GUARD AND TAKE THE MONEY INSIDE...
THEN THEY CAME TO SHUT ME UP.
AH-HA. SO YOU WITNESSED A ROBBERY, HUH?
THIS AREA'S AS ROUGH AS EVER.
WELL SORRY, KID, BUT IF I WERE THE ROBBERS, I WOULDN'T SLEEP WELL UNTIL I KILLED YOU.
HELP THEM OUT AND LET 'EM, EH?
HEY, DON'T BE SO HASTY.
ISN'T THIS A GOOD CHANCE FOR US?
HUH?
THE GOVERNMENT FERRIES HUNDREDS OF MILLIONS AROUND IN THOSE VEHICLES TO KEEP BILLS CIRCULATING.
WE CAN MAKE BANK IF WE BUTT IN ON IT.
WHAT? SO YOU... WANT US TO PROTECT THIS KID?

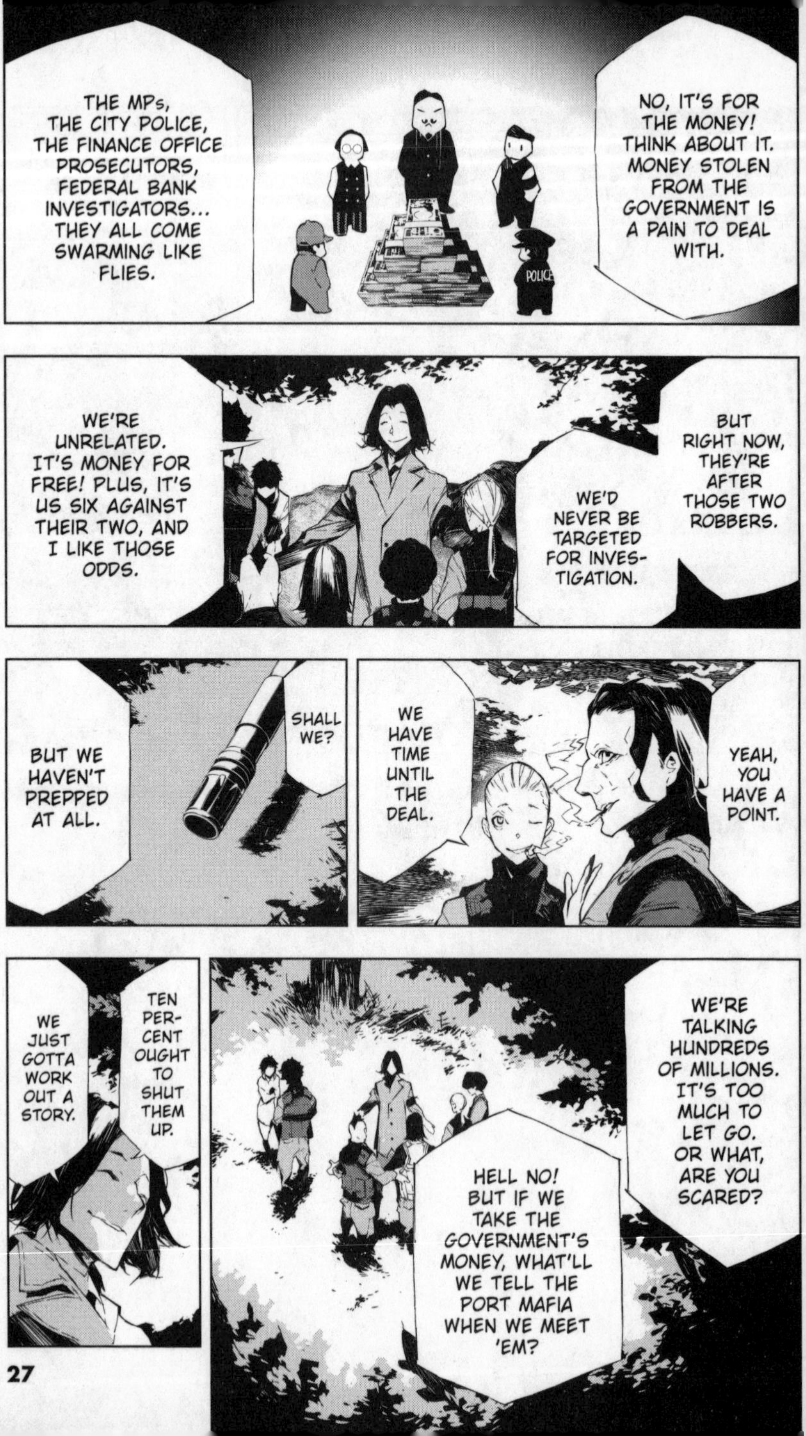

NO, IT'S FOR THE MONEY! THINK ABOUT IT. MONEY STOLEN FROM THE GOVERNMENT IS A PAIN TO DEAL WITH.
THE MPs, THE CITY POLICE, THE FINANCE OFFICE PROSECUTORS, FEDERAL BANK INVESTIGATORS... THEY ALL COME SWARMING LIKE FLIES.
POLICE
BUT RIGHT NOW, THEY'RE AFTER THOSE TWO ROBBERS.
WE'D NEVER BE TARGETED FOR INVES-TIGATION.
WE'RE UNRELATED. IT'S MONEY FOR FREE! PLUS, IT'S US SIX AGAINST THEIR TWO, AND I LIKE THOSE ODDS.
YEAH, YOU HAVE A POINT.
WE HAVE TIME UNTIL THE DEAL.
SHALL WE?
BUT WE HAVEN'T PREPPED AT ALL.
WE'RE TALKING HUNDREDS OF MILLIONS. IT'S TOO MUCH TO LET GO. OR WHAT, ARE YOU SCARED?
HELL NO! BUT IF WE TAKE THE GOVERNMENT'S MONEY, WHAT'LL WE TELL THE PORT MAFIA WHEN WE MEET 'EM?
TEN PER-CENT OUGHT TO SHUT THEM UP.
WE JUST GOTTA WORK OUT A STORY.

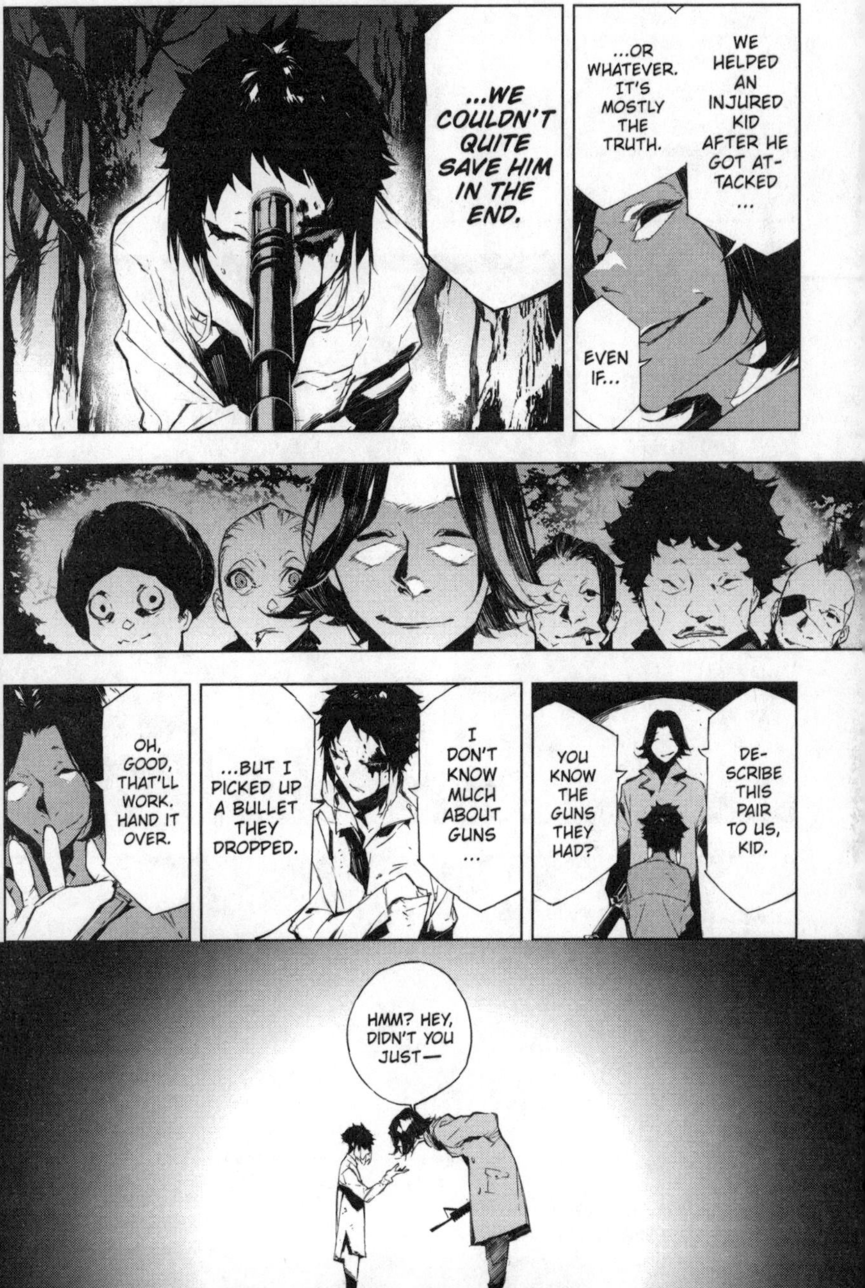
WE HELPED AN INJURED KID AFTER HE GOT AT-TACKED...
...OR WHATEVER. IT'S MOSTLY THE TRUTH.
EVEN IF...
...WE COULDN'T QUITE SAVE HIM IN THE END.
DE-SCRIBE THIS PAIR TO US, KID.
YOU KNOW THE GUNS THEY HAD?
I DON'T KNOW MUCH ABOUT GUNS...
...BUT I PICKED UP A BULLET THEY DROPPED.
OH, GOOD, THAT'LL WORK. HAND IT OVER.
HMM? HEY, DIDN'T YOU JUST—

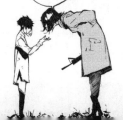

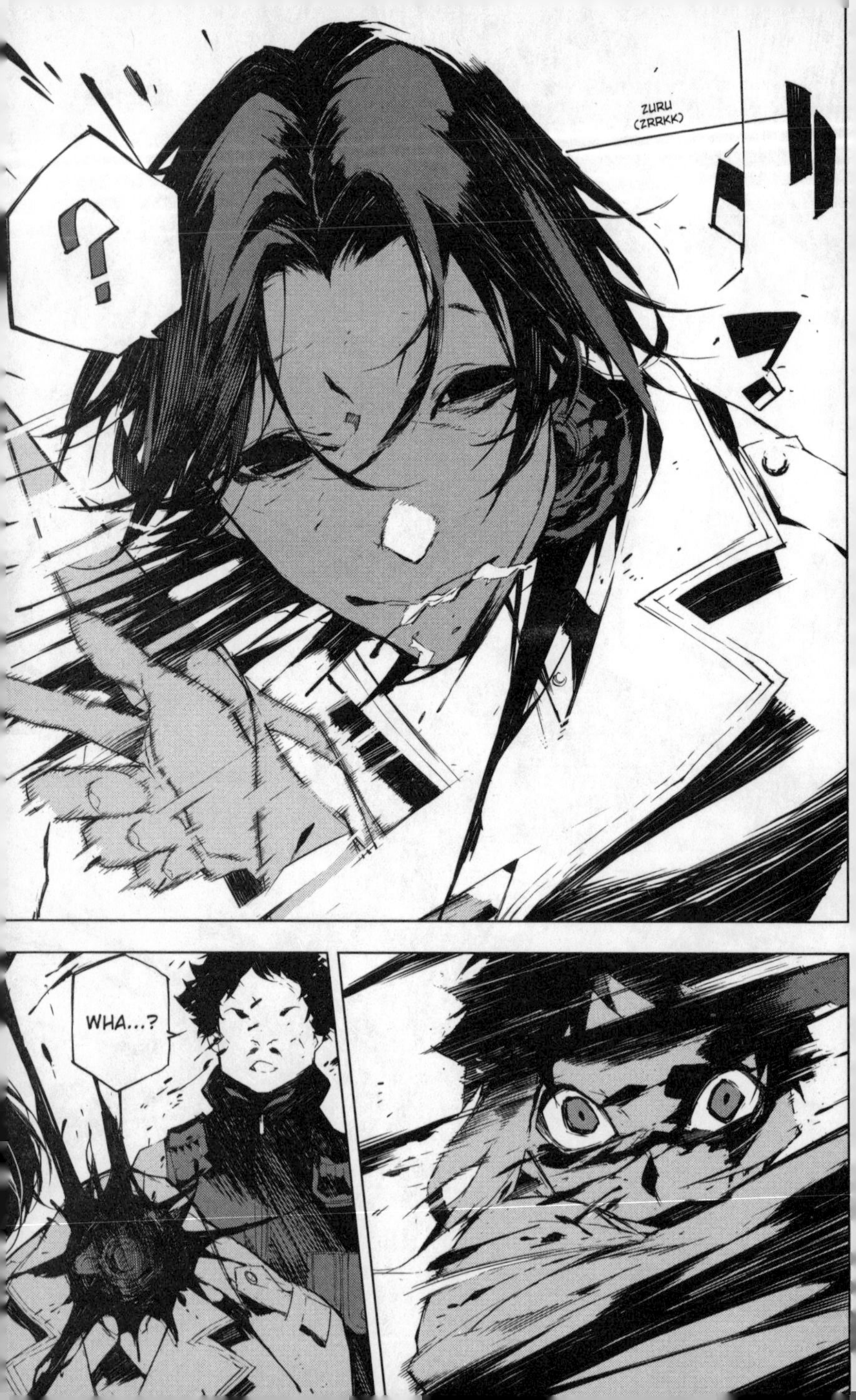
ZURU
(ZRRKK)
?
?
WHA...?

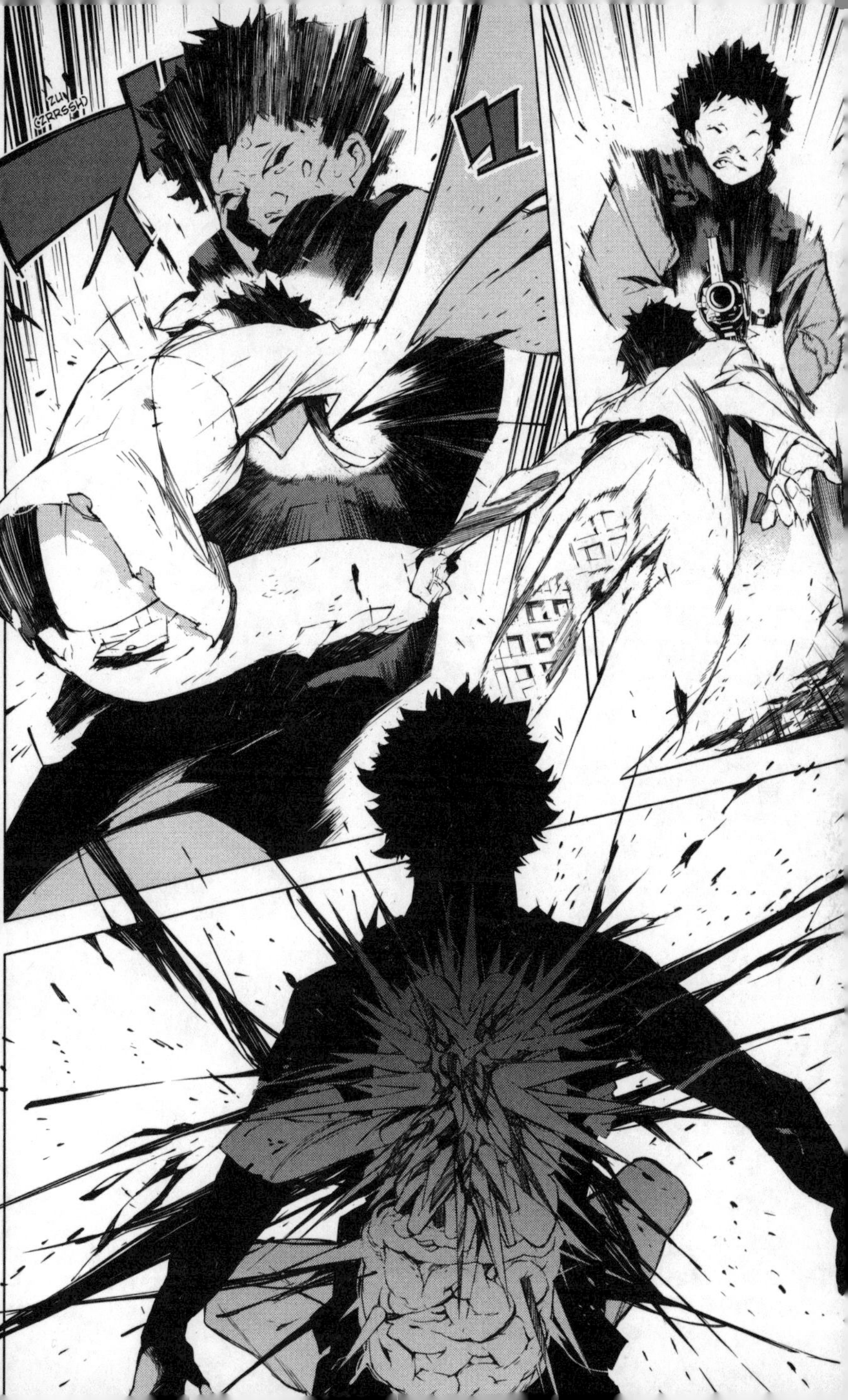
ZUN
(ZRRSSH)

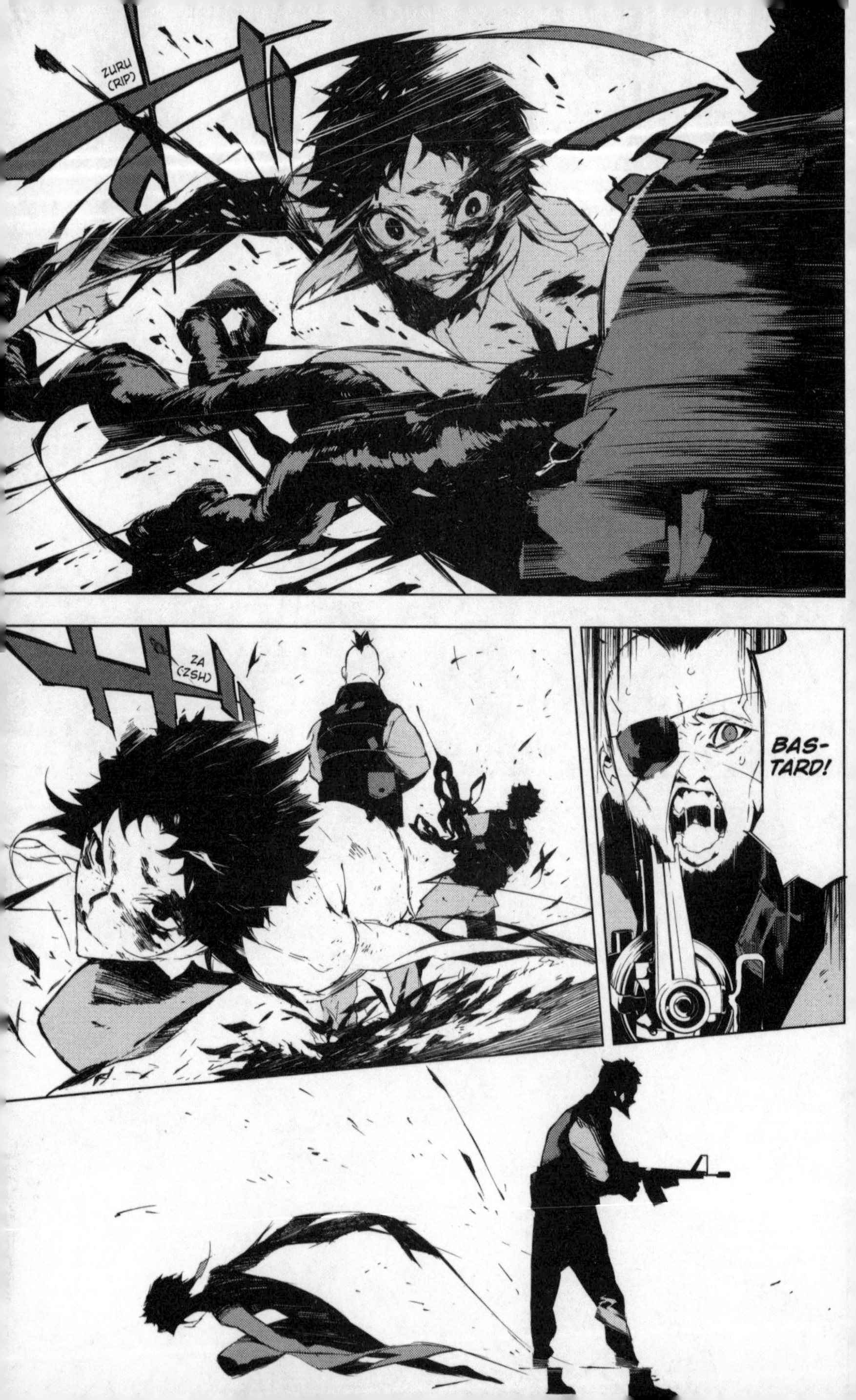
ZURU
(RIP)
BAS-
TARD!
ZA
(ZSH)

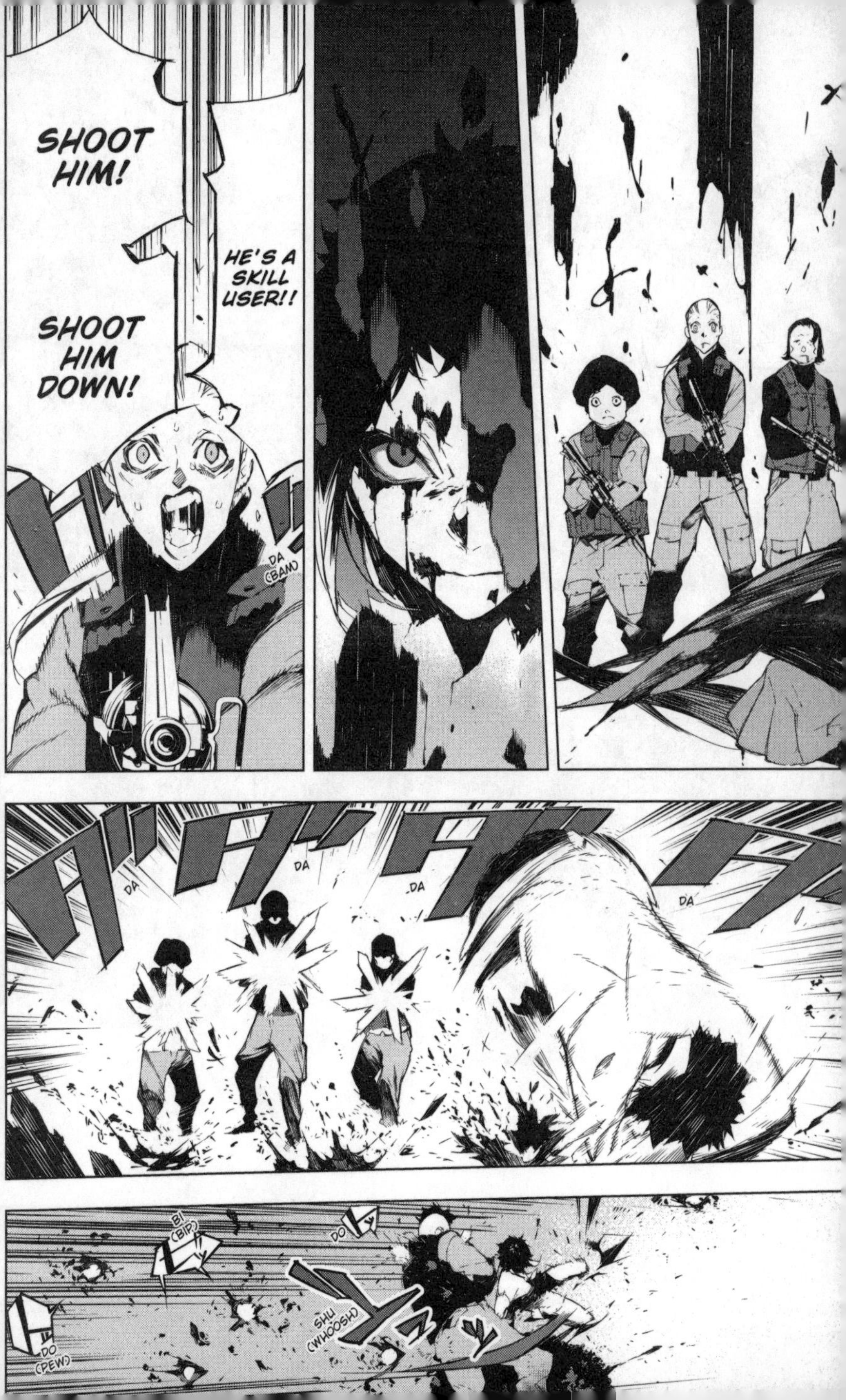

SHOOT HIM!
HE'S A SKILL USER!!
SHOOT HIM DOWN!
DA (BAM)
DA
DA
DA
DA
DO
SHU (WHOOSH)
BI (BIP)
DO (PEW)

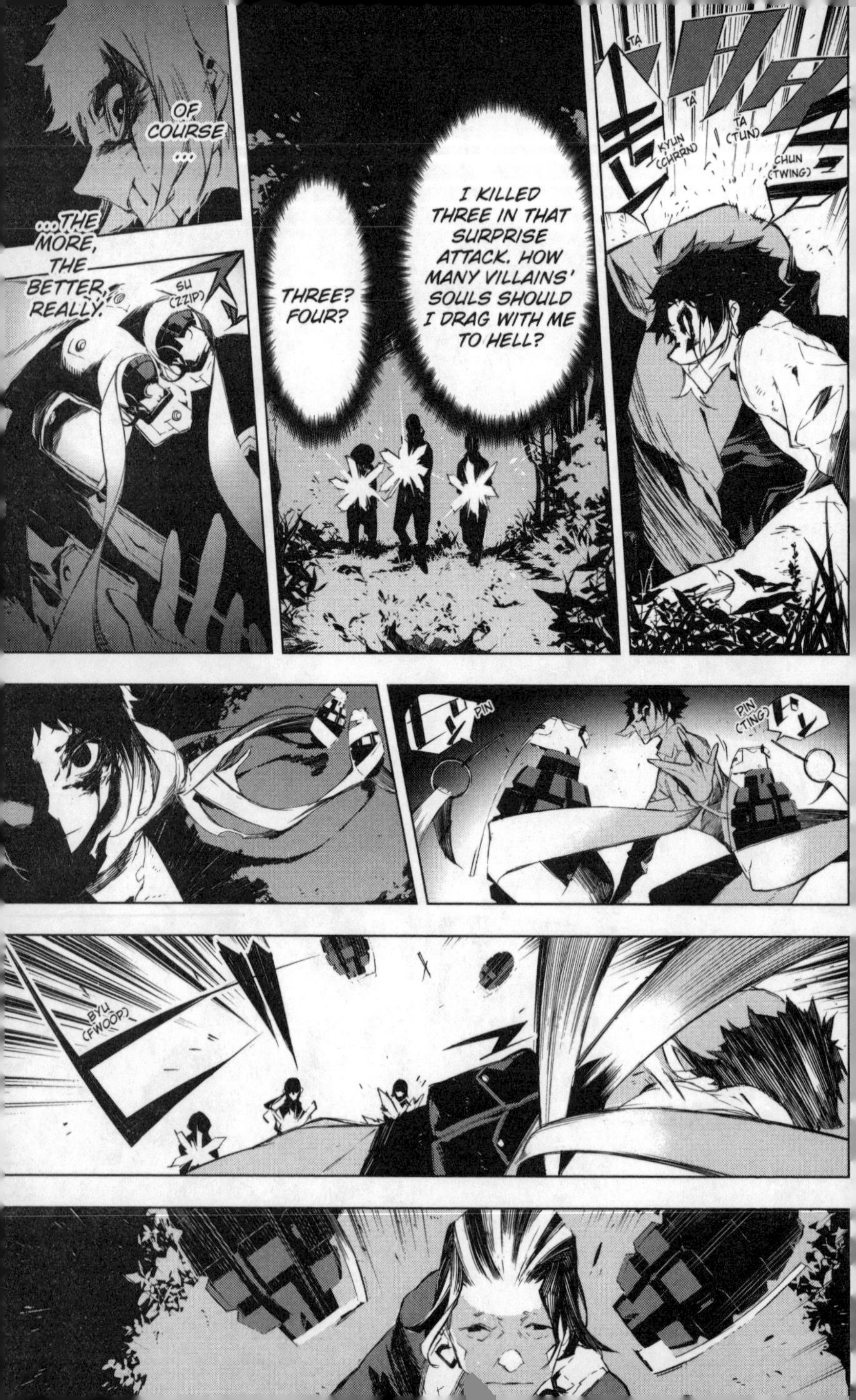
TA
TA
TA (TUN)
CHUN (TWING)
KYUN (CHRRND)
I KILLED THREE IN THAT SURPRISE ATTACK. HOW MANY VILLAINS' SOULS SHOULD I DRAG WITH ME TO HELL?
THREE? FOUR?
OF COURSE ...
...THE MORE, THE BETTER, REALLY.
SU (ZZIP)
PIN (TING)
PIN
BYU (FWOOP)

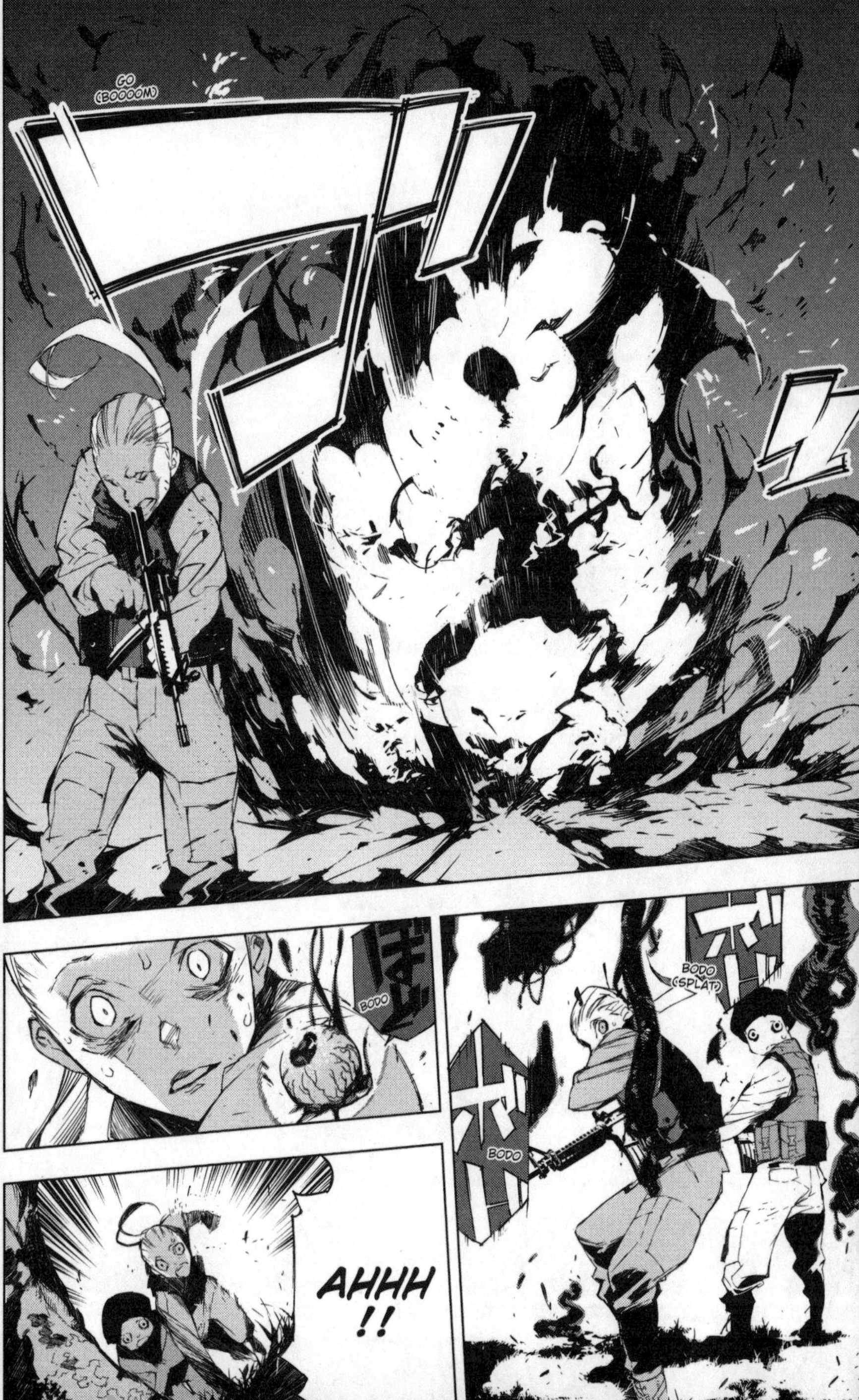
GO
(BOOOOM)
BODO
(SPLAT)
BODO
BODO
AHHH
!!

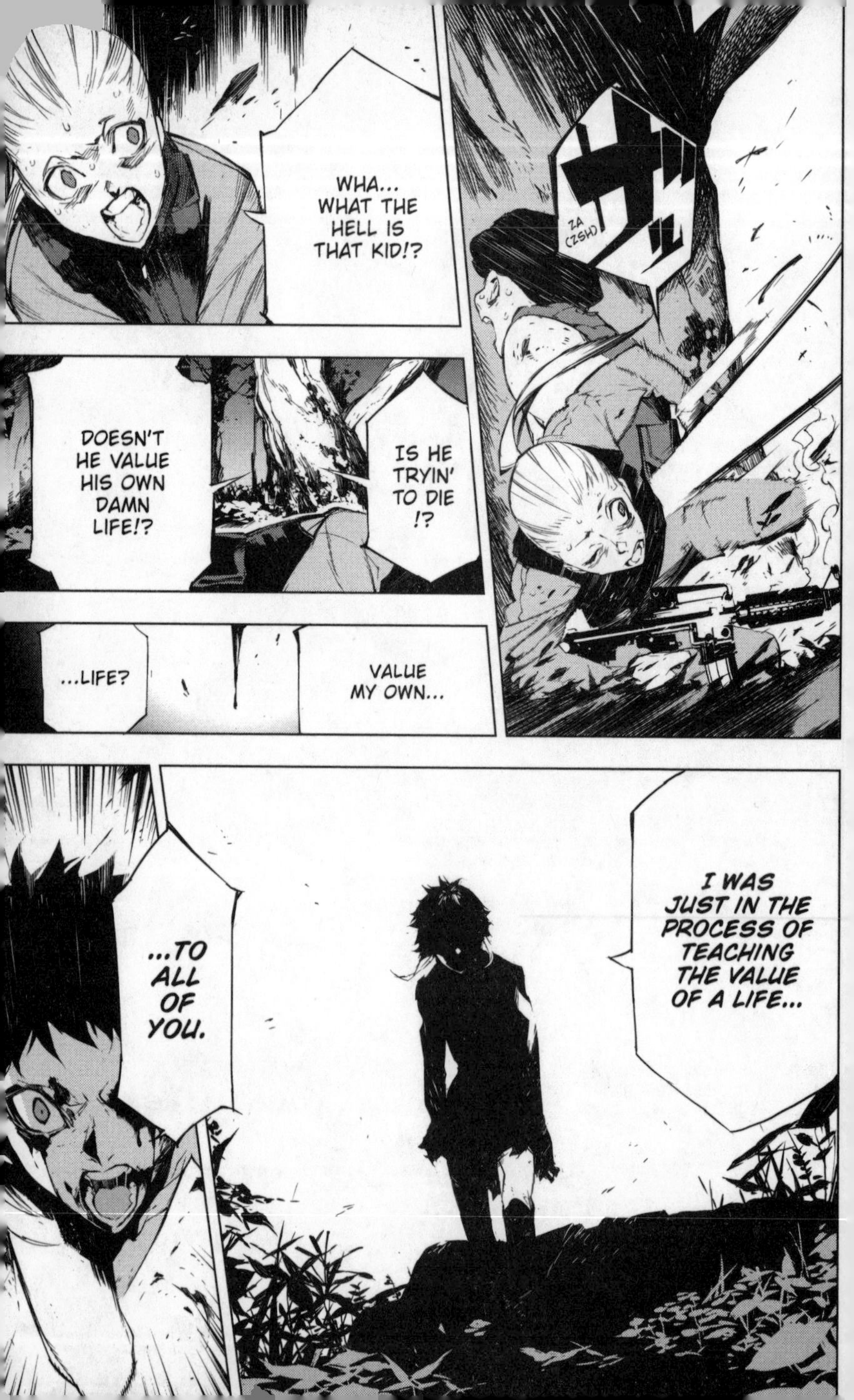
ZA (ZSH)
WHA... WHAT THE HELL IS THAT KID!?
IS HE TRYIN' TO DIE !?
DOESN'T HE VALUE HIS OWN DAMN LIFE!?
VALUE MY OWN...
...LIFE?
I WAS JUST IN THE PROCESS OF TEACHING THE VALUE OF A LIFE...
...TO ALL OF YOU.

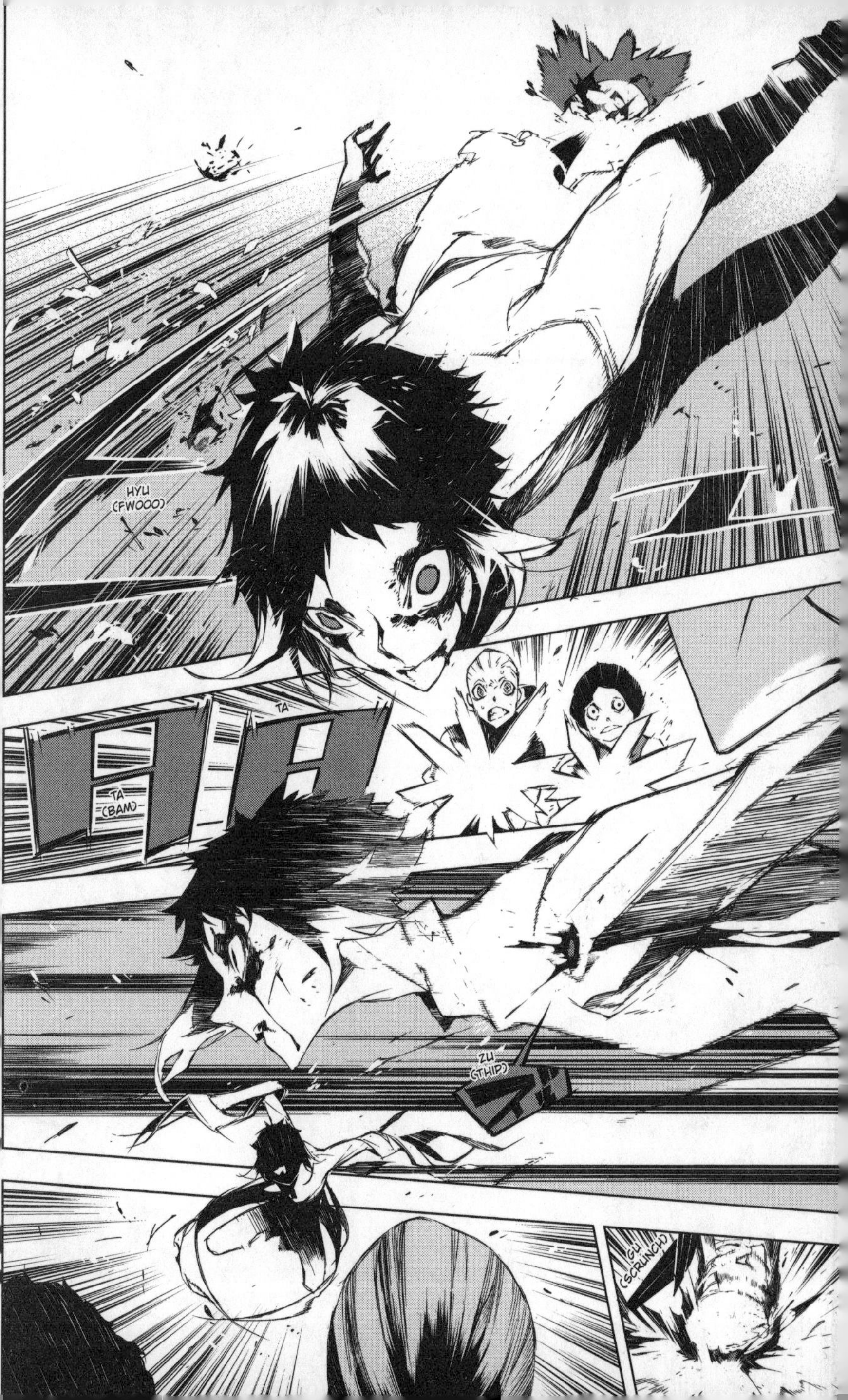
HYU
(FWOOO)
TA
TA
(BAM)
ZU
(THIP)
GU
(SCRUNCH)

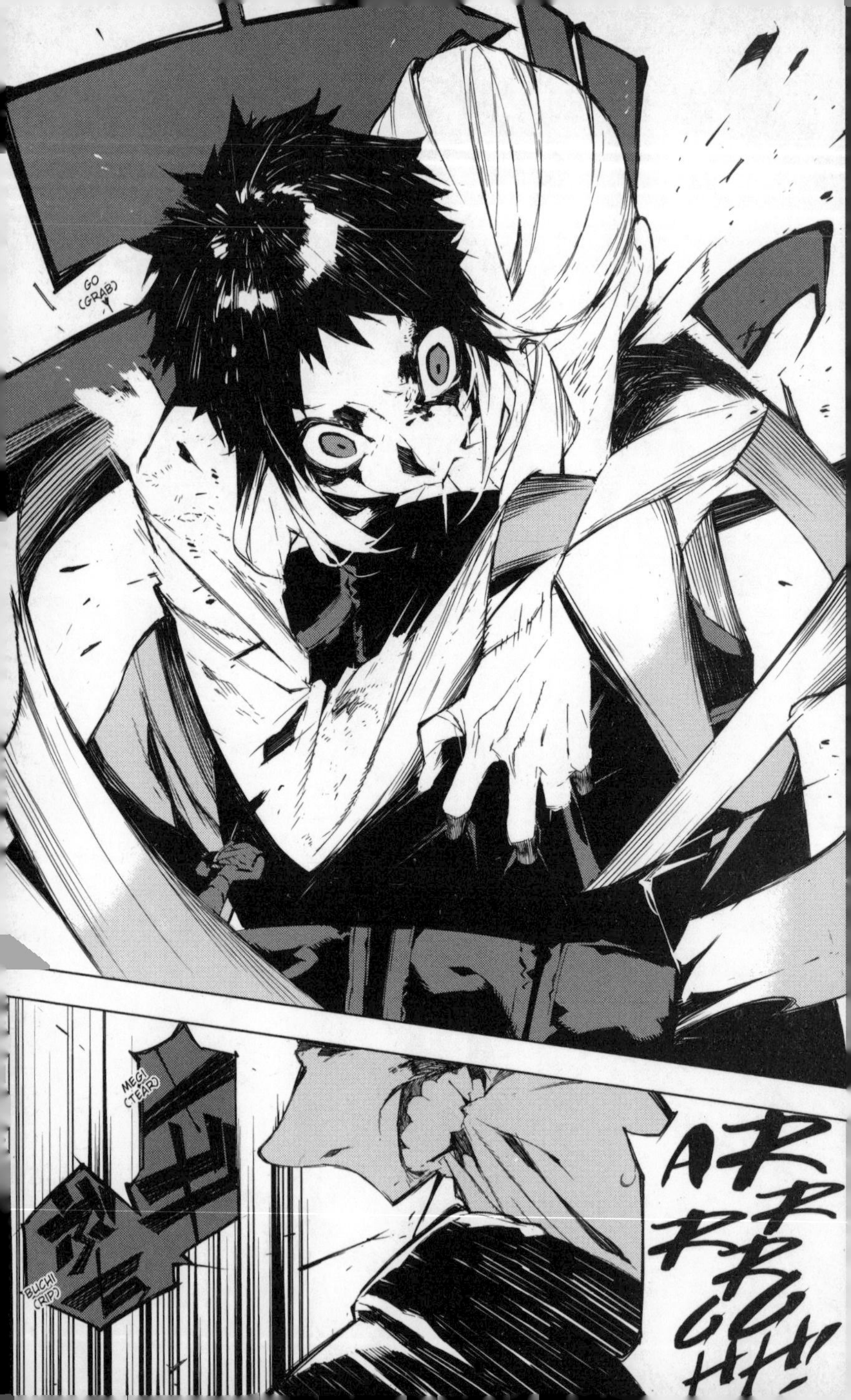
GO
(GRAB)
ARRRRGGHH!!
MEGI
(TEAR)
BUCHI
(RIP)

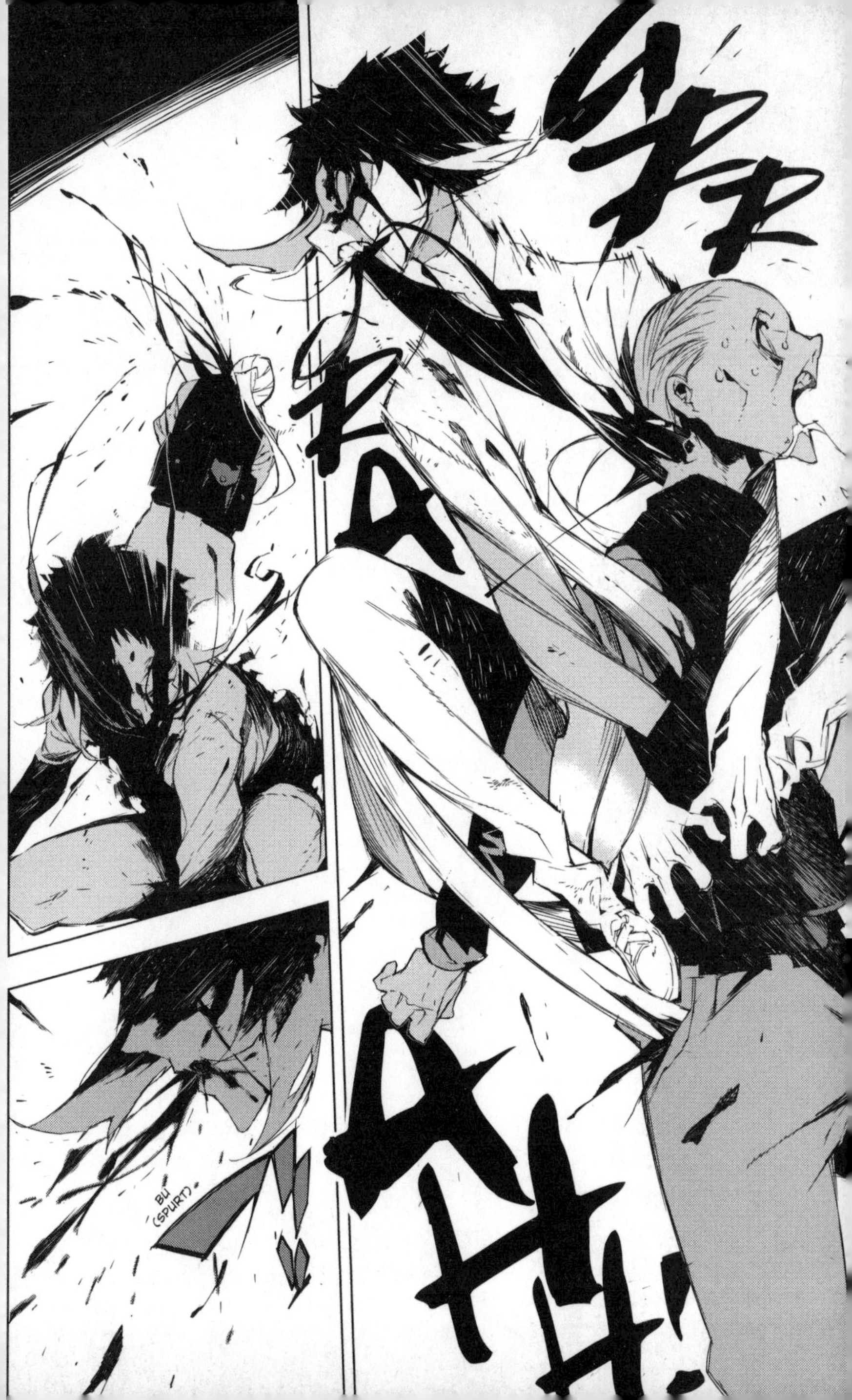
BU (SPURT)

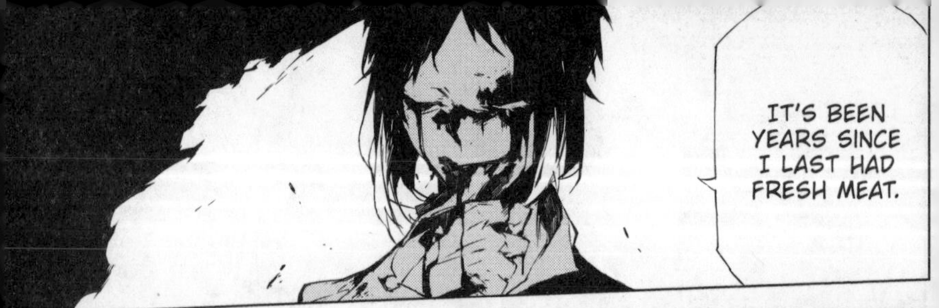
IT'S BEEN YEARS SINCE I LAST HAD FRESH MEAT.
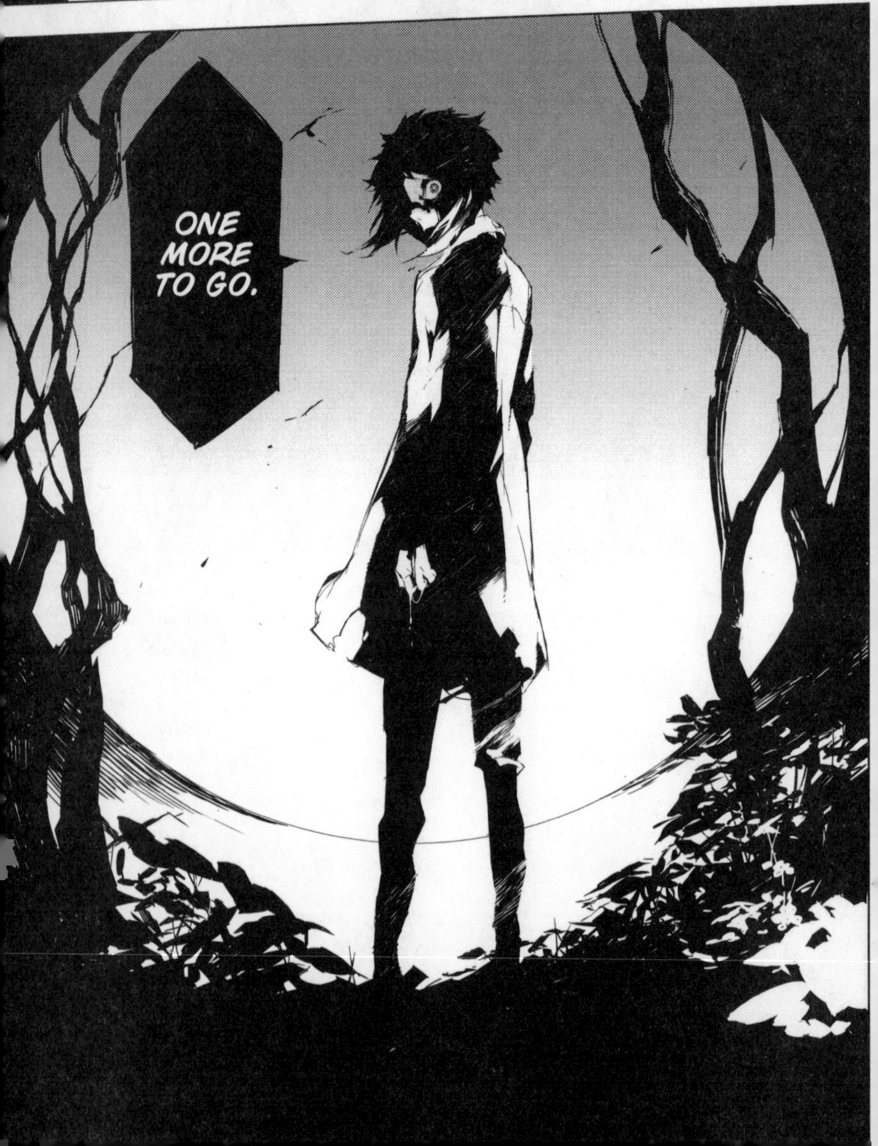
ONE MORE TO GO.

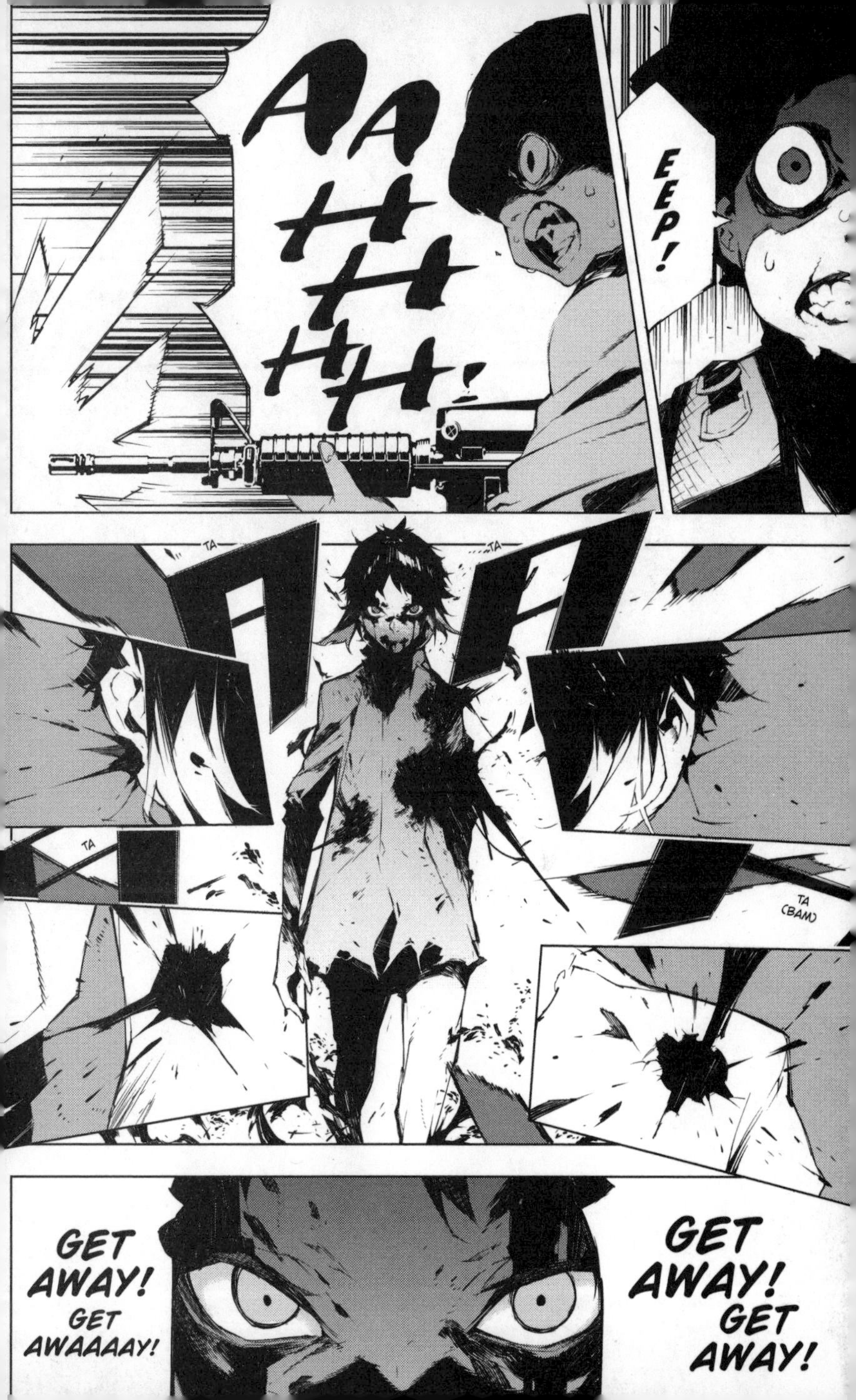
EEP!
AAHHHH!
TA
TA
TA (BAM)
TA
GET AWAY! GET AWAY!
GET AWAY! GET AWAAAAY!

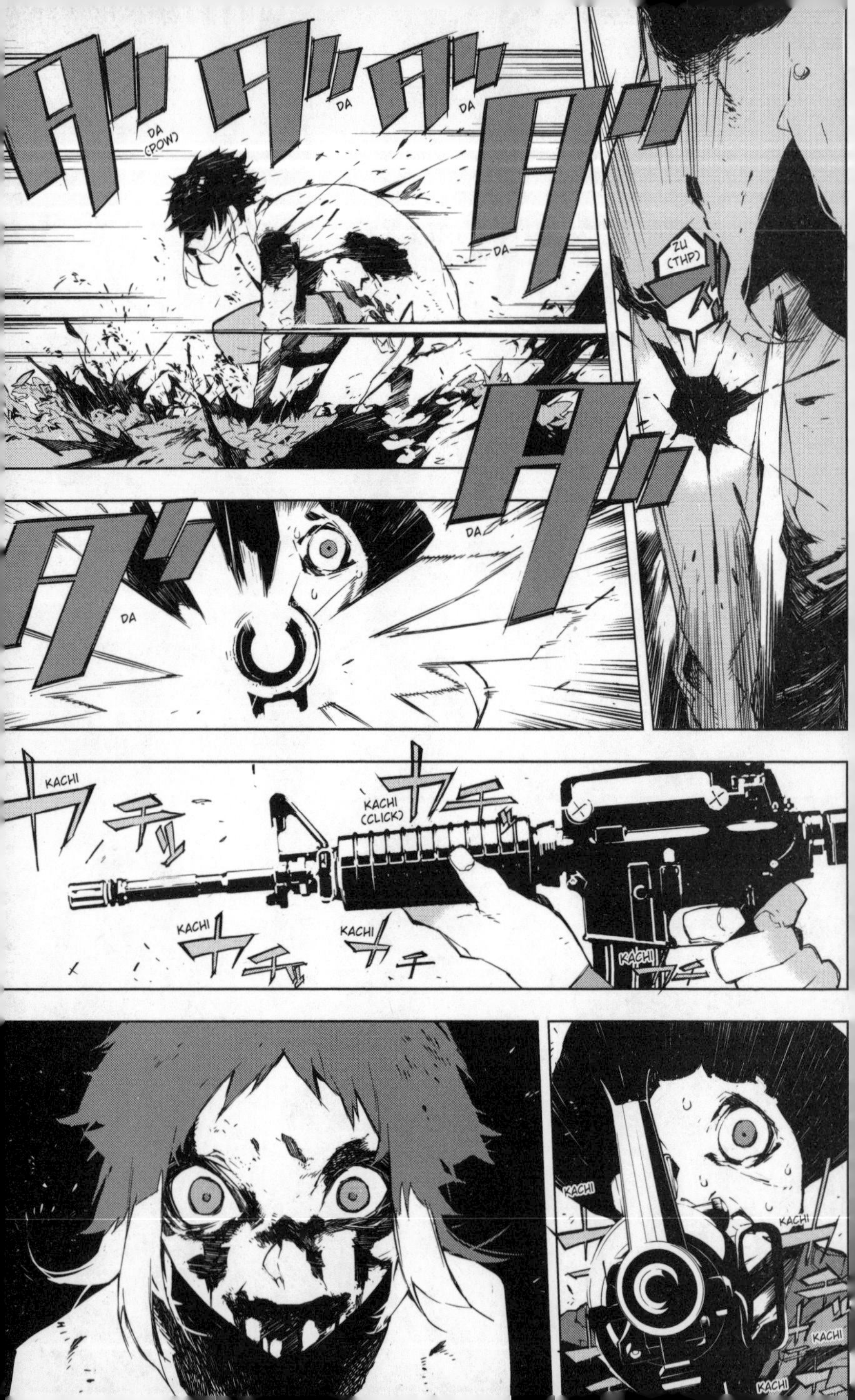
ZU (THP)
DA
DA
DA
DA (POW)
DA
DA
KACHI (CLICK)
KACHI
KACHI
KACHI
KACHI
KACHI
KACHI
KACHI
KACHI

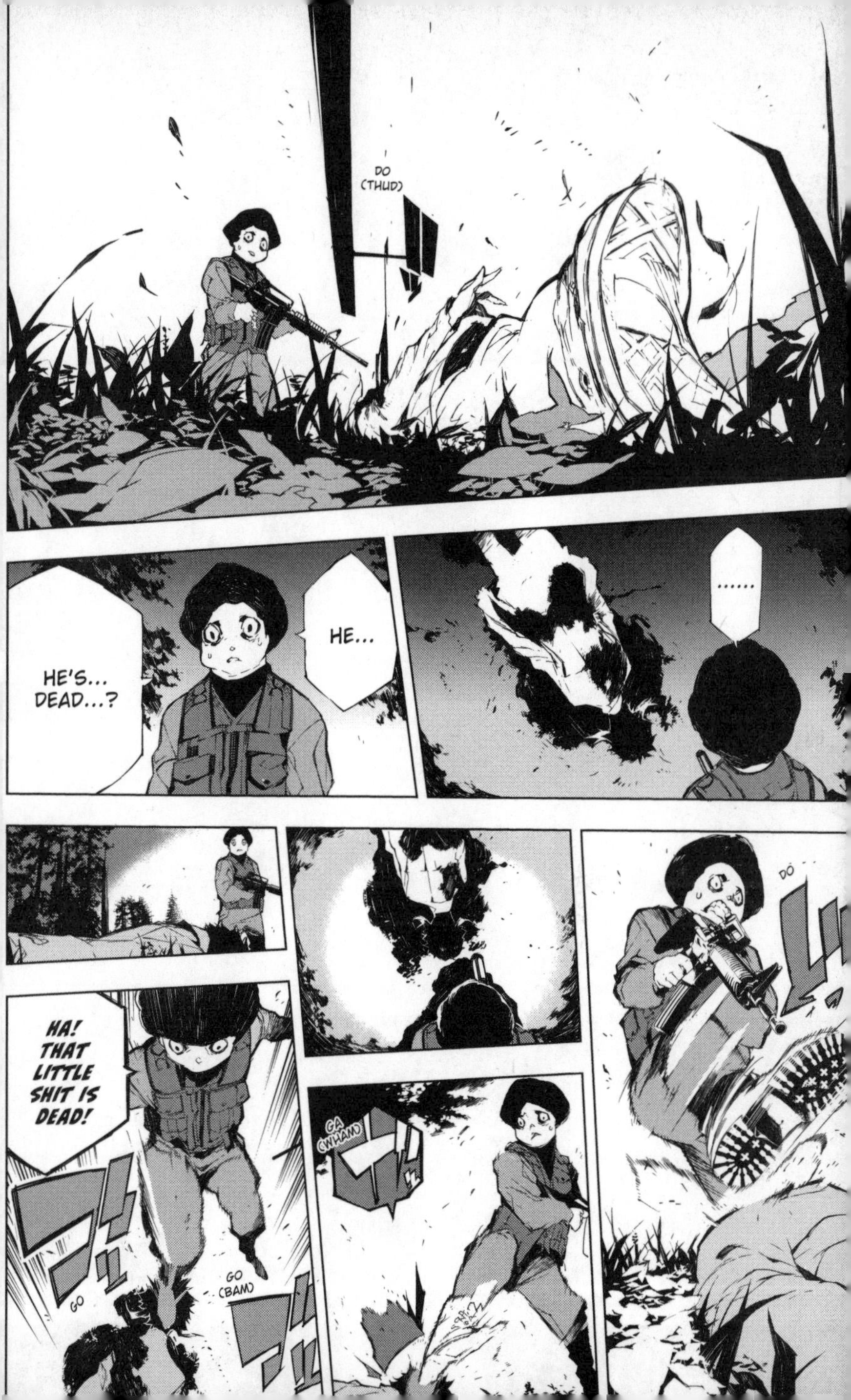
DO
(THUD)
......
HE...
HE'S... DEAD...?
DO
GA
(WHAM)
GO
(BAM)
HA! THAT LITTLE SHIT IS DEAD!
GO

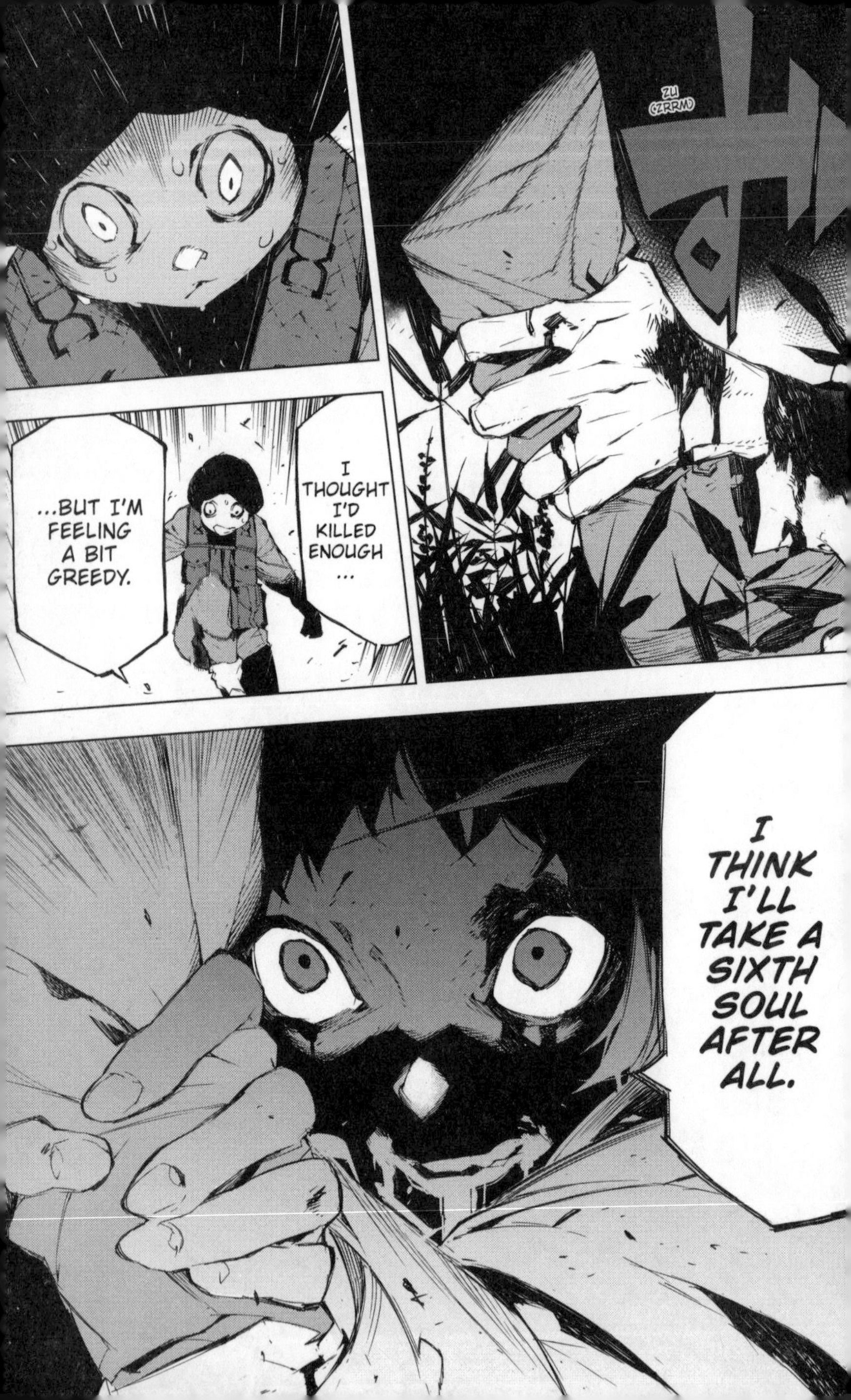
ZU
(ZRRM)
I THOUGHT I'D KILLED ENOUGH...
...BUT I'M FEELING A BIT GREEDY.
I THINK I'LL TAKE A SIXTH SOUL AFTER ALL.

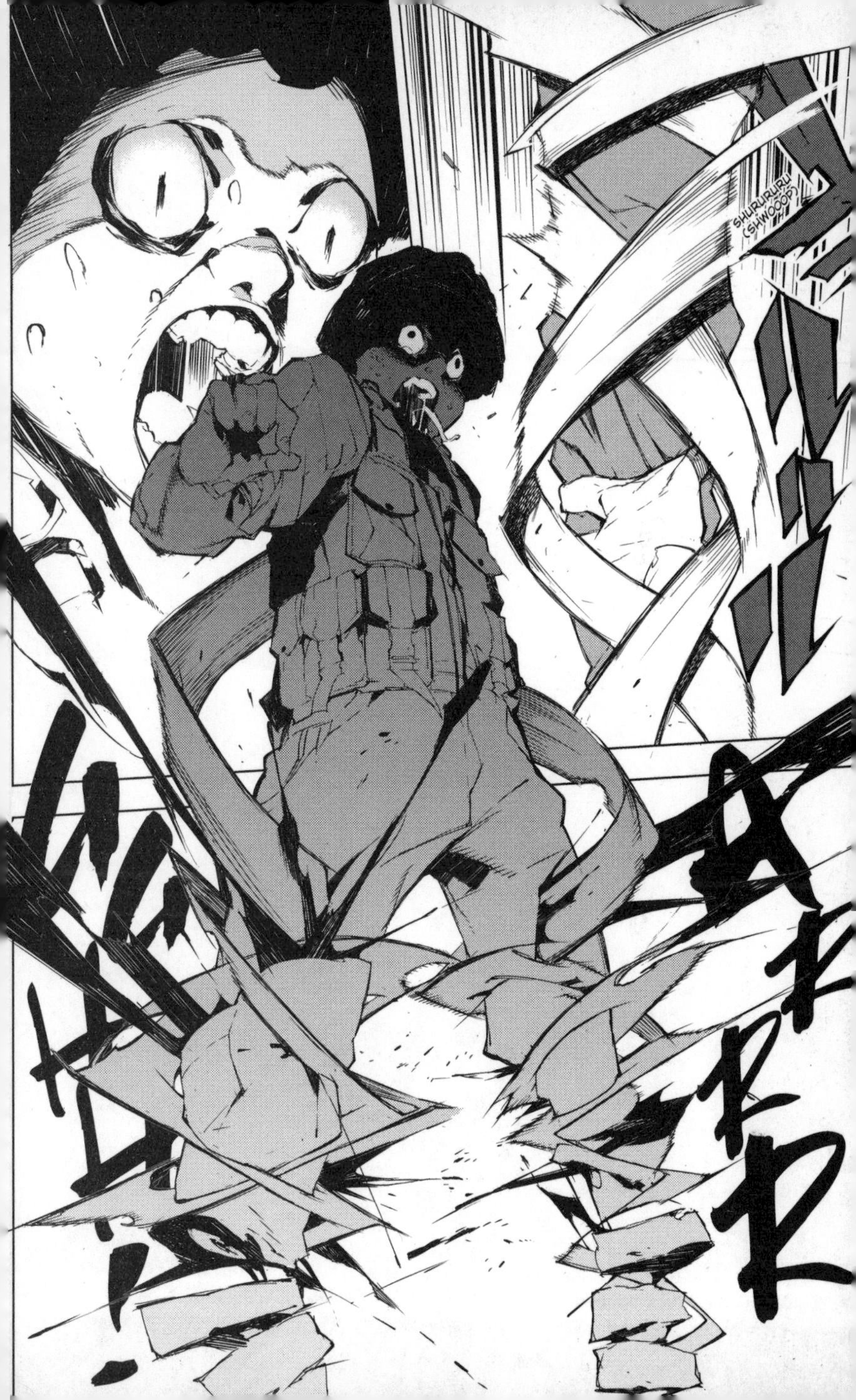
SHURURURU
(SHWOOOP)

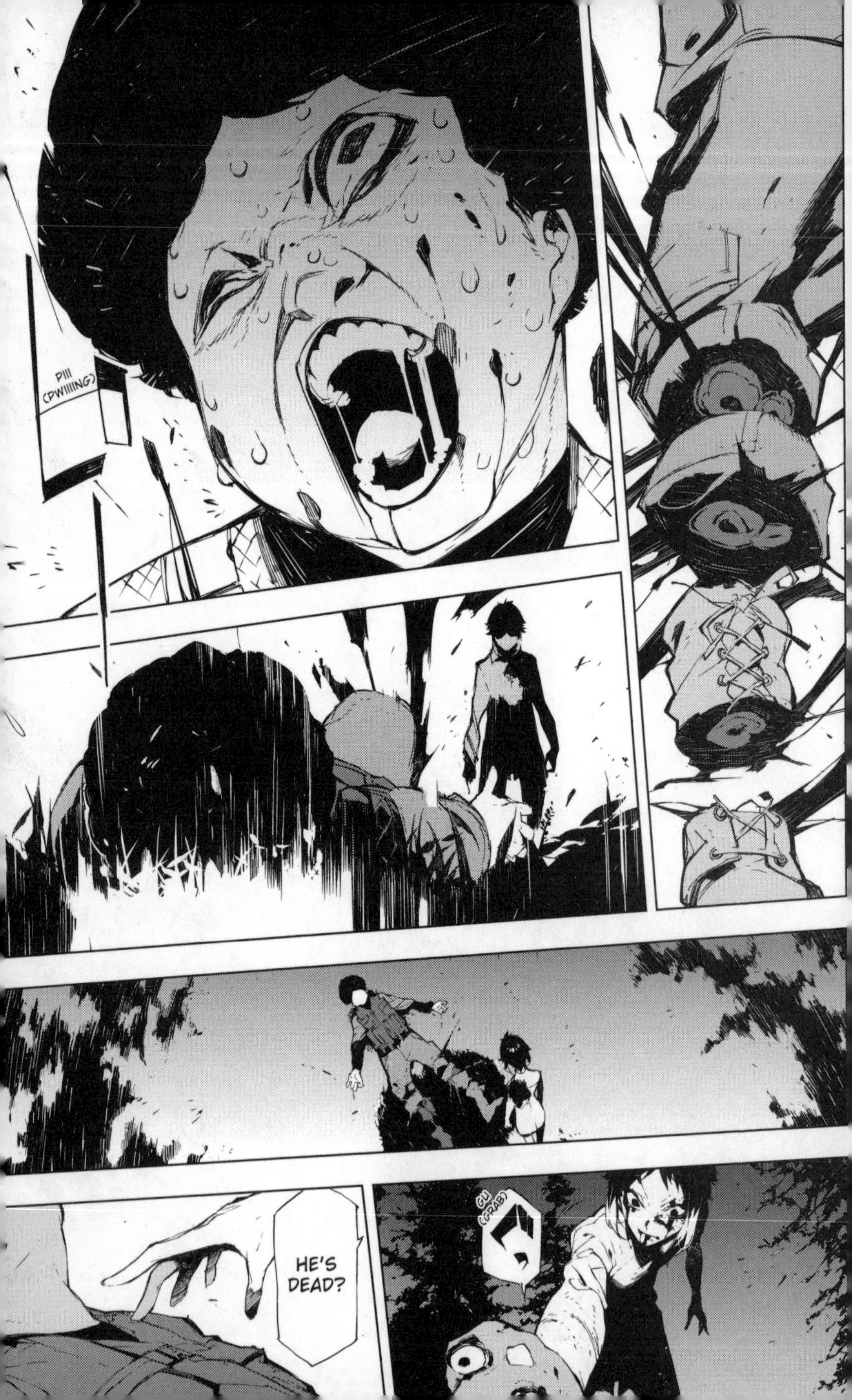
PIII (PWIIIING)
GU (GRAB)
HE'S DEAD?

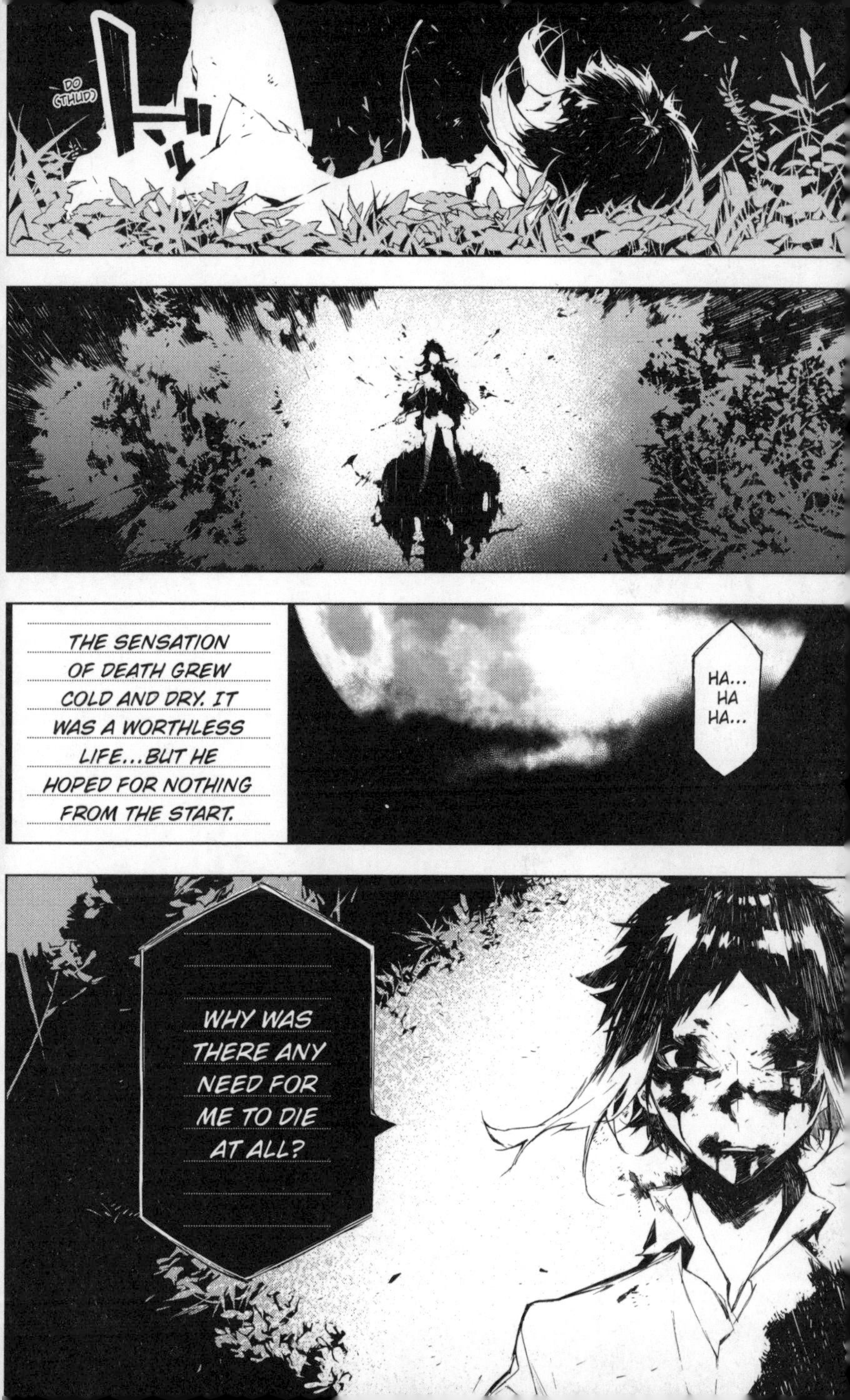
DO (THUD)
THE SENSATION OF DEATH GREW COLD AND DRY. IT WAS A WORTHLESS LIFE...BUT HE HOPED FOR NOTHING FROM THE START.
HA... HA HA...
WHY WAS THERE ANY NEED FOR ME TO DIE AT ALL?

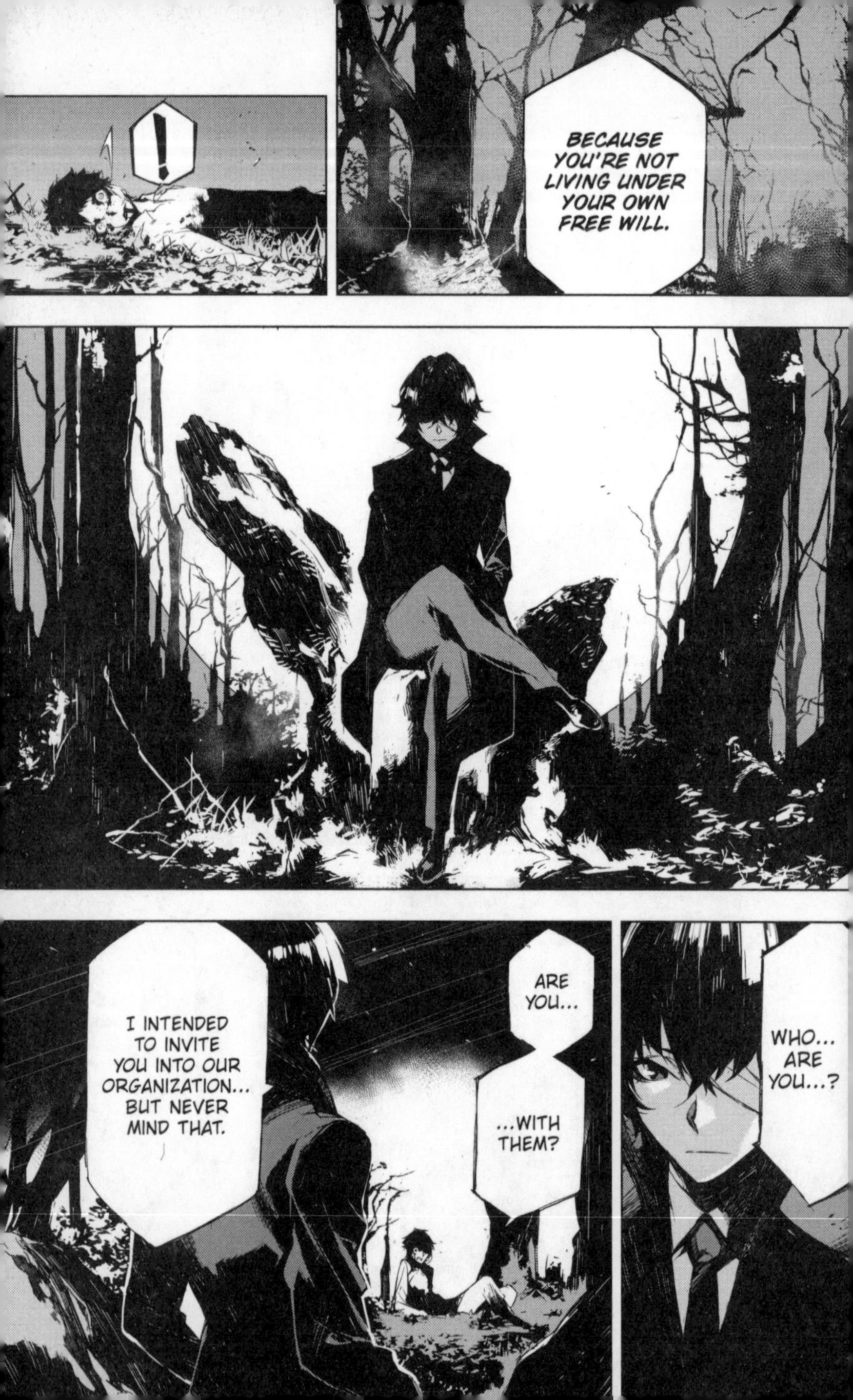
BECAUSE YOU'RE NOT LIVING UNDER YOUR OWN FREE WILL.
!
WHO... ARE YOU...?
ARE YOU...
...WITH THEM?
I INTENDED TO INVITE YOU INTO OUR ORGANIZATION... BUT NEVER MIND THAT.

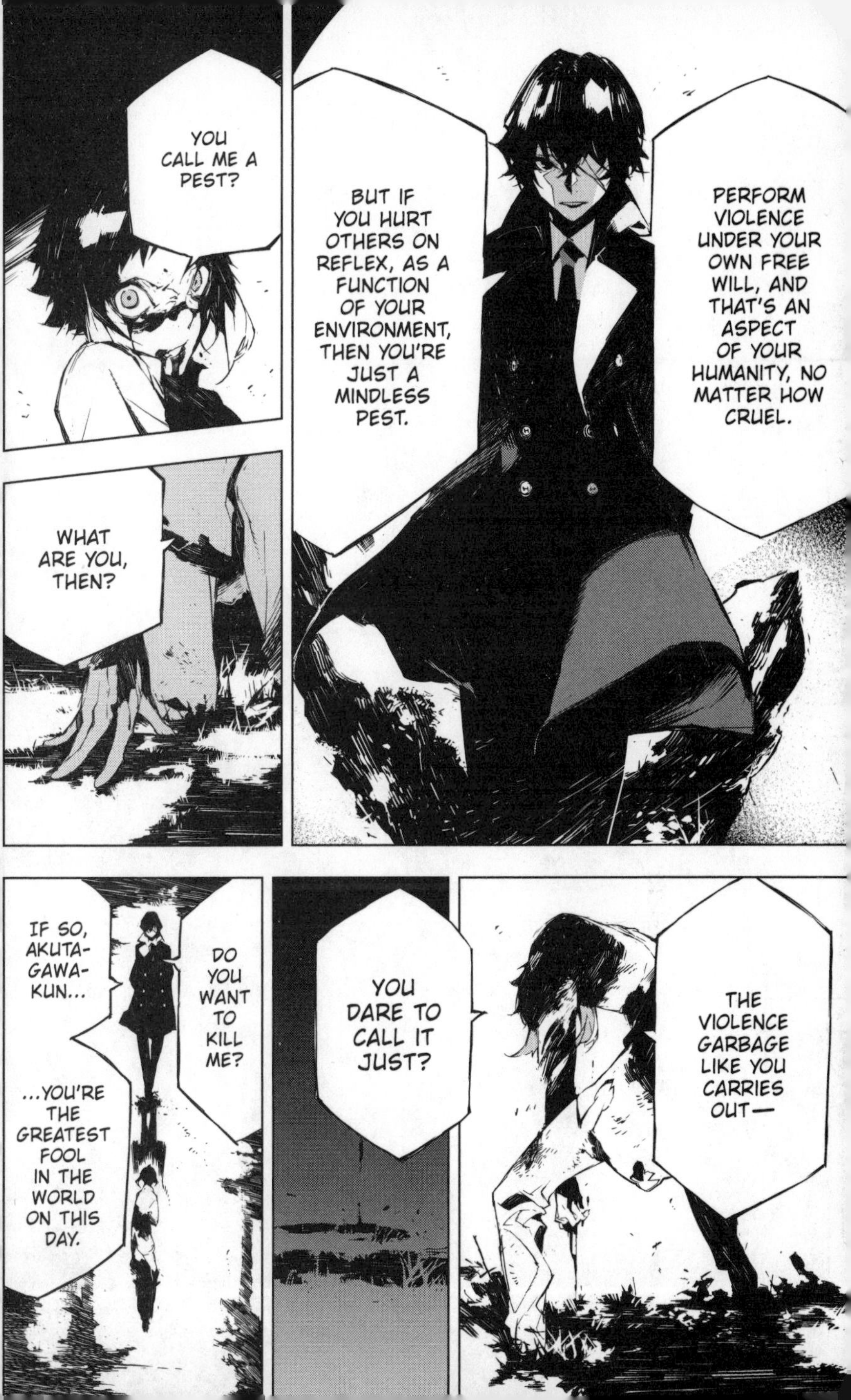
PERFORM VIOLENCE UNDER YOUR OWN FREE WILL, AND THAT'S AN ASPECT OF YOUR HUMANITY, NO MATTER HOW CRUEL.
BUT IF YOU HURT OTHERS ON REFLEX, AS A FUNCTION OF YOUR ENVIRONMENT, THEN YOU'RE JUST A MINDLESS PEST.
YOU CALL ME A PEST?
WHAT ARE YOU, THEN?
THE VIOLENCE GARBAGE LIKE YOU CARRIES OUT—
YOU DARE TO CALL IT JUST?
DO YOU WANT TO KILL ME?
IF SO, AKUTAGAWA-KUN...
...YOU'RE THE GREATEST FOOL IN THE WORLD ON THIS DAY.

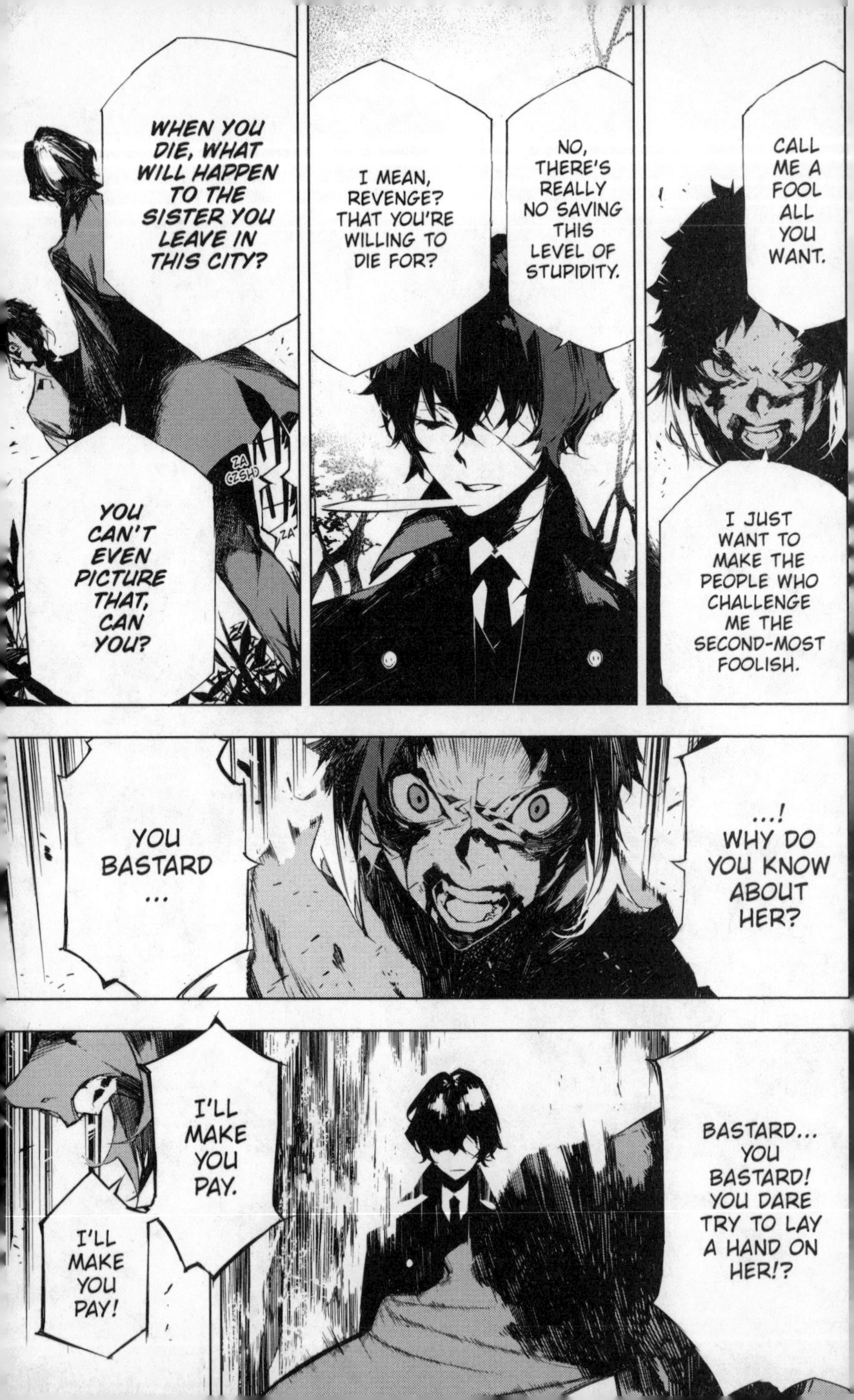
CALL ME A FOOL ALL YOU WANT.
I JUST WANT TO MAKE THE PEOPLE WHO CHALLENGE ME THE SECOND-MOST FOOLISH.
NO, THERE'S REALLY NO SAVING THIS LEVEL OF STUPIDITY.
I MEAN, REVENGE? THAT YOU'RE WILLING TO DIE FOR?
WHEN YOU DIE, WHAT WILL HAPPEN TO THE SISTER YOU LEAVE IN THIS CITY?
YOU CAN'T EVEN PICTURE THAT, CAN YOU?
...! WHY DO YOU KNOW ABOUT HER?
YOU BASTARD ...
BASTARD... YOU BASTARD! YOU DARE TRY TO LAY A HAND ON HER!?
I'LL MAKE YOU PAY.
I'LL MAKE YOU PAY!

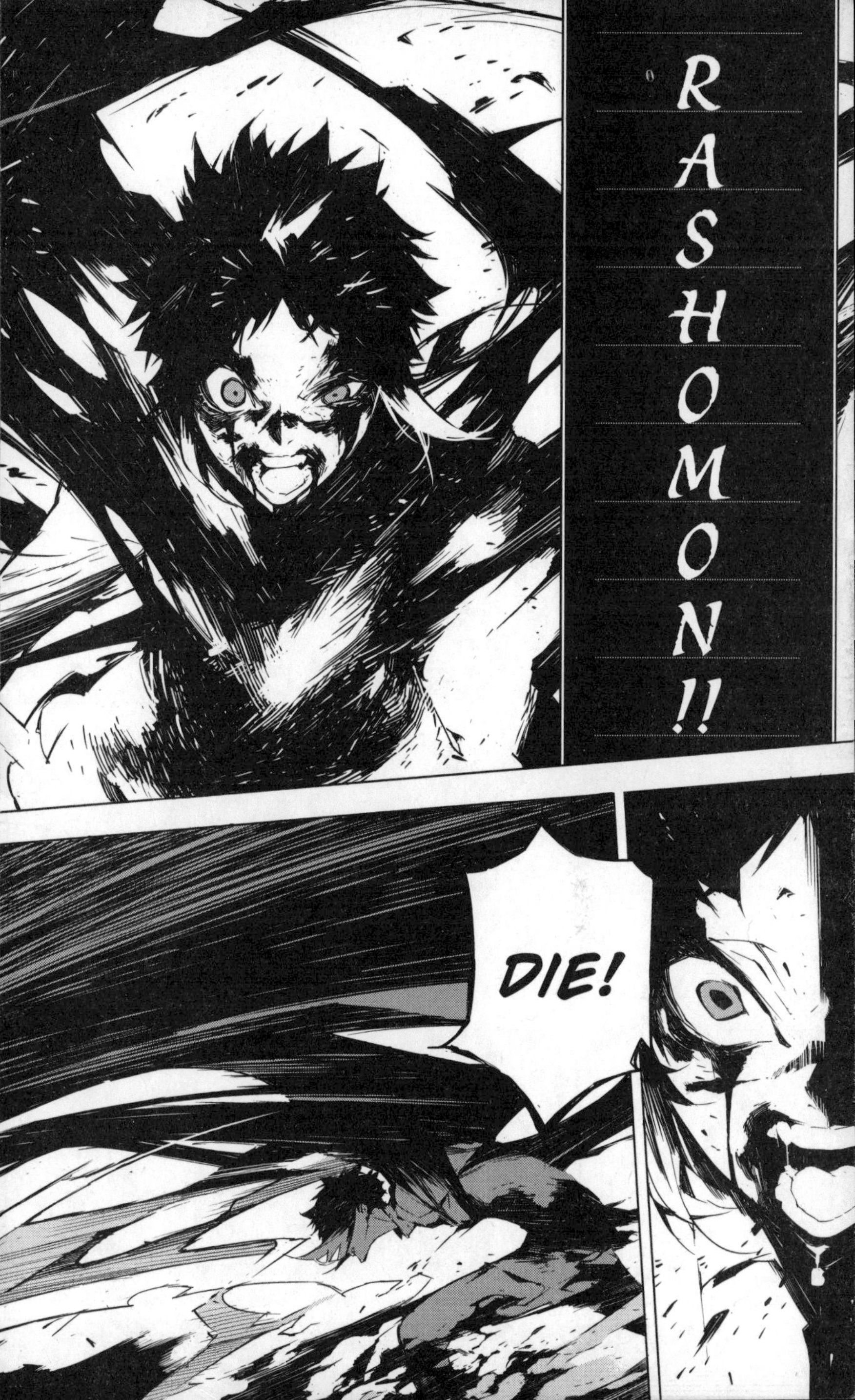
RASHOMON!!
DIE!

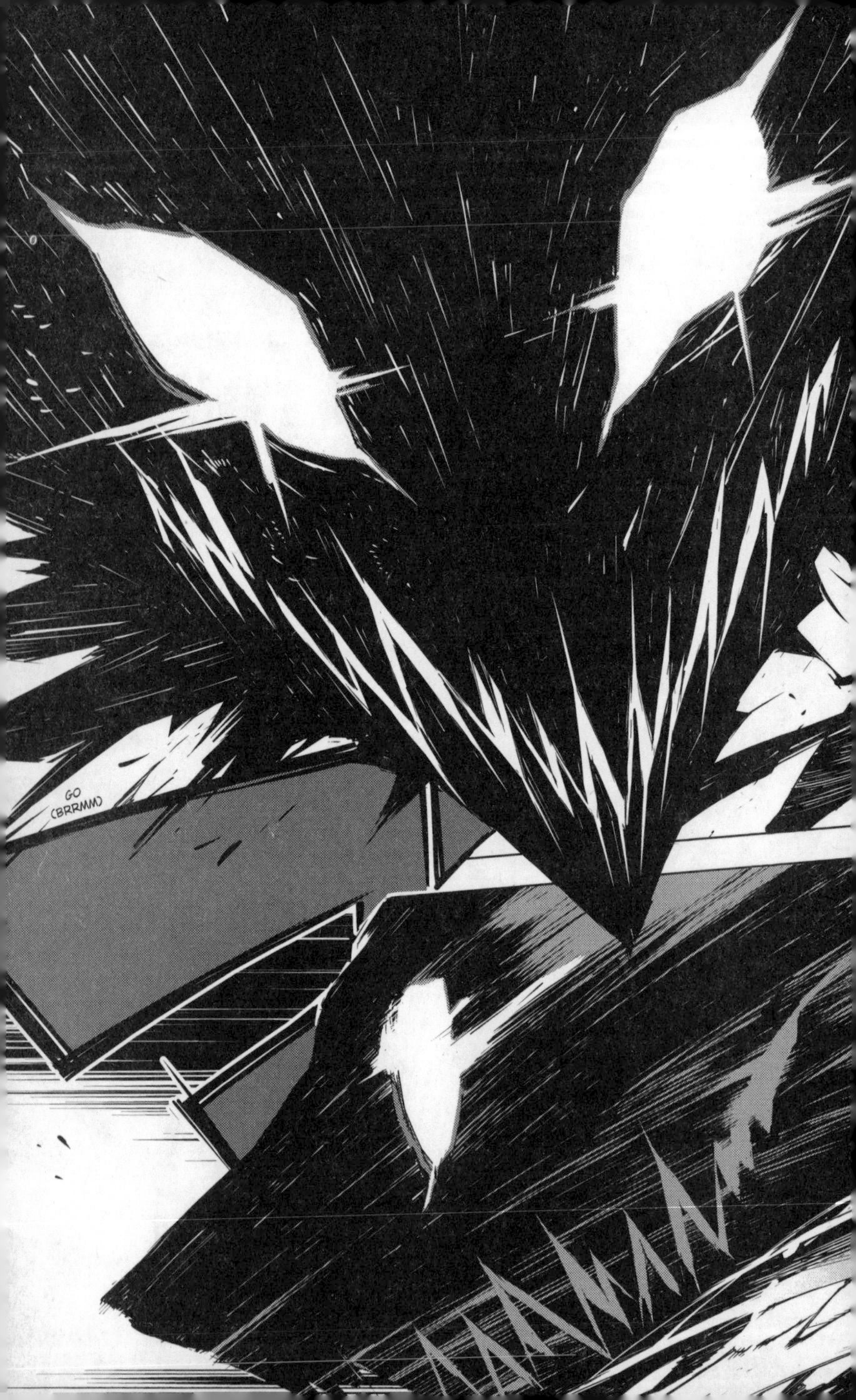
GO
(BRRMM)

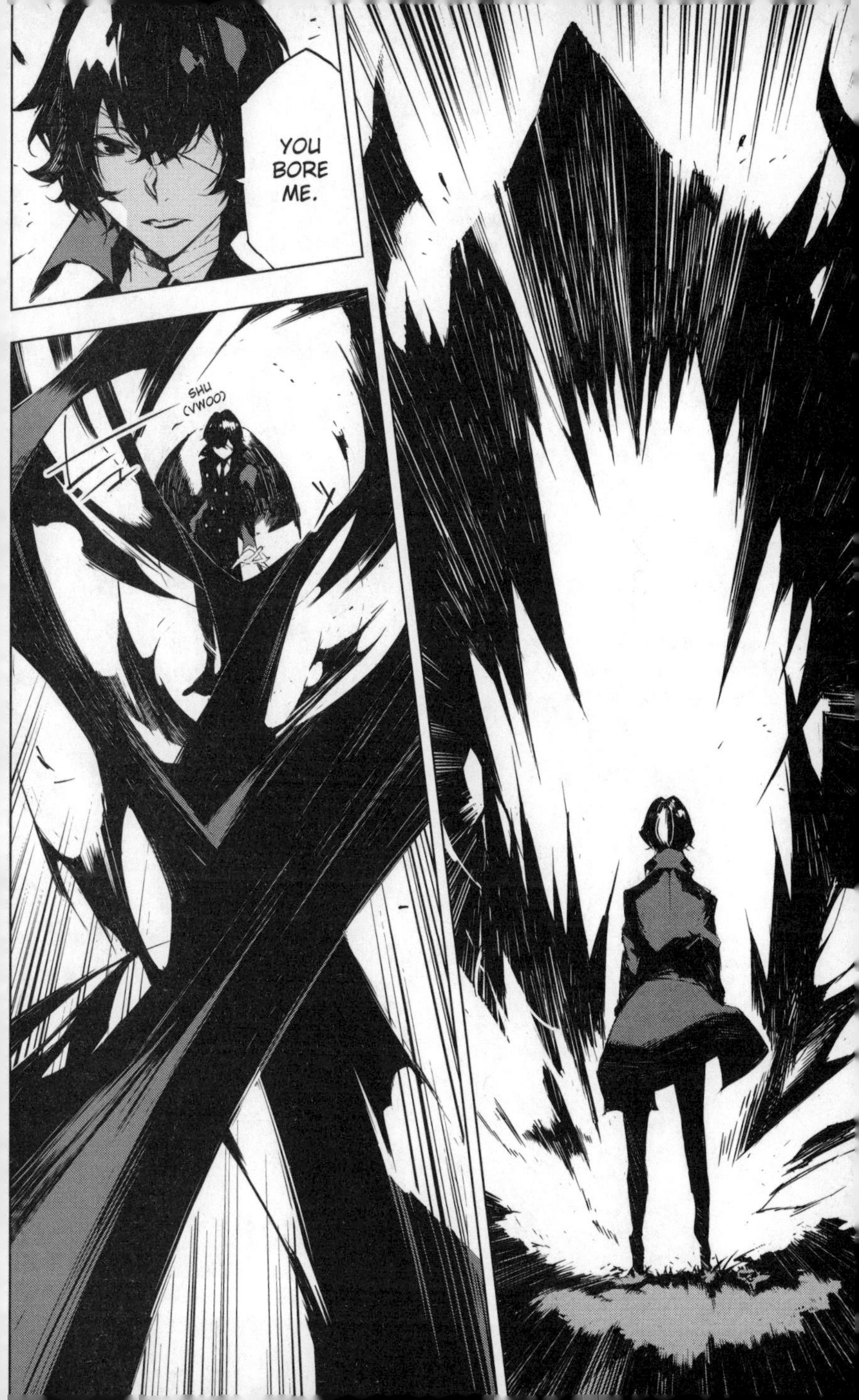
YOU BORE ME.
SHU (VWOO)

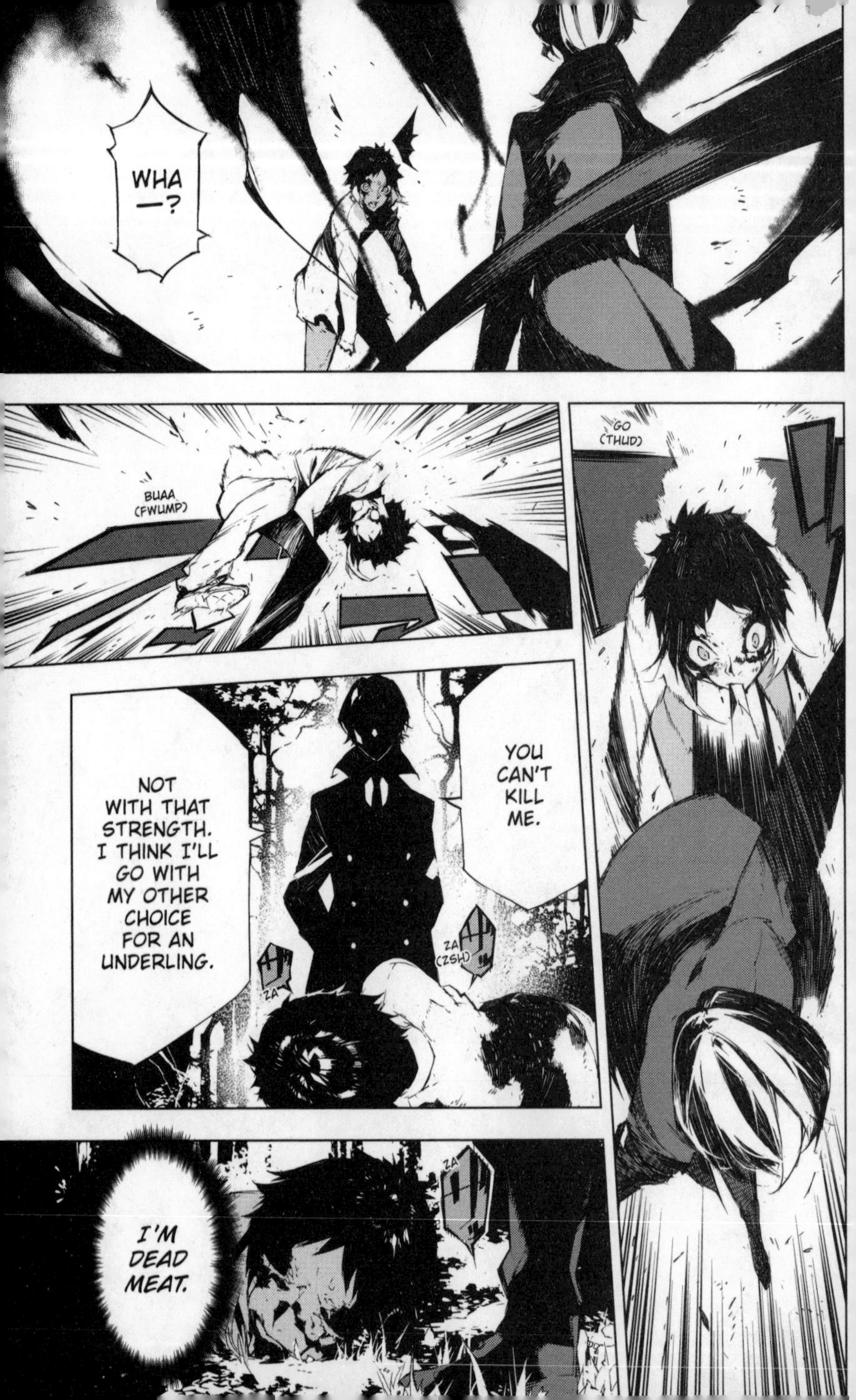
WHA—?
GO (THUD)
BUAA (FWUMP)
YOU CAN'T KILL ME.
ZA (ZSH)
NOT WITH THAT STRENGTH. I THINK I'LL GO WITH MY OTHER CHOICE FOR AN UNDERLING.
ZA
ZA
I'M DEAD MEAT.

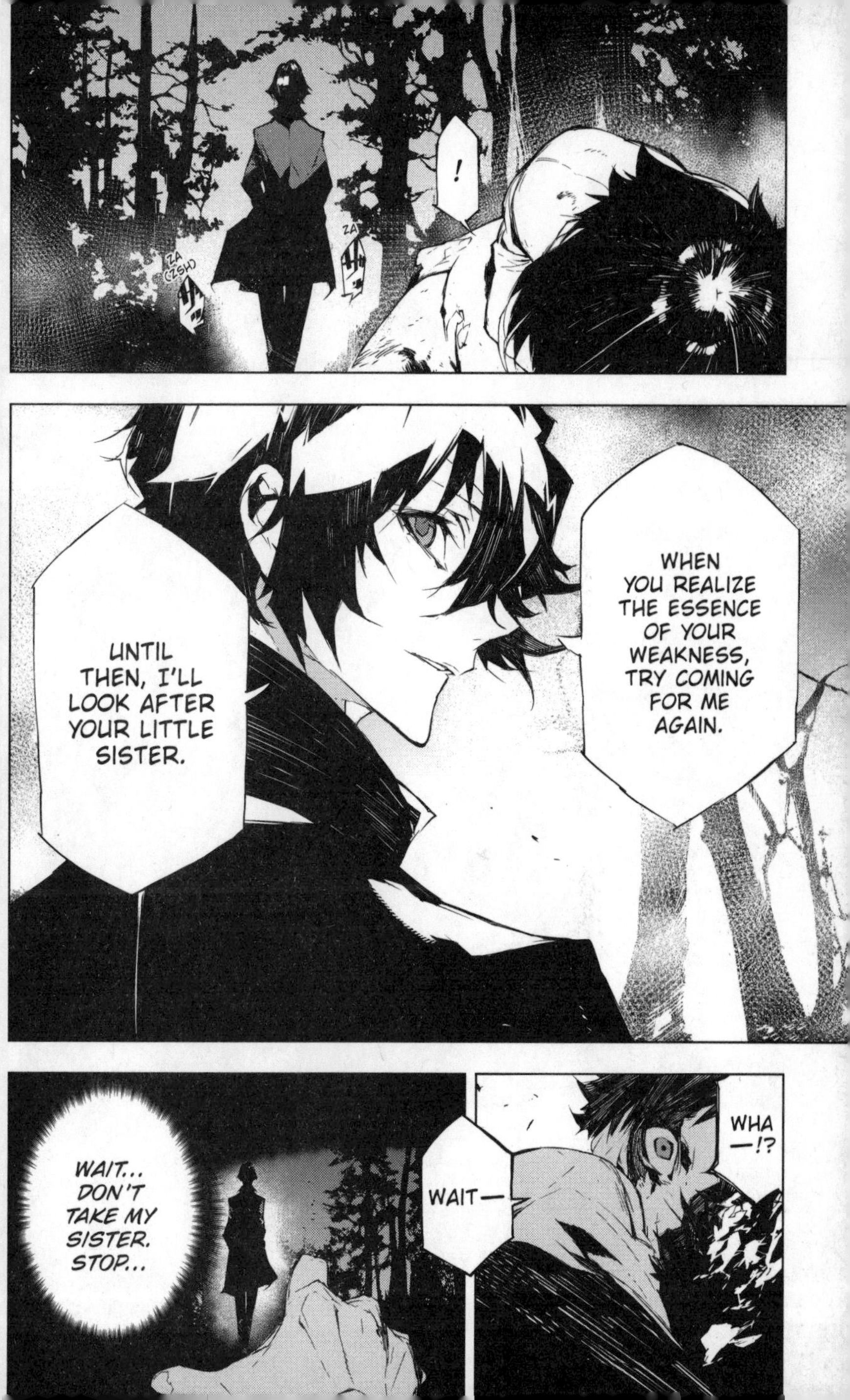
!
ZA
ZA (ZSH)
WHEN YOU REALIZE THE ESSENCE OF YOUR WEAKNESS, TRY COMING FOR ME AGAIN.
UNTIL THEN, I'LL LOOK AFTER YOUR LITTLE SISTER.
WHA—!?
WAIT—
WAIT... DON'T TAKE MY SISTER. STOP...

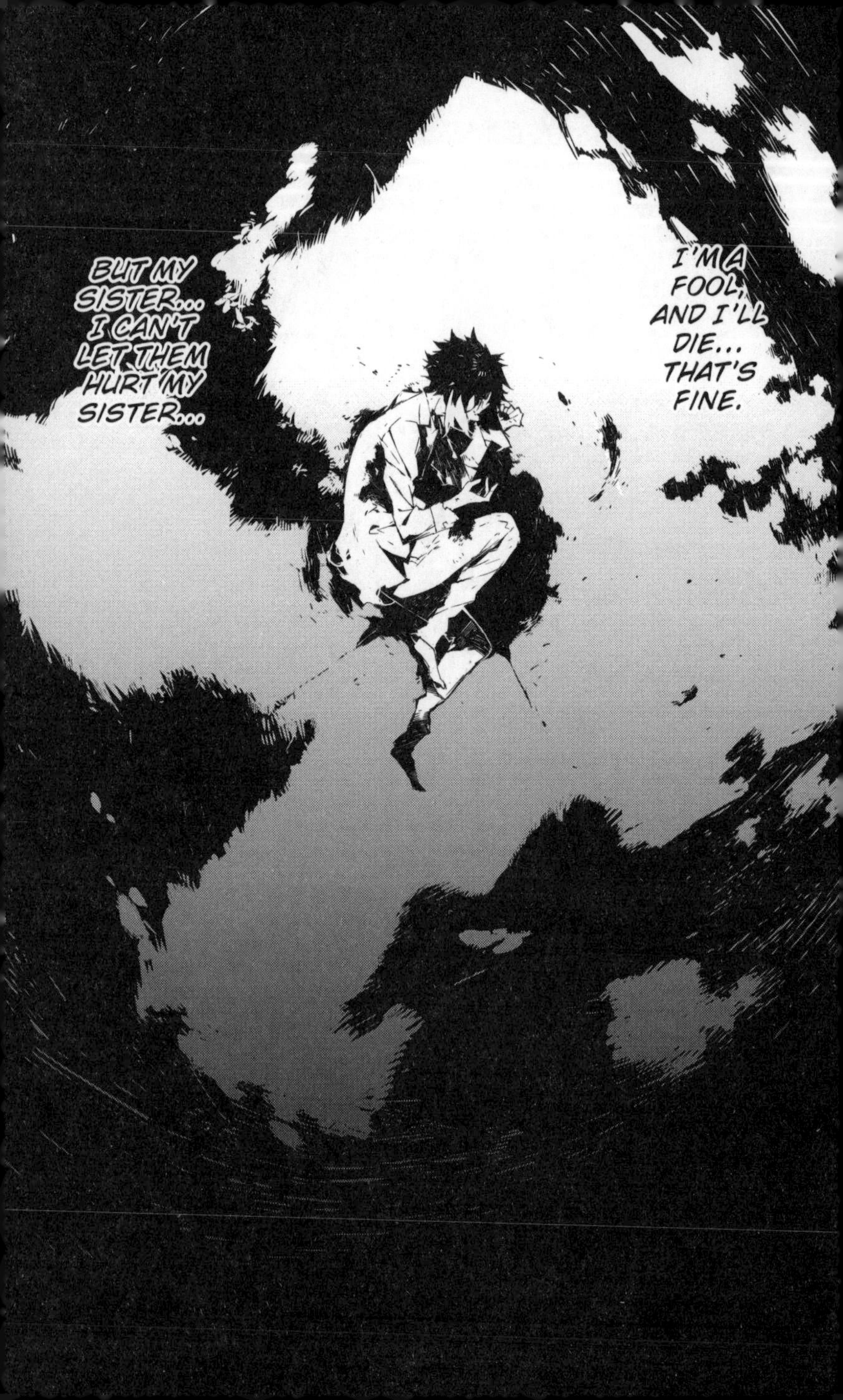
I'M A FOOL, AND I'LL DIE... THAT'S FINE.
BUT MY SISTER... I CAN'T LET THEM HURT MY SISTER...

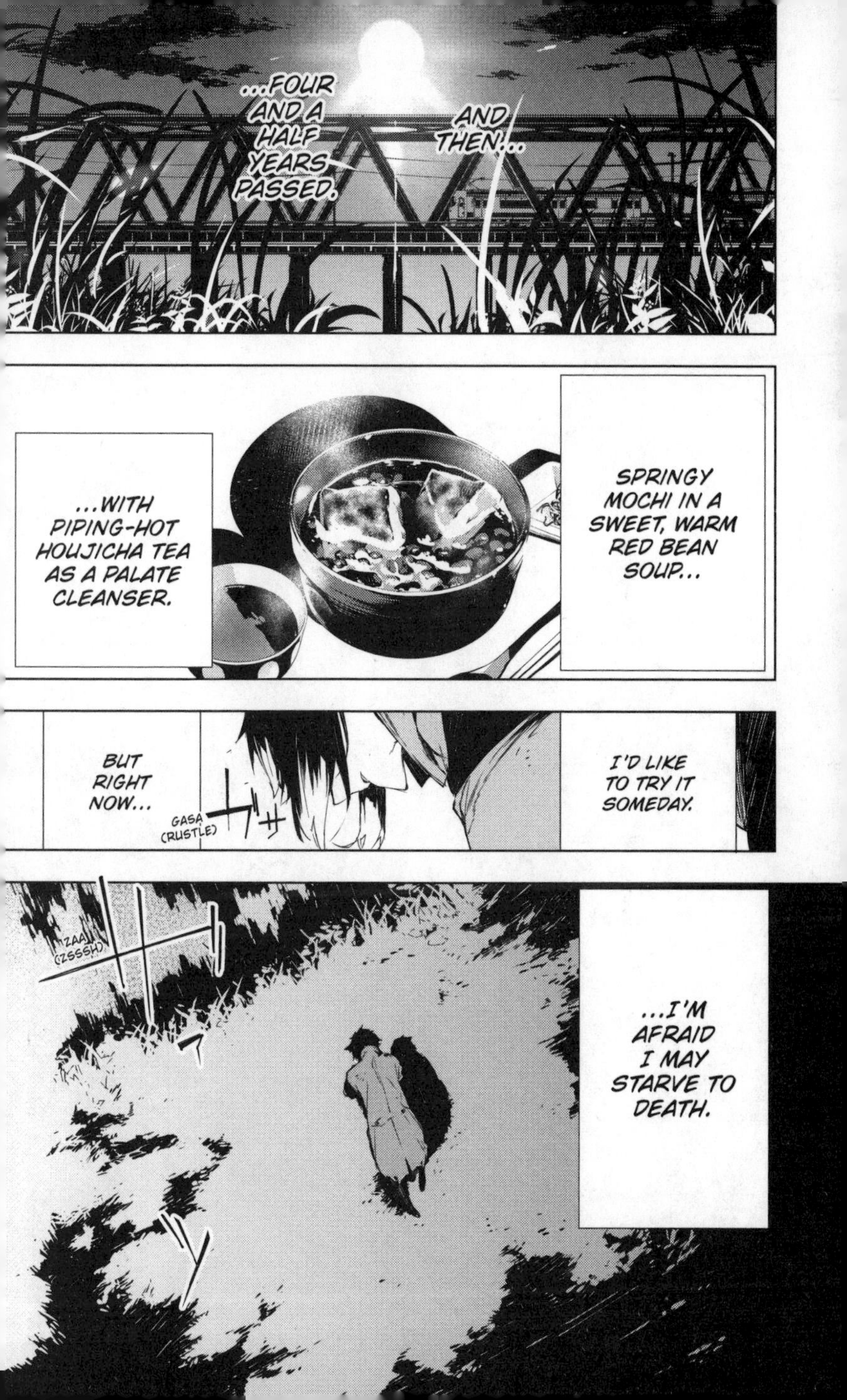
AND THEN...
...FOUR AND A HALF YEARS PASSED.
SPRINGY MOCHI IN A SWEET, WARM RED BEAN SOUP...
...WITH PIPING-HOT HOUJICHA TEA AS A PALATE CLEANSER.
I'D LIKE TO TRY IT SOMEDAY.
GASA (RUSTLE)
BUT RIGHT NOW...
...I'M AFRAID I MAY STARVE TO DEATH.
ZAA (ZSSSH)

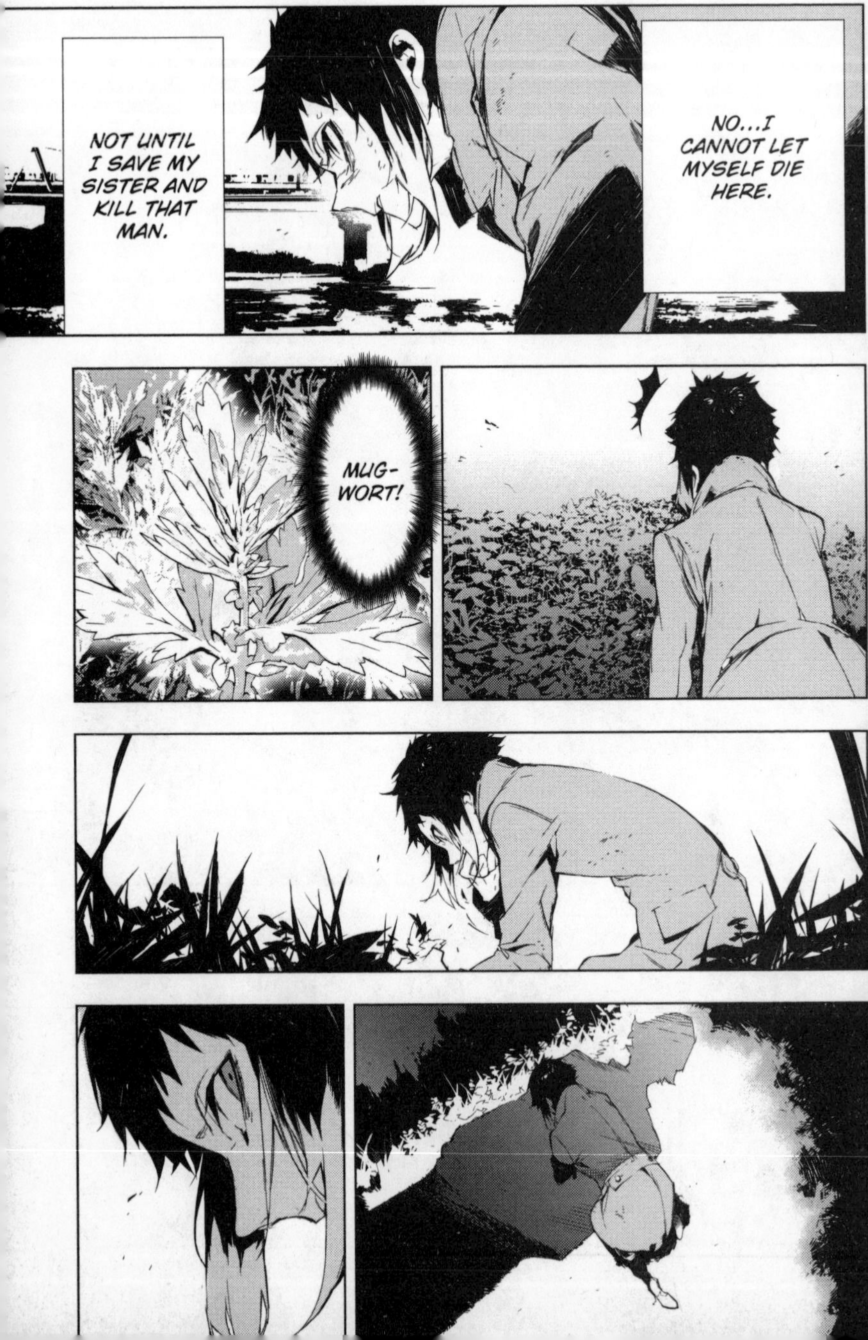
NO...I CANNOT LET MYSELF DIE HERE.
NOT UNTIL I SAVE MY SISTER AND KILL THAT MAN.
MUG-WORT!

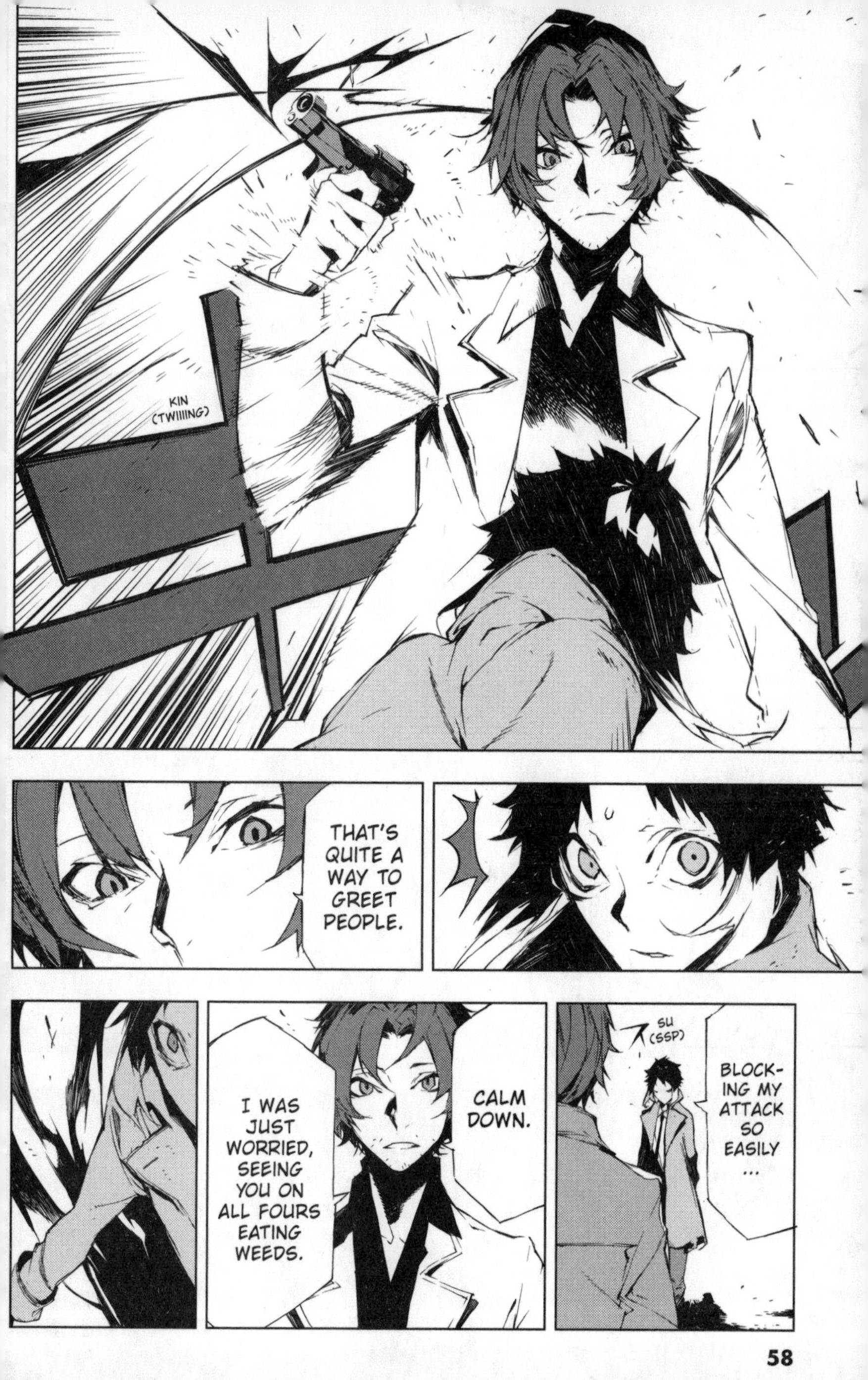
KIN (TWIIIING)
THAT'S QUITE A WAY TO GREET PEOPLE.
SU (SSP)
BLOCKING MY ATTACK SO EASILY ...
CALM DOWN.
I WAS JUST WORRIED, SEEING YOU ON ALL FOURS EATING WEEDS.

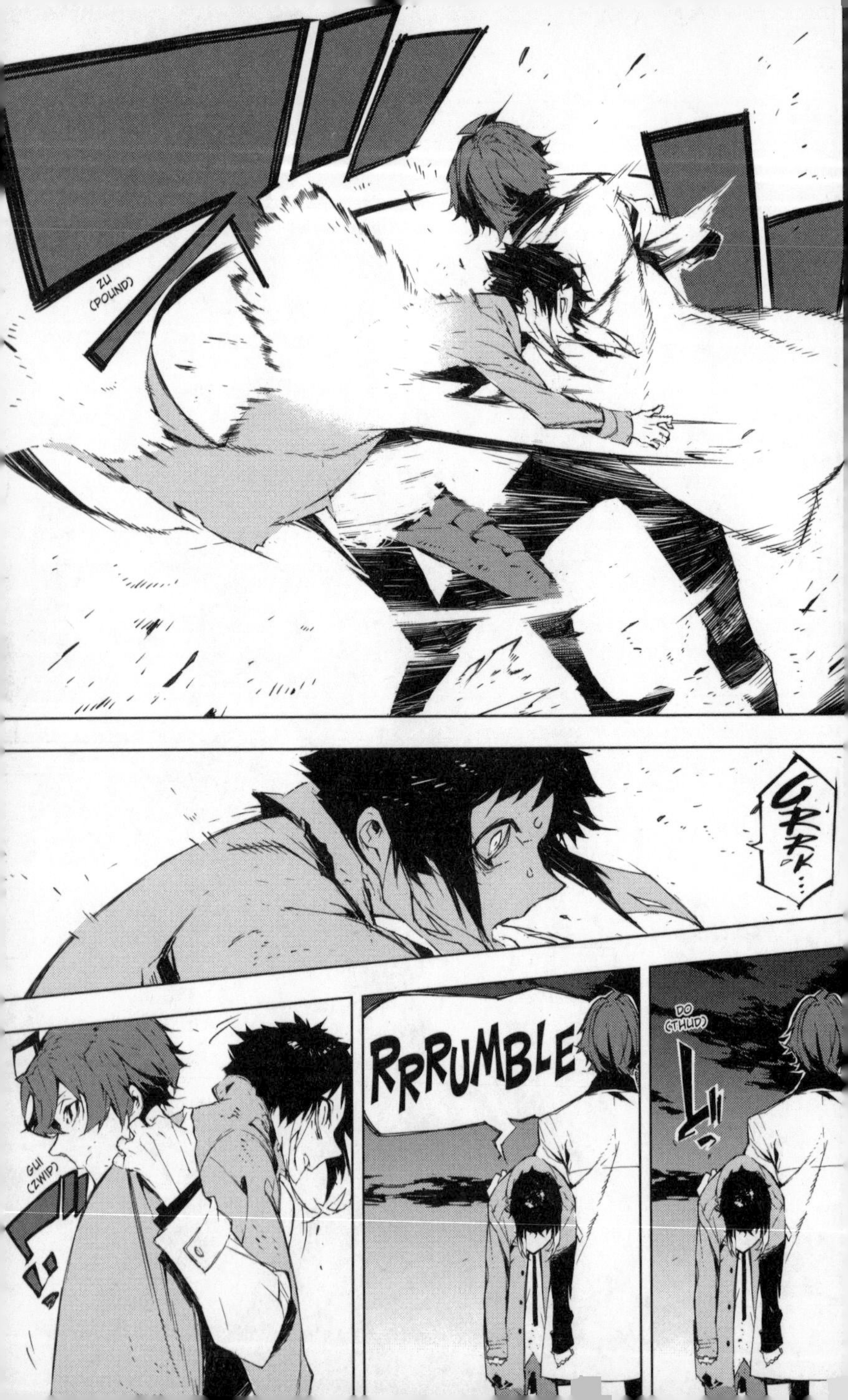
ZU
(POUND)
GRRK...
DO
(THUD)
RRRUMBLE
GUI
(ZWIP)

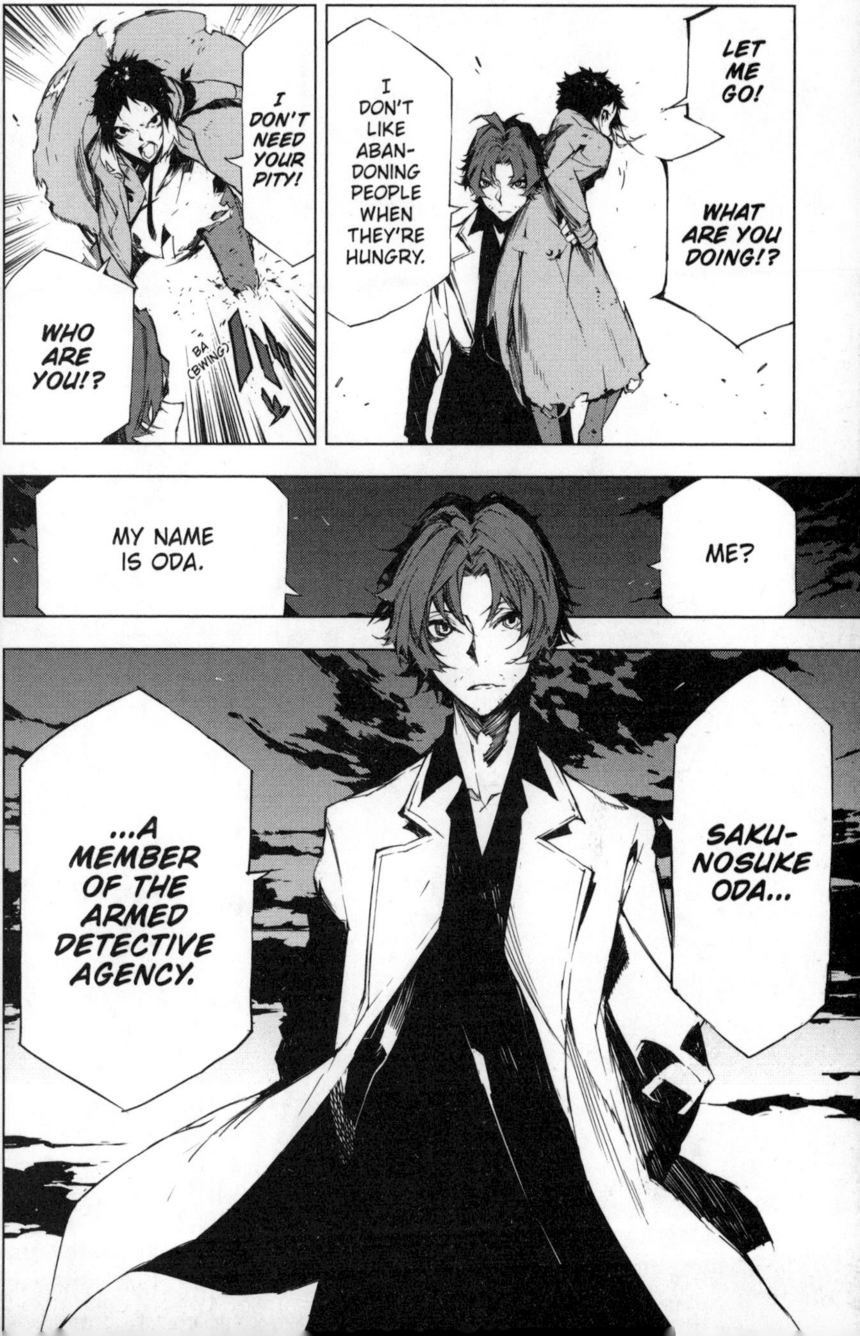
LET ME GO!
WHAT ARE YOU DOING!?
I DON'T LIKE ABAN-DONING PEOPLE WHEN THEY'RE HUNGRY.
I DON'T NEED YOUR PITY!
WHO ARE YOU!?
BA (BWING)
ME?
MY NAME IS ODA.
SAKU-NOSUKE ODA...
...A MEMBER OF THE ARMED DETECTIVE AGENCY.

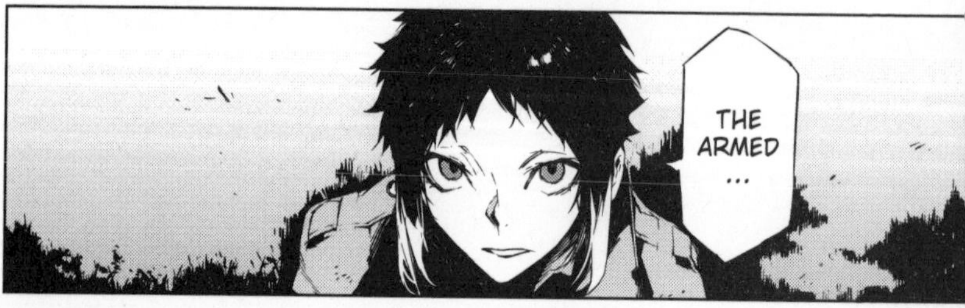
THE ARMED ...
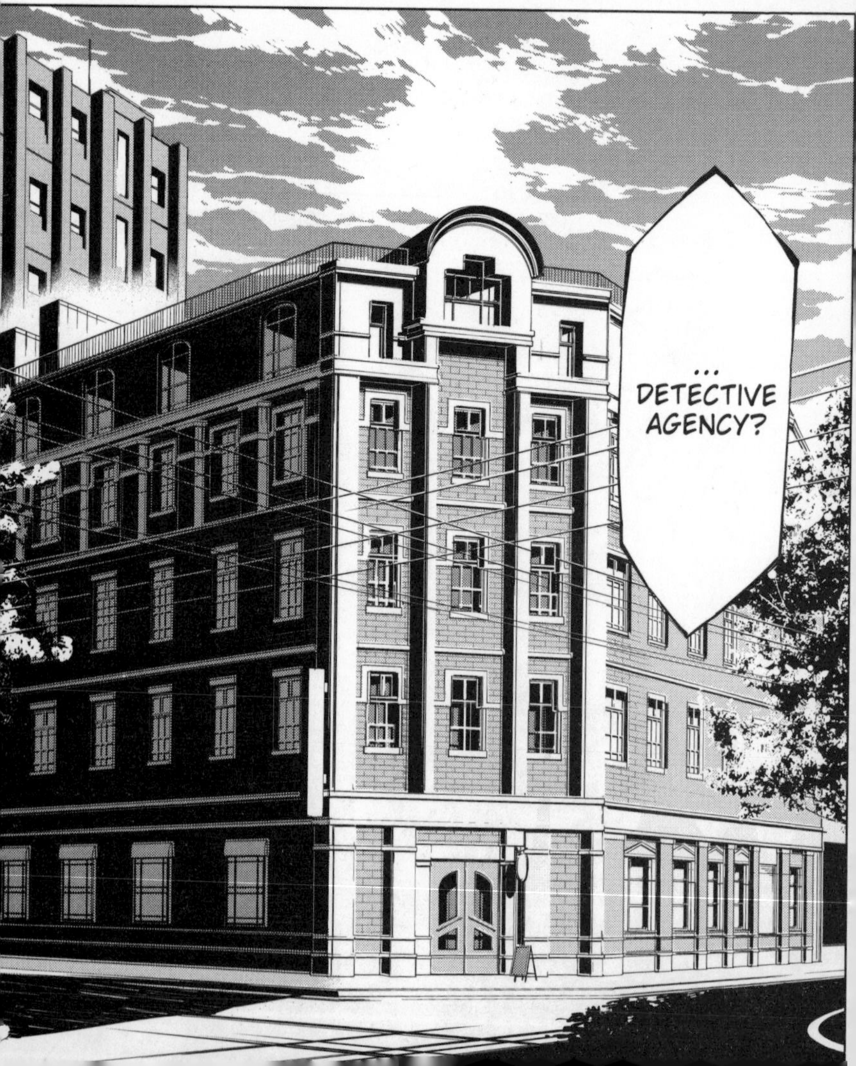
... DETECTIVE AGENCY?

Bungo Stray Dogs

BEAST

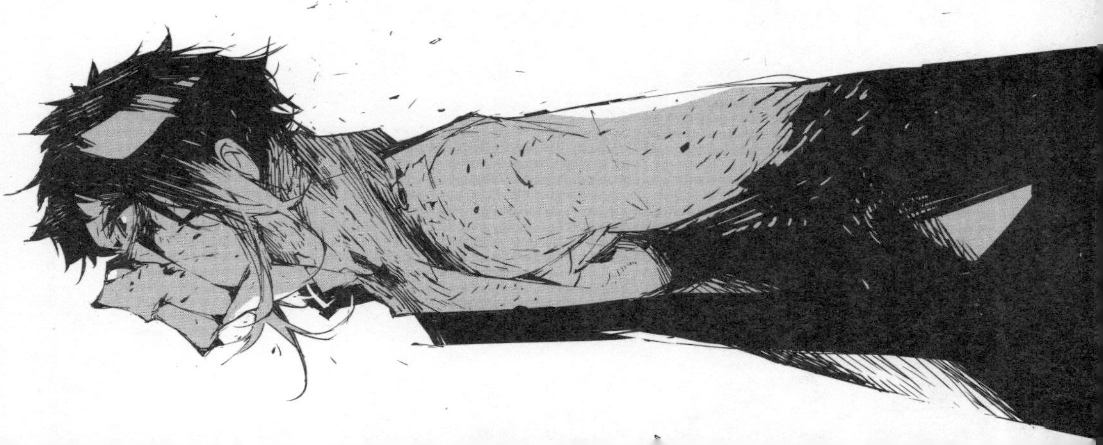

#2: A CERTAIN BOMB

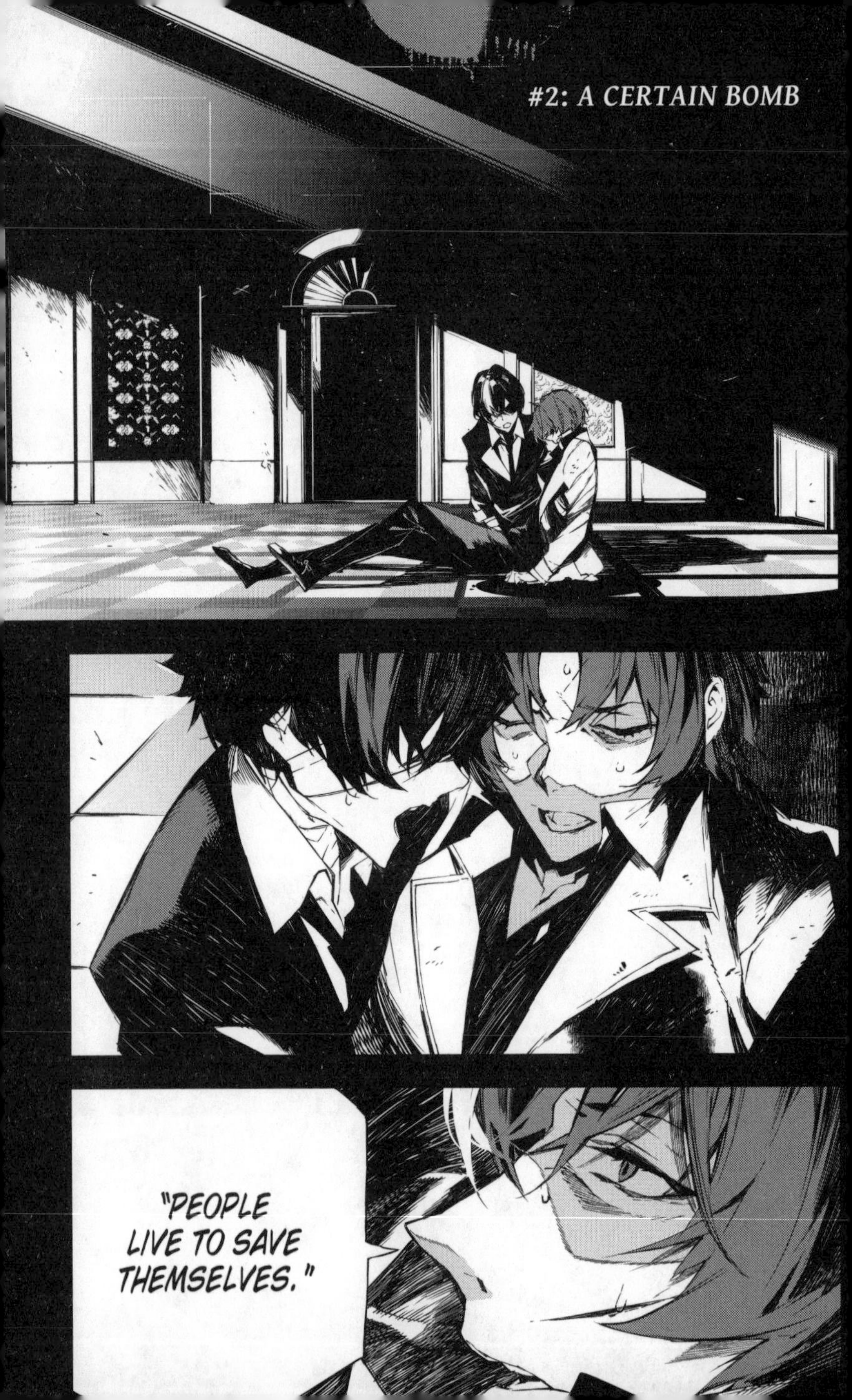
"PEOPLE LIVE TO SAVE THEMSELVES."

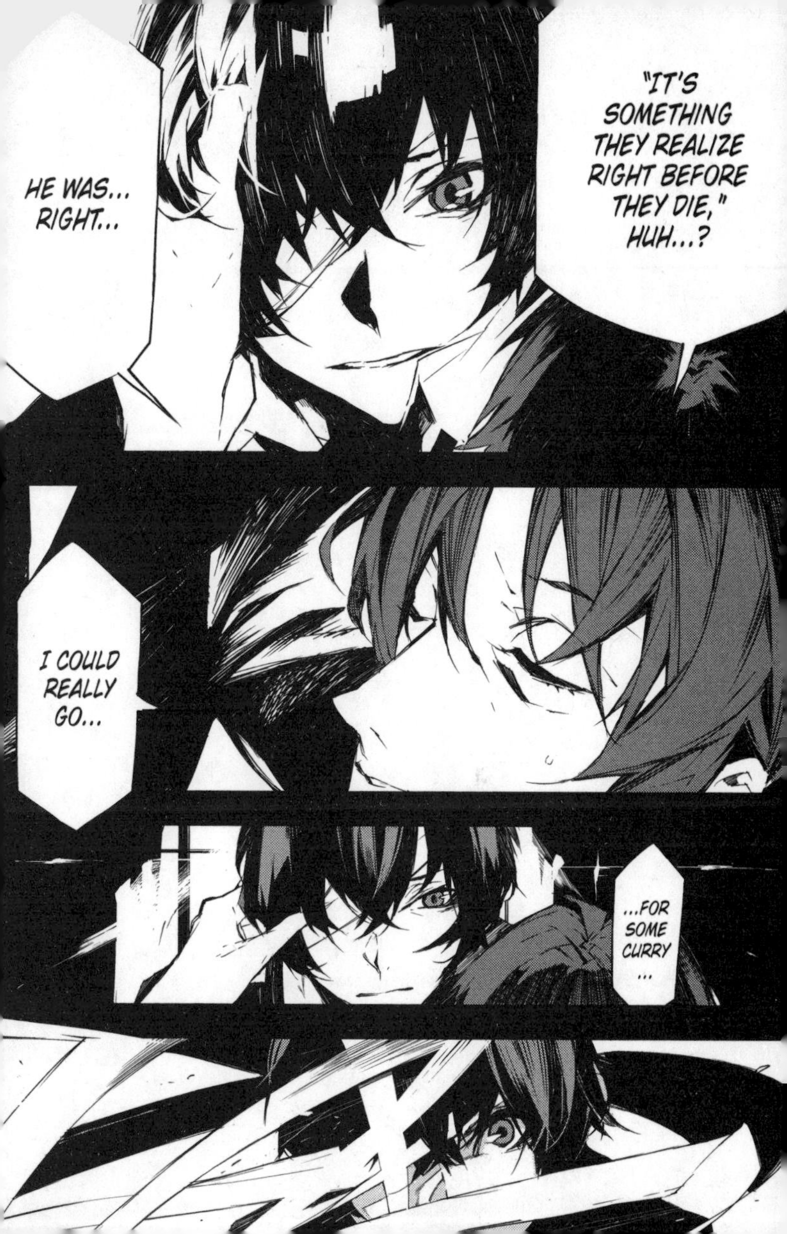
"IT'S SOMETHING THEY REALIZE RIGHT BEFORE THEY DIE," HUH...?
HE WAS... RIGHT...
I COULD REALLY GO...
...FOR SOME CURRY ...

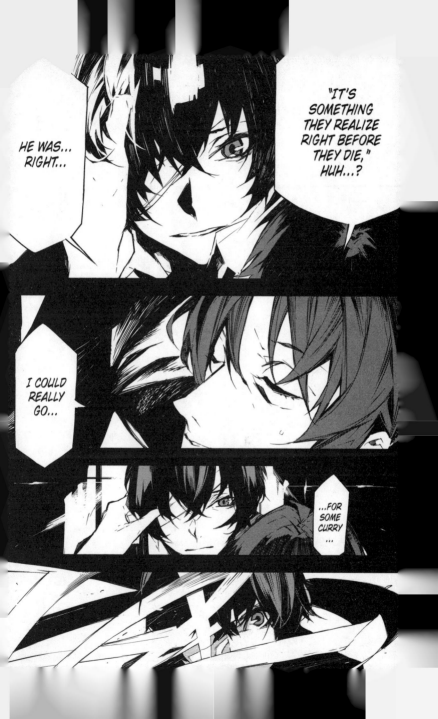

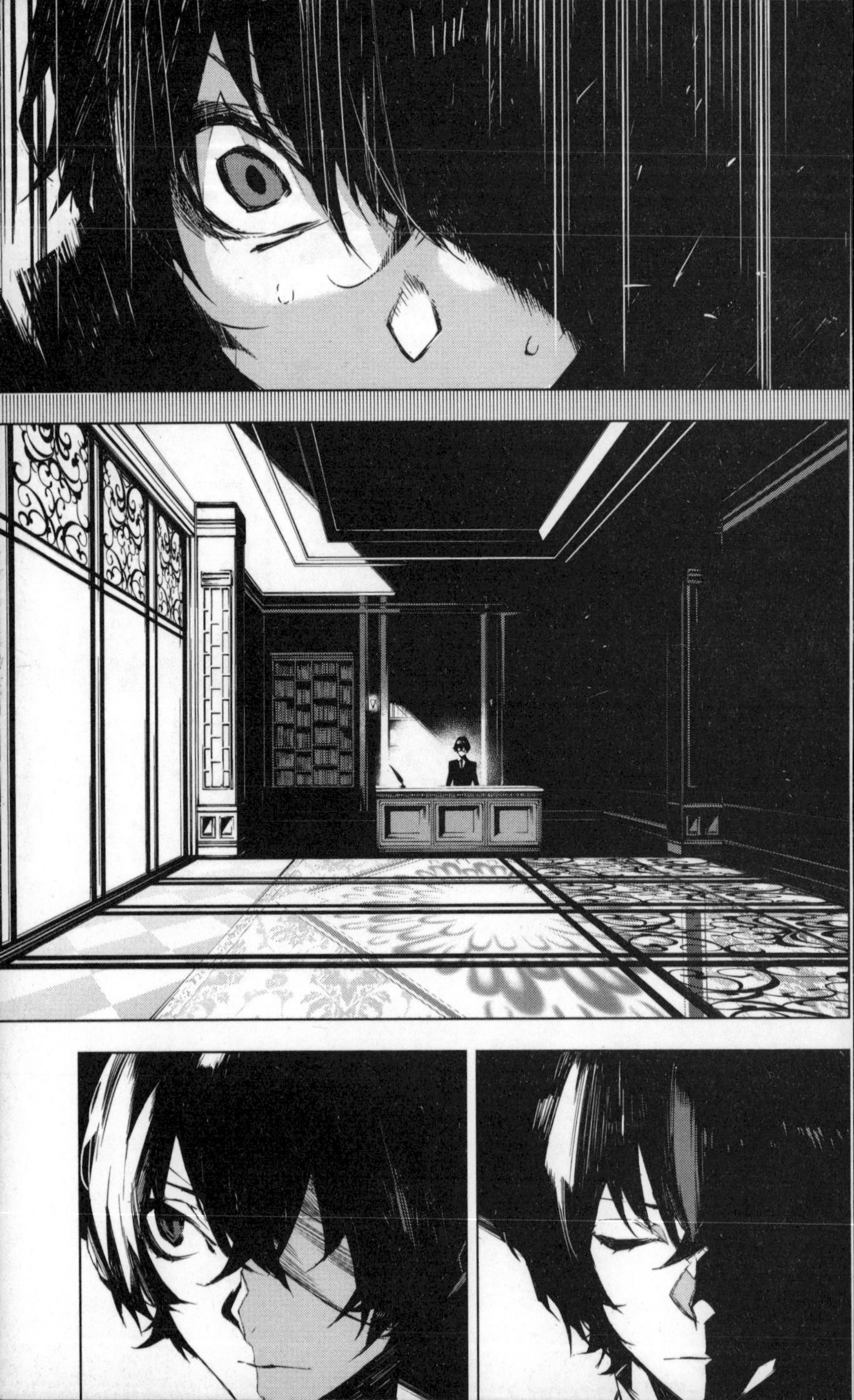

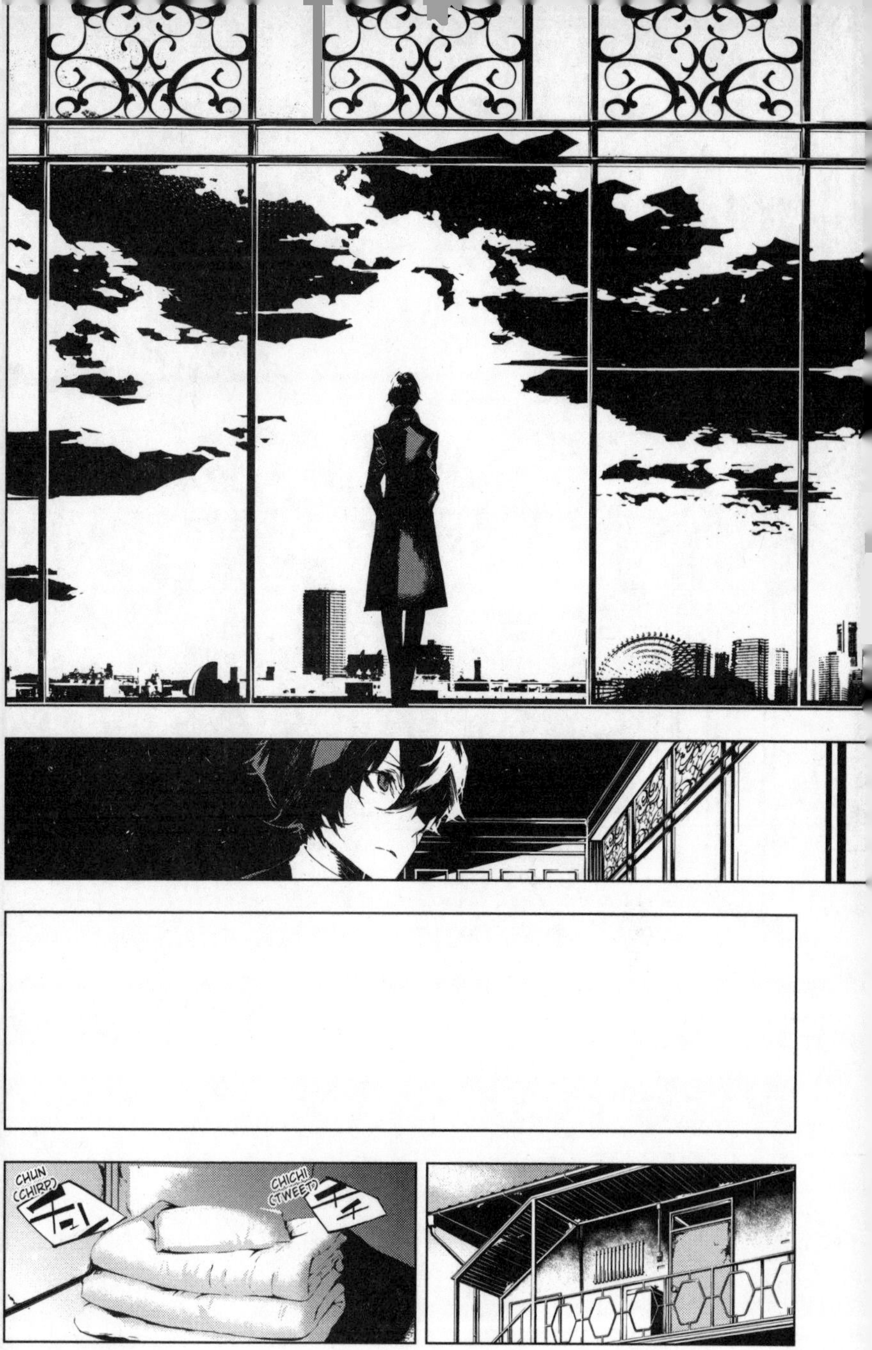
CHICHI (TWEET)
CHUN (CHIRP)

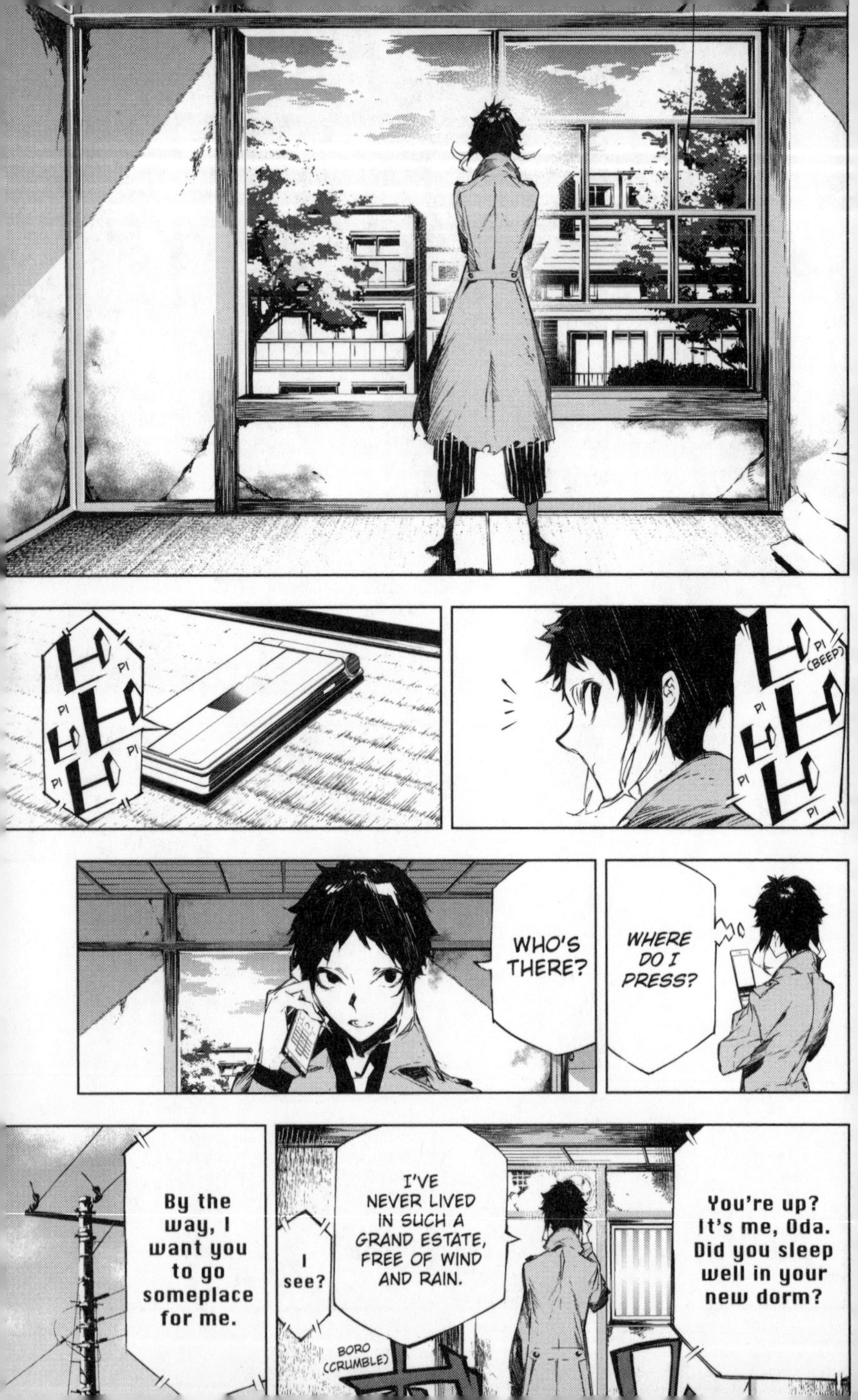
PI (BEEP)
PI
PI
PI
PI
PI
PI
PI
PI
WHERE DO I PRESS?
WHO'S THERE?
You're up? It's me, Oda. Did you sleep well in your new dorm?
I'VE NEVER LIVED IN SUCH A GRAND ESTATE, FREE OF WIND AND RAIN.
I see?
BORO (CRUMBLE)
By the way, I want you to go someplace for me.

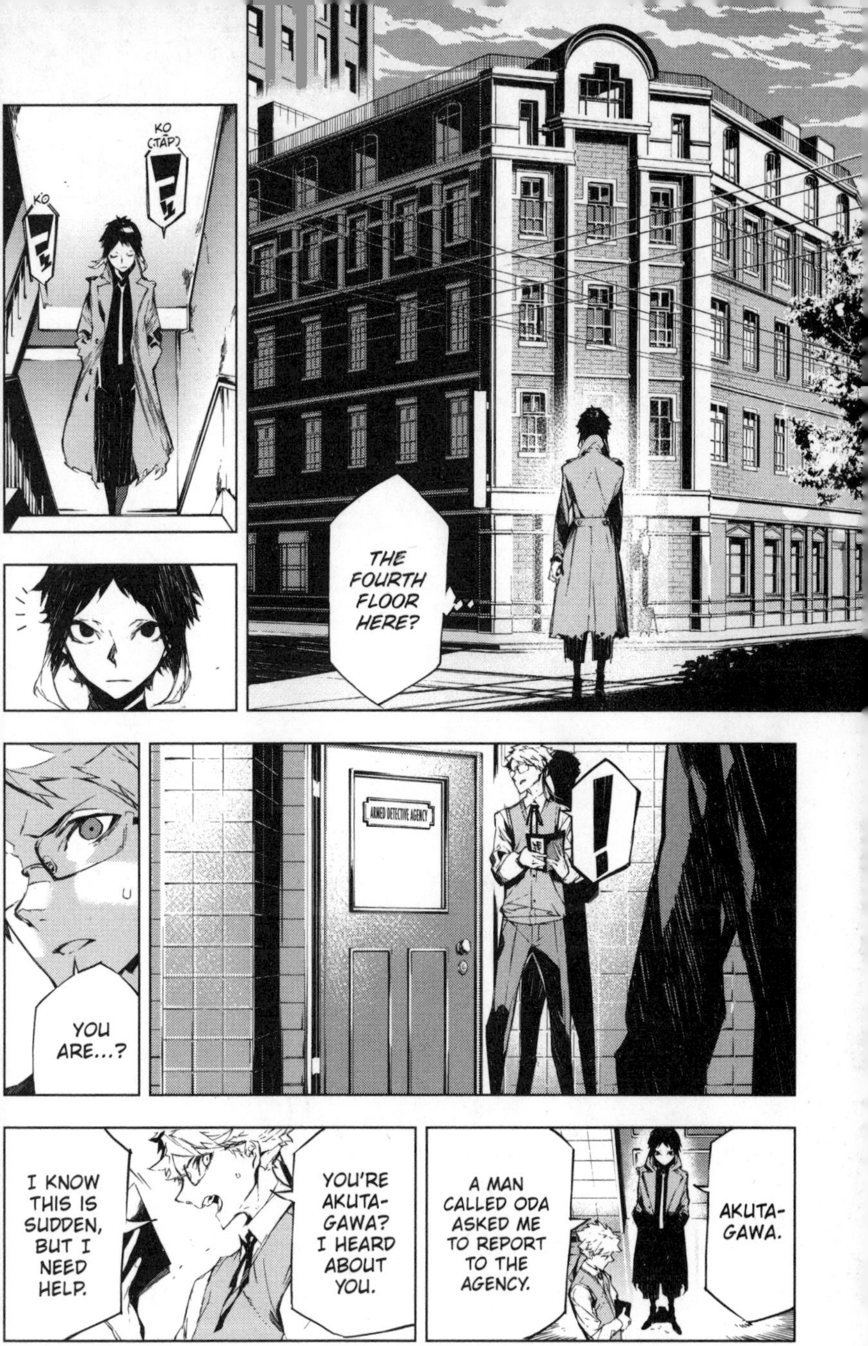
THE FOURTH FLOOR HERE?
KO (TAP)
KO
ARMED DETECTIVE AGENCY
!
YOU ARE...?
AKUTA-GAWA.
A MAN CALLED ODA ASKED ME TO REPORT TO THE AGENCY.
YOU'RE AKUTA-GAWA? I HEARD ABOUT YOU.
I KNOW THIS IS SUDDEN, BUT I NEED HELP.

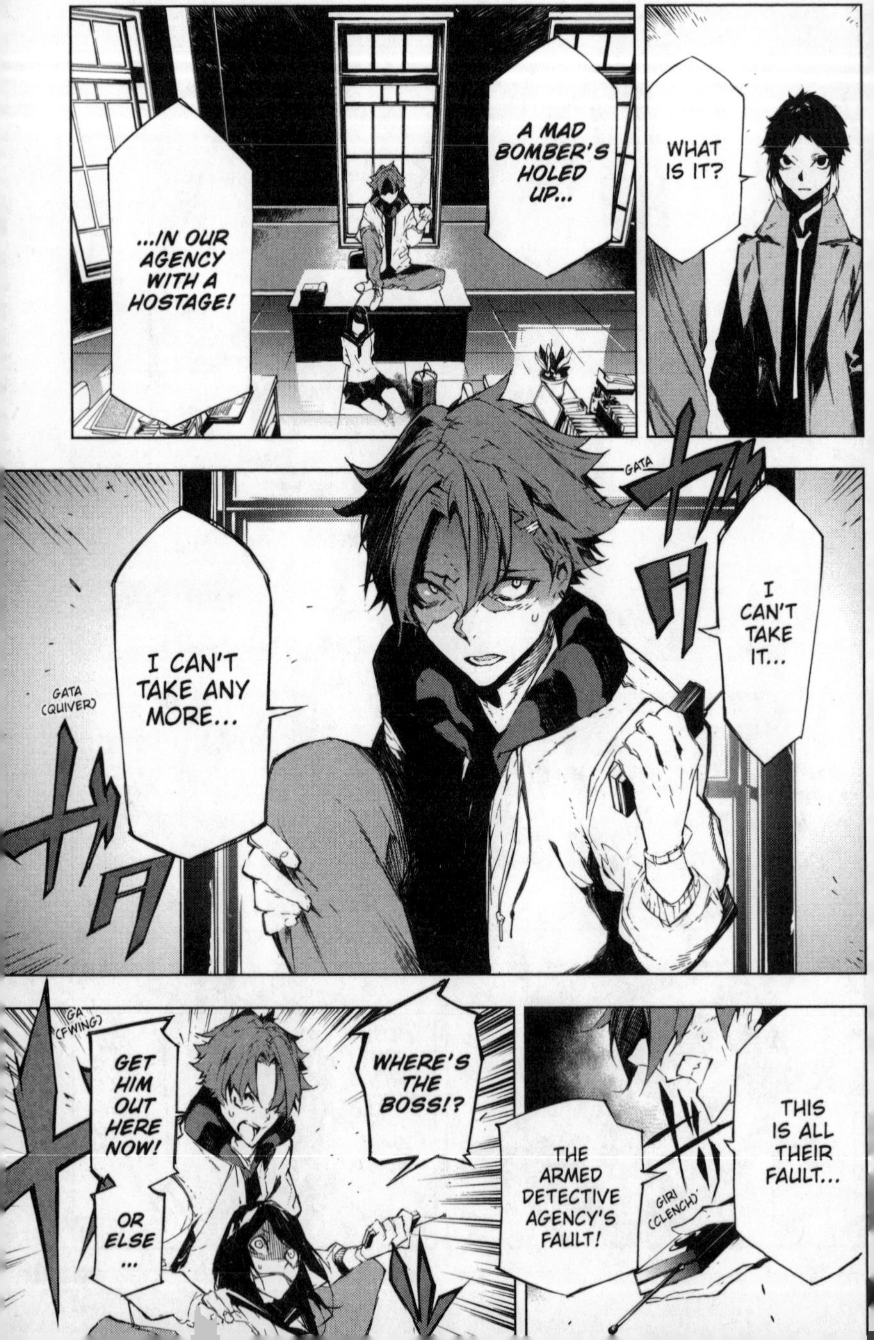
WHAT IS IT?
A MAD BOMBER'S HOLED UP...
...IN OUR AGENCY WITH A HOSTAGE!
GATA
I CAN'T TAKE IT...
I CAN'T TAKE ANY MORE...
GATA (QUIVER)
THIS IS ALL THEIR FAULT...
GIRI (CLENCH)
THE ARMED DETECTIVE AGENCY'S FAULT!
WHERE'S THE BOSS!?
GA (FWING)
GET HIM OUT HERE NOW!
OR ELSE ...

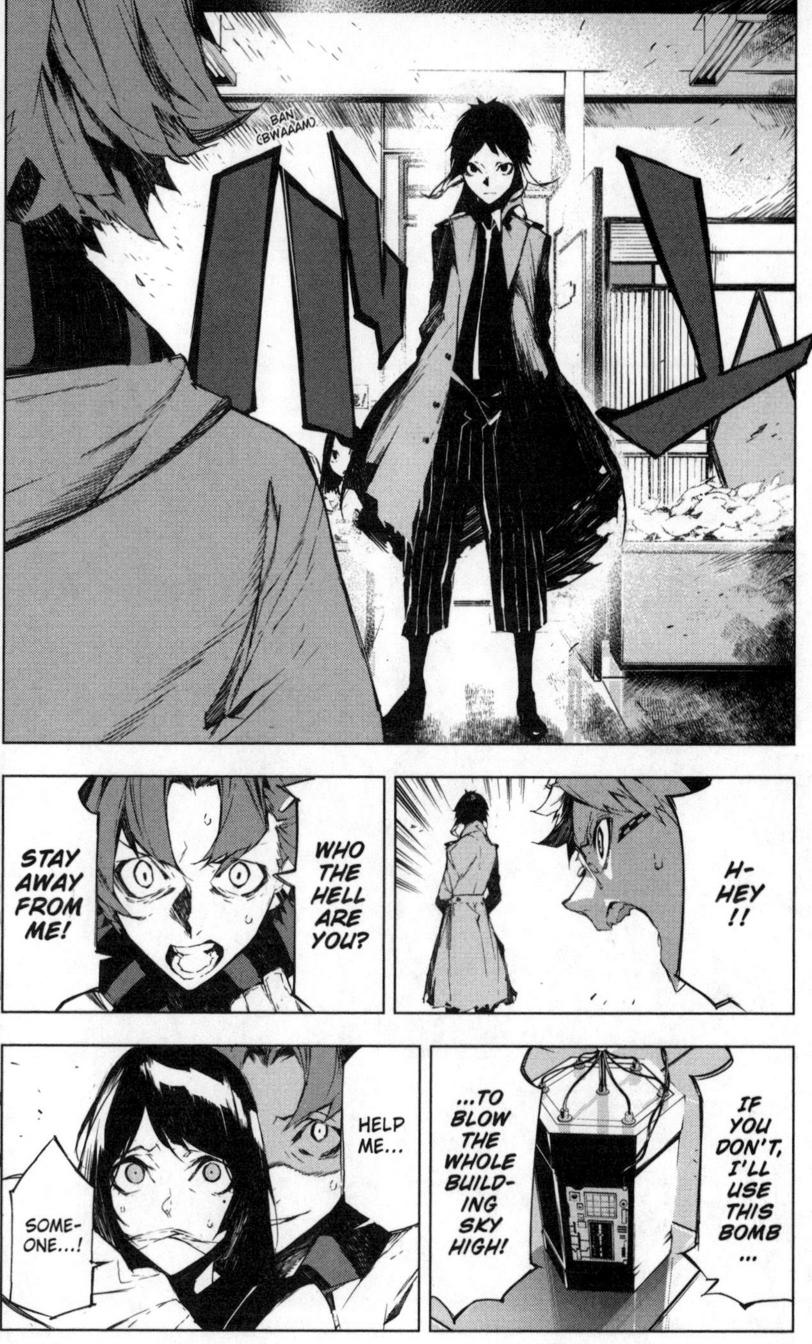
BAN (BWAAAM)
H-HEY!!
WHO THE HELL ARE YOU?
STAY AWAY FROM ME!
IF YOU DON'T, I'LL USE THIS BOMB...
...TO BLOW THE WHOLE BUILDING SKY HIGH!
HELP ME...
SOME-ONE...!

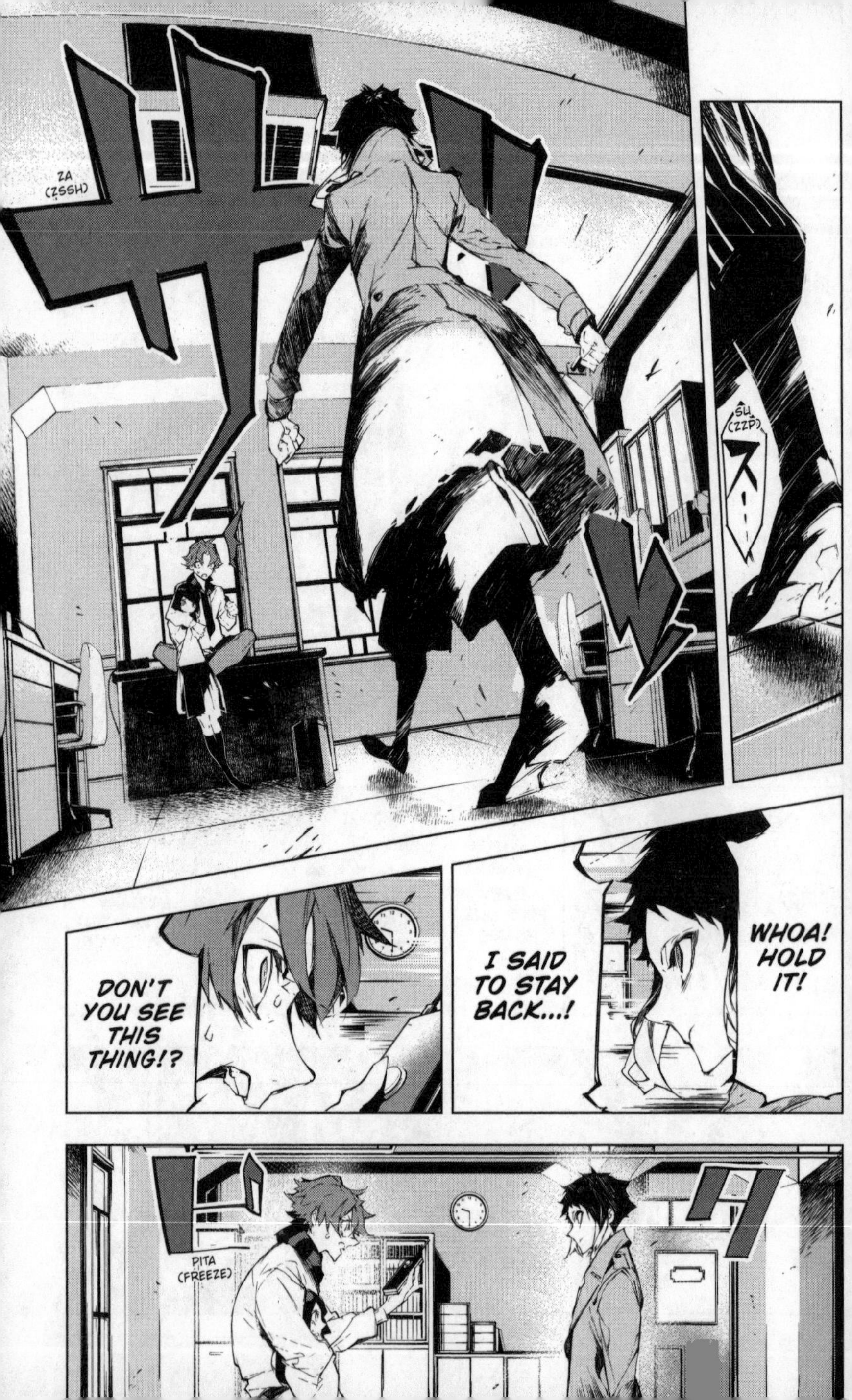
SU
(ZZP)
ZA
(ZSSH)
WHOA! HOLD IT!
I SAID TO STAY BACK...!
DON'T YOU SEE THIS THING!?
PITA
(FREEZE)

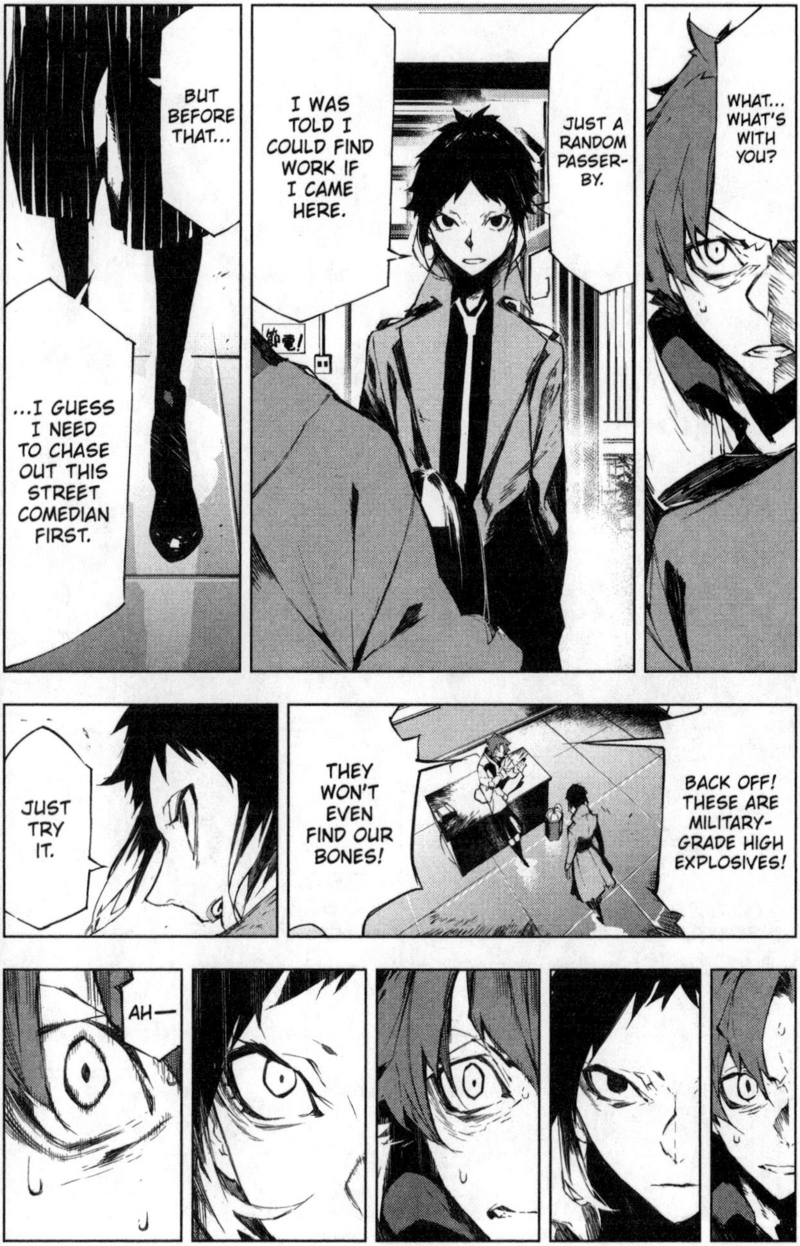
WHAT... WHAT'S WITH YOU?
JUST A RANDOM PASSER-BY.
I WAS TOLD I COULD FIND WORK IF I CAME HERE.
BUT BEFORE THAT...
...I GUESS I NEED TO CHASE OUT THIS STREET COMEDIAN FIRST.
BACK OFF! THESE ARE MILITARY-GRADE HIGH EXPLOSIVES!
THEY WON'T EVEN FIND OUR BONES!
JUST TRY IT.
AH—

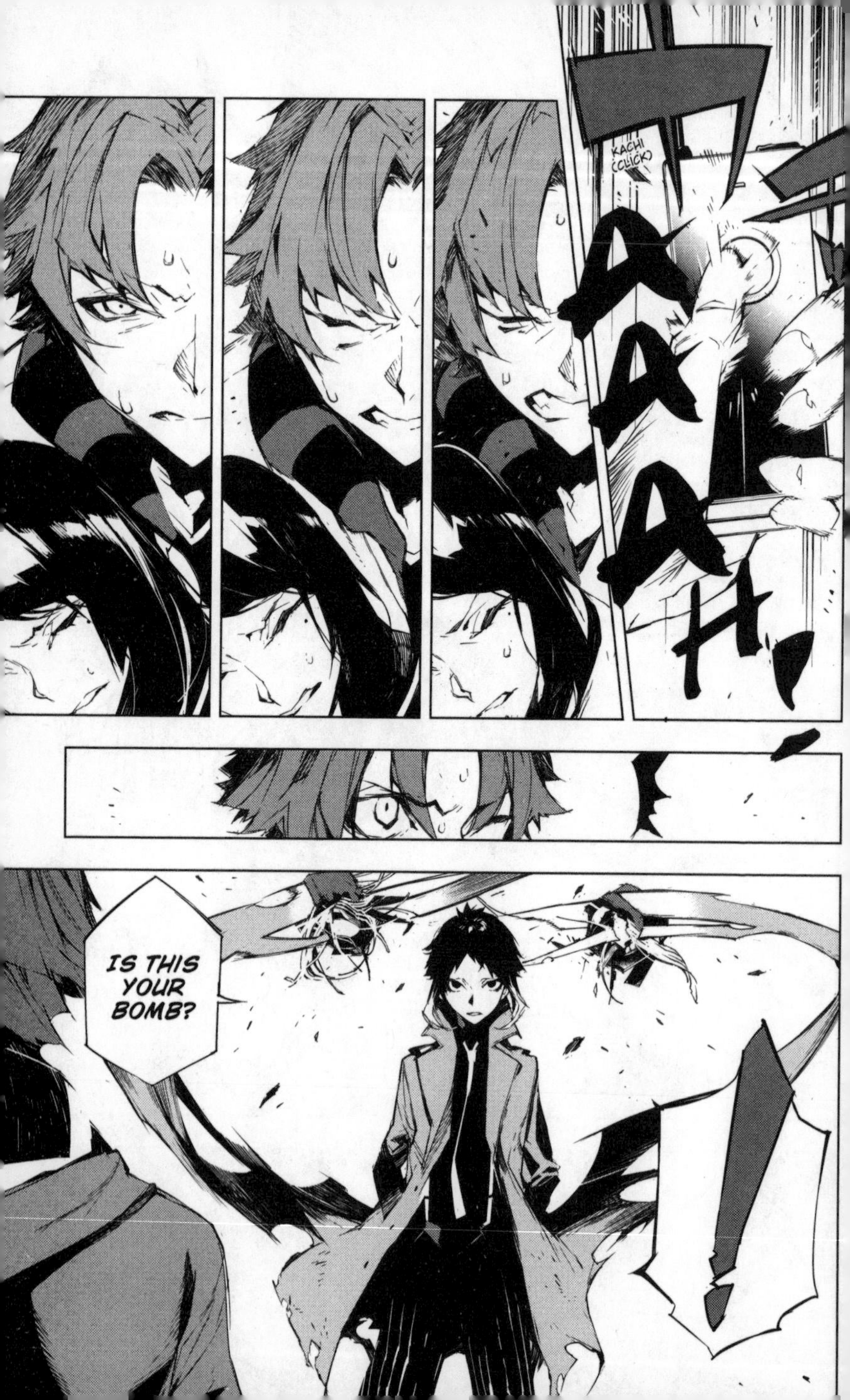
KACHI (CLICK)
AAAH
IS THIS YOUR BOMB?

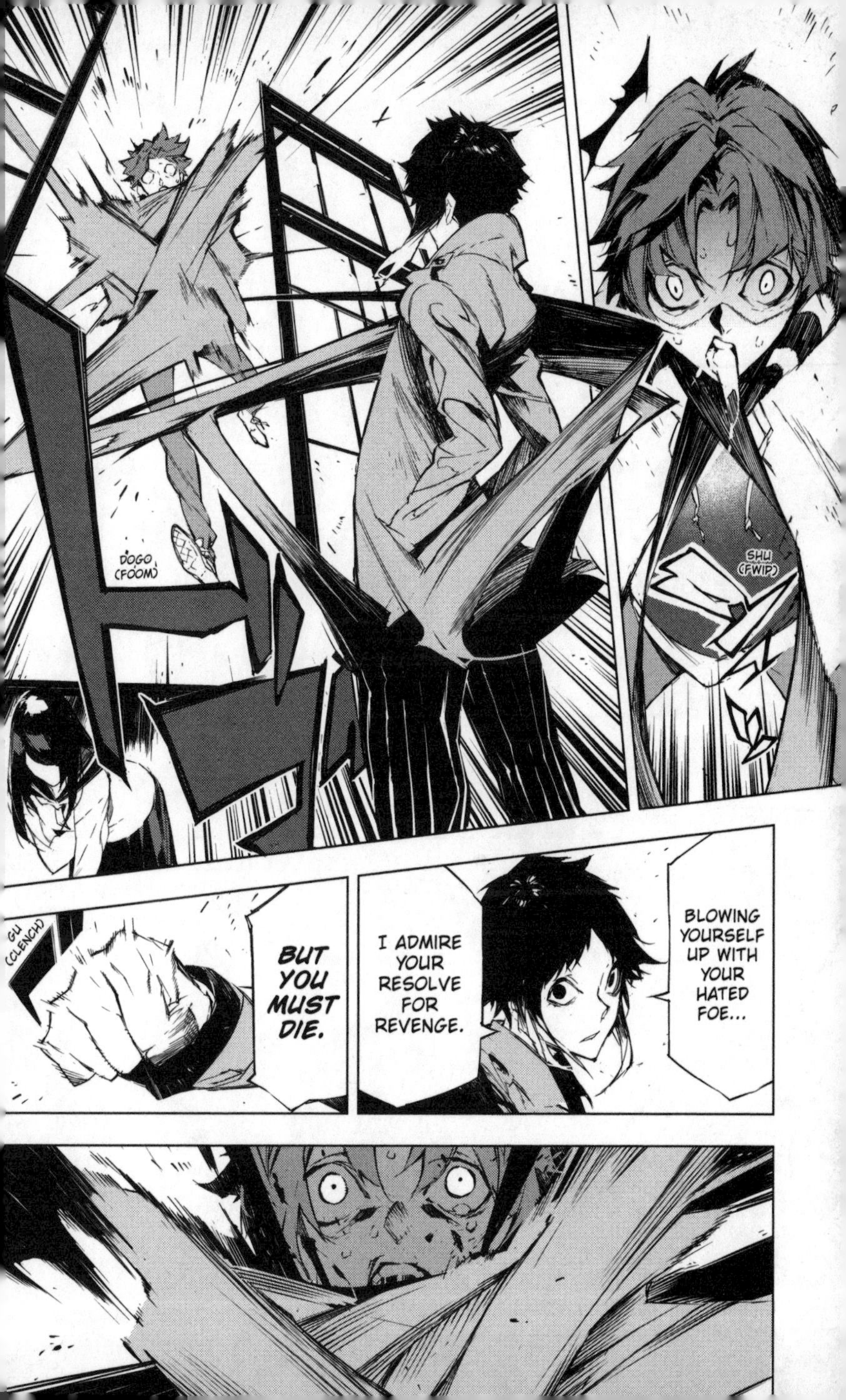
SHU (FWIP)
DOGO (FOOM)
BLOWING YOURSELF UP WITH YOUR HATED FOE...
I ADMIRE YOUR RESOLVE FOR REVENGE.
BUT YOU MUST DIE.
GU (CLENCH)

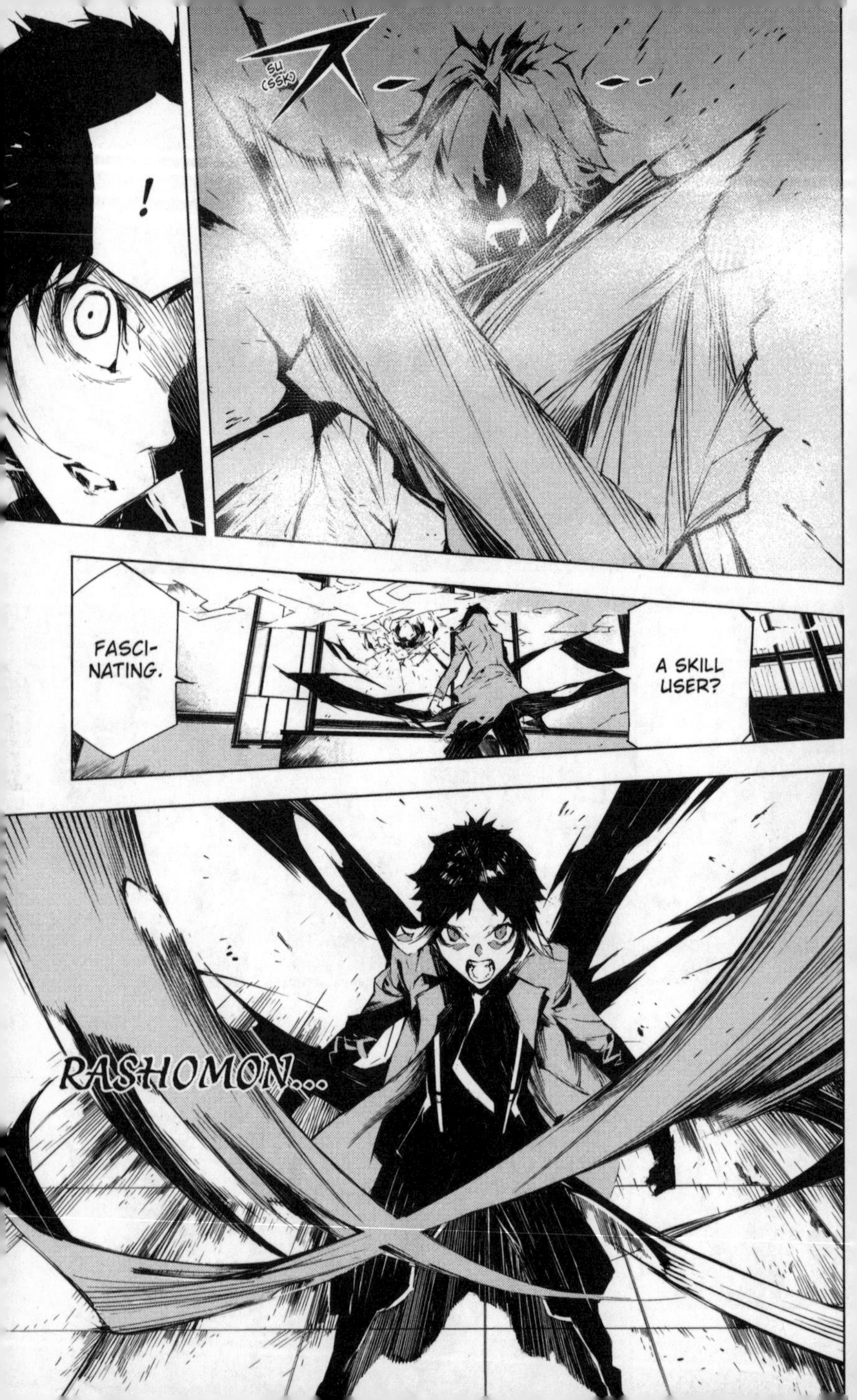
SU (SSK)
!
A SKILL USER?
FASCI-NATING.
RASHOMON...

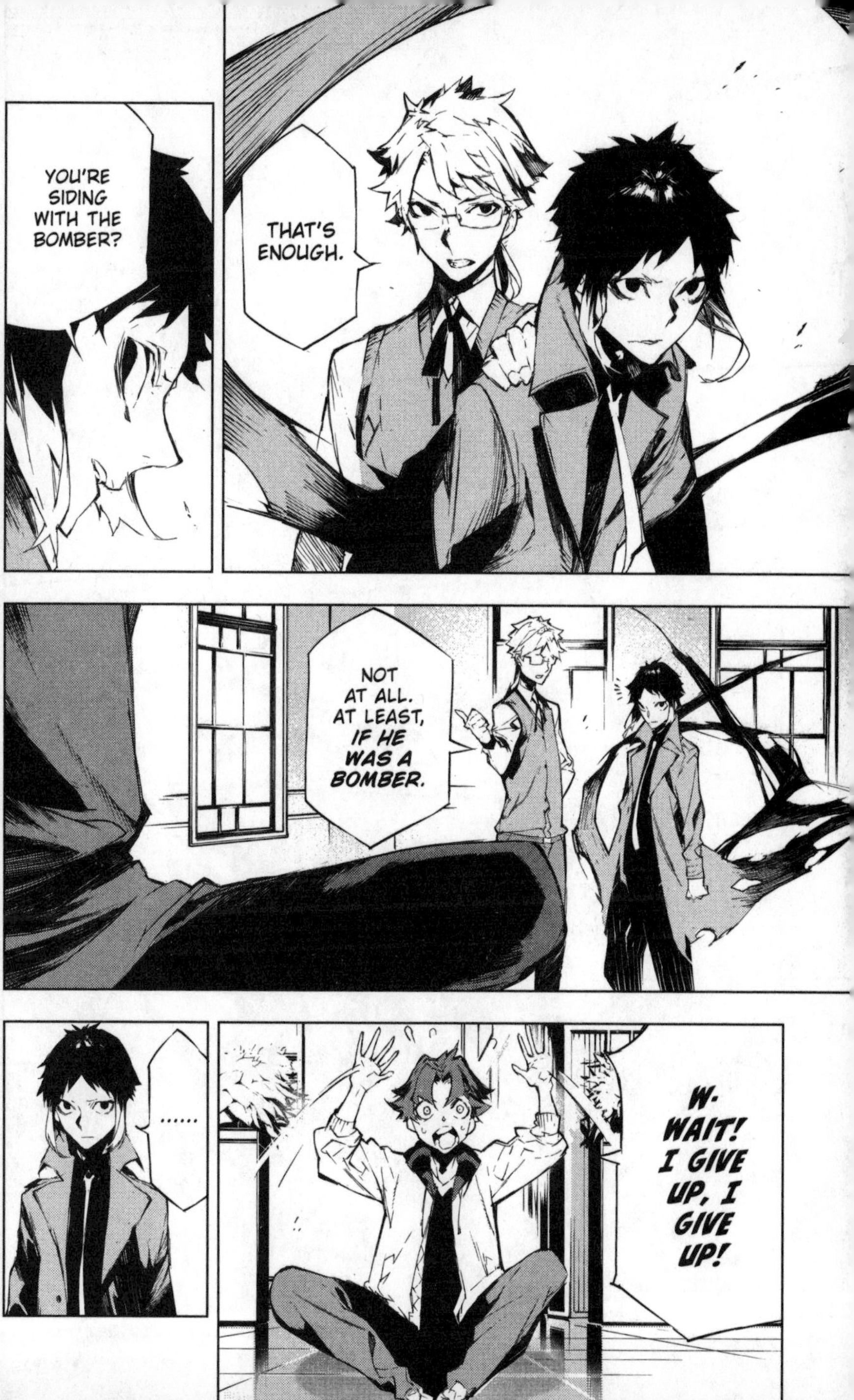
THAT'S ENOUGH.
YOU'RE SIDING WITH THE BOMBER?
NOT AT ALL. AT LEAST, *IF HE WAS A BOMBER.*
W-WAIT! I GIVE UP, I GIVE UP!
......

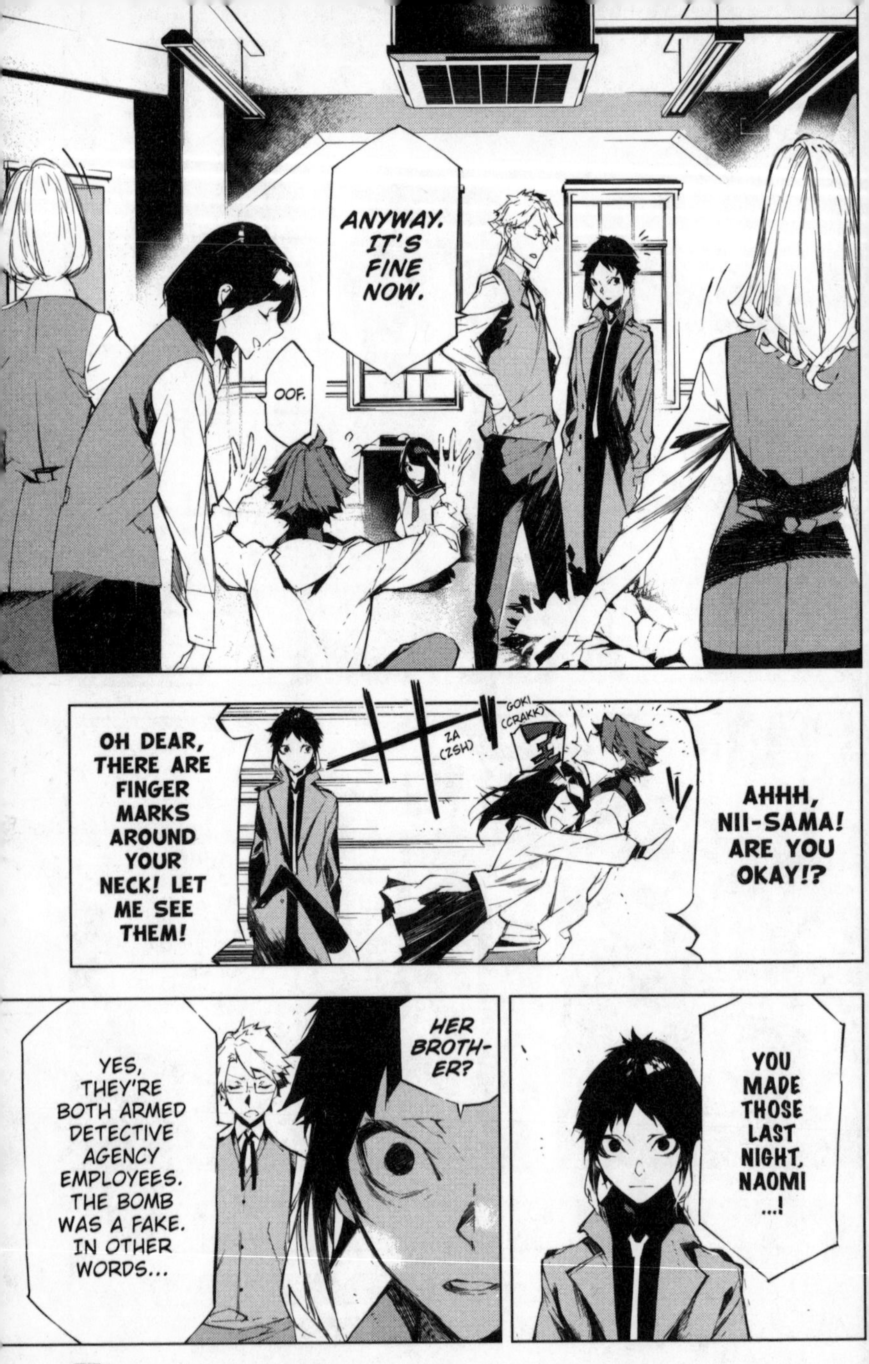
ANYWAY. IT'S FINE NOW.
OOF.
AHHH, NII-SAMA! ARE YOU OKAY!?
GOKI (CRAKK)
ZA (ZSH)
OH DEAR, THERE ARE FINGER MARKS AROUND YOUR NECK! LET ME SEE THEM!
YOU MADE THOSE LAST NIGHT, NAOMI ...!
HER BROTH-ER?
YES, THEY'RE BOTH ARMED DETECTIVE AGENCY EMPLOYEES. THE BOMB WAS A FAKE. IN OTHER WORDS...

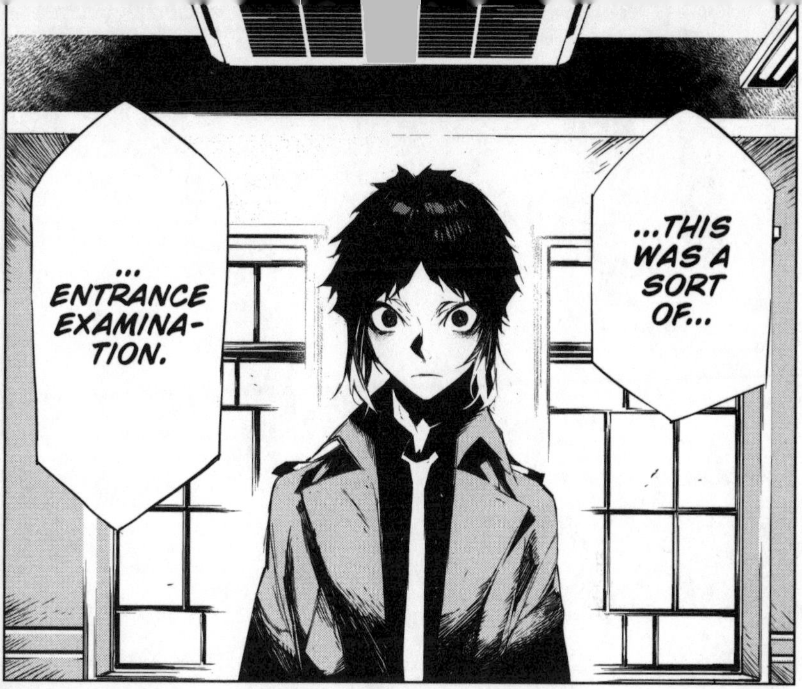
...THIS WAS A SORT OF...
... ENTRANCE EXAMINATION.

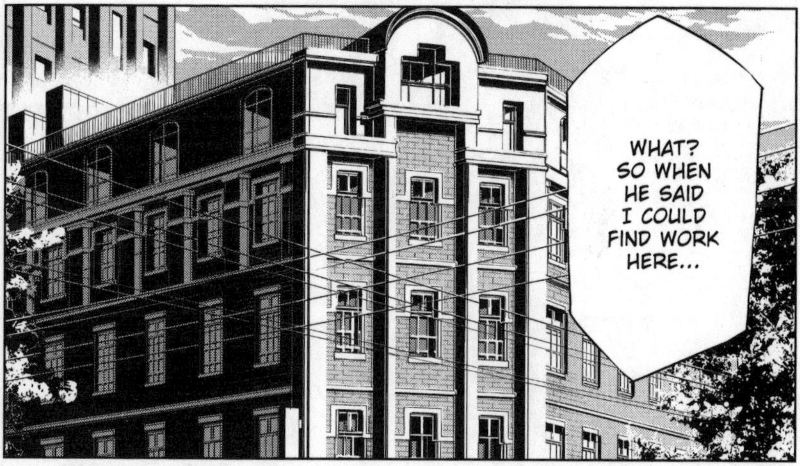
WHAT? SO WHEN HE SAID I COULD FIND WORK HERE...

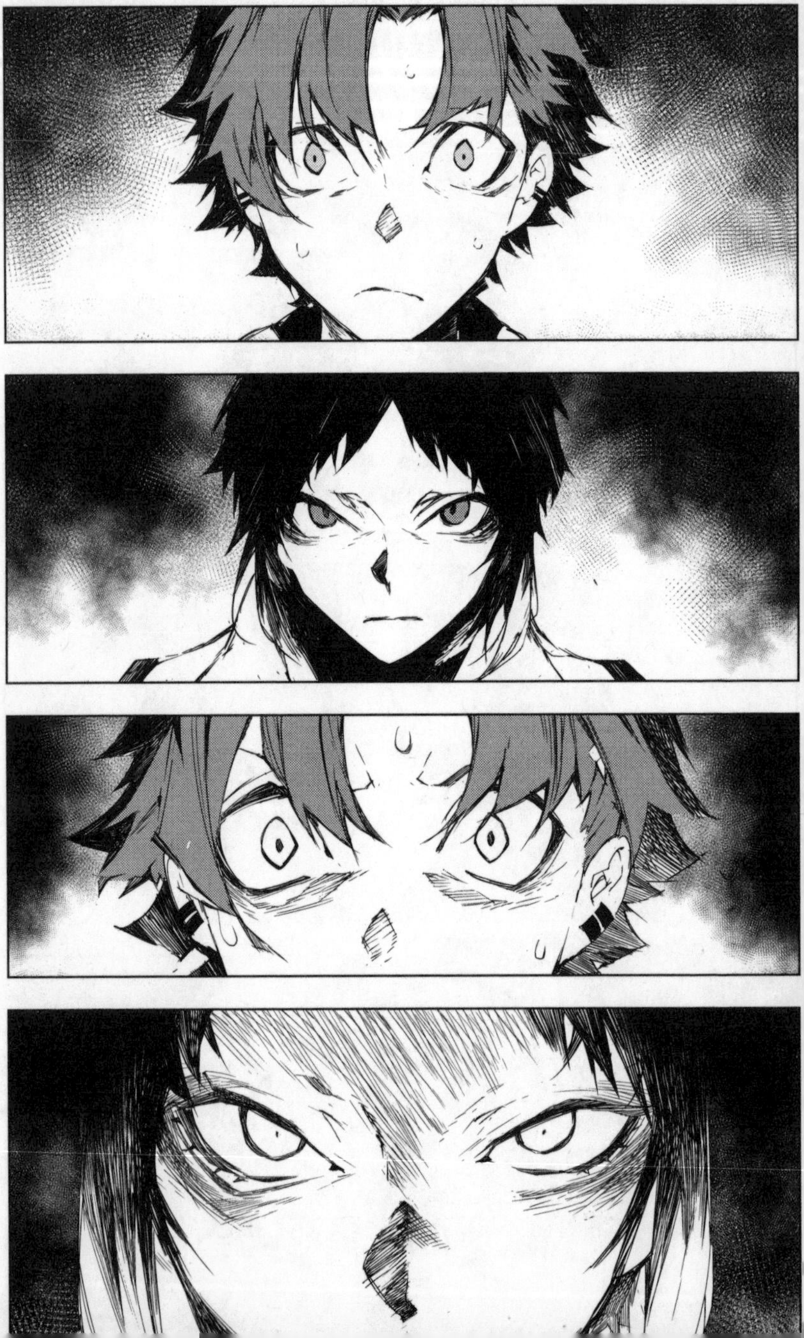

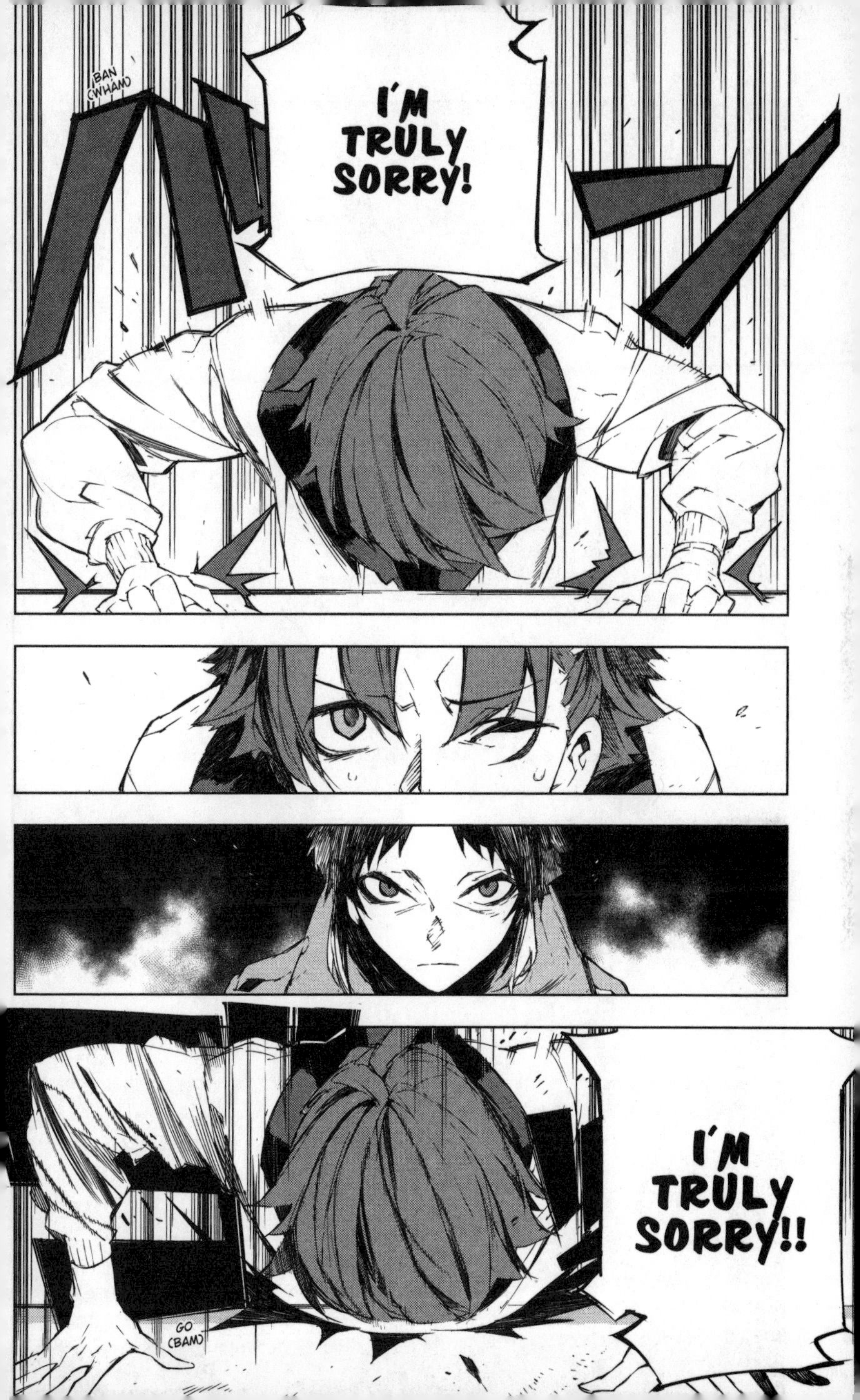
I'M TRULY SORRY!
BAN (WHAM)
I'M TRULY SORRY!!
GO (BAM)

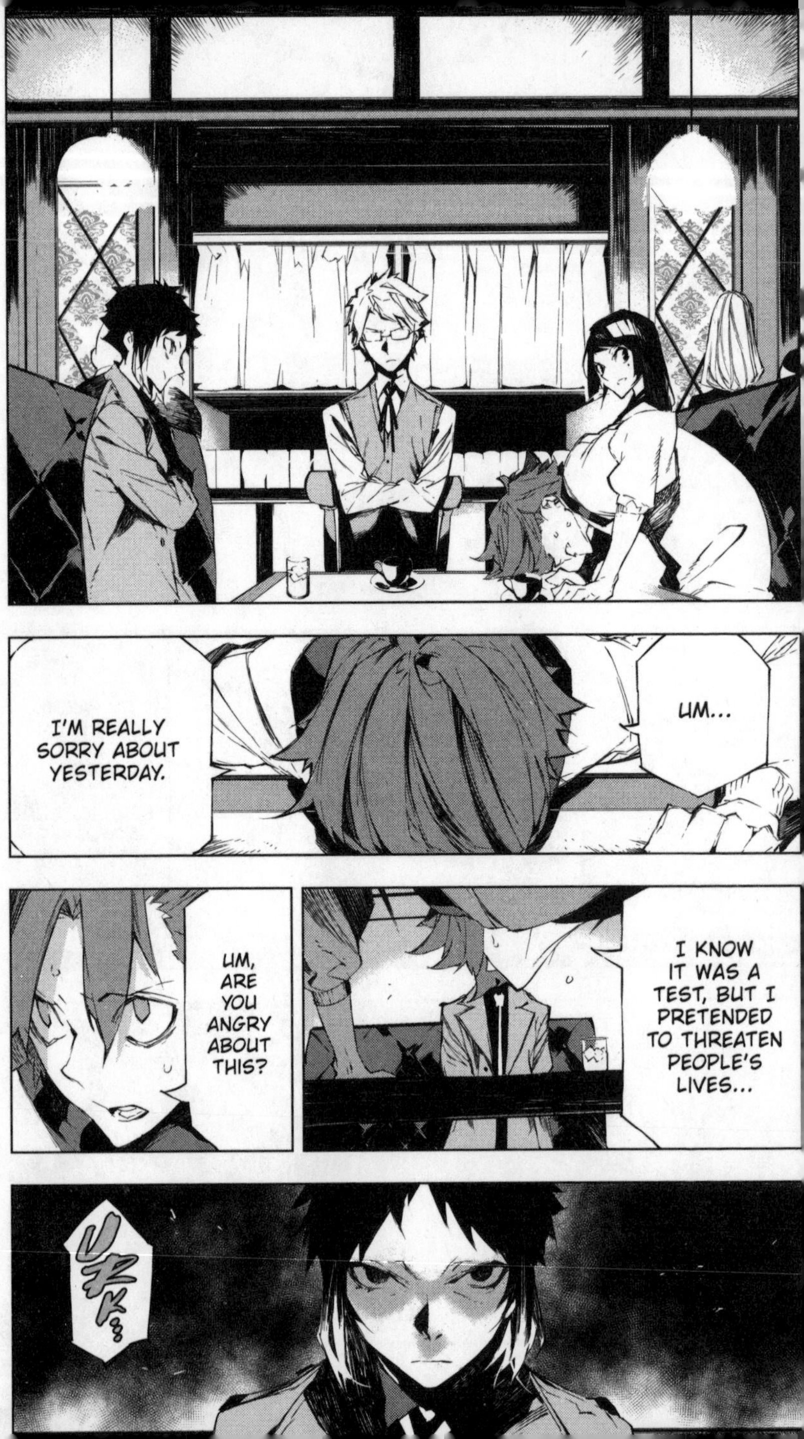
UM...
I'M REALLY SORRY ABOUT YESTERDAY.
I KNOW IT WAS A TEST, BUT I PRETENDED TO THREATEN PEOPLE'S LIVES...
UM, ARE YOU ANGRY ABOUT THIS?
URK

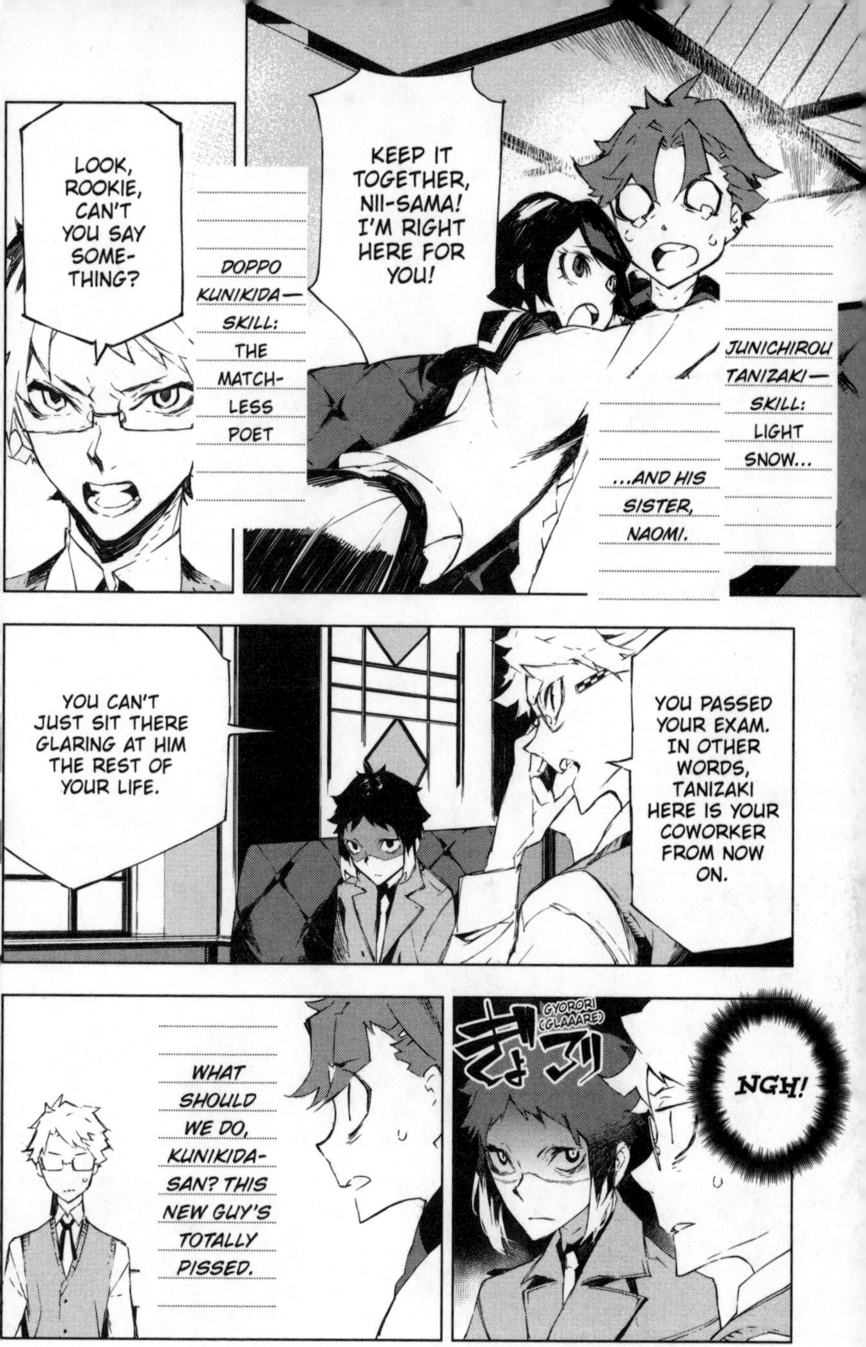
KEEP IT TOGETHER, NII-SAMA! I'M RIGHT HERE FOR YOU!
JUNICHIROU TANIZAKI—SKILL: LIGHT SNOW...
...AND HIS SISTER, NAOMI.
DOPPO KUNIKIDA—SKILL: THE MATCHLESS POET
LOOK, ROOKIE, CAN'T YOU SAY SOME-THING?
YOU PASSED YOUR EXAM. IN OTHER WORDS, TANIZAKI HERE IS YOUR COWORKER FROM NOW ON.
YOU CAN'T JUST SIT THERE GLARING AT HIM THE REST OF YOUR LIFE.
NGH!
GYORORI (GLAAARE)
WHAT SHOULD WE DO, KUNIKIDA-SAN? THIS NEW GUY'S TOTALLY PISSED.

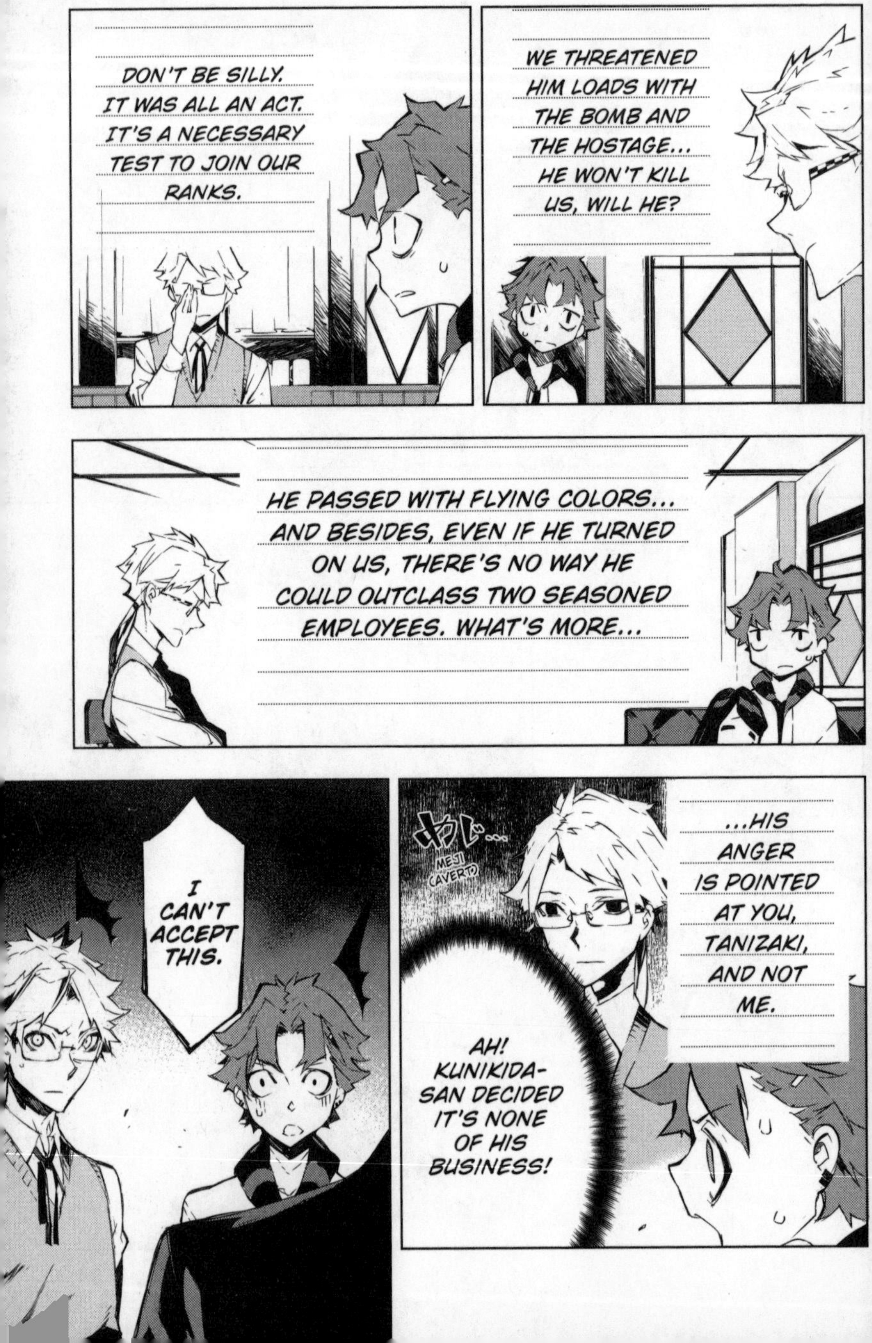
WE THREATENED HIM LOADS WITH THE BOMB AND THE HOSTAGE... HE WON'T KILL US, WILL HE?
DON'T BE SILLY. IT WAS ALL AN ACT. IT'S A NECESSARY TEST TO JOIN OUR RANKS.
HE PASSED WITH FLYING COLORS... AND BESIDES, EVEN IF HE TURNED ON US, THERE'S NO WAY HE COULD OUTCLASS TWO SEASONED EMPLOYEES. WHAT'S MORE...
...HIS ANGER IS POINTED AT YOU, TANIZAKI, AND NOT ME.
MEJI (AVERT)
AH! KUNIKIDA-SAN DECIDED IT'S NONE OF HIS BUSINESS!
I CAN'T ACCEPT THIS.

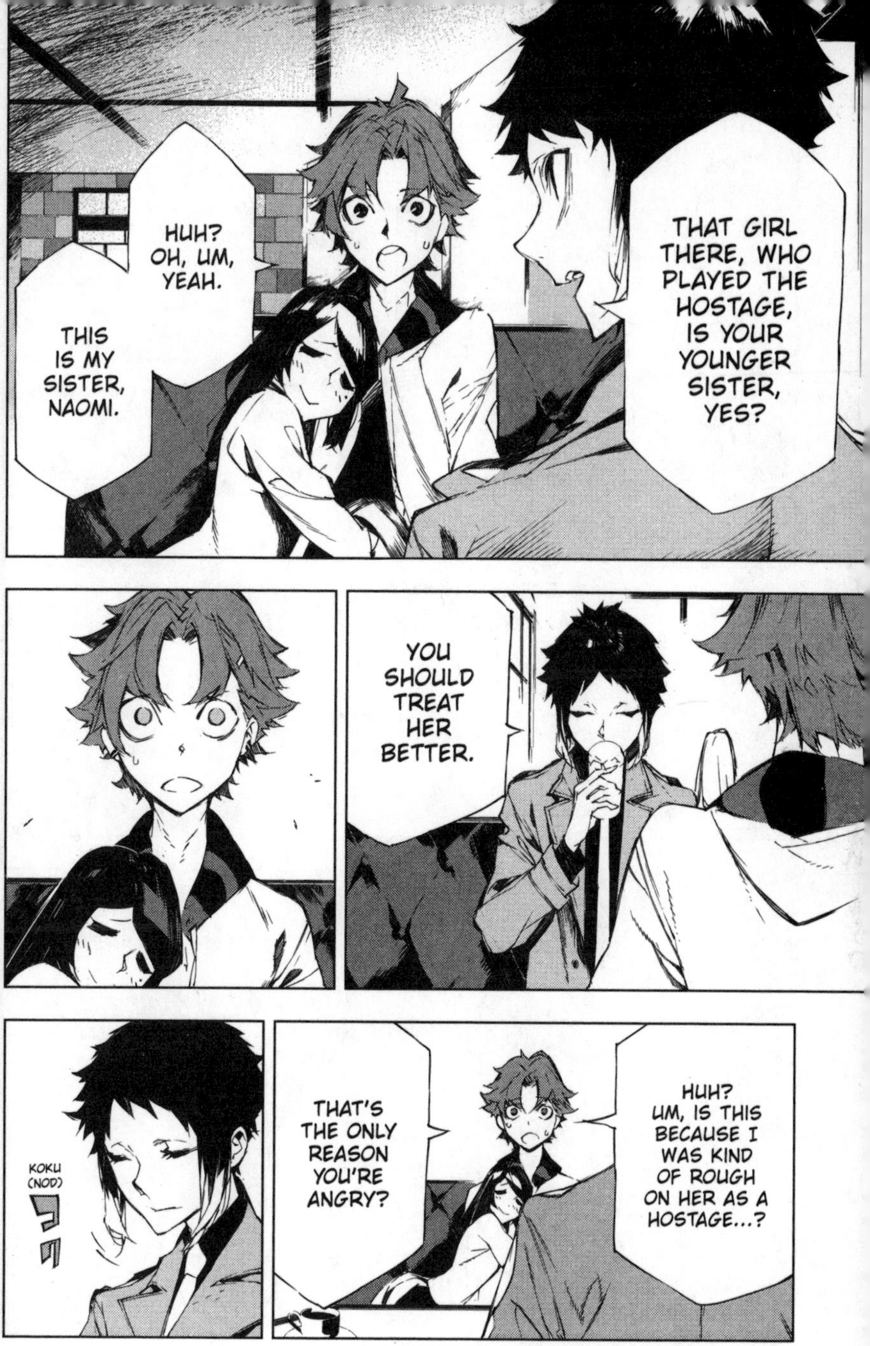
THAT GIRL THERE, WHO PLAYED THE HOSTAGE, IS YOUR YOUNGER SISTER, YES?
HUH? OH, UM, YEAH.
THIS IS MY SISTER, NAOMI.
YOU SHOULD TREAT HER BETTER.
HUH? UM, IS THIS BECAUSE I WAS KIND OF ROUGH ON HER AS A HOSTAGE...?
THAT'S THE ONLY REASON YOU'RE ANGRY?
KOKU (NOD)

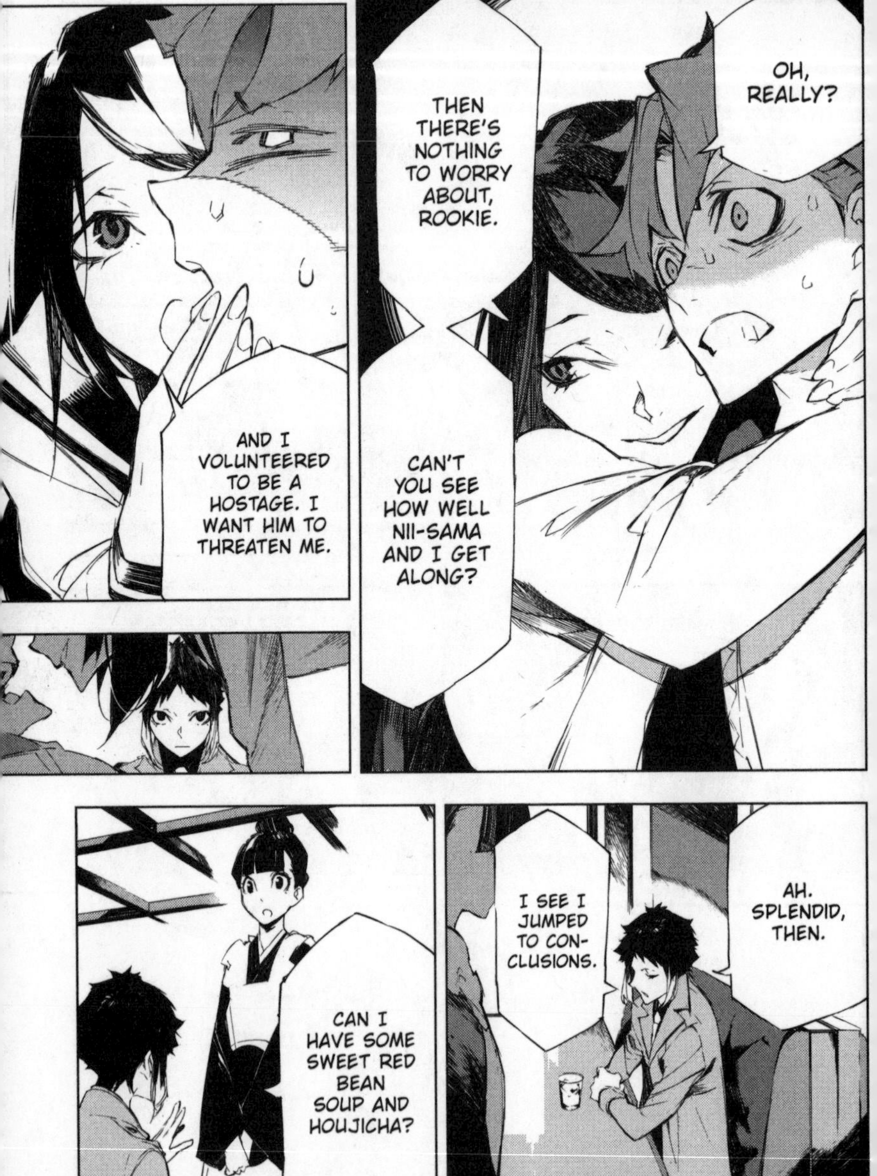
OH, REALLY?
THEN THERE'S NOTHING TO WORRY ABOUT, ROOKIE.
CAN'T YOU SEE HOW WELL NII-SAMA AND I GET ALONG?
AND I VOLUNTEERED TO BE A HOSTAGE. I WANT HIM TO THREATEN ME.
AH. SPLENDID, THEN.
I SEE I JUMPED TO CON-CLUSIONS.
CAN I HAVE SOME SWEET RED BEAN SOUP AND HOUJICHA?

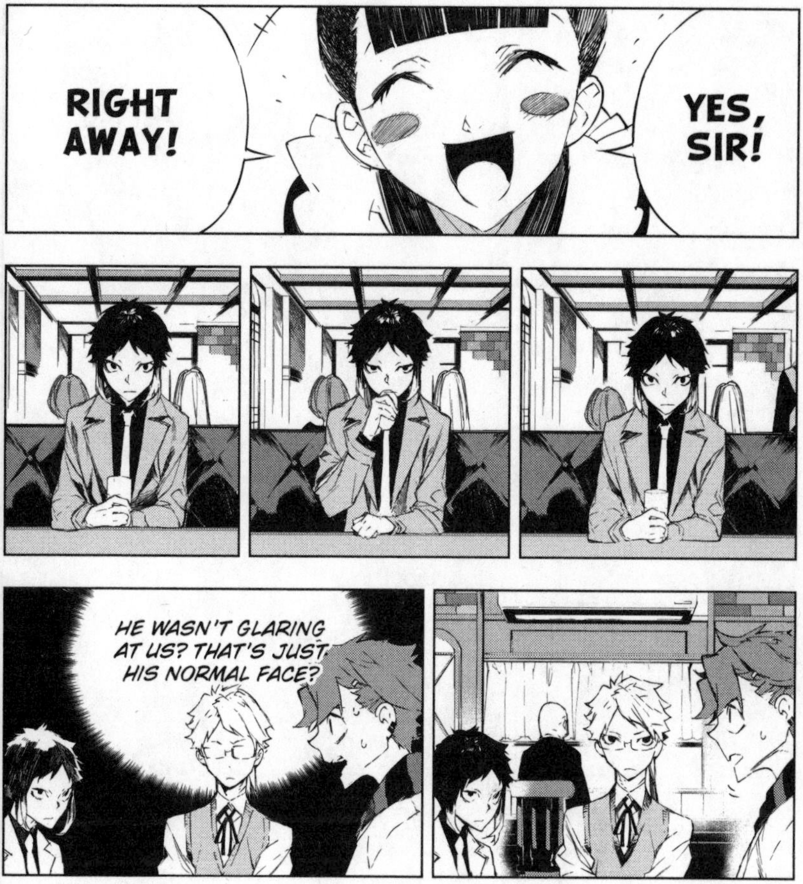
YES, SIR!
RIGHT AWAY!
HE WASN'T GLARING AT US? THAT'S JUST HIS NORMAL FACE?
BUT WHY IS THAT MAN NOT HERE YET?
IT'S LONG PAST THE APPOINTED TIME. HONESTLY...
THE VERY MAN WHO PICKS UP A NEAR-STARVED ORPHAN BY THE RIVER AND SUGGESTS HIM FOR THE FIRM JUST ABANDONS HIM?

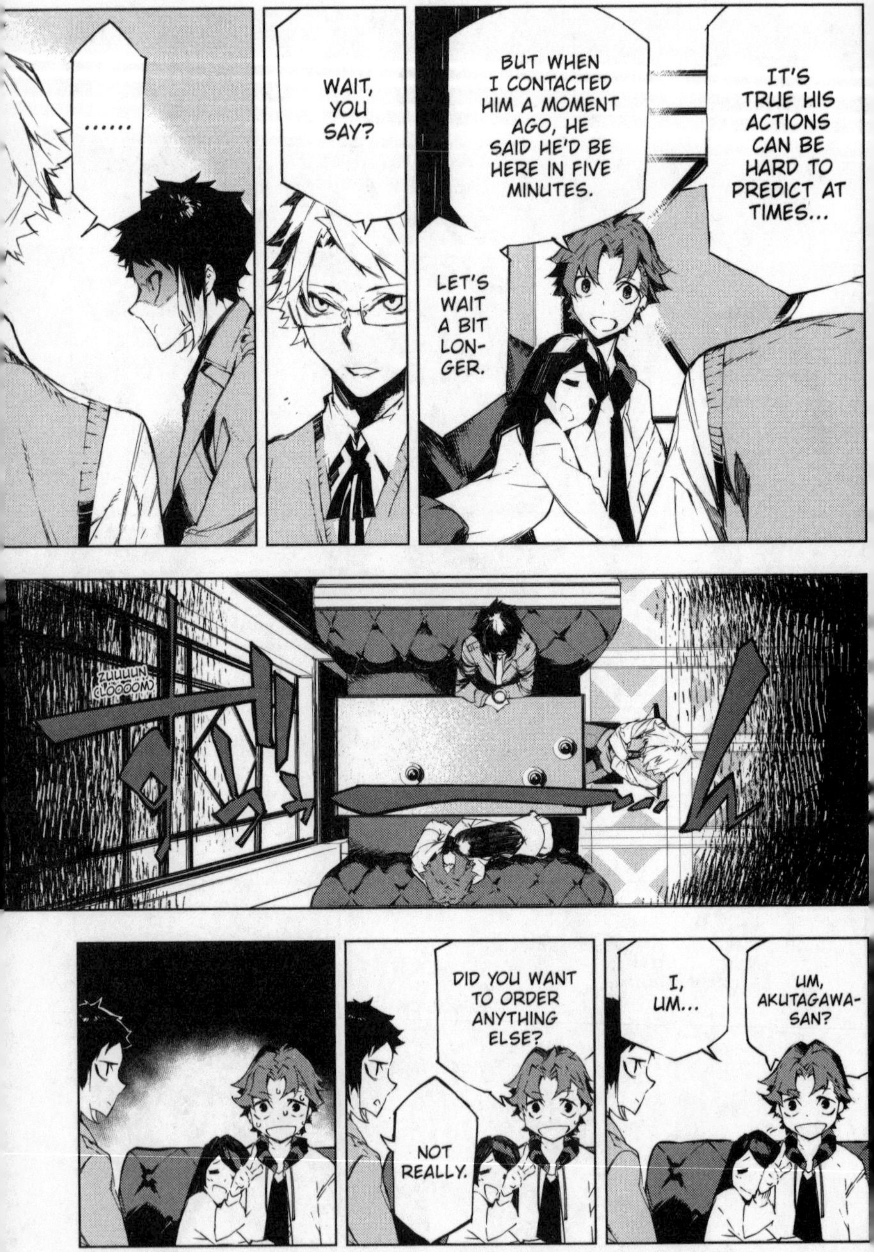
IT'S TRUE HIS ACTIONS CAN BE HARD TO PREDICT AT TIMES...
BUT WHEN I CONTACTED HIM A MOMENT AGO, HE SAID HE'D BE HERE IN FIVE MINUTES.
LET'S WAIT A BIT LON-GER.
WAIT, YOU SAY?
......
ZUUUUN (LOOOOOM)
UM, AKUTAGAWA-SAN?
I, UM...
DID YOU WANT TO ORDER ANYTHING ELSE?
NOT REALLY.

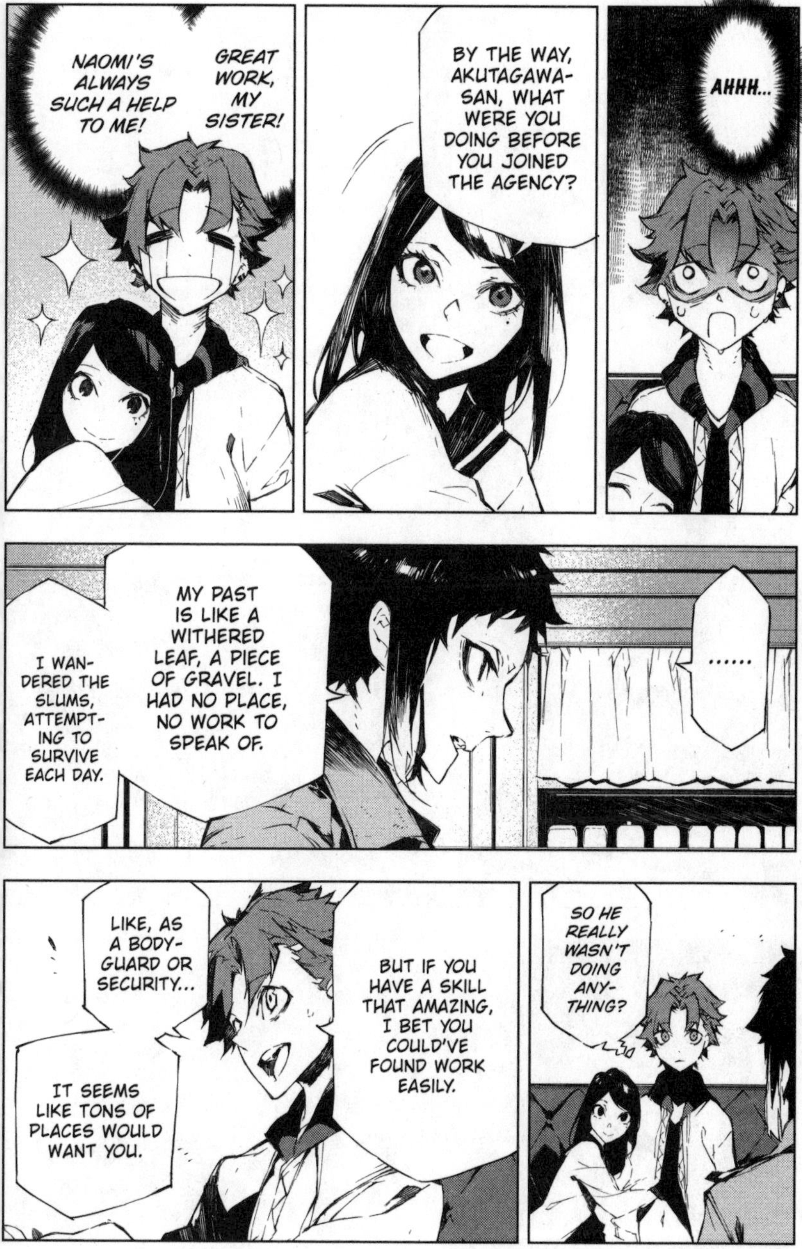
AHHH...
BY THE WAY, AKUTAGAWA-SAN, WHAT WERE YOU DOING BEFORE YOU JOINED THE AGENCY?
GREAT WORK, MY SISTER!
NAOMI'S ALWAYS SUCH A HELP TO ME!
......
MY PAST IS LIKE A WITHERED LEAF, A PIECE OF GRAVEL. I HAD NO PLACE, NO WORK TO SPEAK OF.
I WANDERED THE SLUMS, ATTEMPTING TO SURVIVE EACH DAY.
SO HE REALLY WASN'T DOING ANYTHING?
BUT IF YOU HAVE A SKILL THAT AMAZING, I BET YOU COULD'VE FOUND WORK EASILY.
LIKE, AS A BODYGUARD OR SECURITY...
IT SEEMS LIKE TONS OF PLACES WOULD WANT YOU.

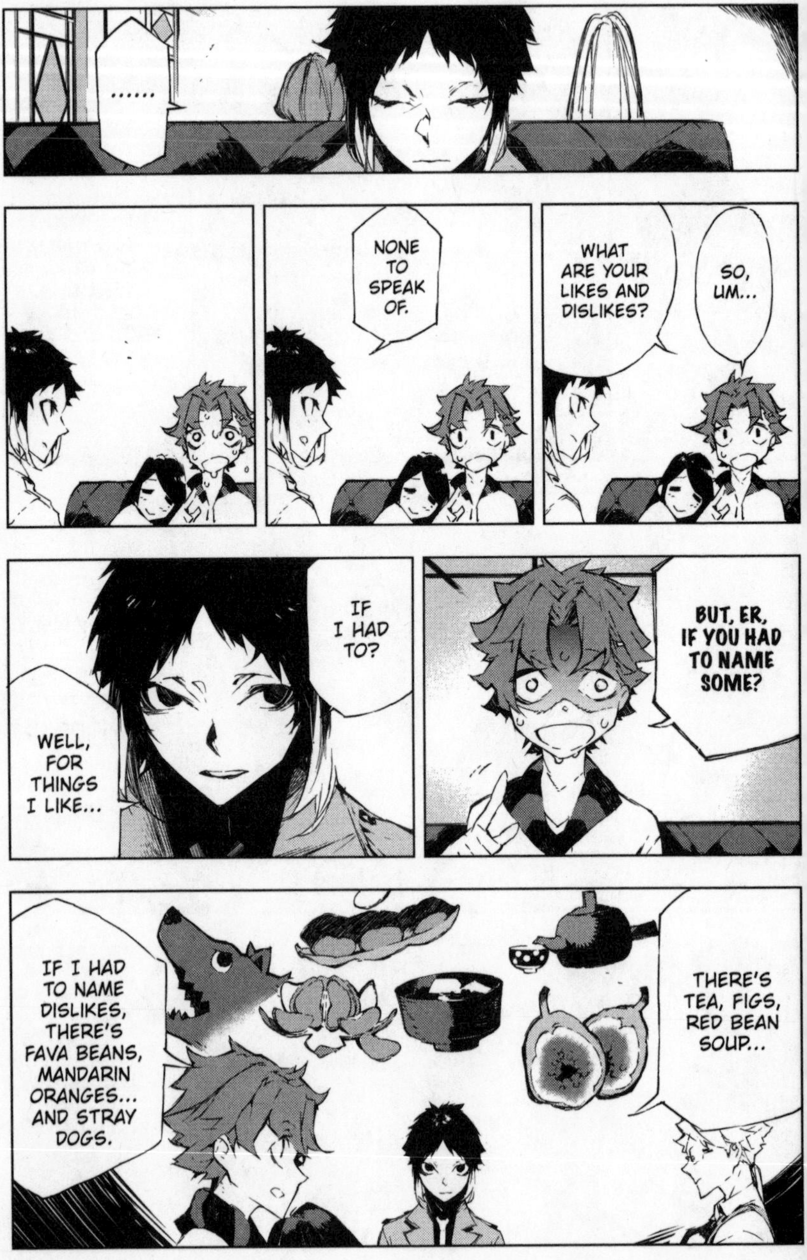
......
SO, UM...
WHAT ARE YOUR LIKES AND DISLIKES?
NONE TO SPEAK OF.
BUT, ER, IF YOU HAD TO NAME SOME?
IF I HAD TO?
WELL, FOR THINGS I LIKE...
THERE'S TEA, FIGS, RED BEAN SOUP...
IF I HAD TO NAME DISLIKES, THERE'S FAVA BEANS, MANDARIN ORANGES... AND STRAY DOGS.

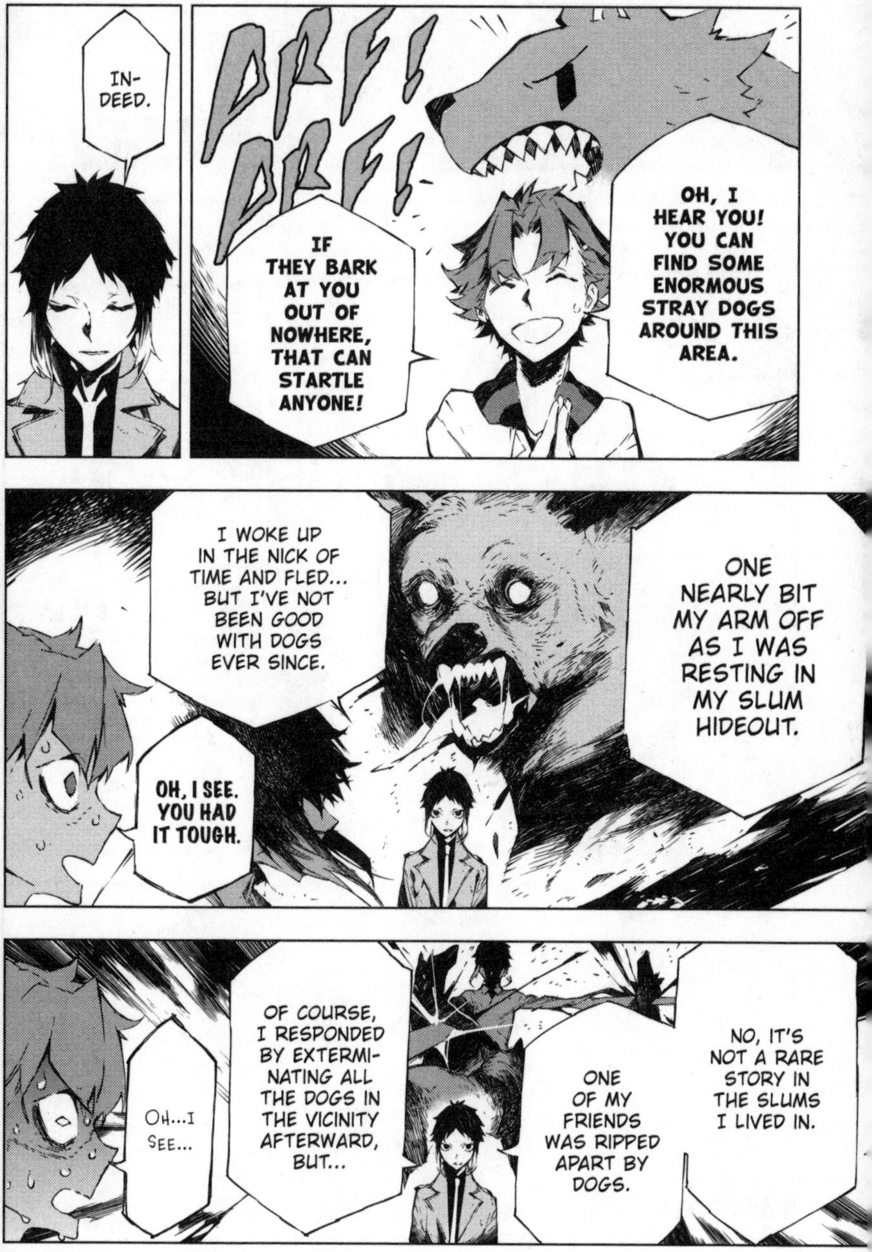
DRF! DRF!
OH, I HEAR YOU! YOU CAN FIND SOME ENORMOUS STRAY DOGS AROUND THIS AREA.
IF THEY BARK AT YOU OUT OF NOWHERE, THAT CAN STARTLE ANYONE!
IN-DEED.
ONE NEARLY BIT MY ARM OFF AS I WAS RESTING IN MY SLUM HIDEOUT.
I WOKE UP IN THE NICK OF TIME AND FLED... BUT I'VE NOT BEEN GOOD WITH DOGS EVER SINCE.
OH, I SEE. YOU HAD IT TOUGH.
NO, IT'S NOT A RARE STORY IN THE SLUMS I LIVED IN.
ONE OF MY FRIENDS WAS RIPPED APART BY DOGS.
OF COURSE, I RESPONDED BY EXTERMINATING ALL THE DOGS IN THE VICINITY AFTERWARD, BUT...
OH...I SEE...

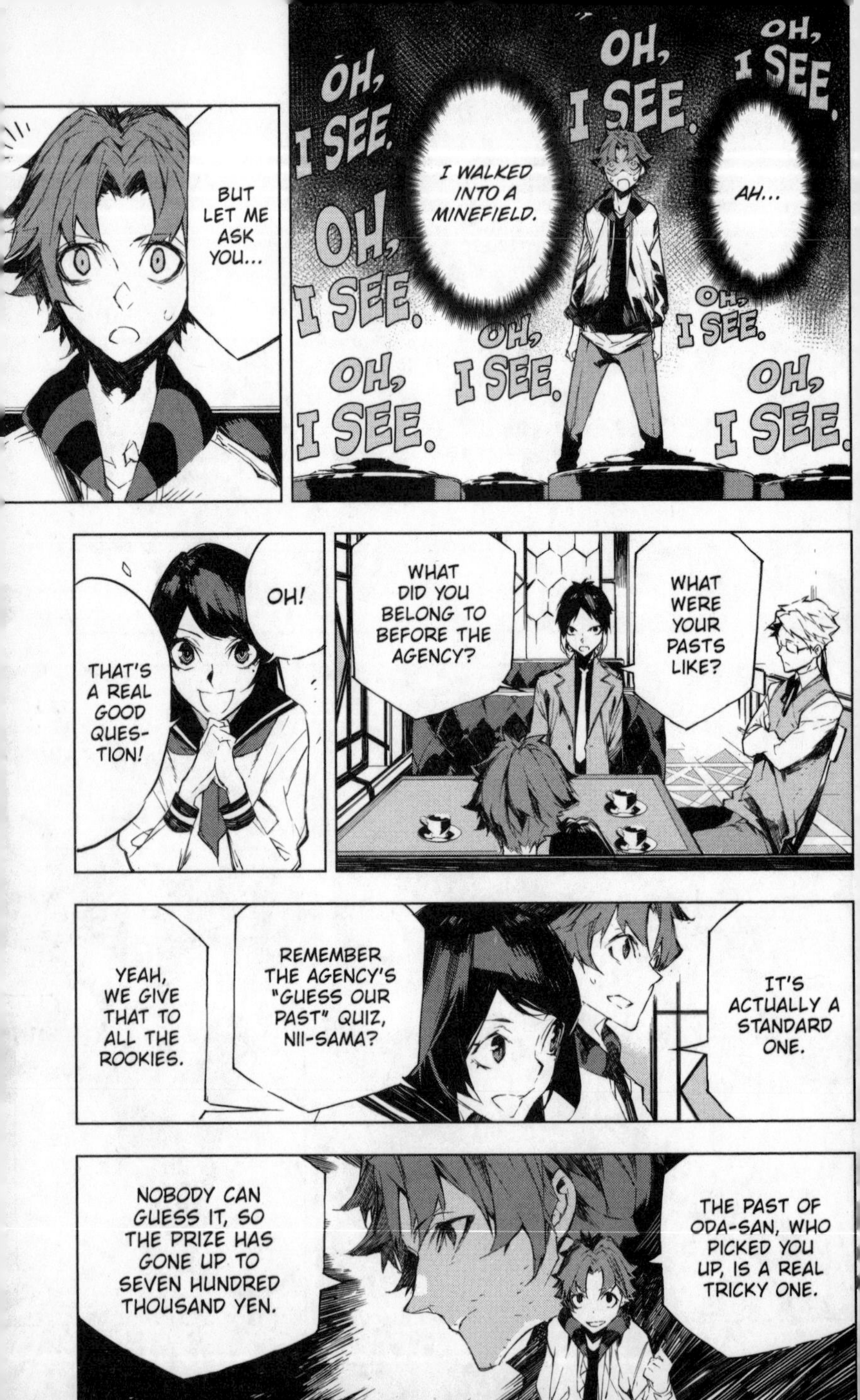
OH, I SEE.
OH, I SEE.
OH, I SEE.
AH...
I WALKED INTO A MINEFIELD.
OH, I SEE.
OH, I SEE.
OH, I SEE.
OH, I SEE.
OH, I SEE.
BUT LET ME ASK YOU...
WHAT WERE YOUR PASTS LIKE?
WHAT DID YOU BELONG TO BEFORE THE AGENCY?
OH!
THAT'S A REAL GOOD QUESTION!
IT'S ACTUALLY A STANDARD ONE.
REMEMBER THE AGENCY'S "GUESS OUR PAST" QUIZ, NII-SAMA?
YEAH, WE GIVE THAT TO ALL THE ROOKIES.
THE PAST OF ODA-SAN, WHO PICKED YOU UP, IS A REAL TRICKY ONE.
NOBODY CAN GUESS IT, SO THE PRIZE HAS GONE UP TO SEVEN HUNDRED THOUSAND YEN.

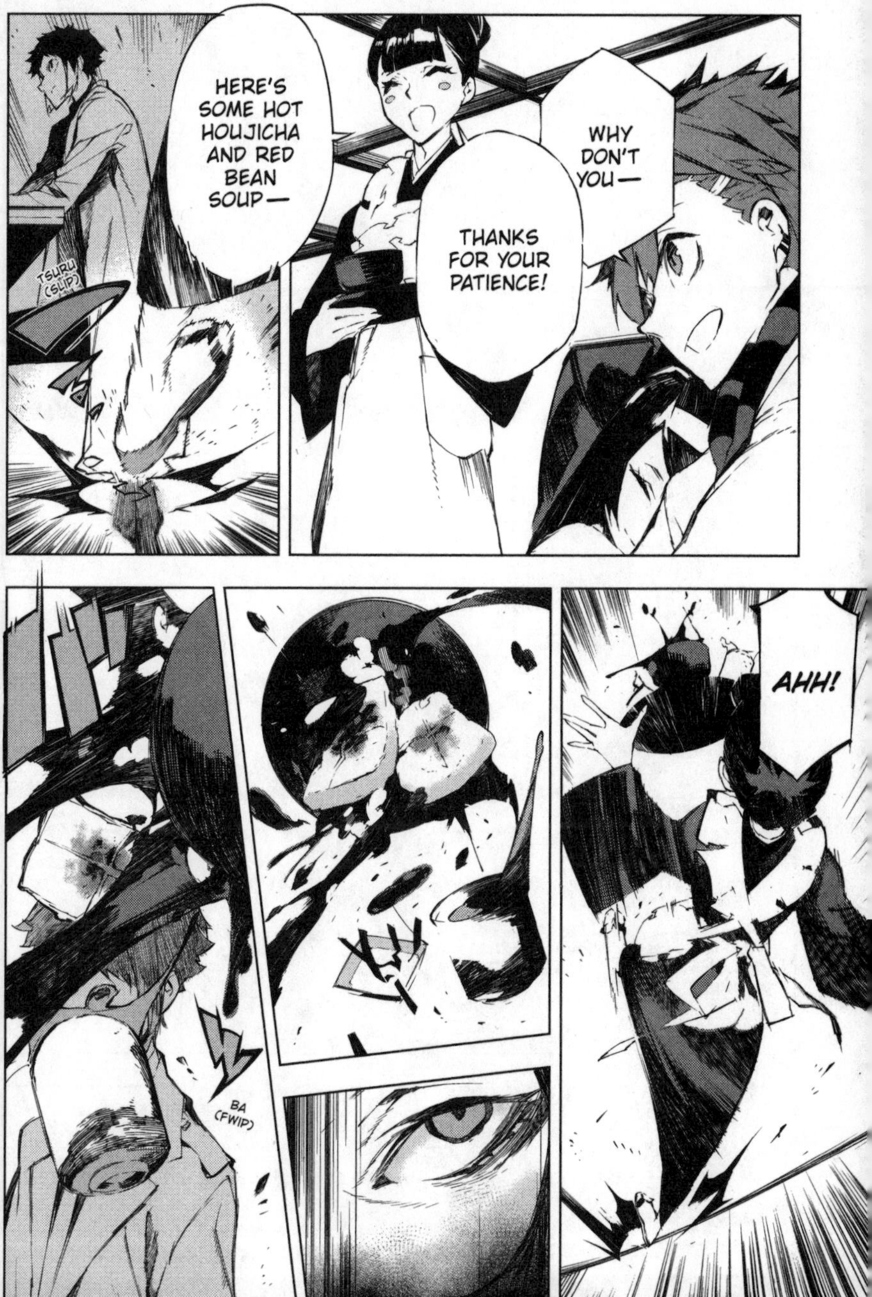
WHY DON'T YOU—
THANKS FOR YOUR PATIENCE!
HERE'S SOME HOT HOUJICHA AND RED BEAN SOUP—
TSURU (SLIP)
AHH!
BA (FWIP)

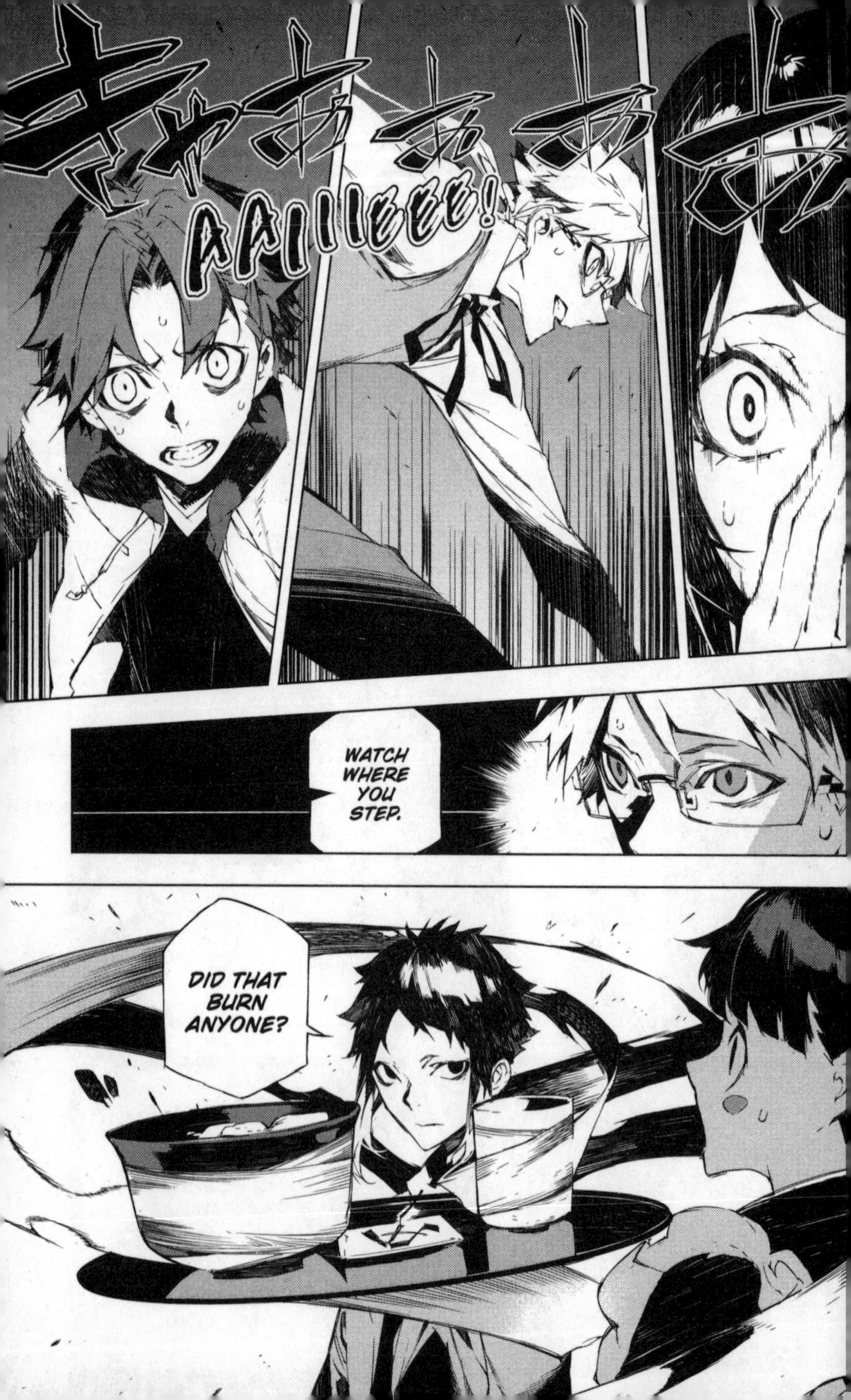
AAIIIEEEE!
WATCH WHERE YOU STEP.
DID THAT BURN ANYONE?

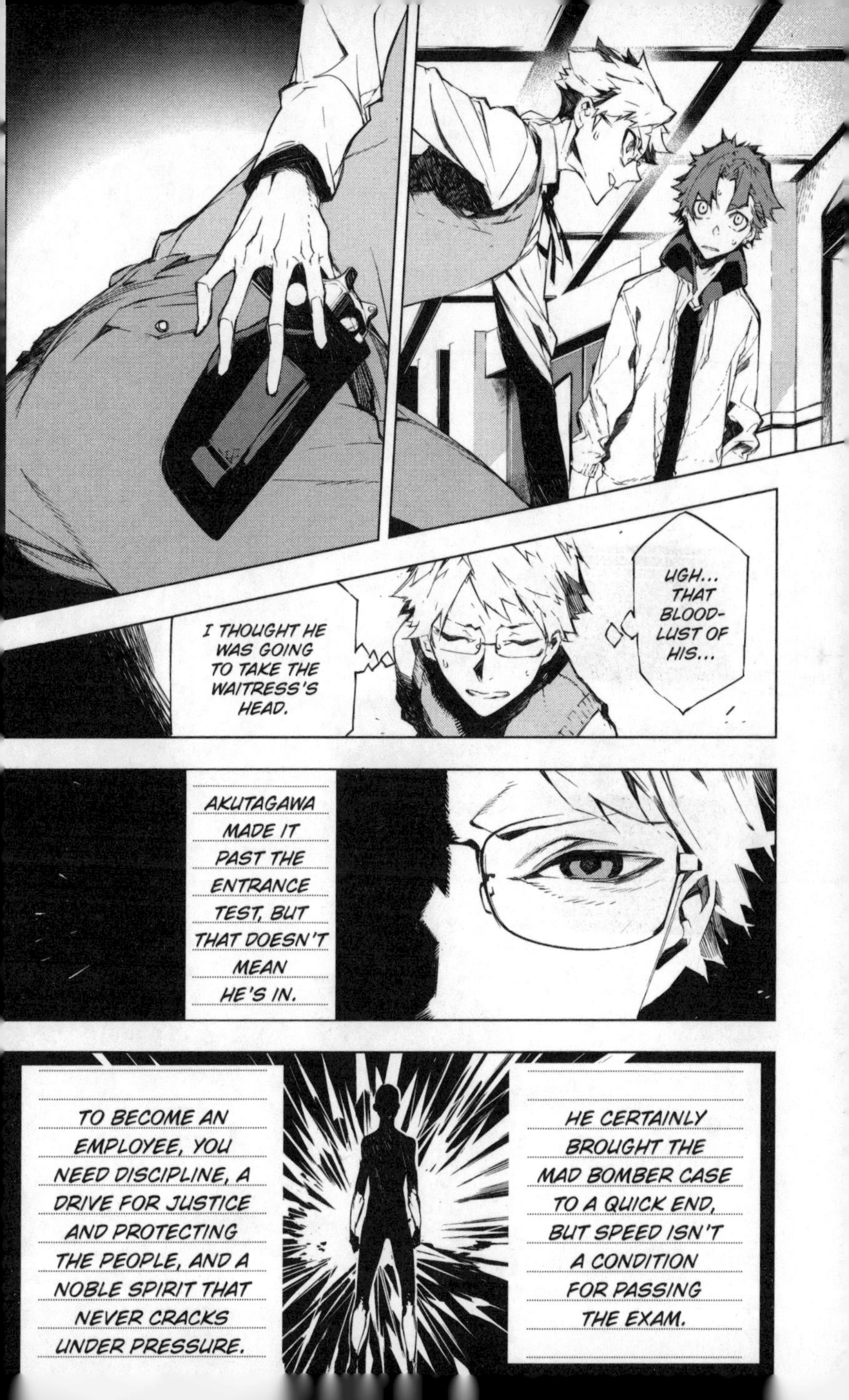
UGH... THAT BLOODLUST OF HIS...
I THOUGHT HE WAS GOING TO TAKE THE WAITRESS'S HEAD.
AKUTAGAWA MADE IT PAST THE ENTRANCE TEST, BUT THAT DOESN'T MEAN HE'S IN.
HE CERTAINLY BROUGHT THE MAD BOMBER CASE TO A QUICK END, BUT SPEED ISN'T A CONDITION FOR PASSING THE EXAM.
TO BECOME AN EMPLOYEE, YOU NEED DISCIPLINE, A DRIVE FOR JUSTICE AND PROTECTING THE PEOPLE, AND A NOBLE SPIRIT THAT NEVER CRACKS UNDER PRESSURE.

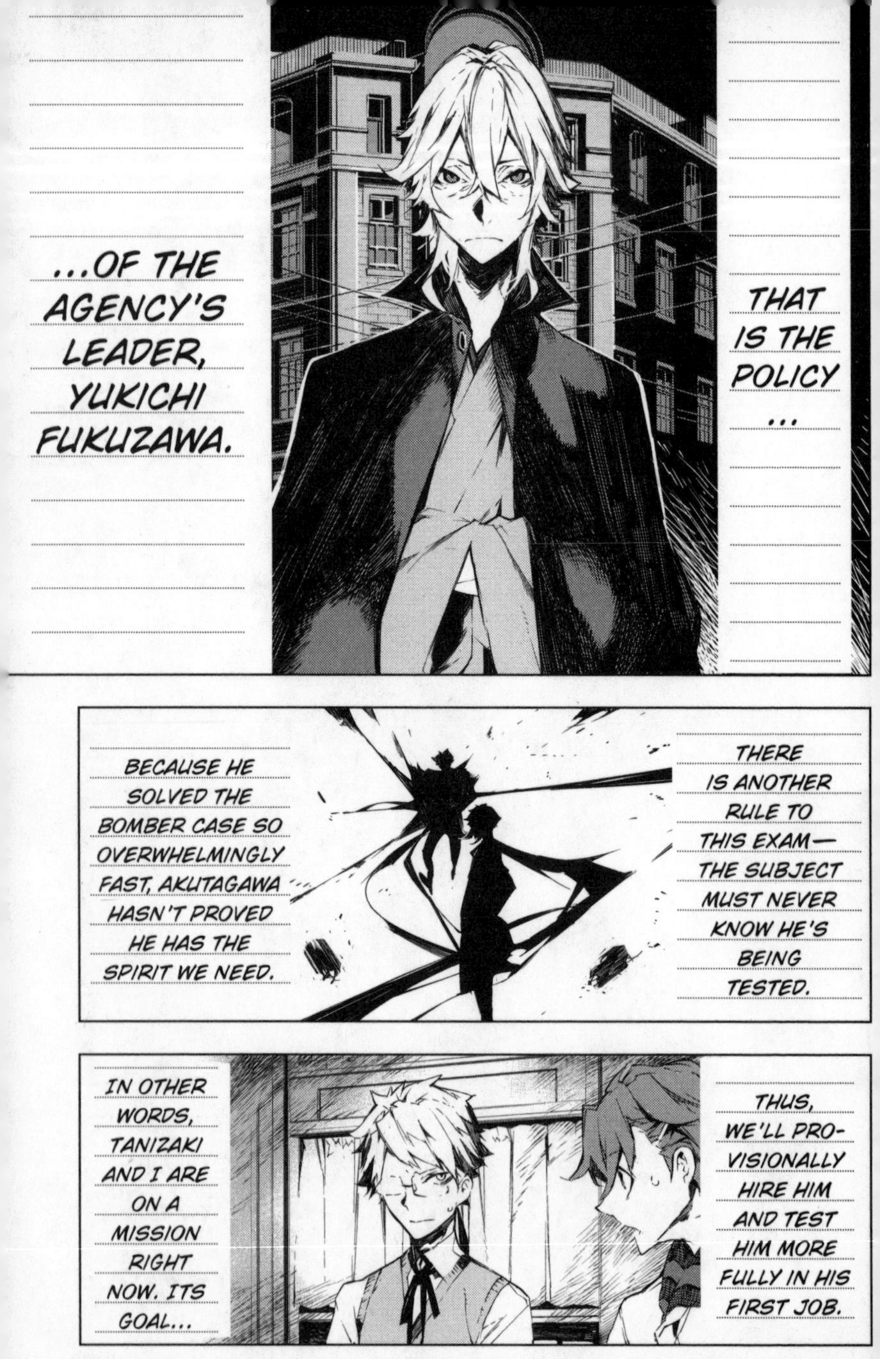
THAT IS THE POLICY ...
...OF THE AGENCY'S LEADER, YUKICHI FUKUZAWA.
THERE IS ANOTHER RULE TO THIS EXAM—THE SUBJECT MUST NEVER KNOW HE'S BEING TESTED.
BECAUSE HE SOLVED THE BOMBER CASE SO OVERWHELMINGLY FAST, AKUTAGAWA HASN'T PROVED HE HAS THE SPIRIT WE NEED.
THUS, WE'LL PRO-VISIONALLY HIRE HIM AND TEST HIM MORE FULLY IN HIS FIRST JOB.
IN OTHER WORDS, TANIZAKI AND I ARE ON A MISSION RIGHT NOW. ITS GOAL...

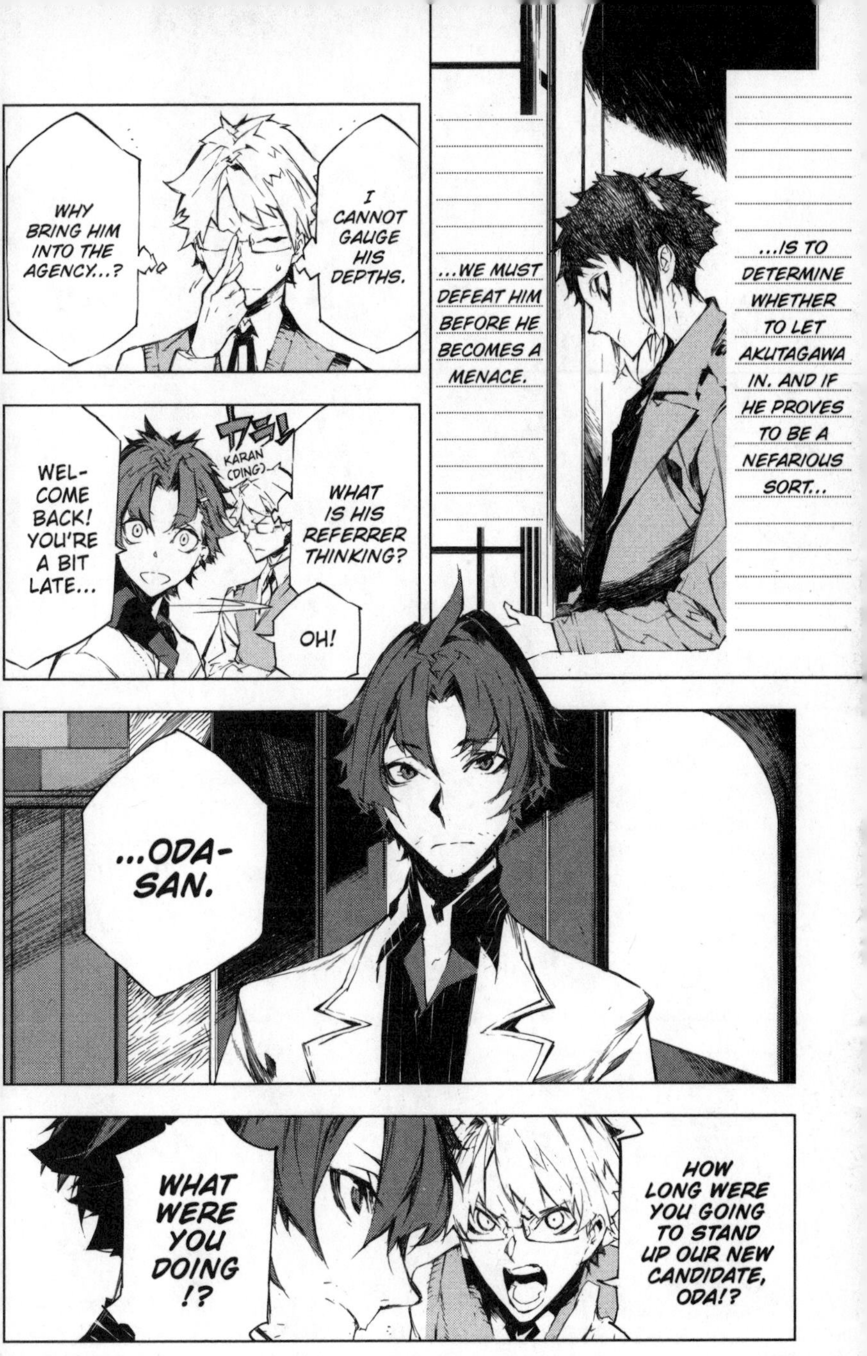
...IS TO DETERMINE WHETHER TO LET AKUTAGAWA IN. AND IF HE PROVES TO BE A NEFARIOUS SORT...
...WE MUST DEFEAT HIM BEFORE HE BECOMES A MENACE.
I CANNOT GAUGE HIS DEPTHS.
WHY BRING HIM INTO THE AGENCY...?
WHAT IS HIS REFERRER THINKING?
KARAN (DING)
WEL-COME BACK! YOU'RE A BIT LATE...
OH!
...ODA-SAN.
HOW LONG WERE YOU GOING TO STAND UP OUR NEW CANDIDATE, ODA!?
WHAT WERE YOU DOING!?

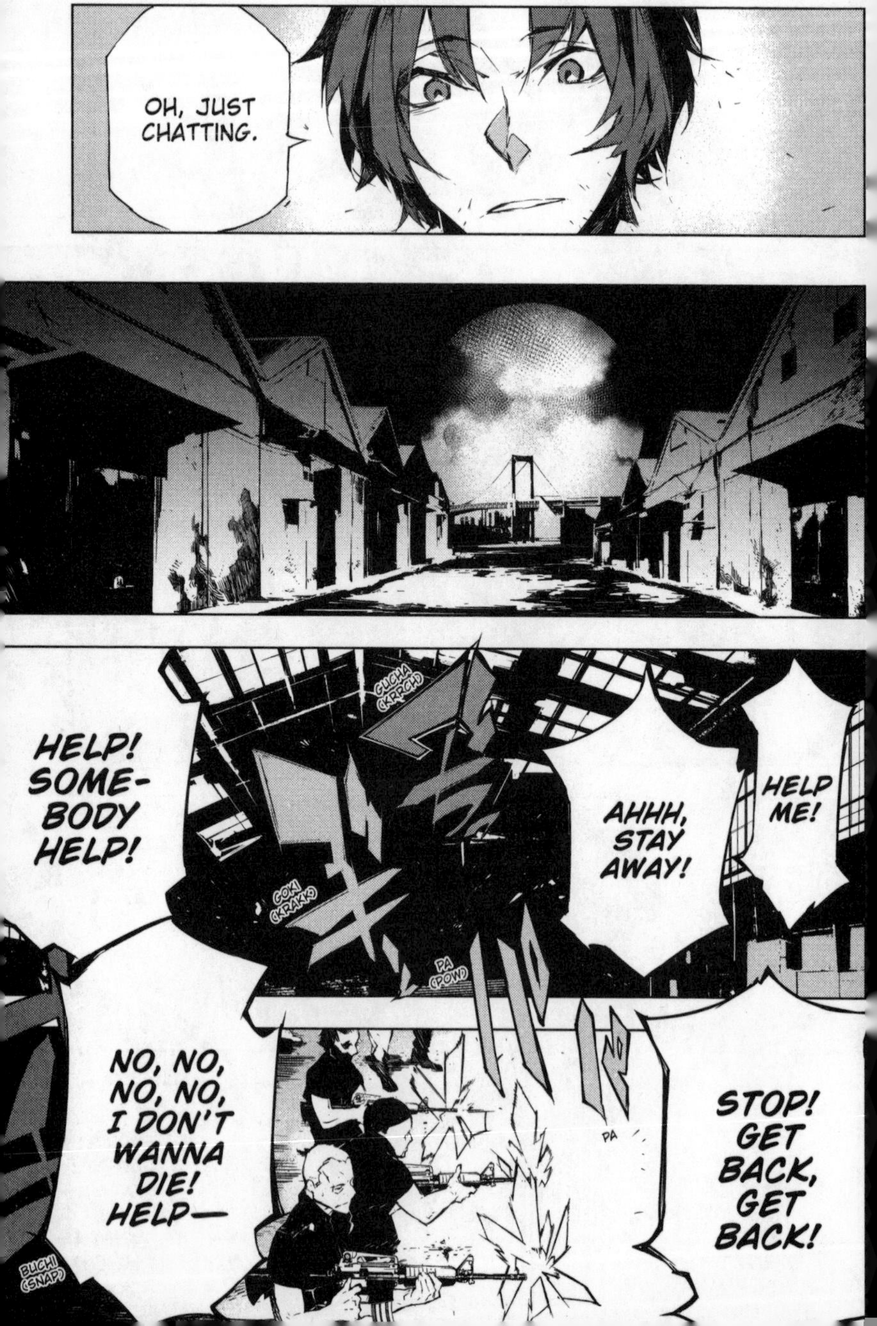
OH, JUST CHATTING.
HELP ME!
AHHH, STAY AWAY!
GUCHA (KRRCH)
HELP! SOME-BODY HELP!
GOKI (KRAKK)
PA (POW)
STOP! GET BACK, GET BACK!
PA
NO, NO, NO, NO, I DON'T WANNA DIE! HELP—
BUCHI (SNAP)

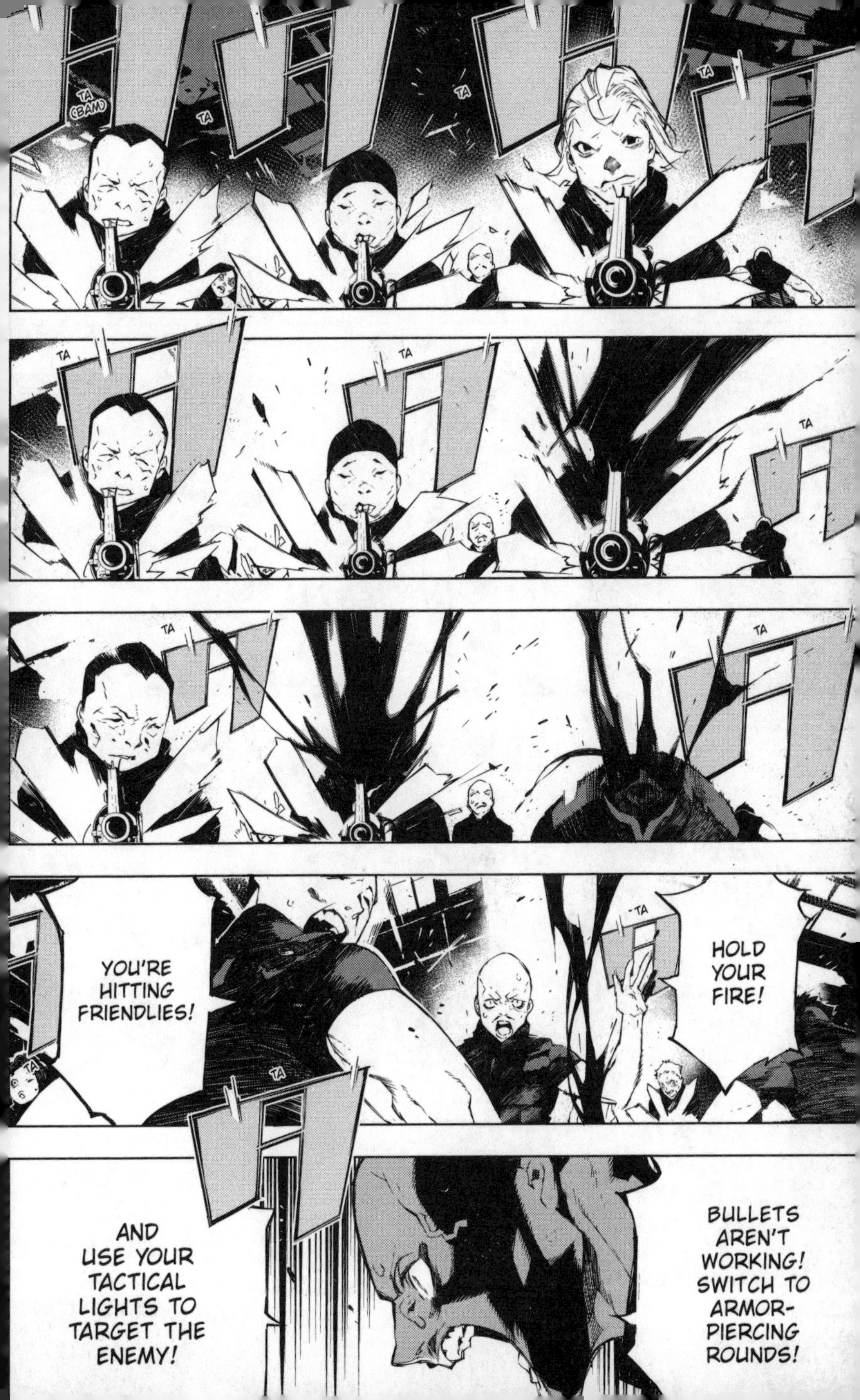
TA
TA
TA
TA
(BAM)
TA
TA
TA
TA
TA
HOLD YOUR FIRE!
TA
YOU'RE HITTING FRIENDLIES!
TA
TA
BULLETS AREN'T WORKING! SWITCH TO ARMOR-PIERCING ROUNDS!
AND USE YOUR TACTICAL LIGHTS TO TARGET THE ENEMY!

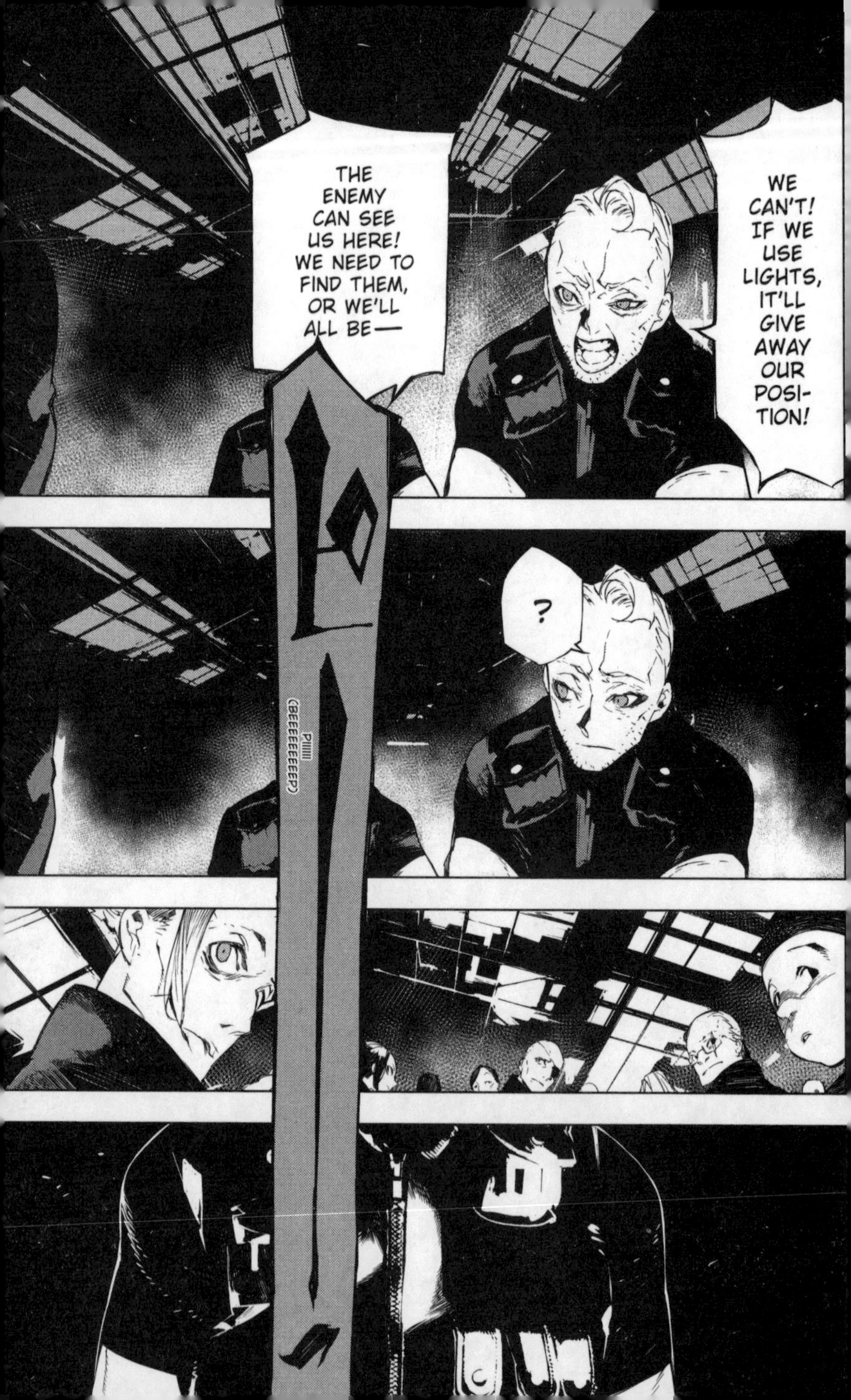
WE CAN'T! IF WE USE LIGHTS, IT'LL GIVE AWAY OUR POSI-TION!
THE ENEMY CAN SEE US HERE! WE NEED TO FIND THEM, OR WE'LL ALL BE—
?
PIIIII
(BEEEEEEEEEEP)

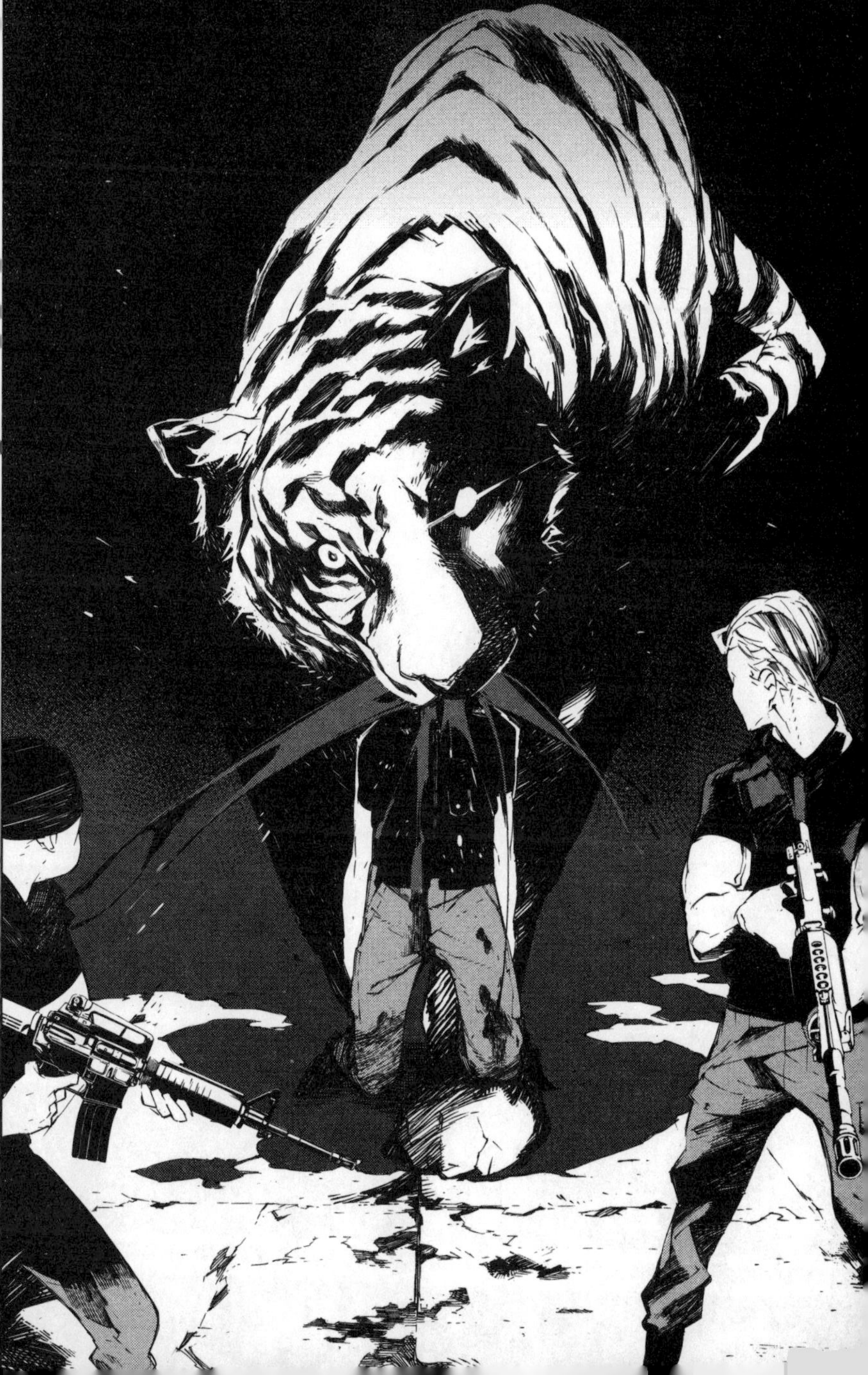

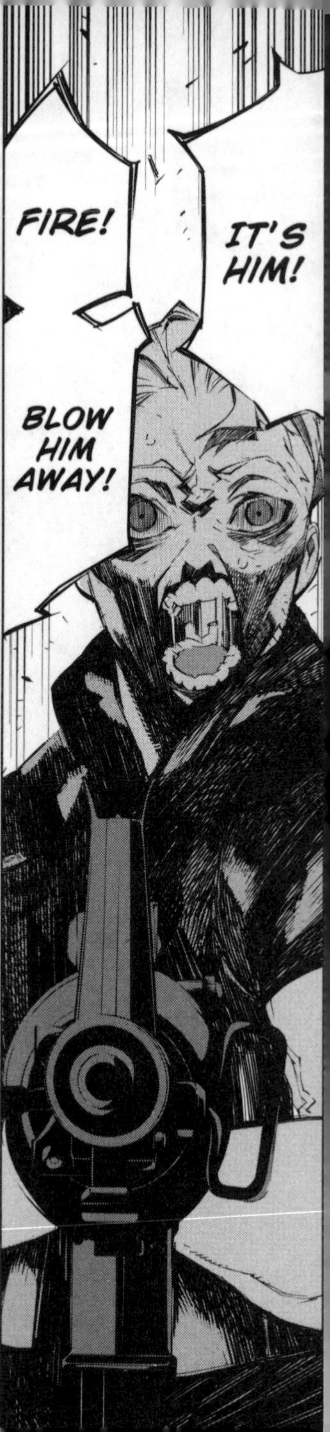
IT'S HIM!
FIRE!
BLOW HIM AWAY!

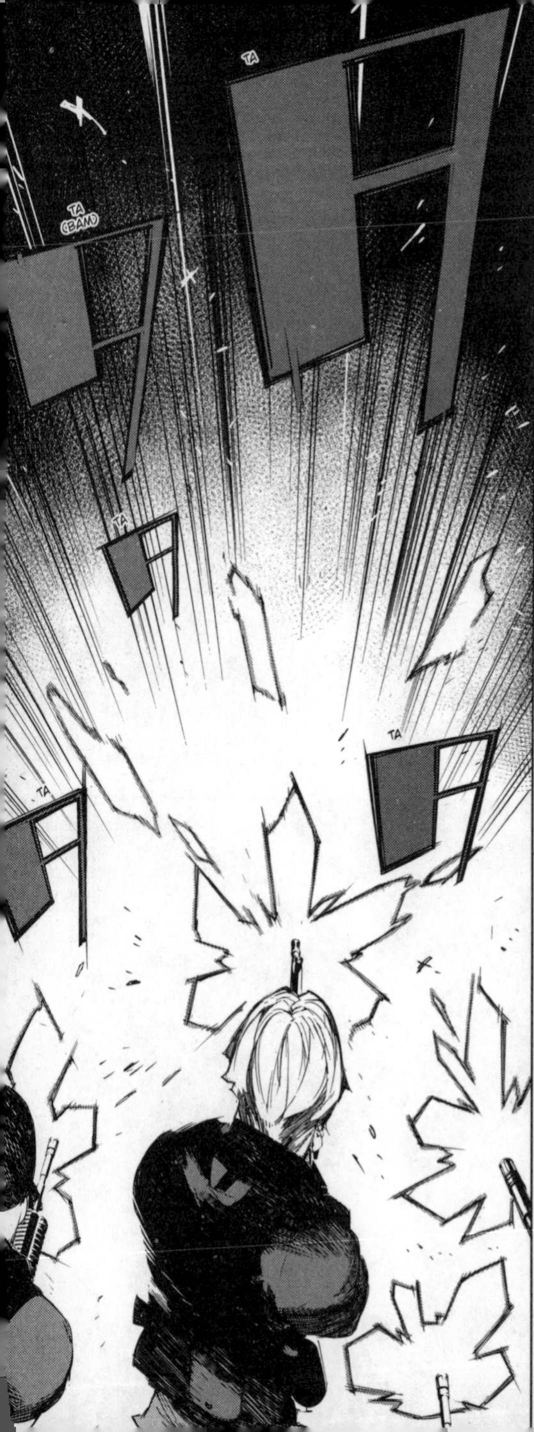
TA
TA
(BAM)
TA
TA
TA

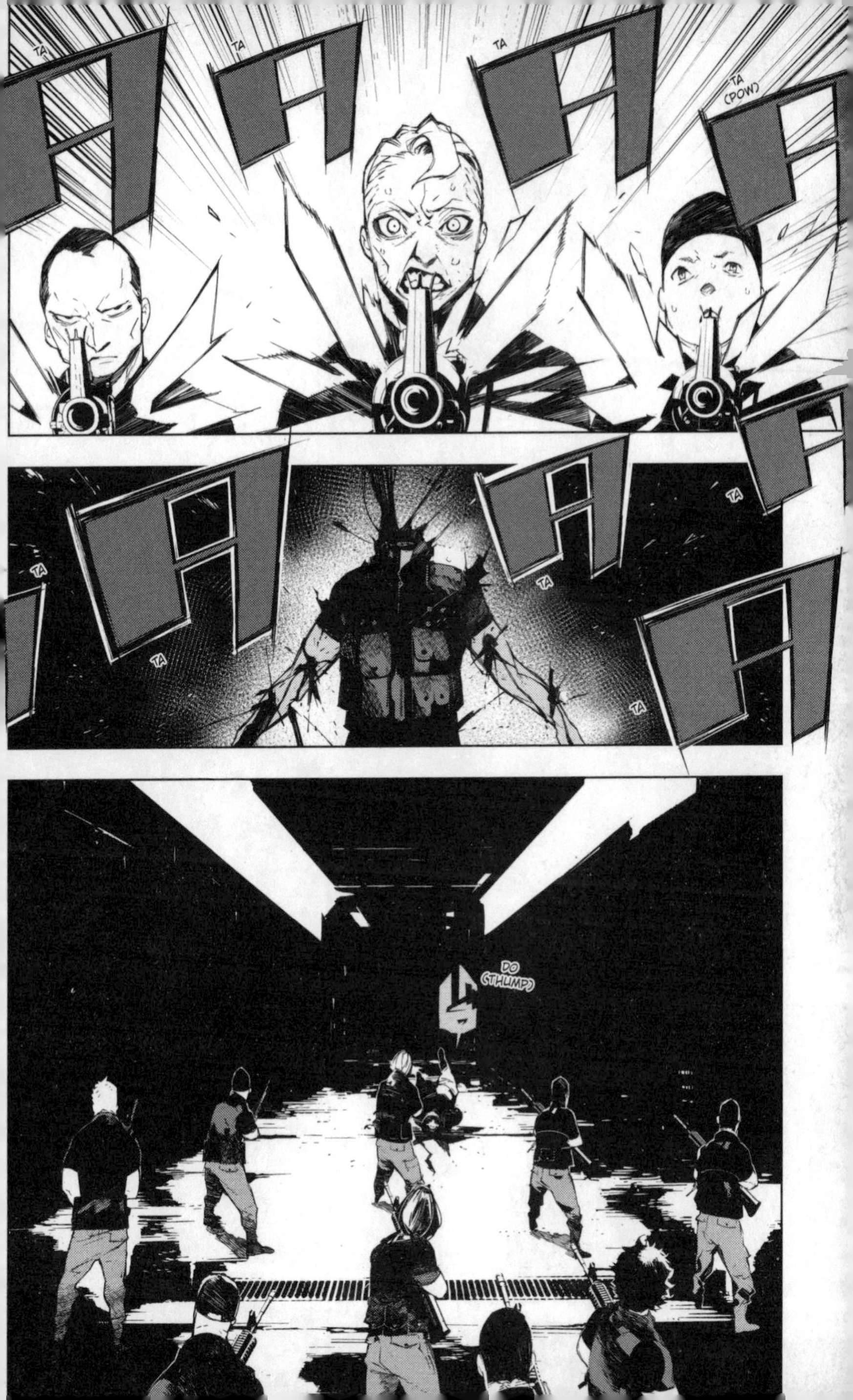
TA
(POW)
TA
TA
TA
TA
TA
TA
TA
TA
DO
(THUMP)

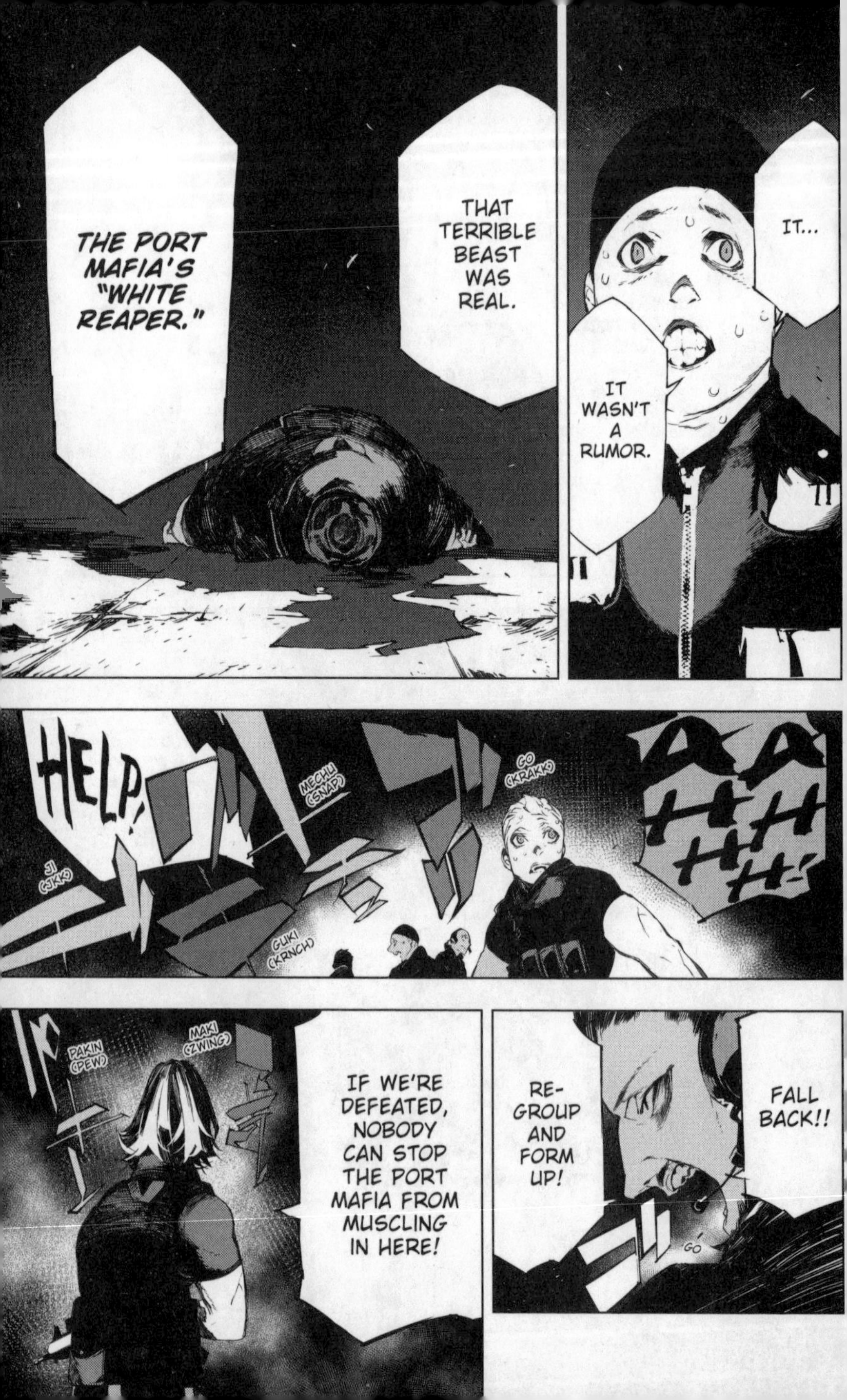
IT...
IT WASN'T A RUMOR.
THAT TERRIBLE BEAST WAS REAL.
THE PORT MAFIA'S "WHITE REAPER."
AAHHHHHHH-!
GO (KRAKK)
MECHU (SNAP)
HELP!
JI (JIKK)
GUKI (KRNCH)
FALL BACK!!
RE-GROUP AND FORM UP!
GO
IF WE'RE DEFEATED, NOBODY CAN STOP THE PORT MAFIA FROM MUSCLING IN HERE!
MAKI (ZWING)
PAKIN (PEW)

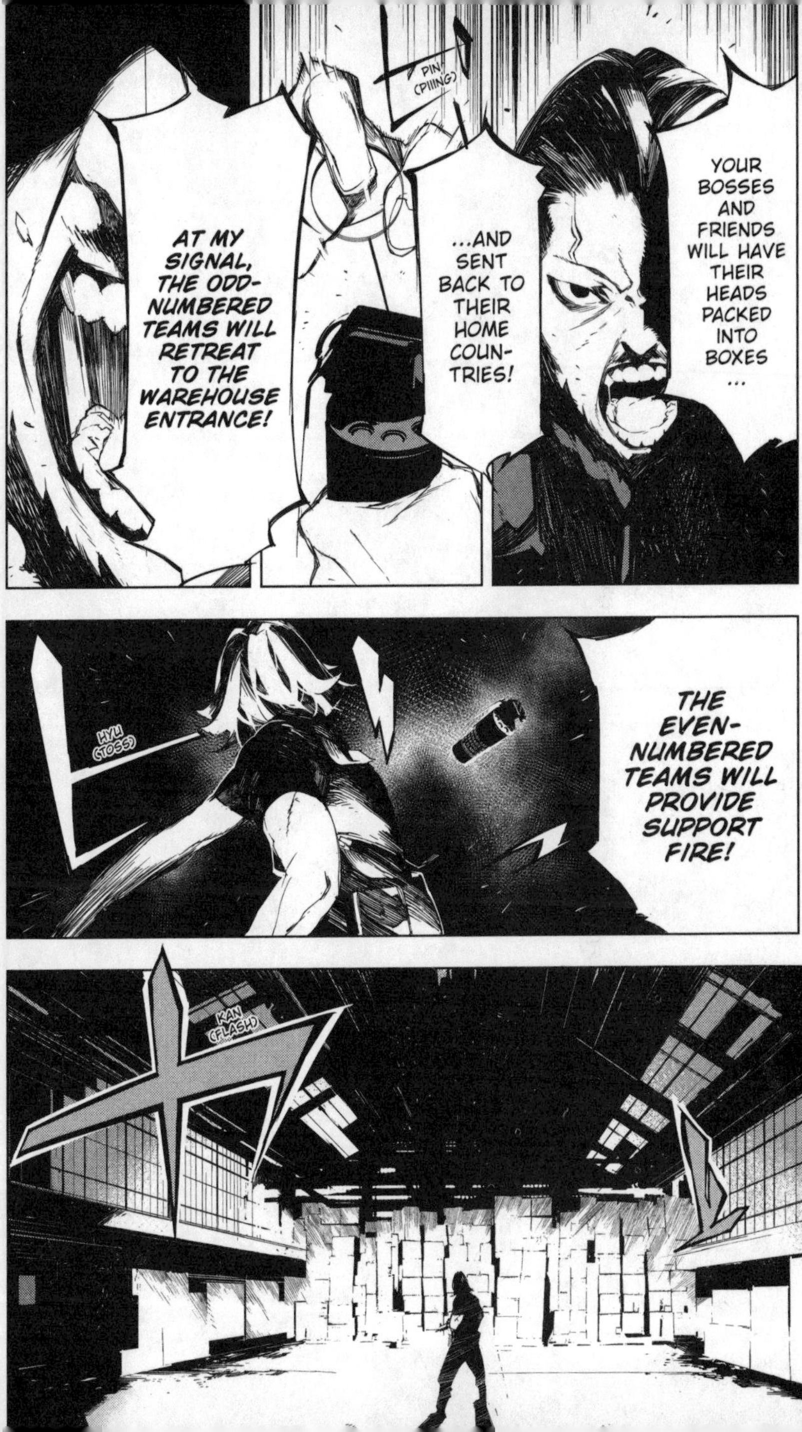
YOUR BOSSES AND FRIENDS WILL HAVE THEIR HEADS PACKED INTO BOXES ...
PIN (PIIING)
...AND SENT BACK TO THEIR HOME COUN-TRIES!
AT MY SIGNAL, THE ODD-NUMBERED TEAMS WILL RETREAT TO THE WAREHOUSE ENTRANCE!
THE EVEN-NUMBERED TEAMS WILL PROVIDE SUPPORT FIRE!
HYU (TOSS)
KAN (FLASH)

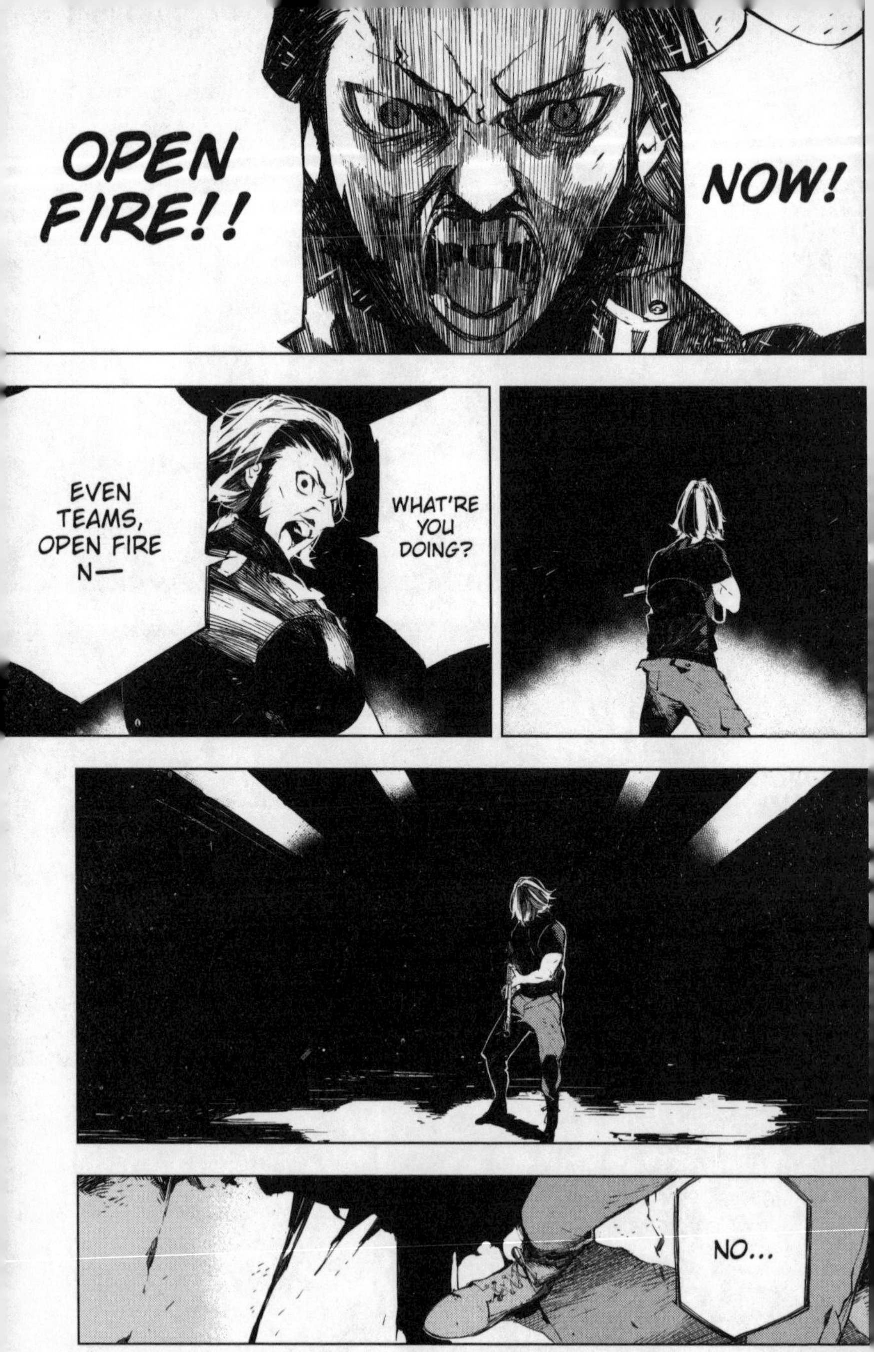
NOW!
OPEN FIRE!!
WHAT'RE YOU DOING?
EVEN TEAMS, OPEN FIRE N—
NO...

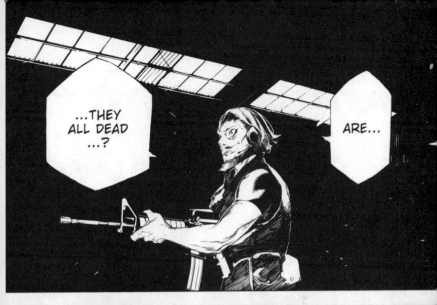

...THEY ALL DEAD ...?

ARE...

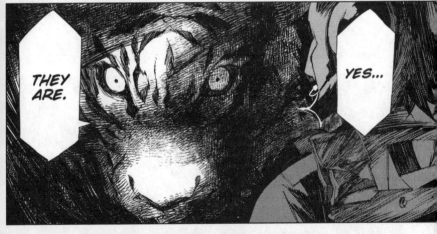

THEY ARE.

YES...

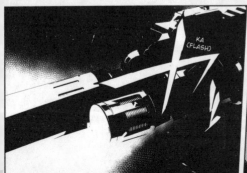

KA
(FLASH)

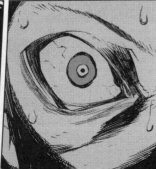

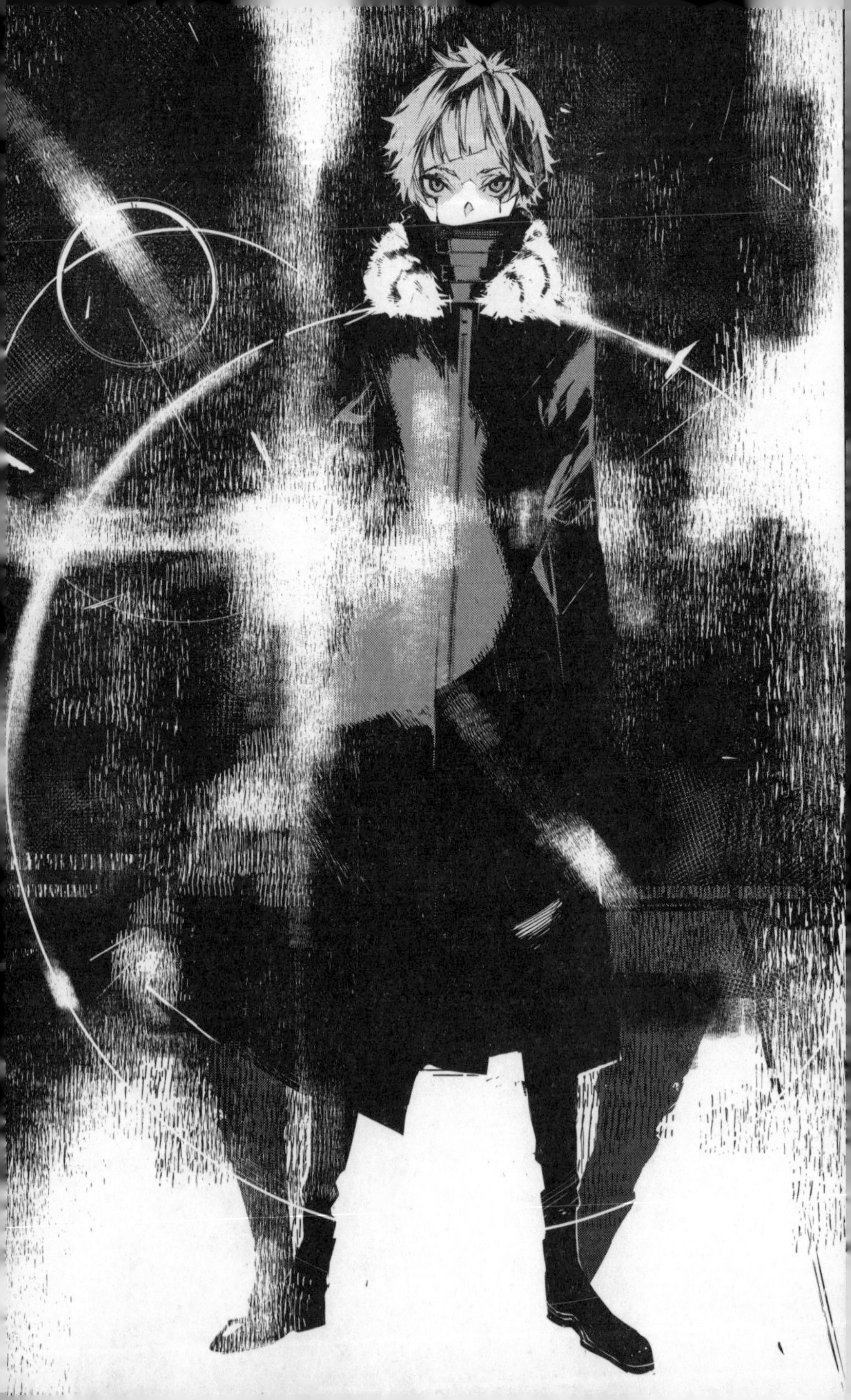

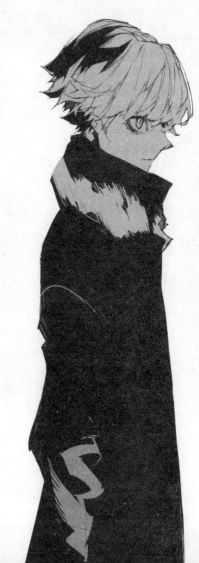

Bungo Stray Dogs

B E A S T

#3: THE WHITE REAPER

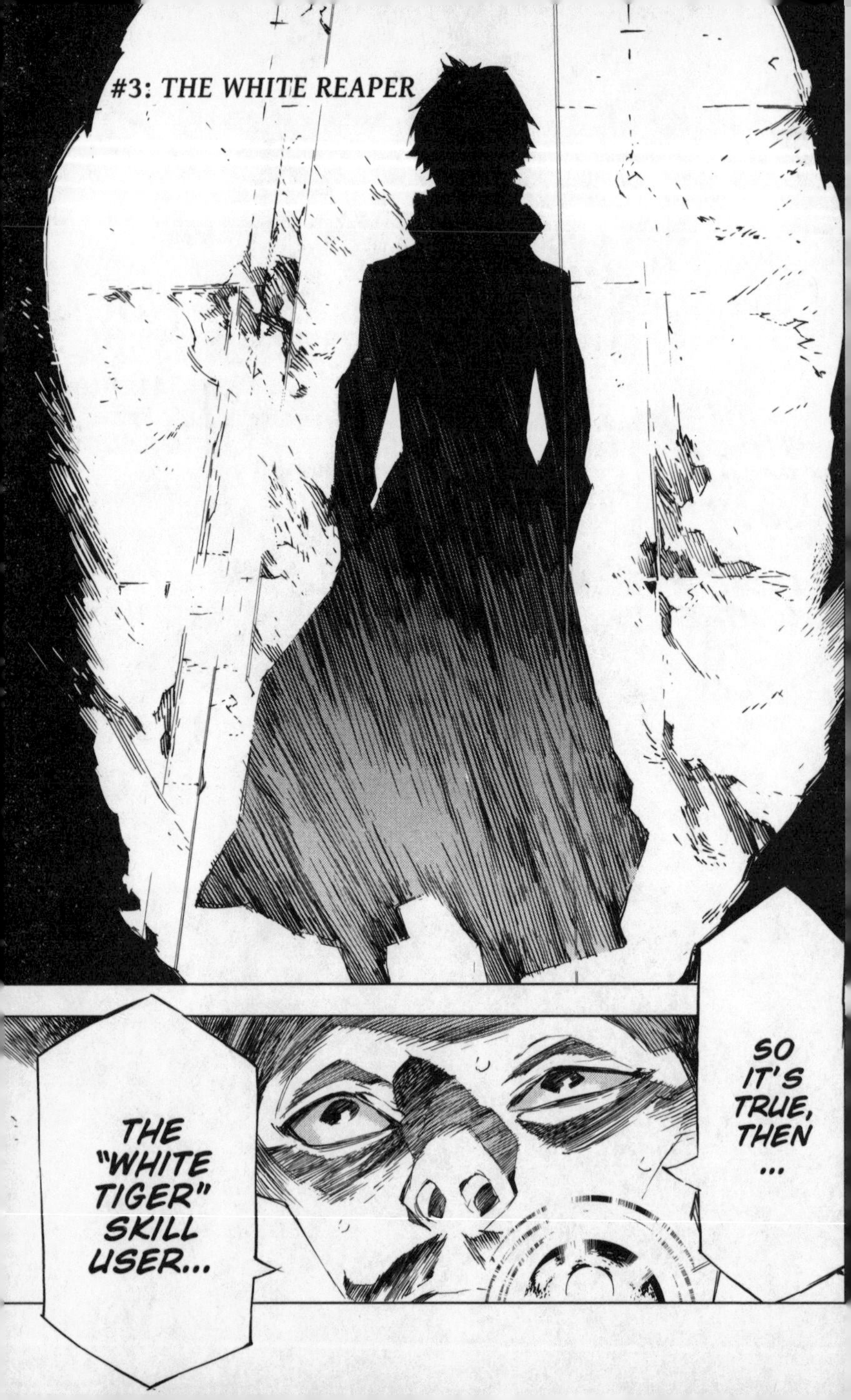

SO IT'S TRUE, THEN...
THE "WHITE TIGER" SKILL USER...

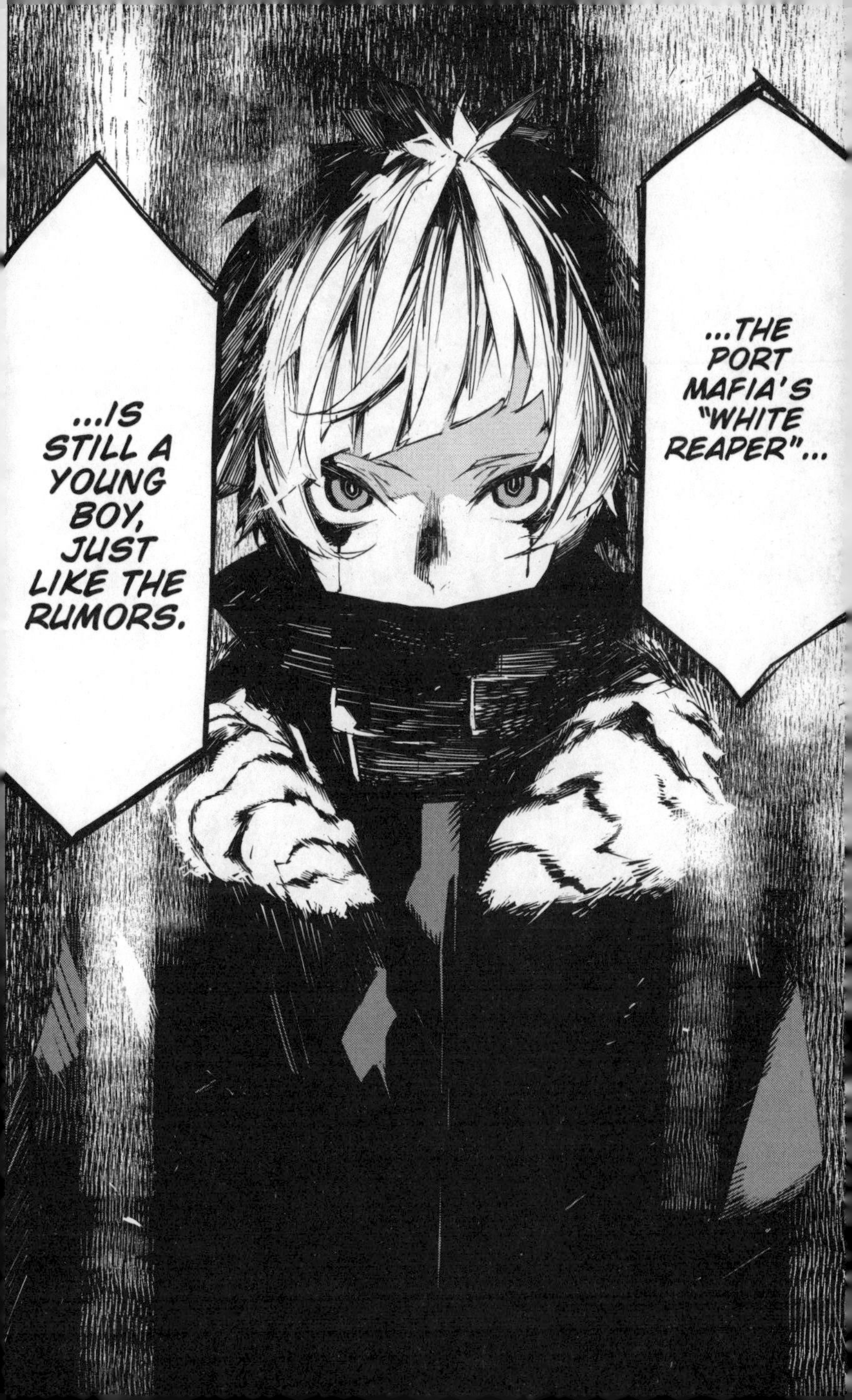
...THE PORT MAFIA'S "WHITE REAPER"...
...IS STILL A YOUNG BOY, JUST LIKE THE RUMORS.

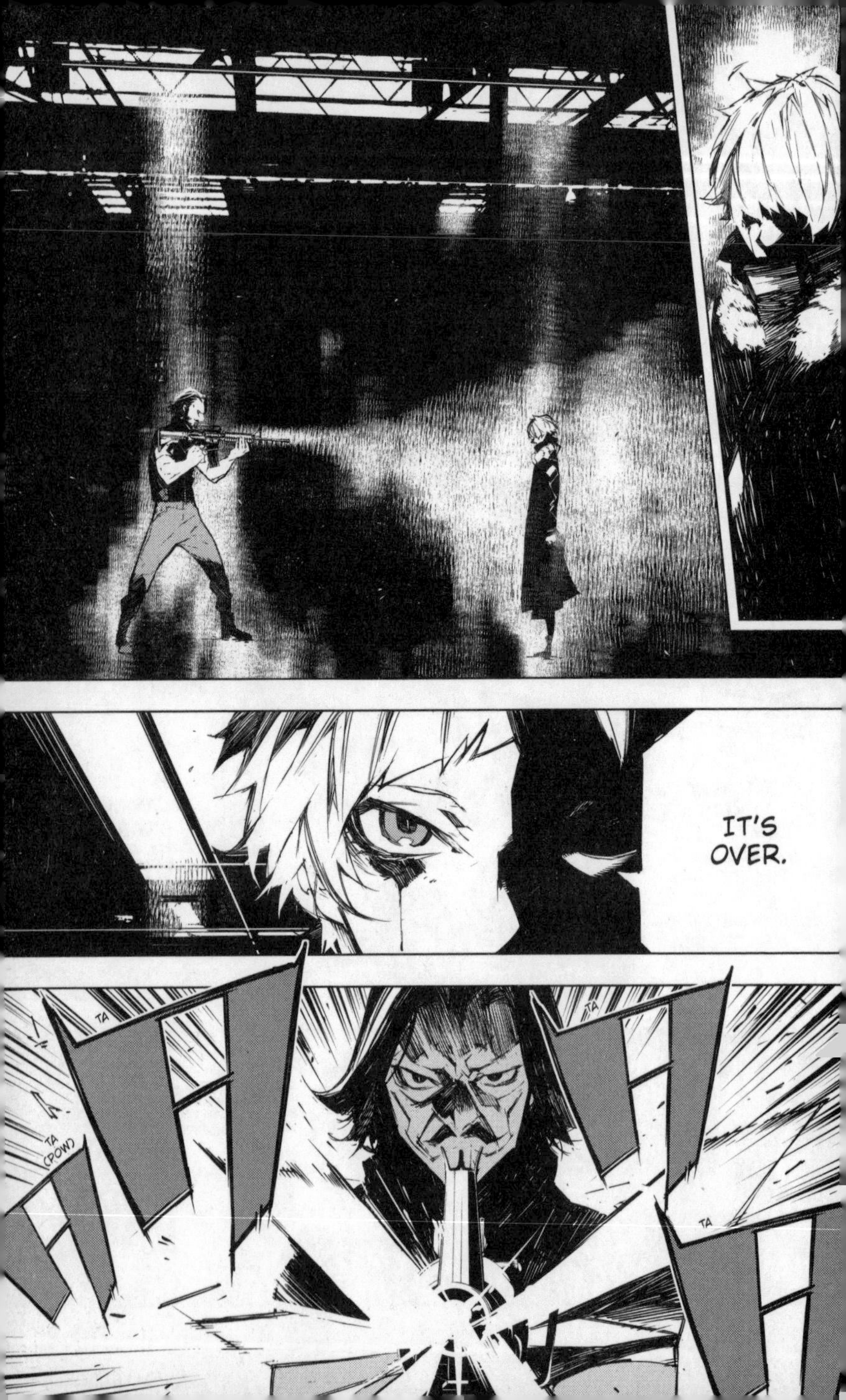
IT'S OVER.
TA
TA
TA
(POW)
TA

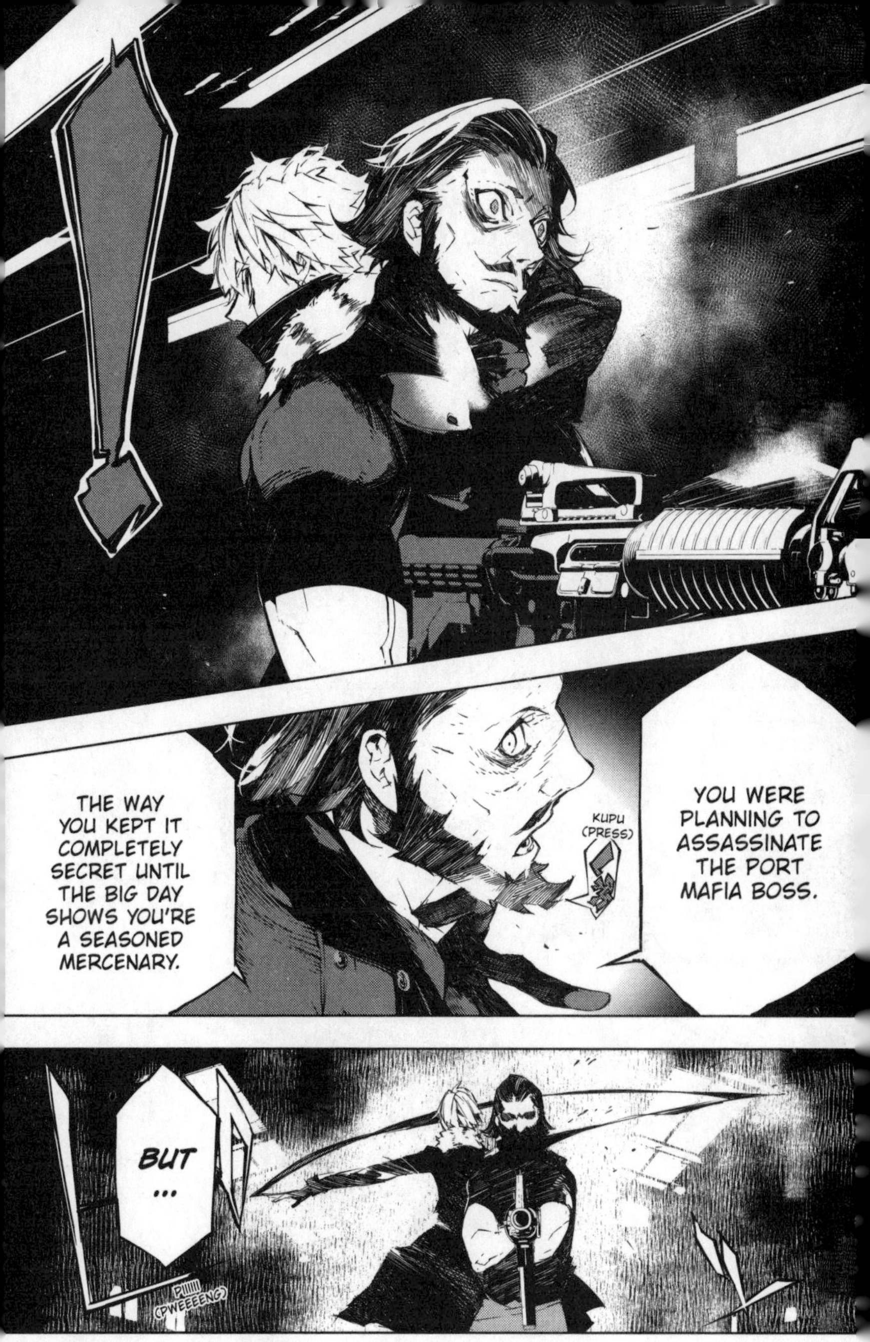
YOU WERE PLANNING TO ASSASSINATE THE PORT MAFIA BOSS.
KUPU (PRESS)
THE WAY YOU KEPT IT COMPLETELY SECRET UNTIL THE BIG DAY SHOWS YOU'RE A SEASONED MERCENARY.
BUT ...
PIIIIII (PWEEEENG)

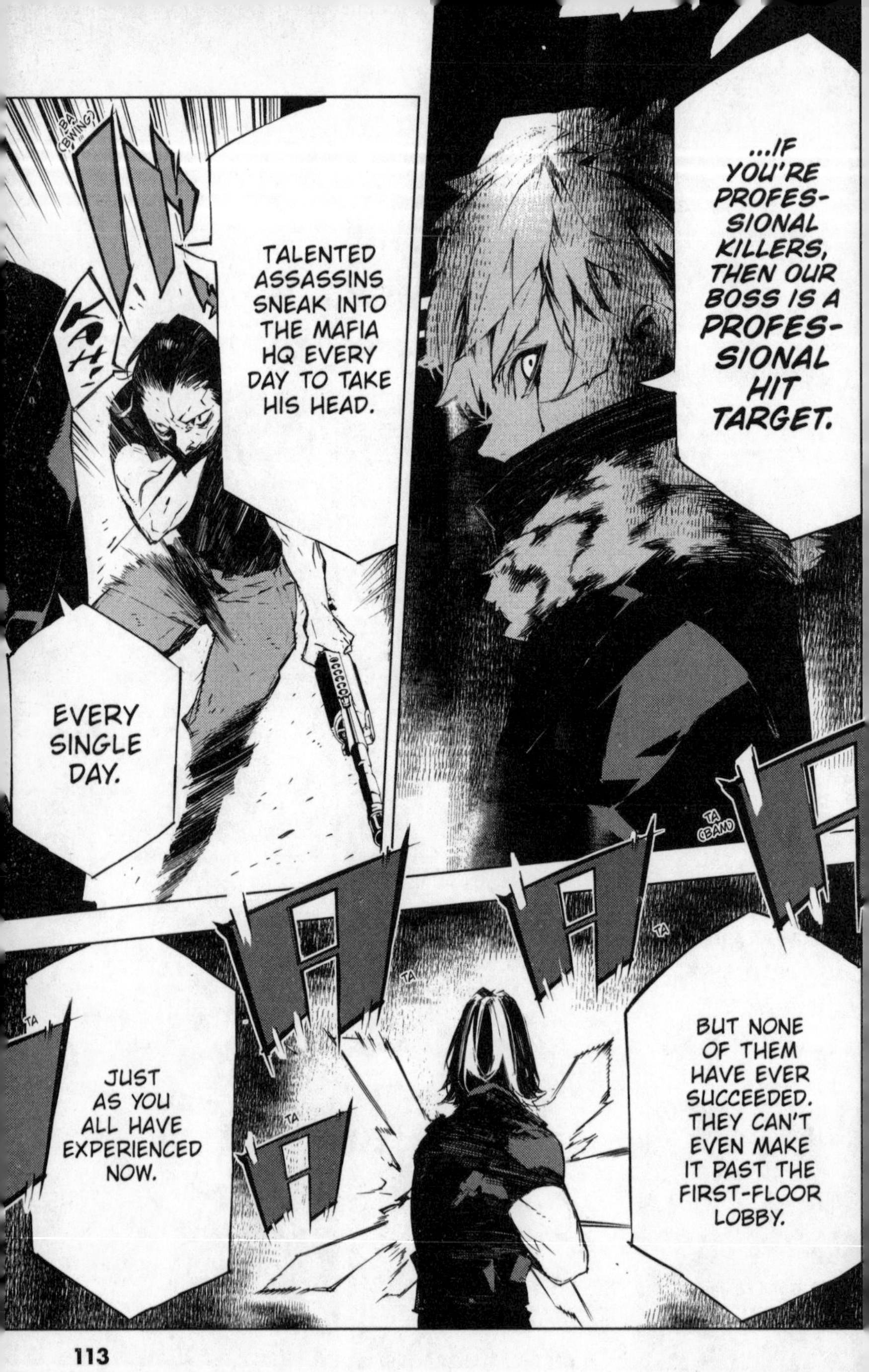
...IF YOU'RE PROFES-SIONAL KILLERS, THEN OUR BOSS IS A PROFES-SIONAL HIT TARGET.
TA (BAM)
BA (BWING?)
KAH!
TALENTED ASSASSINS SNEAK INTO THE MAFIA HQ EVERY DAY TO TAKE HIS HEAD.
EVERY SINGLE DAY.
TA
BUT NONE OF THEM HAVE EVER SUCCEEDED. THEY CAN'T EVEN MAKE IT PAST THE FIRST-FLOOR LOBBY.
TA
TA
TA
JUST AS YOU ALL HAVE EXPERIENCED NOW.

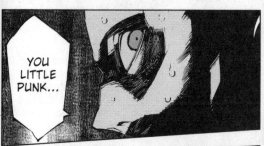

YOU LITTLE PUNK...

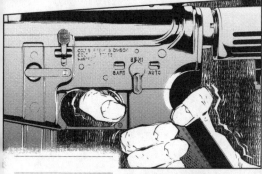

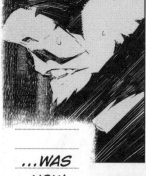

THE FINGER OF THIS WAR-HARDENED SOLDIER, WHO NEVER SWEATED ONCE IN BATTLE, NOT EVEN AGAINST GREAT ARMIES...

...WAS NOW QUIVERING AT THE HANDS OF A SINGLE BOY.

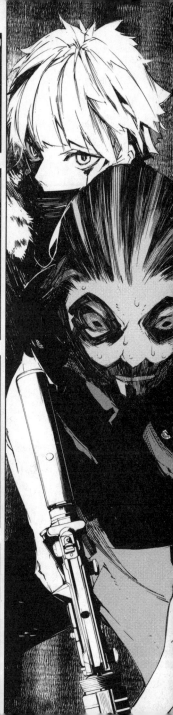

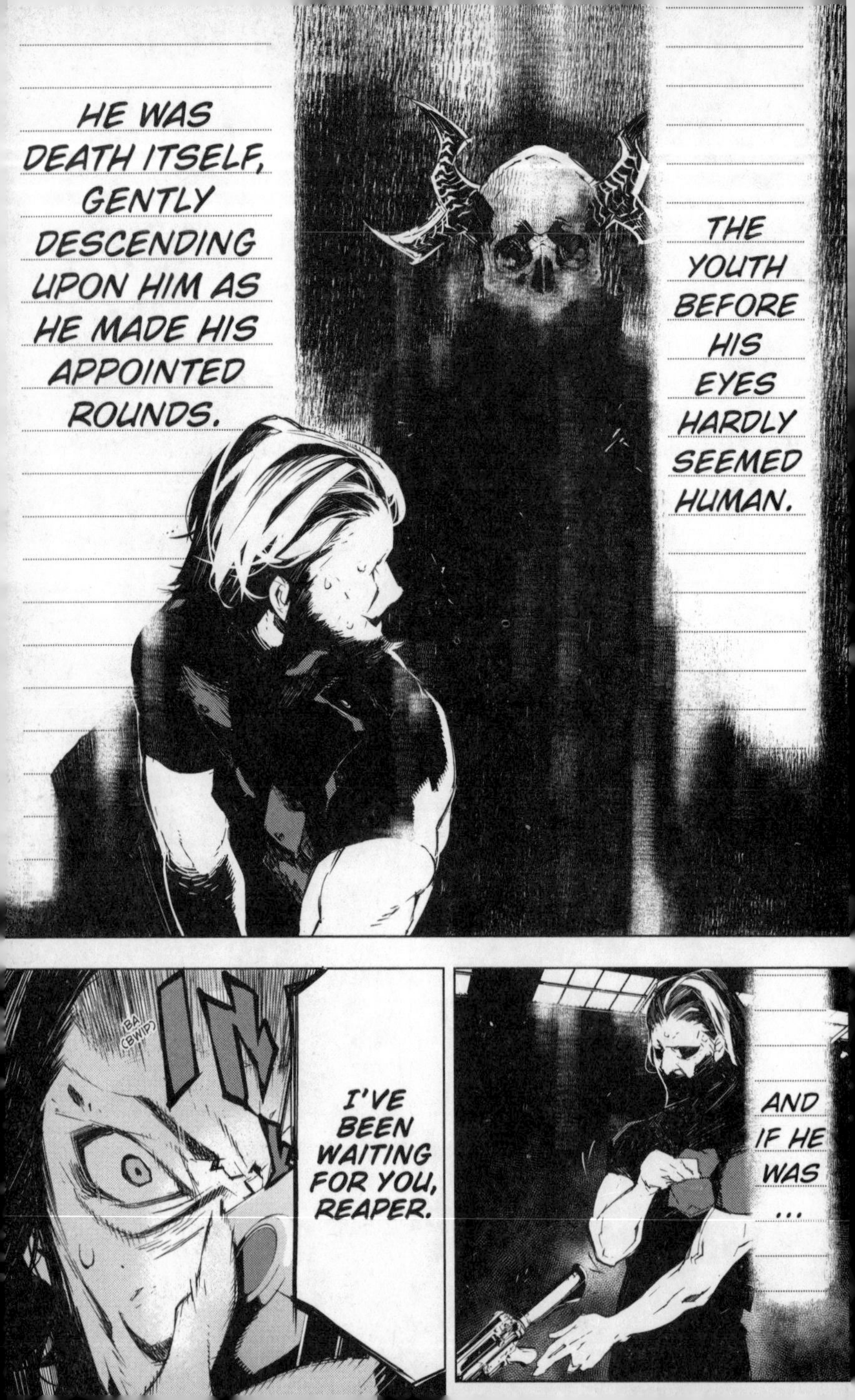
THE YOUTH BEFORE HIS EYES HARDLY SEEMED HUMAN.
HE WAS DEATH ITSELF, GENTLY DESCENDING UPON HIM AS HE MADE HIS APPOINTED ROUNDS.
AND IF HE WAS...
BA (BWIP)
I'VE BEEN WAITING FOR YOU, REAPER.

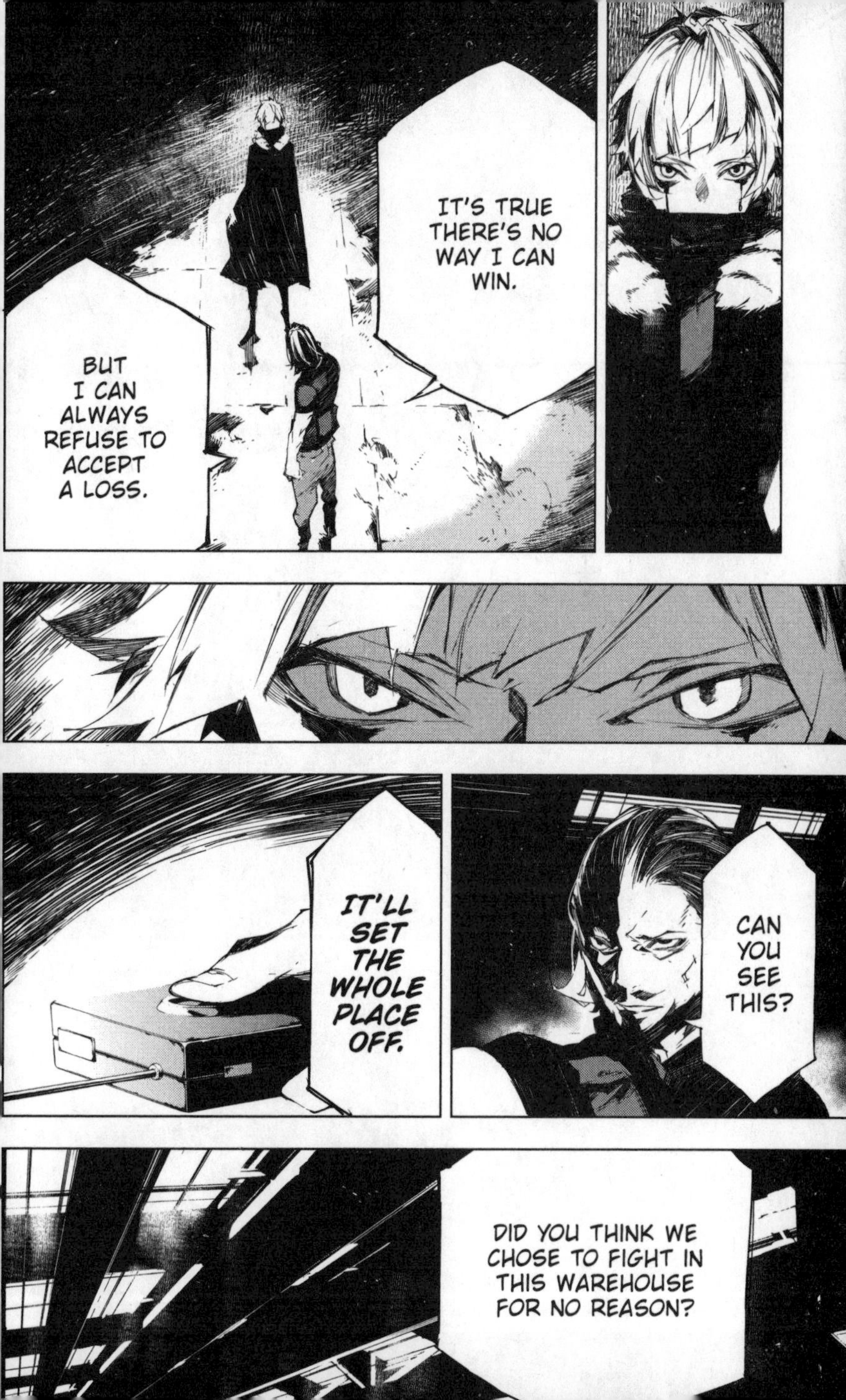
IT'S TRUE THERE'S NO WAY I CAN WIN.
BUT I CAN ALWAYS REFUSE TO ACCEPT A LOSS.
CAN YOU SEE THIS?
IT'LL SET THE WHOLE PLACE OFF.
DID YOU THINK WE CHOSE TO FIGHT IN THIS WAREHOUSE FOR NO REASON?

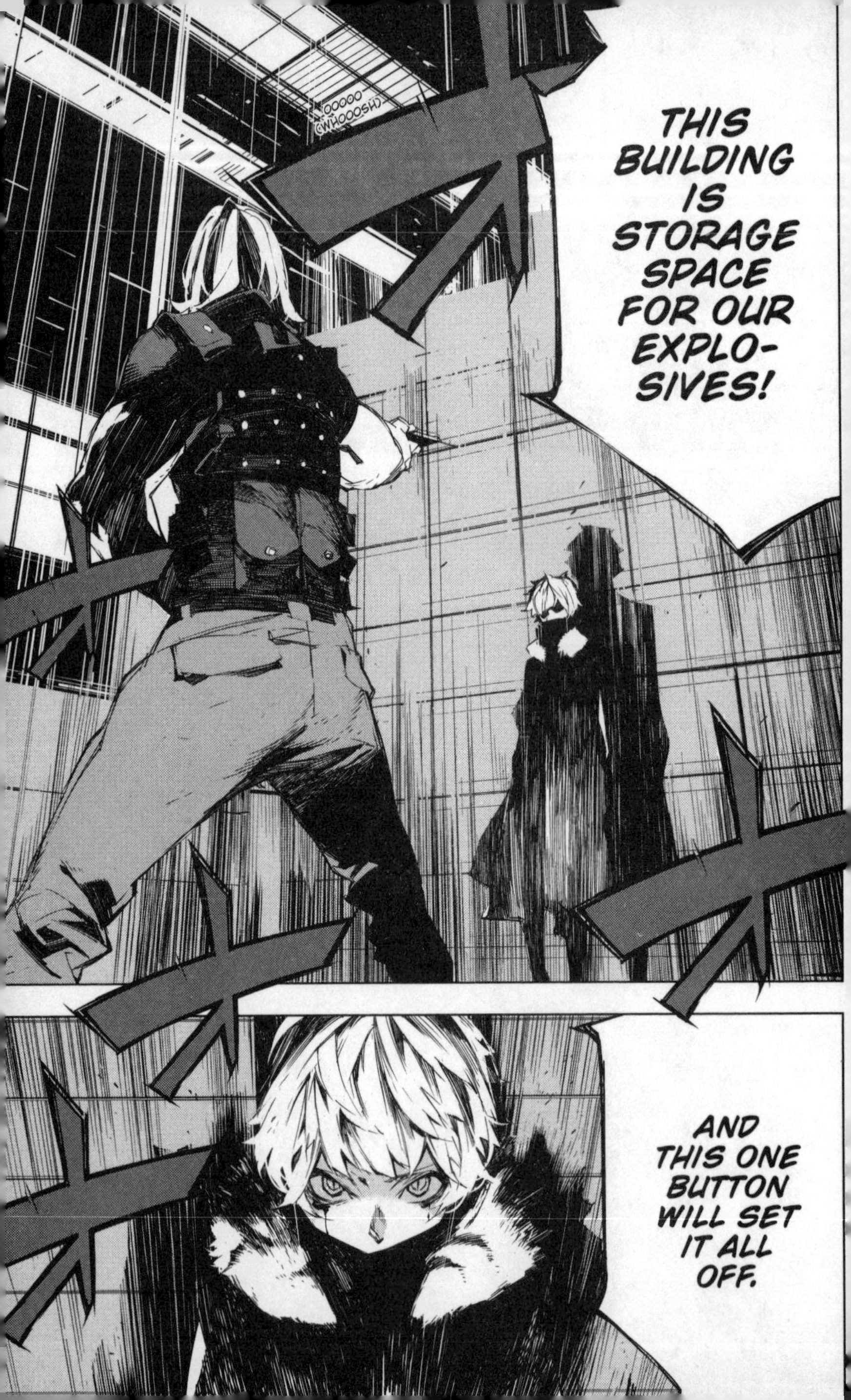
THIS BUILDING IS STORAGE SPACE FOR OUR EXPLO-SIVES!
AND THIS ONE BUTTON WILL SET IT ALL OFF.

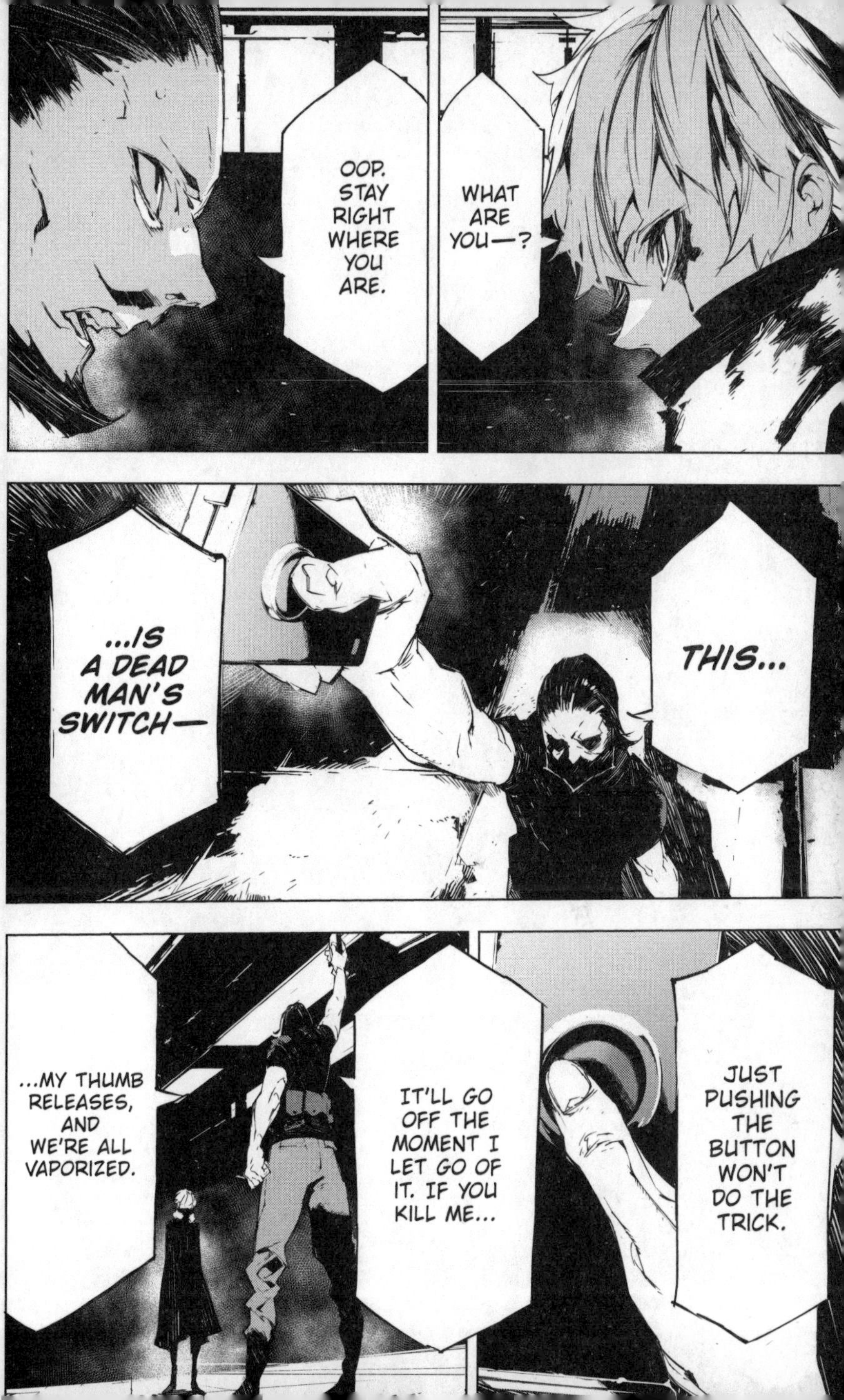
WHAT ARE YOU—?
OOP. STAY RIGHT WHERE YOU ARE.
THIS...
...IS A DEAD MAN'S SWITCH—
JUST PUSHING THE BUTTON WON'T DO THE TRICK.
IT'LL GO OFF THE MOMENT I LET GO OF IT. IF YOU KILL ME...
...MY THUMB RELEASES, AND WE'RE ALL VAPORIZED.

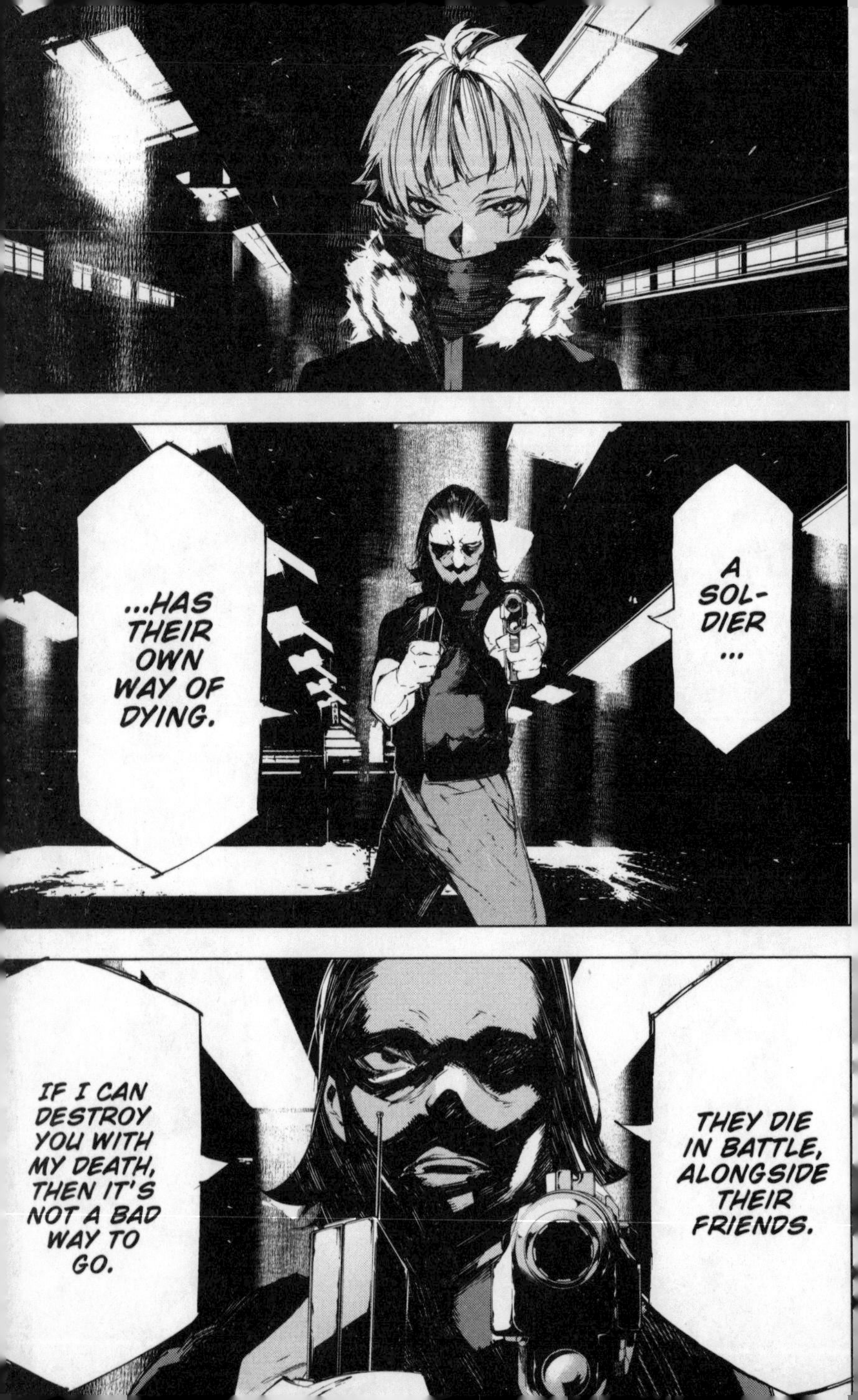
A SOL-DIER ...
...HAS THEIR OWN WAY OF DYING.
THEY DIE IN BATTLE, ALONGSIDE THEIR FRIENDS.
IF I CAN DESTROY YOU WITH MY DEATH, THEN IT'S NOT A BAD WAY TO GO.

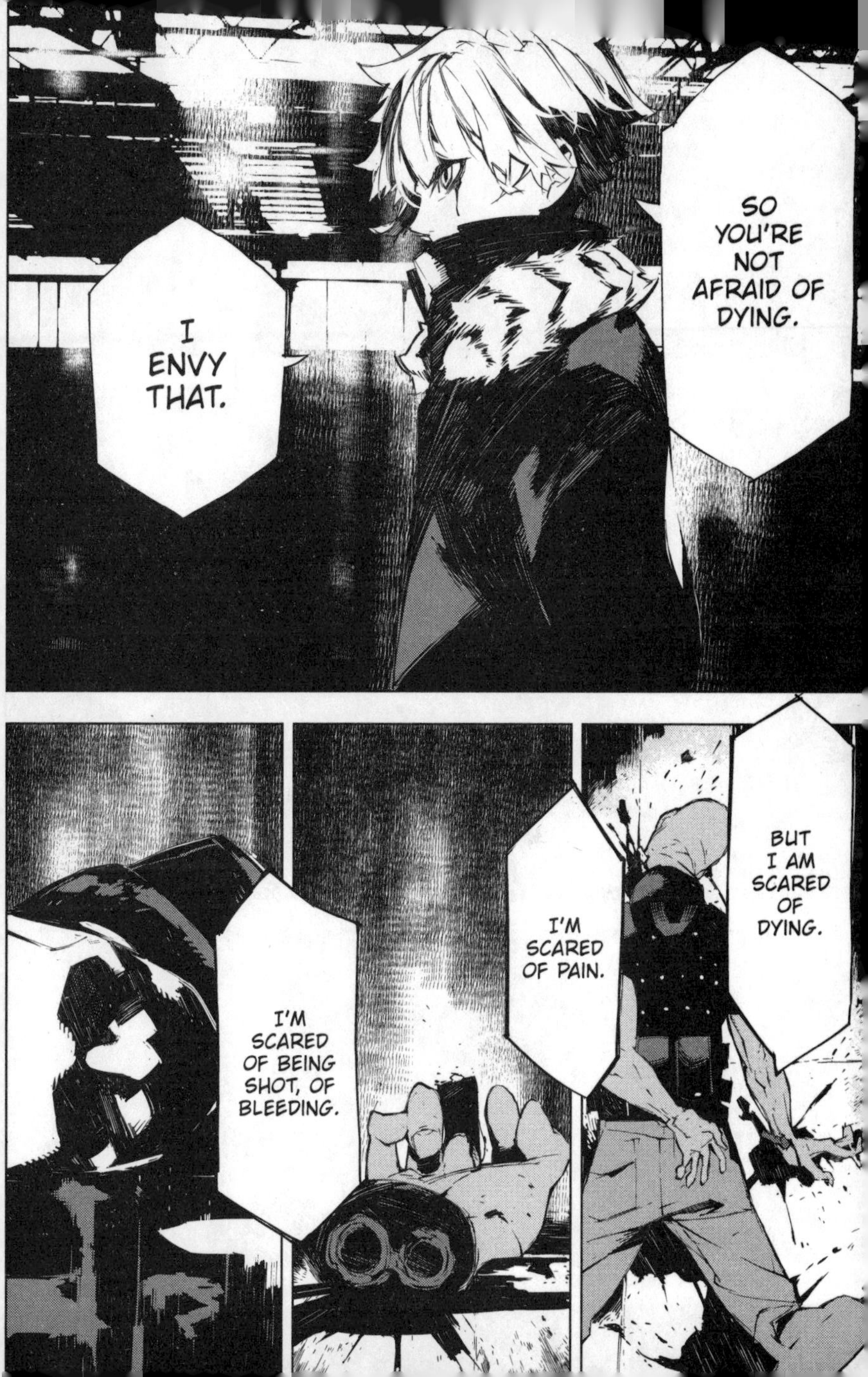
SO YOU'RE NOT AFRAID OF DYING.
I ENVY THAT.
BUT I AM SCARED OF DYING.
I'M SCARED OF PAIN.
I'M SCARED OF BEING SHOT, OF BLEEDING.

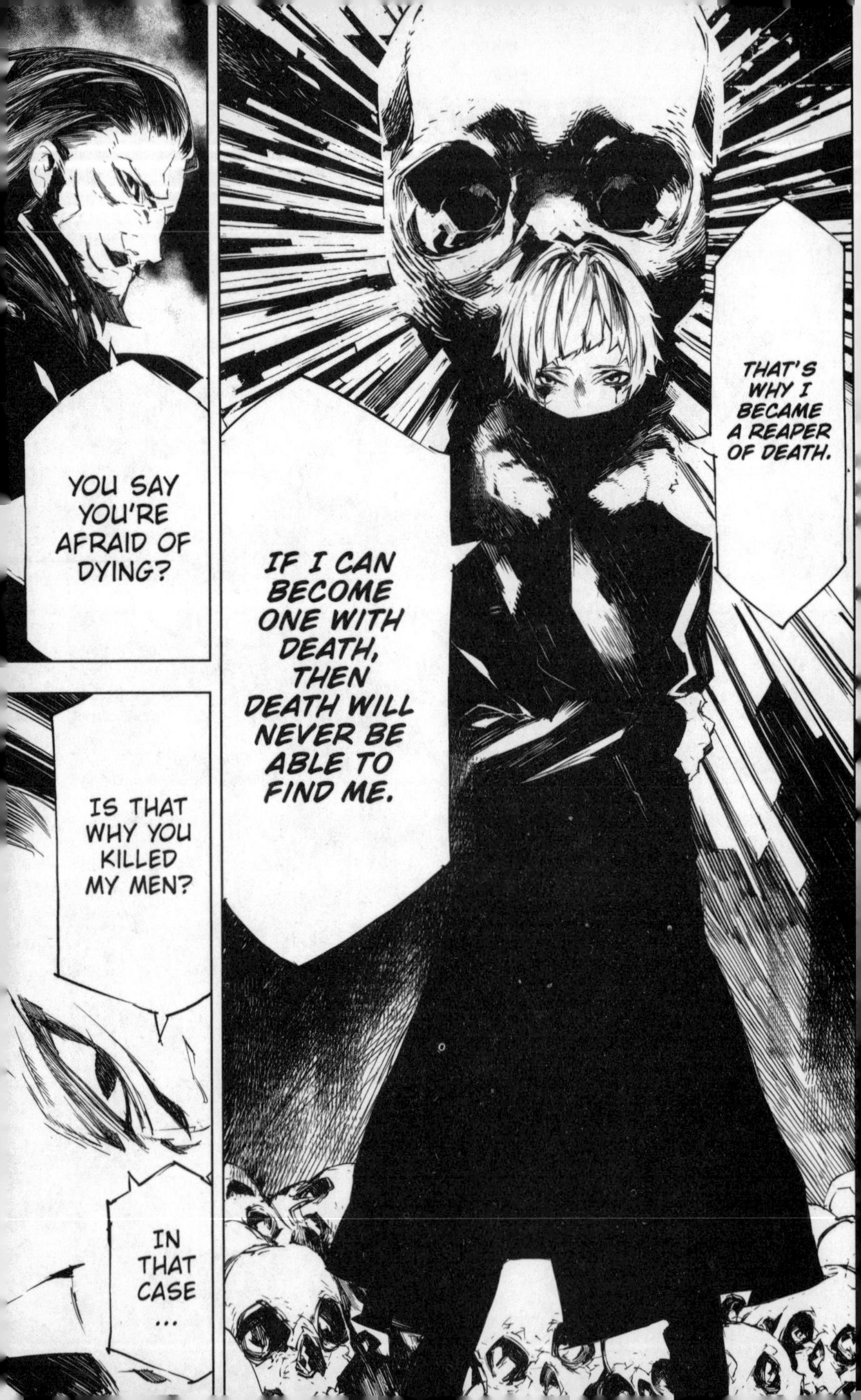
THAT'S WHY I BECAME A REAPER OF DEATH.
IF I CAN BECOME ONE WITH DEATH, THEN DEATH WILL NEVER BE ABLE TO FIND ME.
YOU SAY YOU'RE AFRAID OF DYING?
IS THAT WHY YOU KILLED MY MEN?
IN THAT CASE ...

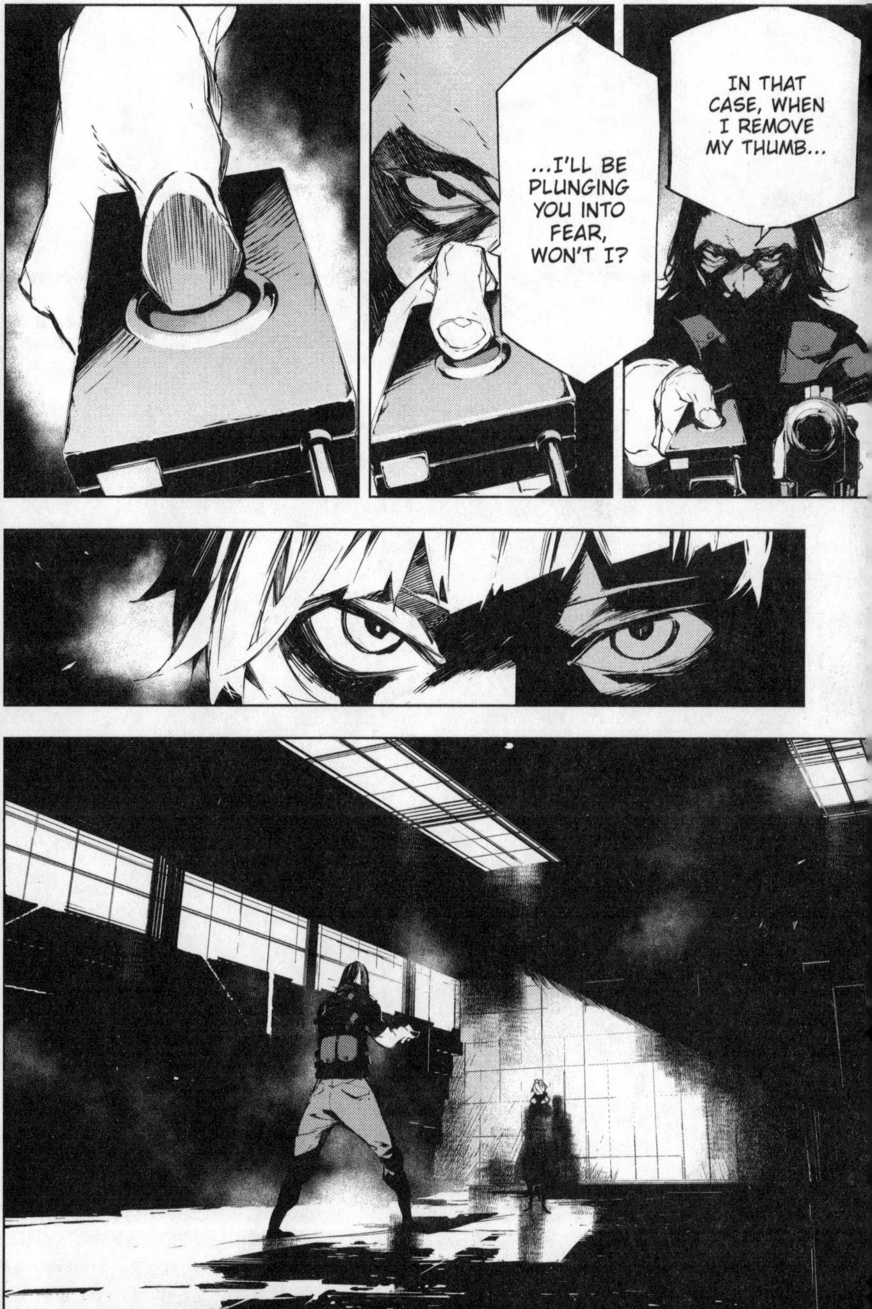
IN THAT CASE, WHEN I REMOVE MY THUMB...
...I'LL BE PLUNGING YOU INTO FEAR, WON'T I?

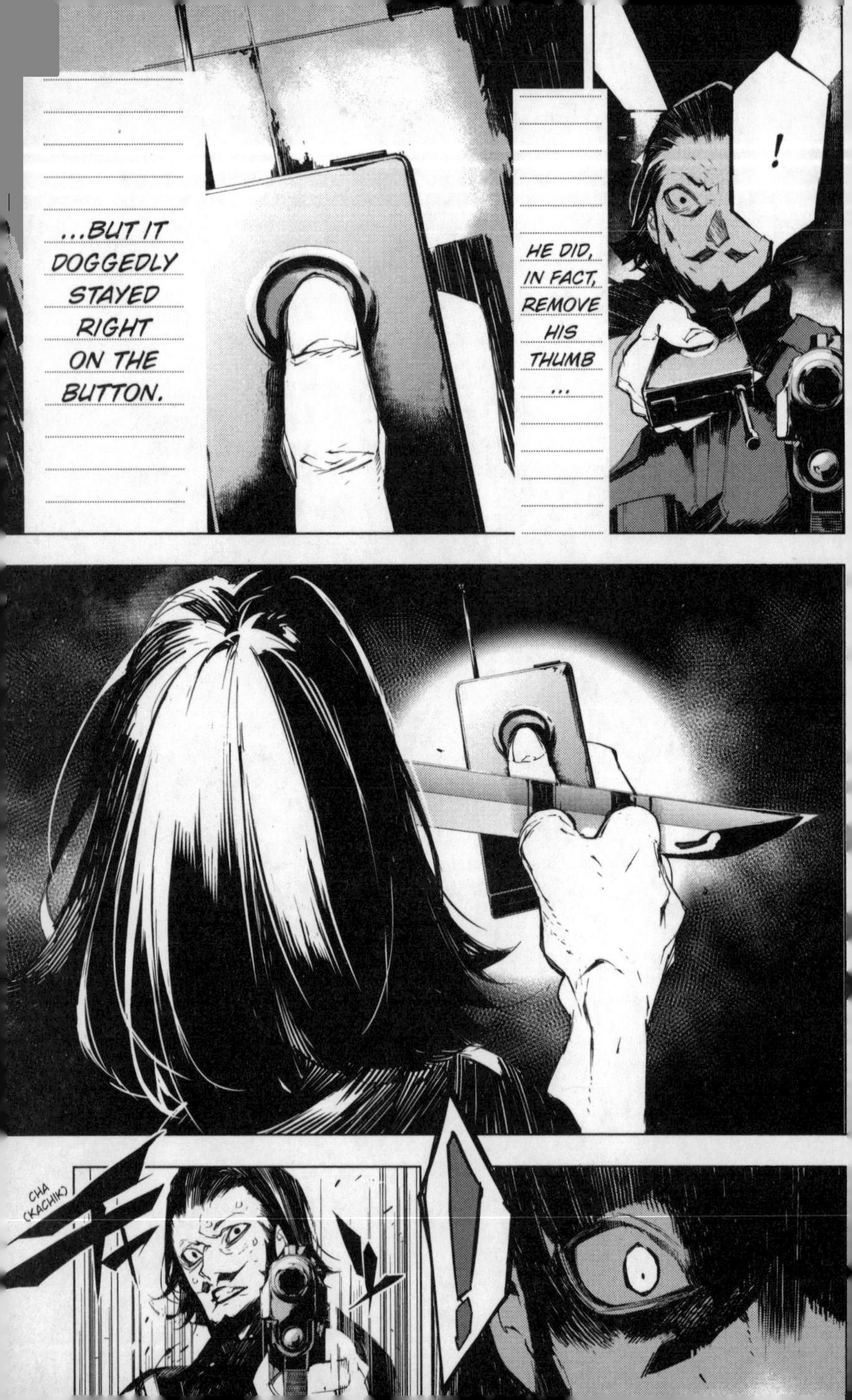
!
HE DID, IN FACT, REMOVE HIS THUMB ...
...BUT IT DOGGEDLY STAYED RIGHT ON THE BUTTON.
!
CHA (KACHIK)

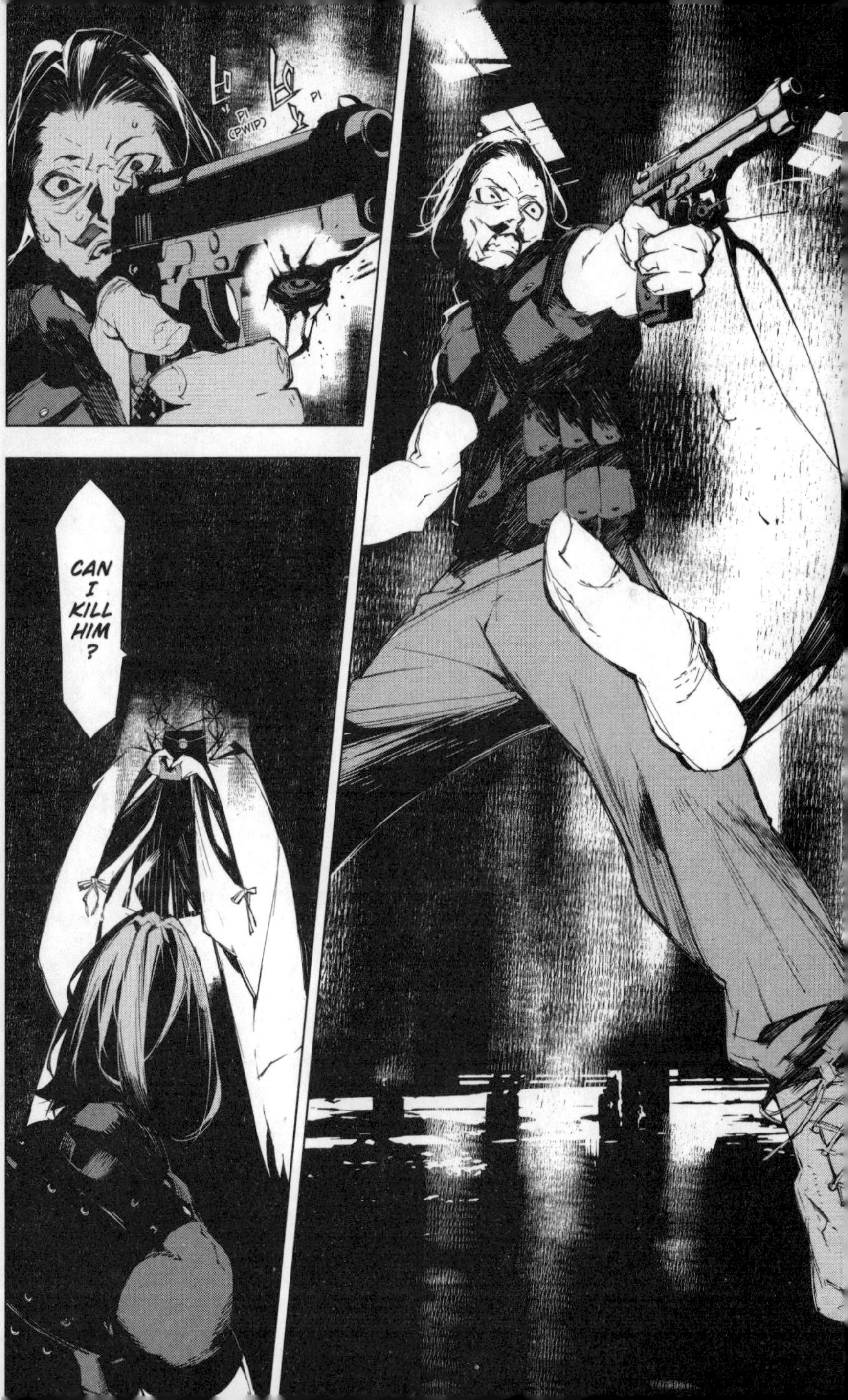
PI
PI
(PWIP)
CAN I KILL HIM?

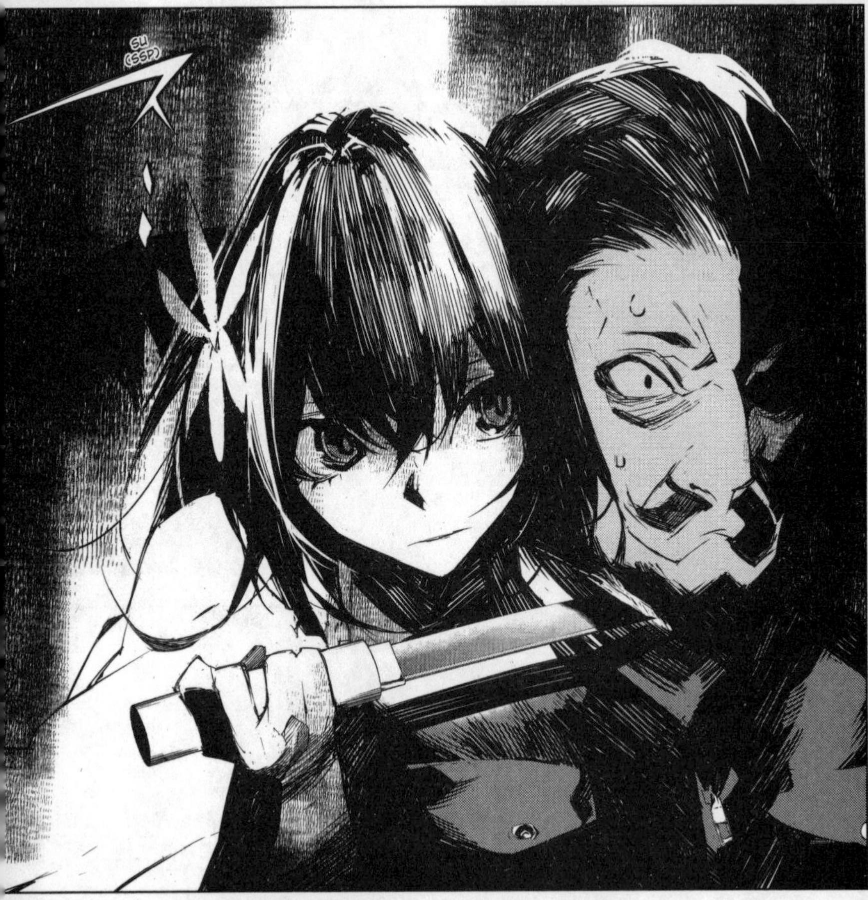
SU
(SSP)
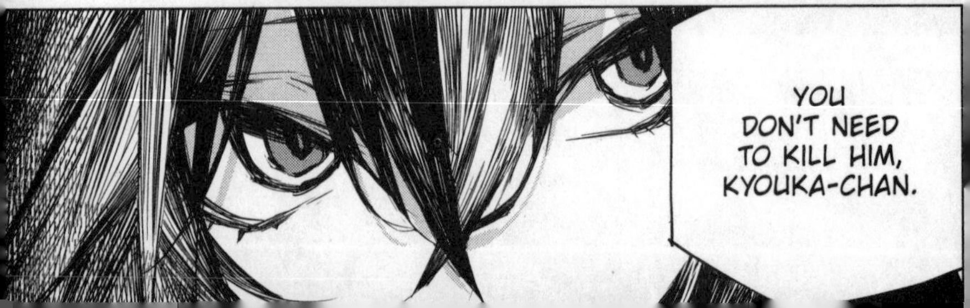
YOU DON'T NEED TO KILL HIM, KYOUKA-CHAN.

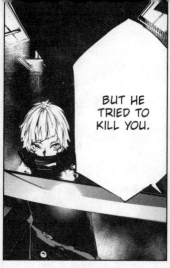

BUT HE TRIED TO KILL YOU.

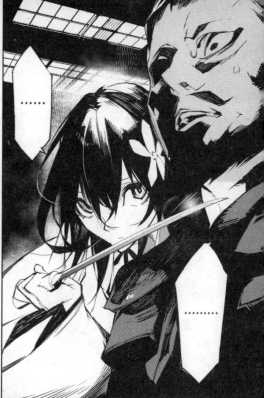

......

....

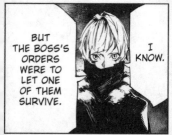

BUT THE BOSS'S ORDERS WERE TO LET ONE OF THEM SURVIVE.

I KNOW.

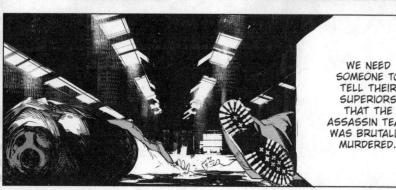

WE NEED SOMEONE TO TELL THEIR SUPERIORS THAT THE ASSASSIN TEAM WAS BRUTALLY MURDERED.

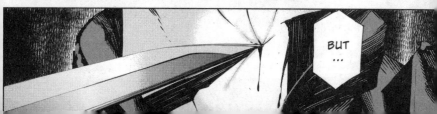

BUT ...

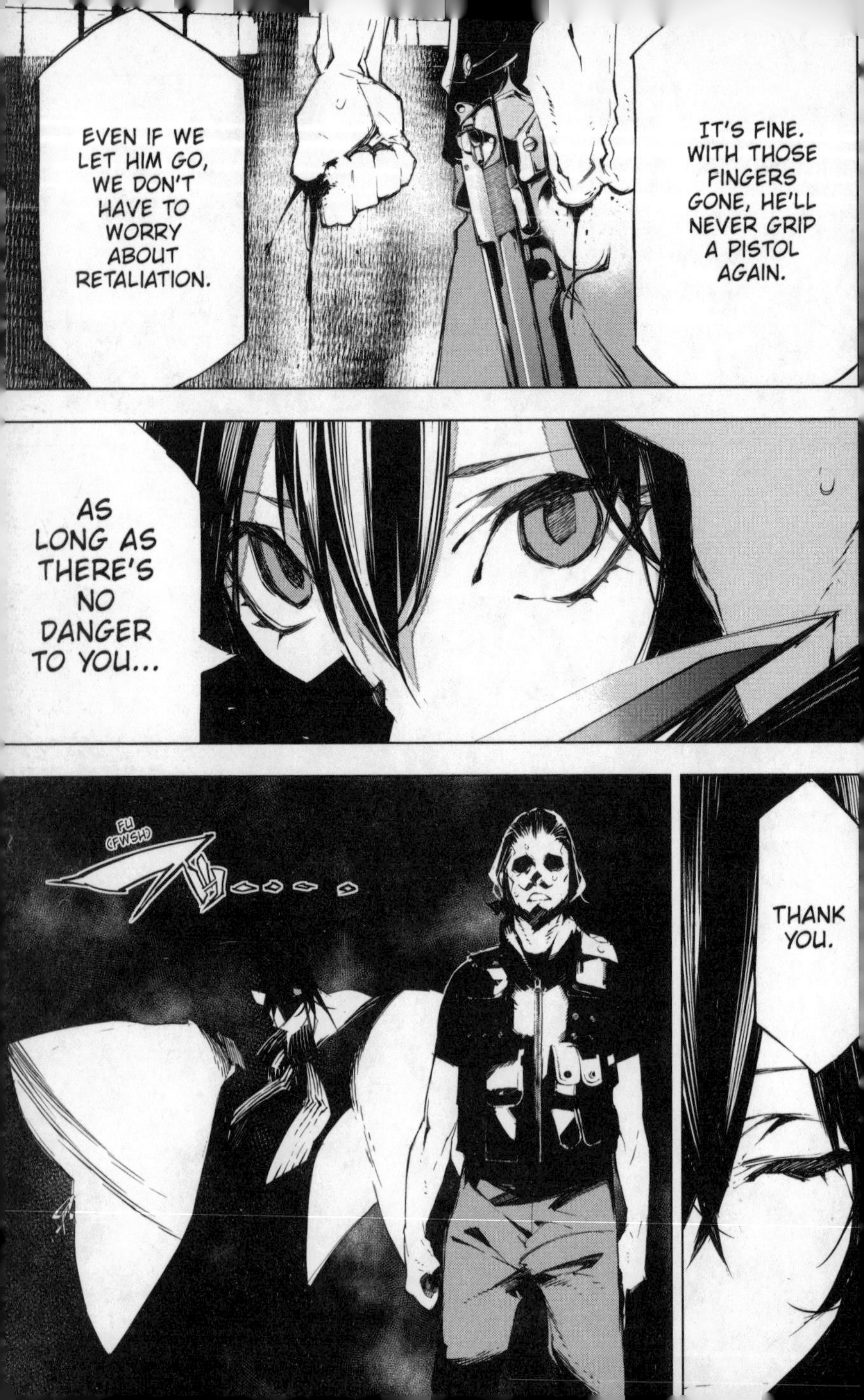
IT'S FINE. WITH THOSE FINGERS GONE, HE'LL NEVER GRIP A PISTOL AGAIN.
EVEN IF WE LET HIM GO, WE DON'T HAVE TO WORRY ABOUT RETALIATION.
AS LONG AS THERE'S NO DANGER TO YOU...
THANK YOU.
FU (FWSH)

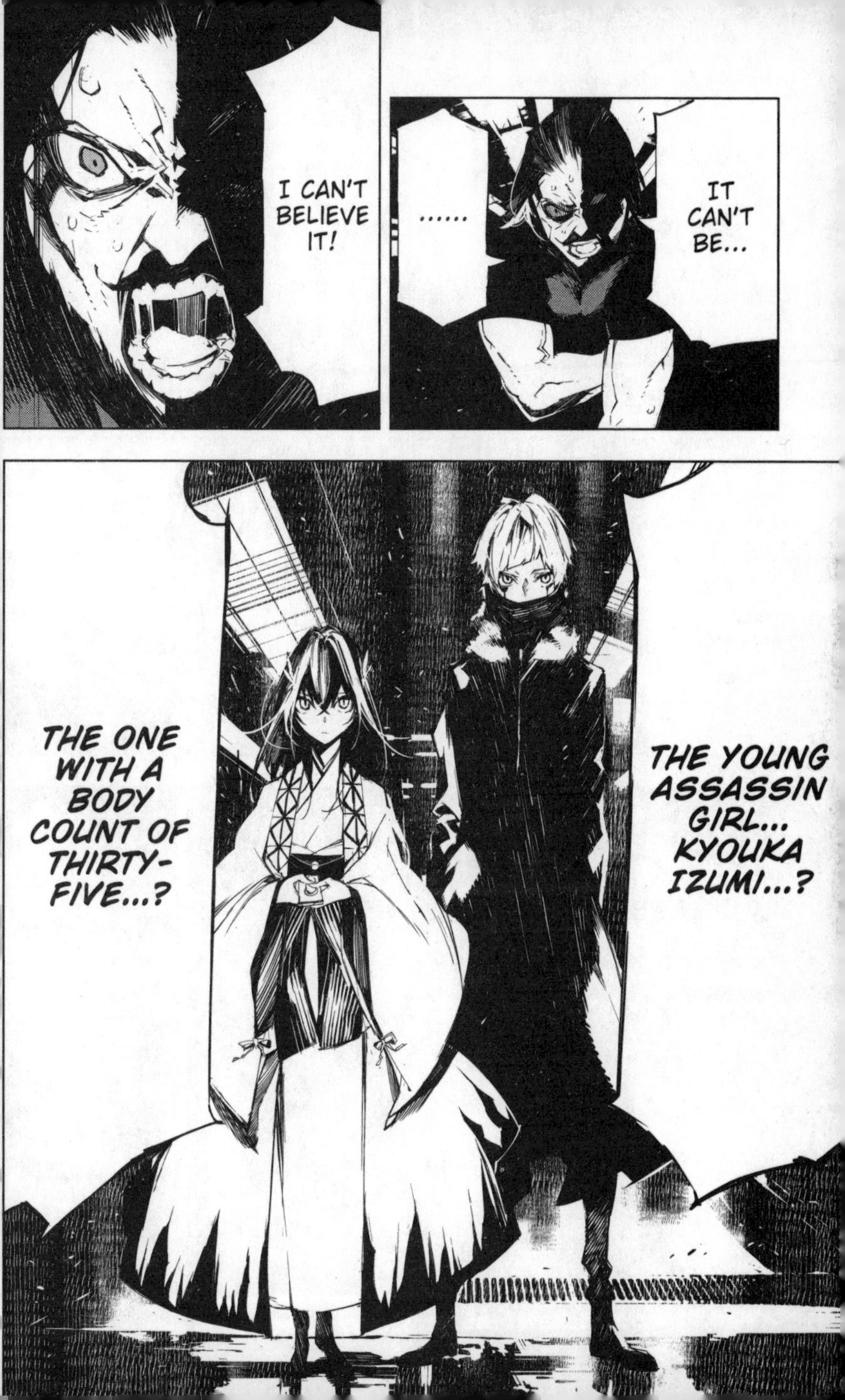
IT CAN'T BE...
......
I CAN'T BELIEVE IT!
THE YOUNG ASSASSIN GIRL... KYOUKA IZUMI...?
THE ONE WITH A BODY COUNT OF THIRTY-FIVE...?

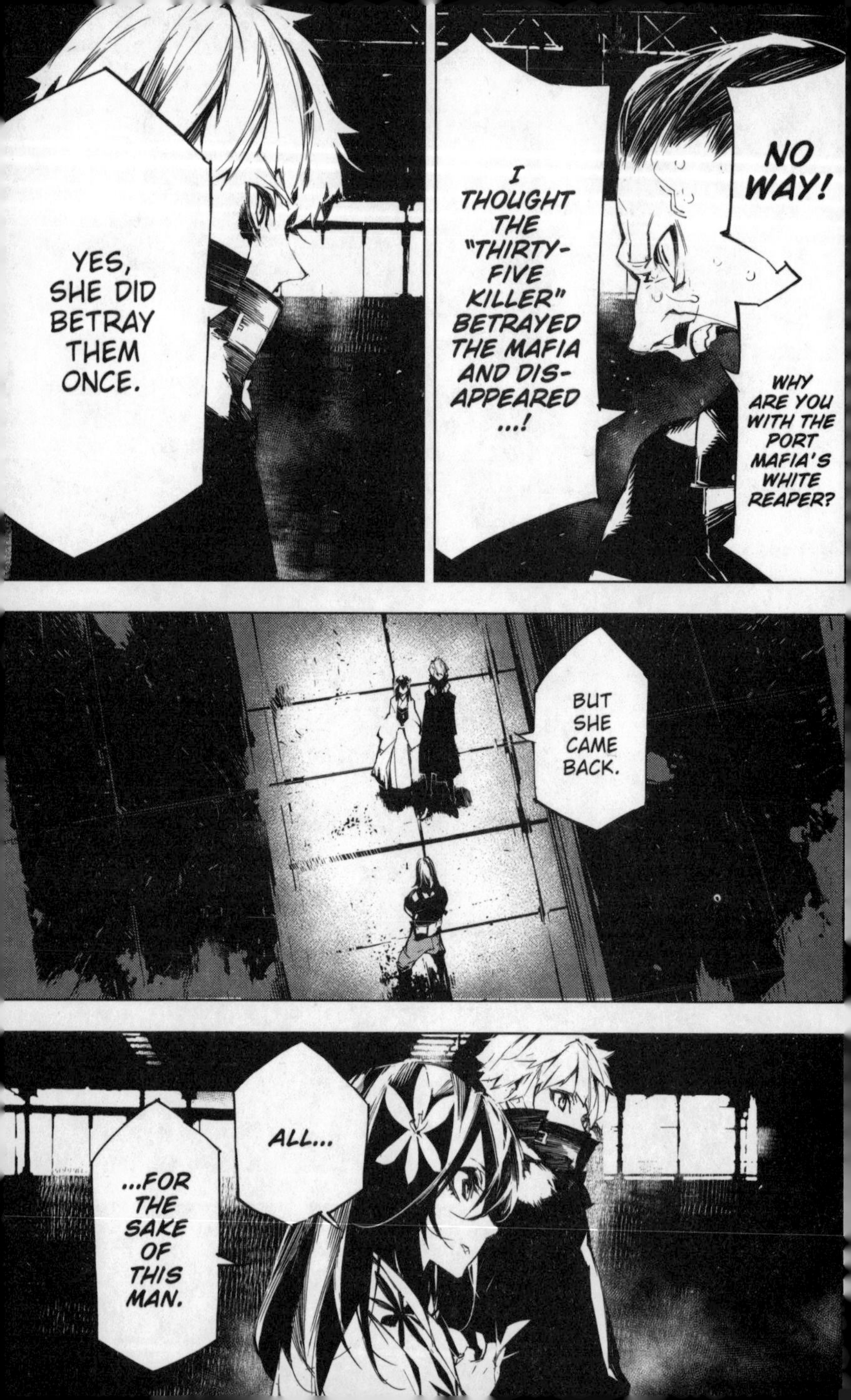
NO WAY!
I THOUGHT THE "THIRTY-FIVE KILLER" BETRAYED THE MAFIA AND DIS-APPEARED...!
WHY ARE YOU WITH THE PORT MAFIA'S WHITE REAPER?
YES, SHE DID BETRAY THEM ONCE.
BUT SHE CAME BACK.
ALL...
...FOR THE SAKE OF THIS MAN.

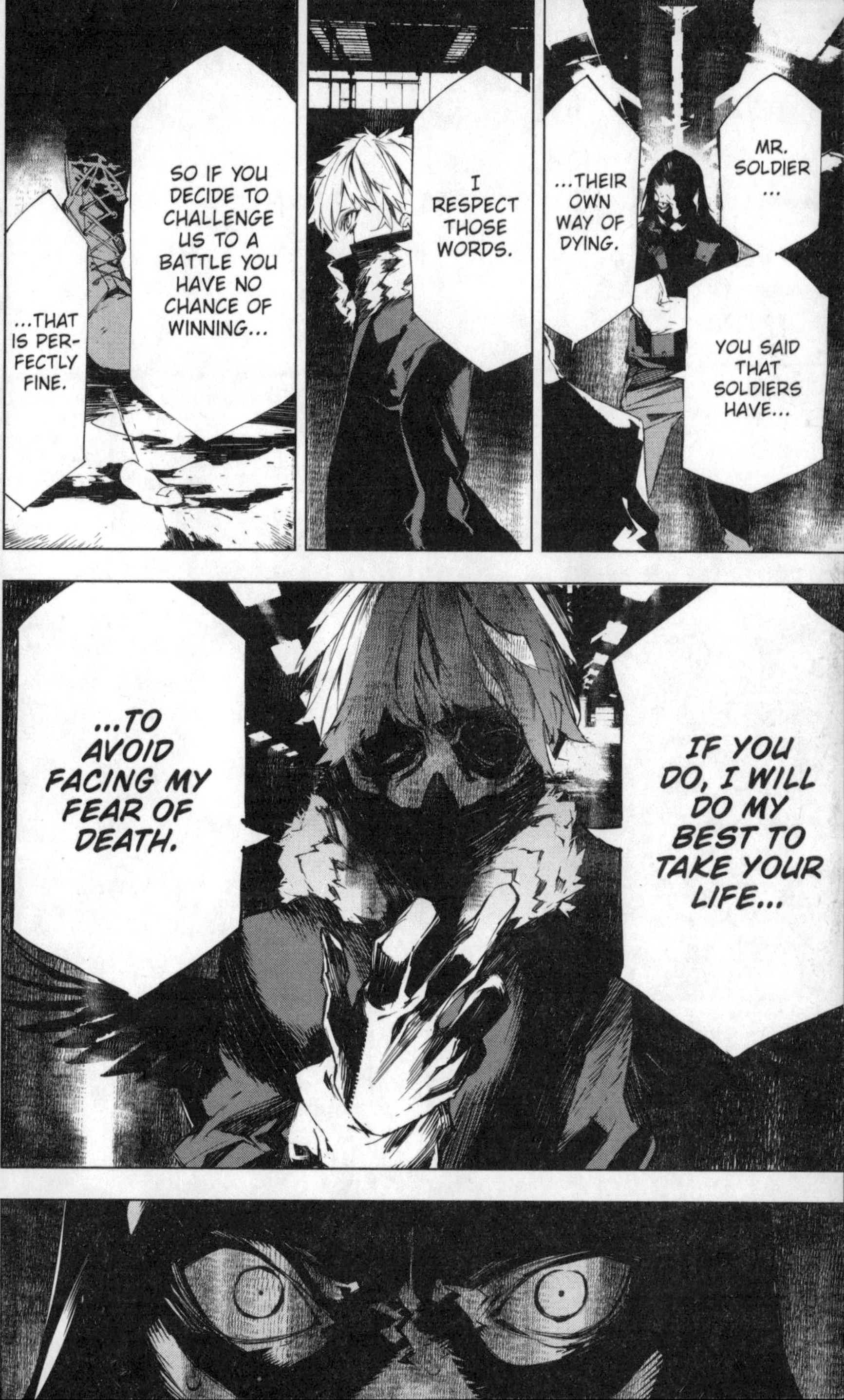

MR. SOLDIER...
YOU SAID THAT SOLDIERS HAVE...
...THEIR OWN WAY OF DYING.
I RESPECT THOSE WORDS.
SO IF YOU DECIDE TO CHALLENGE US TO A BATTLE YOU HAVE NO CHANCE OF WINNING...
...THAT IS PER-FECTLY FINE.
IF YOU DO, I WILL DO MY BEST TO TAKE YOUR LIFE...
...TO AVOID FACING MY FEAR OF DEATH.

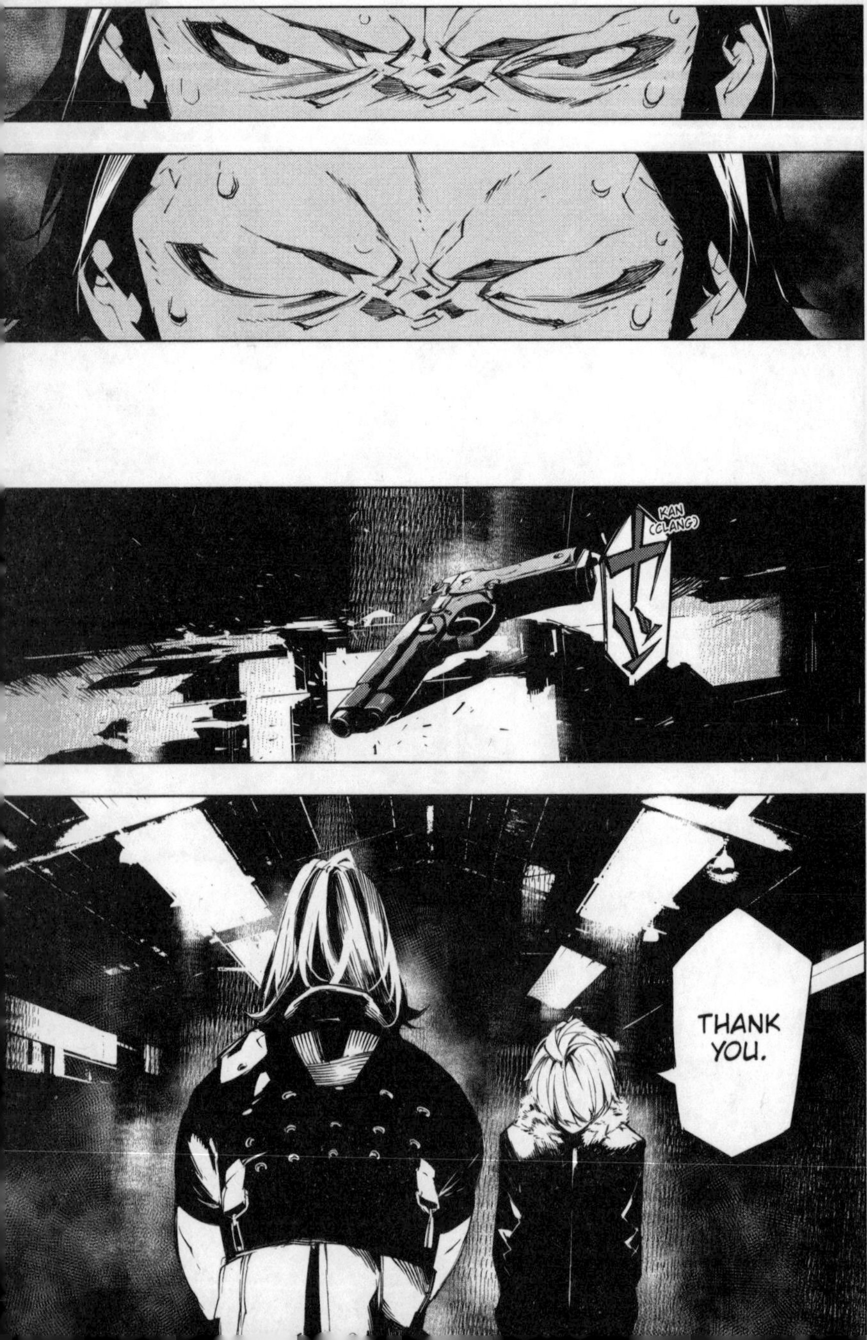
KAN
(CLANG)
THANK YOU.

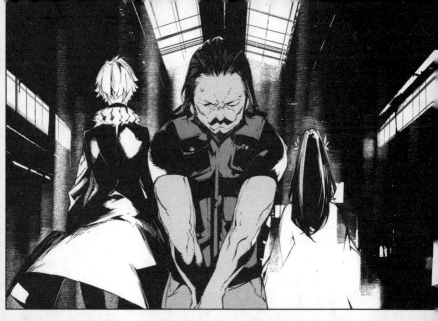

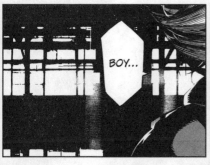

BOY...

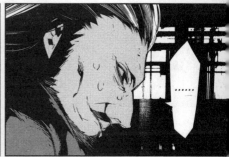

......

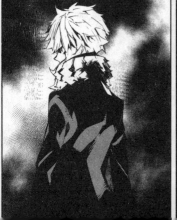

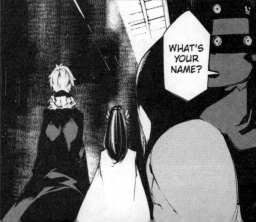

WHAT'S YOUR NAME?

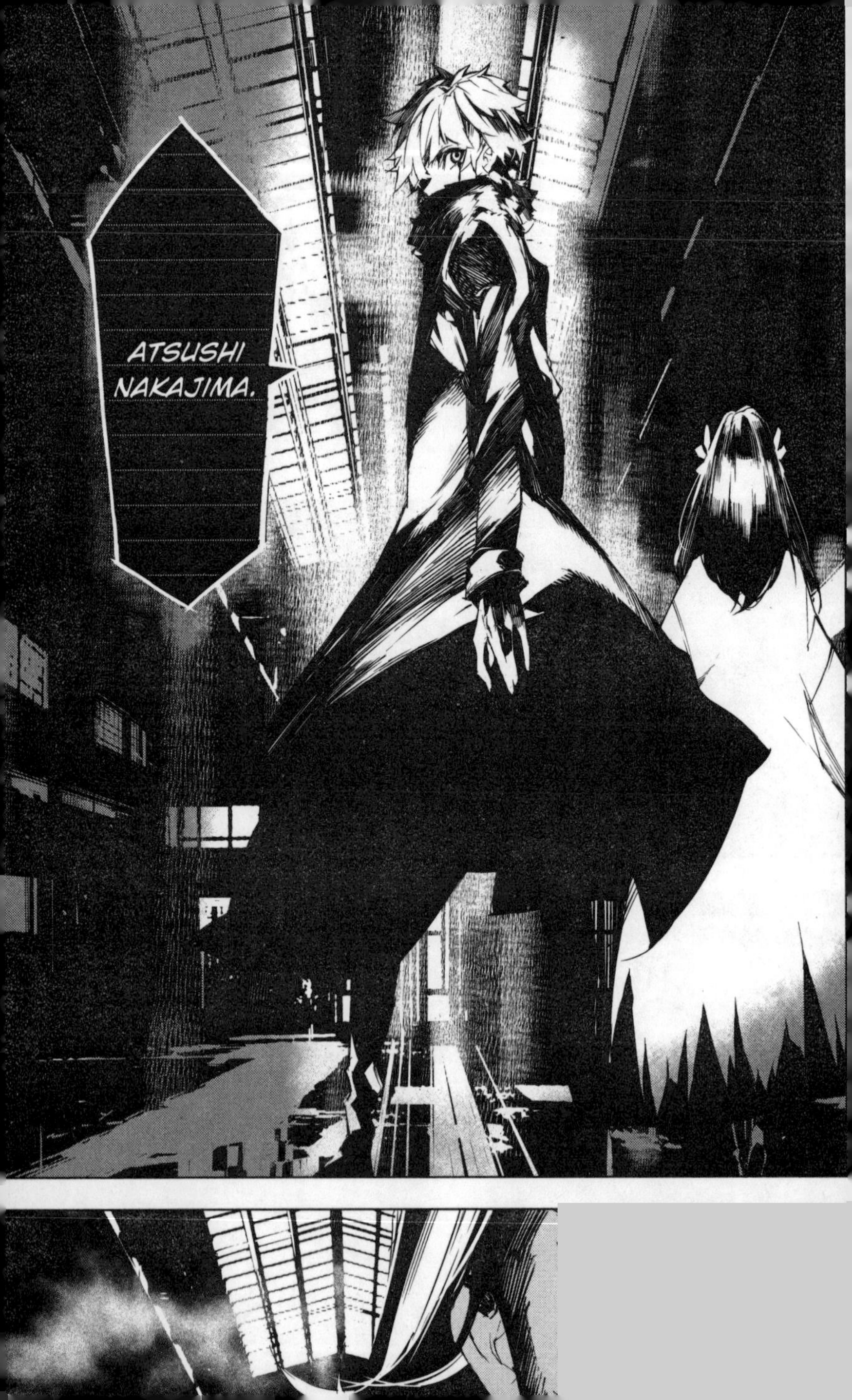
ATSUSHI NAKAJIMA.

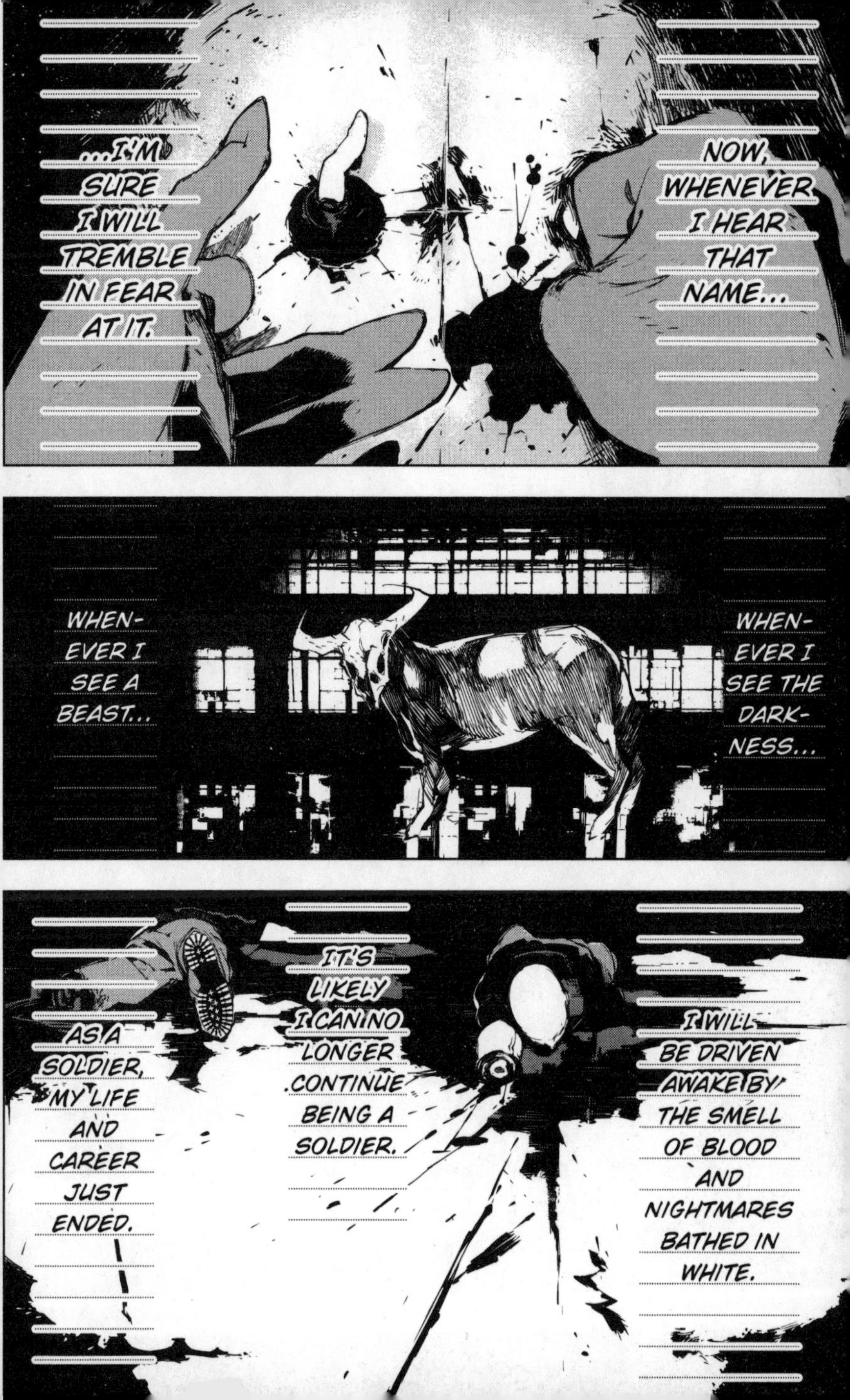
NOW, WHENEVER I HEAR THAT NAME...
...I'M SURE I WILL TREMBLE IN FEAR AT IT.
WHEN-EVER I SEE THE DARK-NESS...
WHEN-EVER I SEE A BEAST...
I WILL BE DRIVEN AWAKE BY THE SMELL OF BLOOD AND NIGHTMARES BATHED IN WHITE.
IT'S LIKELY I CAN NO LONGER CONTINUE BEING A SOLDIER.
AS A SOLDIER, MY LIFE AND CAREER JUST ENDED.

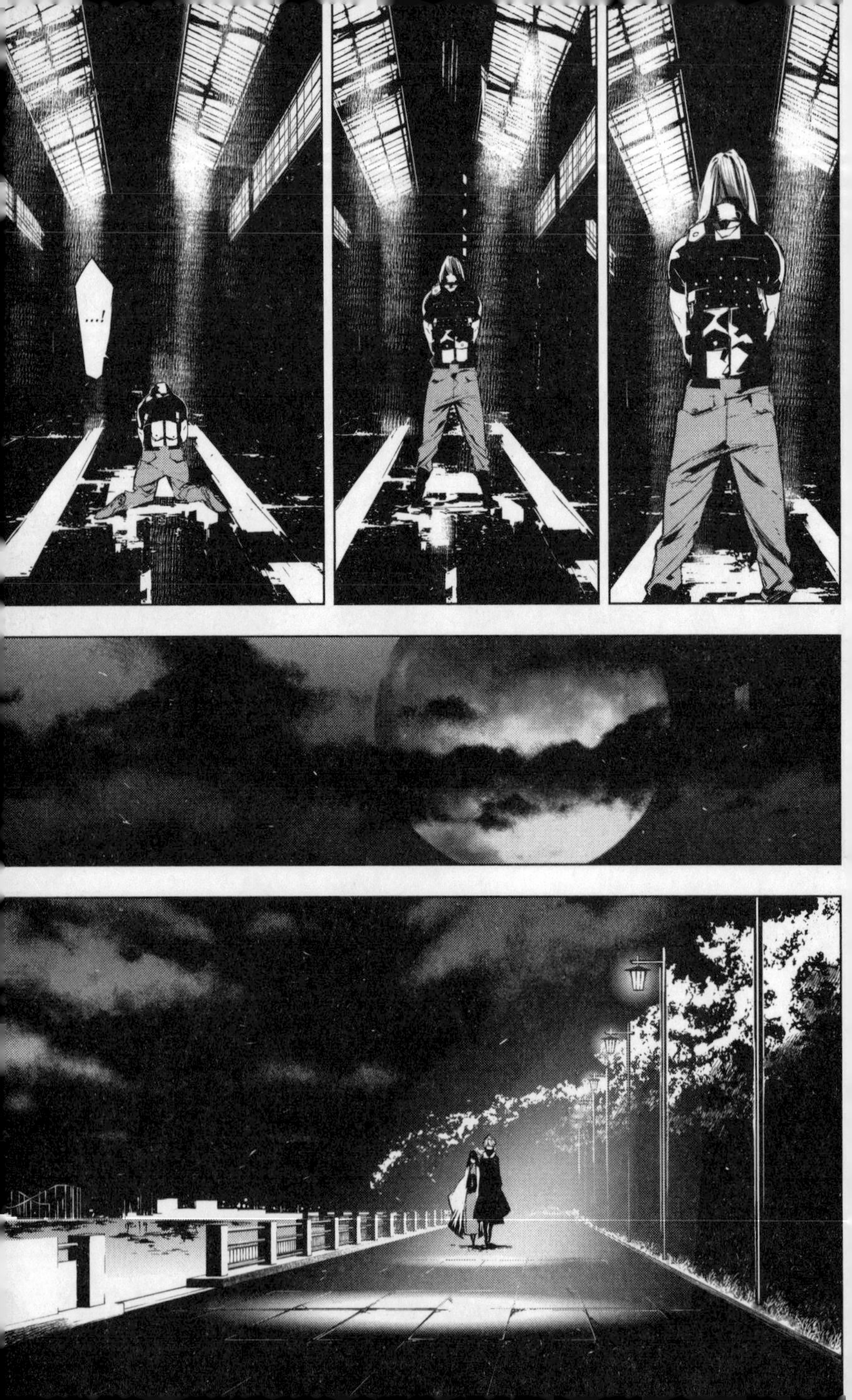
...!

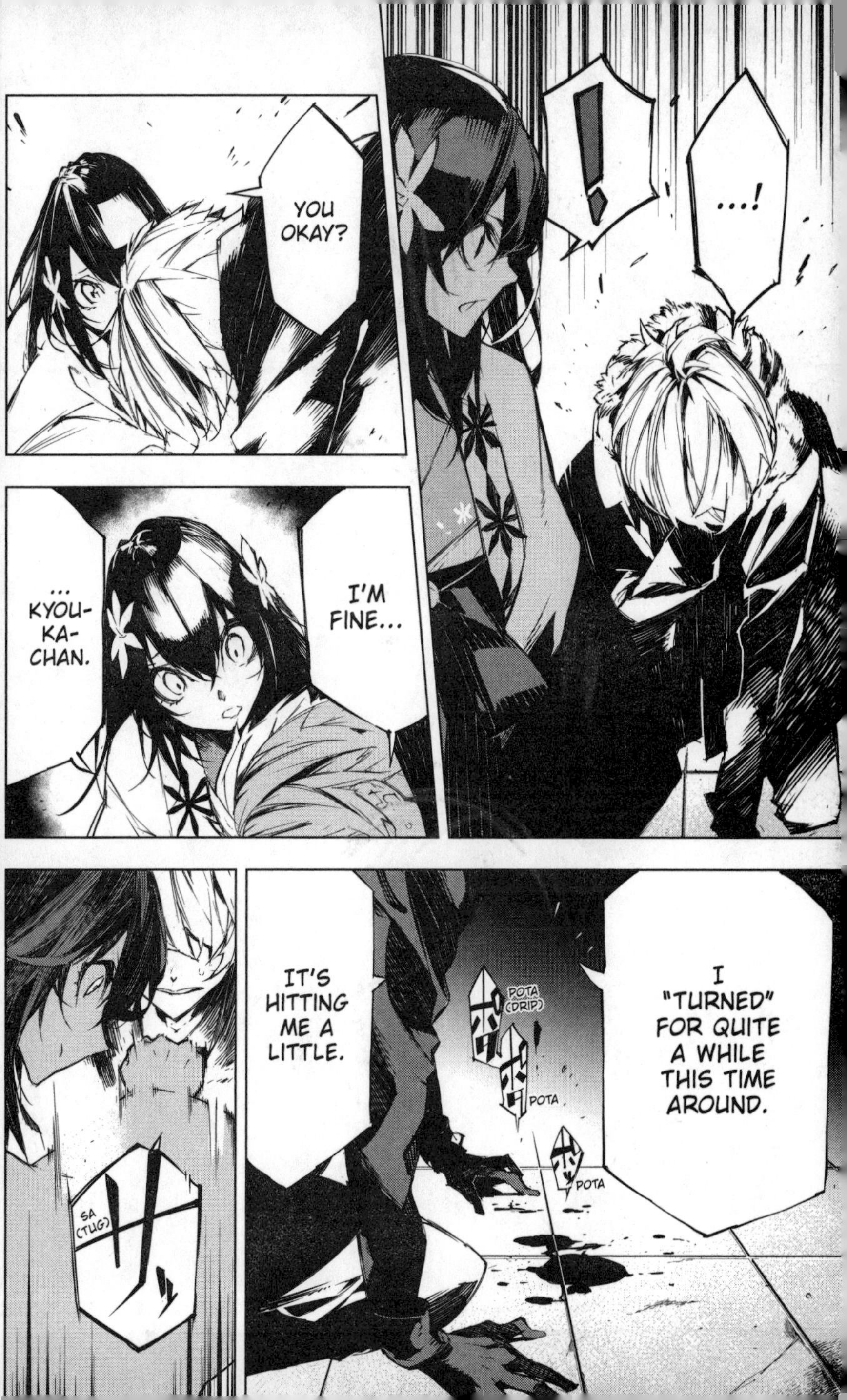
!
...!
YOU OKAY?
I'M FINE...
... KYOU-KA-CHAN.
I "TURNED" FOR QUITE A WHILE THIS TIME AROUND.
POTA (DRIP)
POTA
POTA
IT'S HITTING ME A LITTLE.
SA (TUG)

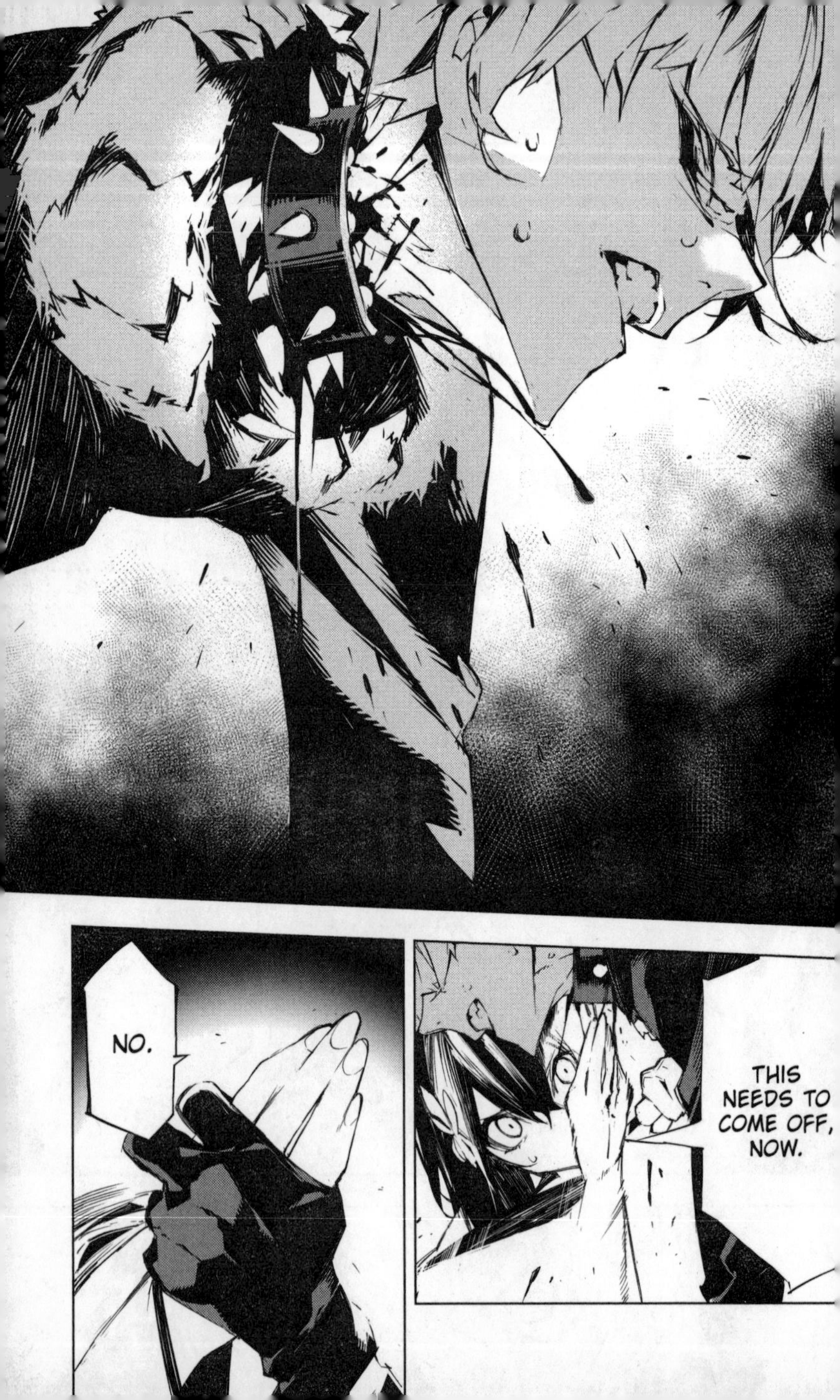
THIS NEEDS TO COME OFF, NOW.
NO.

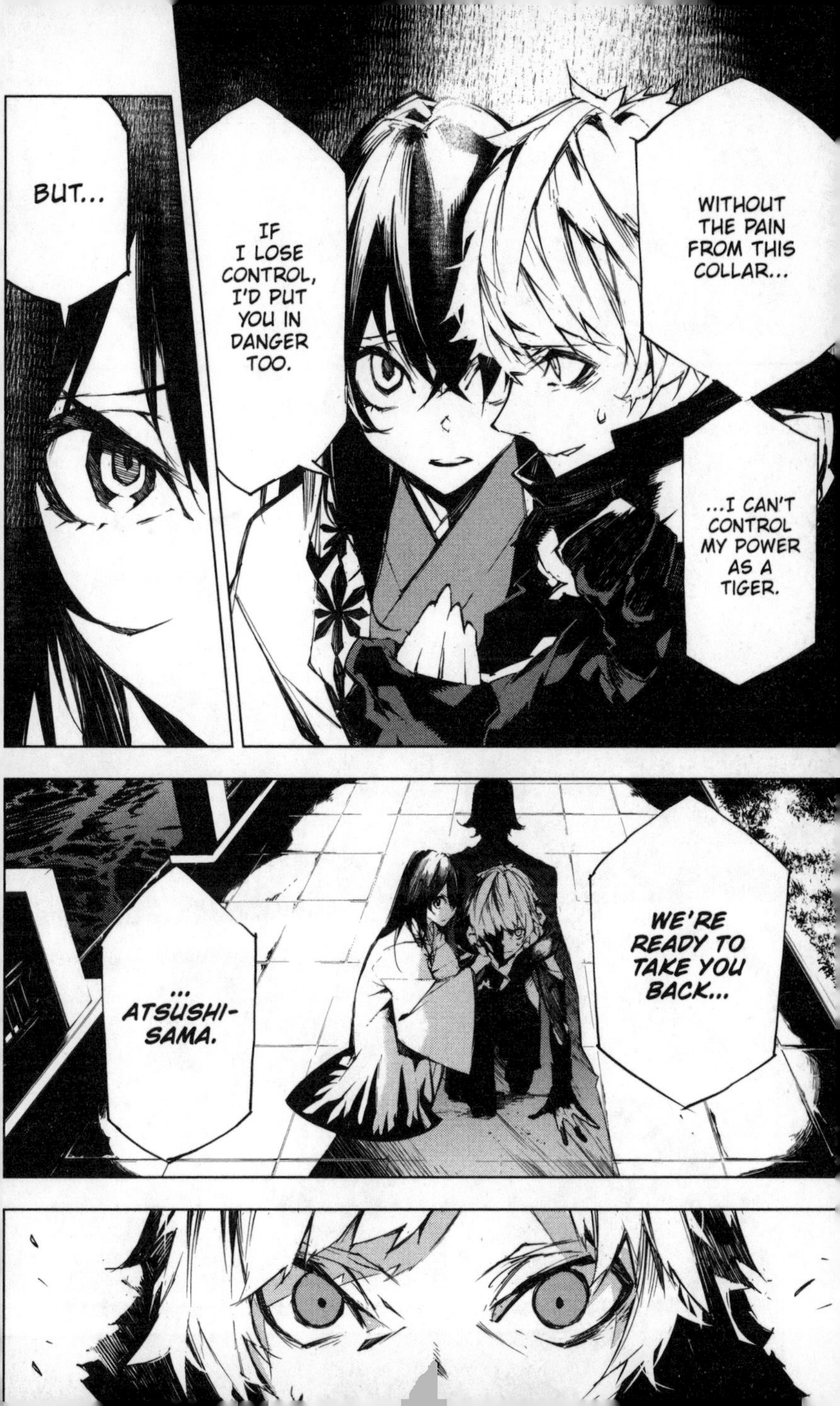
WITHOUT THE PAIN FROM THIS COLLAR...
...I CAN'T CONTROL MY POWER AS A TIGER.
IF I LOSE CONTROL, I'D PUT YOU IN DANGER TOO.
BUT...
WE'RE READY TO TAKE YOU BACK...
...ATSUSHI-SAMA.

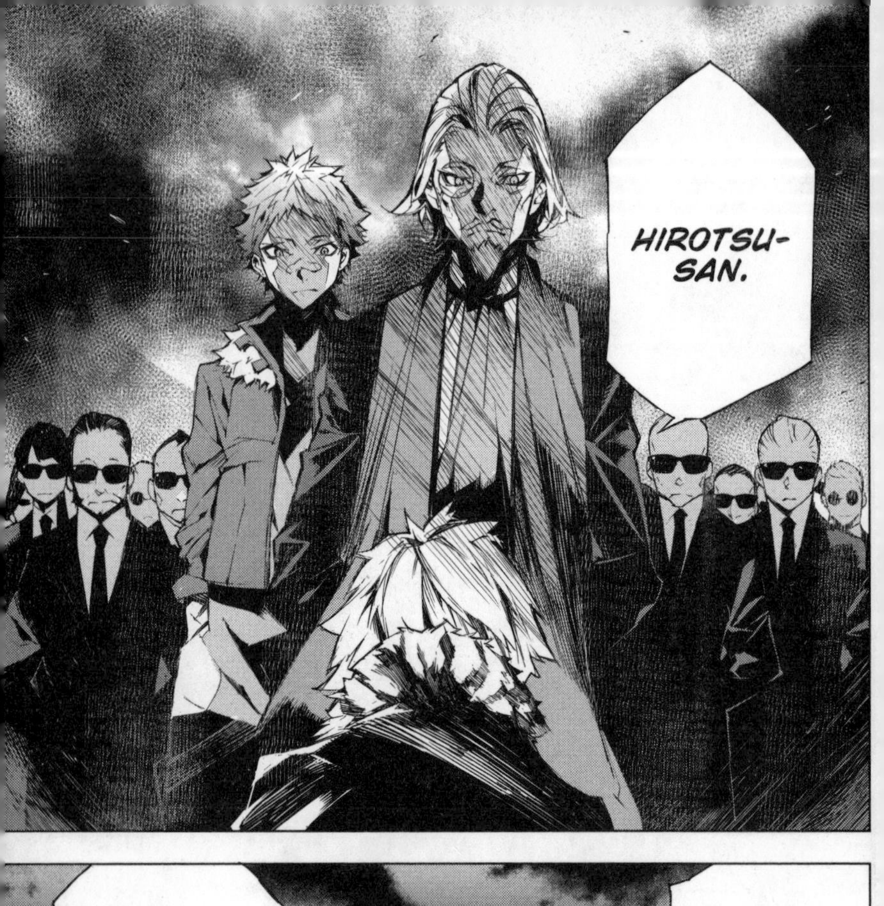
HIROTSU-SAN.

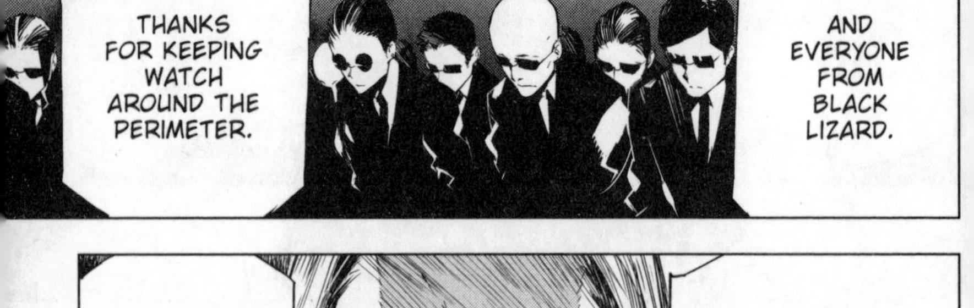
AND EVERYONE FROM BLACK LIZARD.
THANKS FOR KEEPING WATCH AROUND THE PERIMETER.

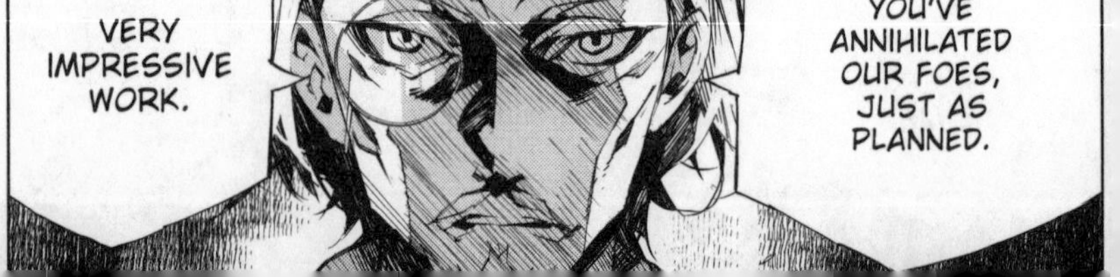
YOU'VE ANNIHILATED OUR FOES, JUST AS PLANNED.
VERY IMPRESSIVE WORK.

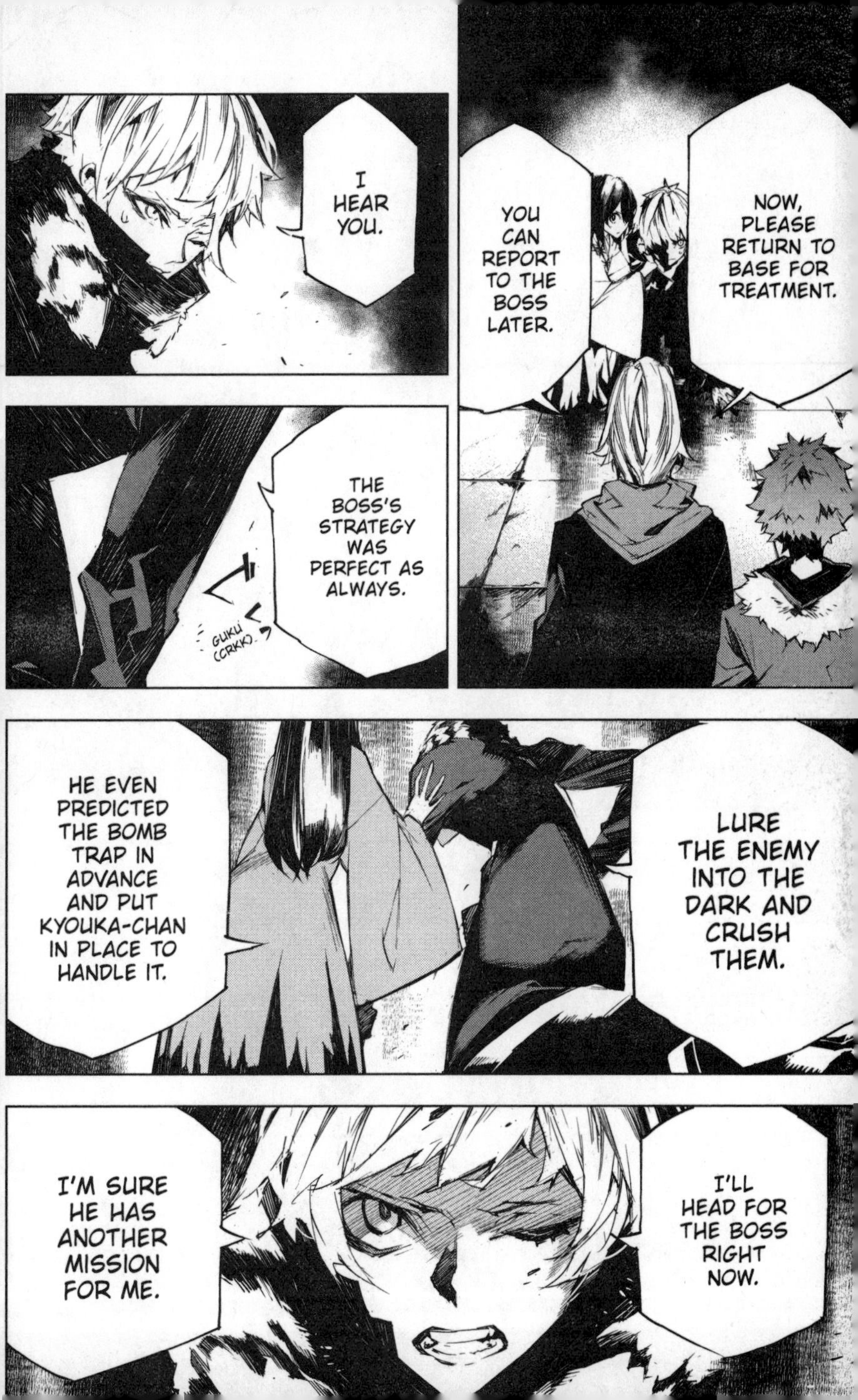
NOW, PLEASE RETURN TO BASE FOR TREATMENT.
YOU CAN REPORT TO THE BOSS LATER.
I HEAR YOU.
THE BOSS'S STRATEGY WAS PERFECT AS ALWAYS.
GUKU (CRKK)
LURE THE ENEMY INTO THE DARK AND CRUSH THEM.
HE EVEN PREDICTED THE BOMB TRAP IN ADVANCE AND PUT KYOUKA-CHAN IN PLACE TO HANDLE IT.
I'LL HEAD FOR THE BOSS RIGHT NOW.
I'M SURE HE HAS ANOTHER MISSION FOR ME.

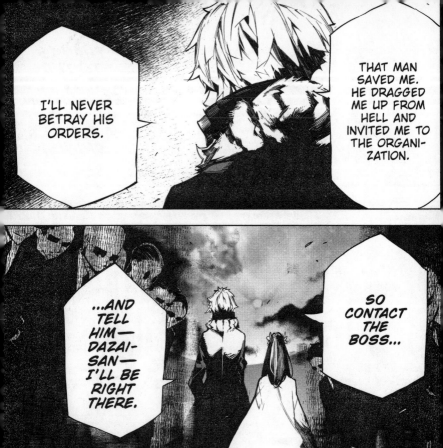

THAT MAN SAVED ME. HE DRAGGED ME UP FROM HELL AND INVITED ME TO THE ORGANIZATION.

I'LL NEVER BETRAY HIS ORDERS.

SO CONTACT THE BOSS...

...AND TELL HIM— DAZAI-SAN— I'LL BE RIGHT THERE.

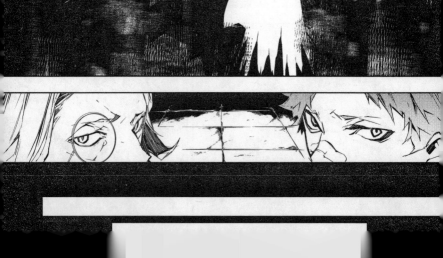

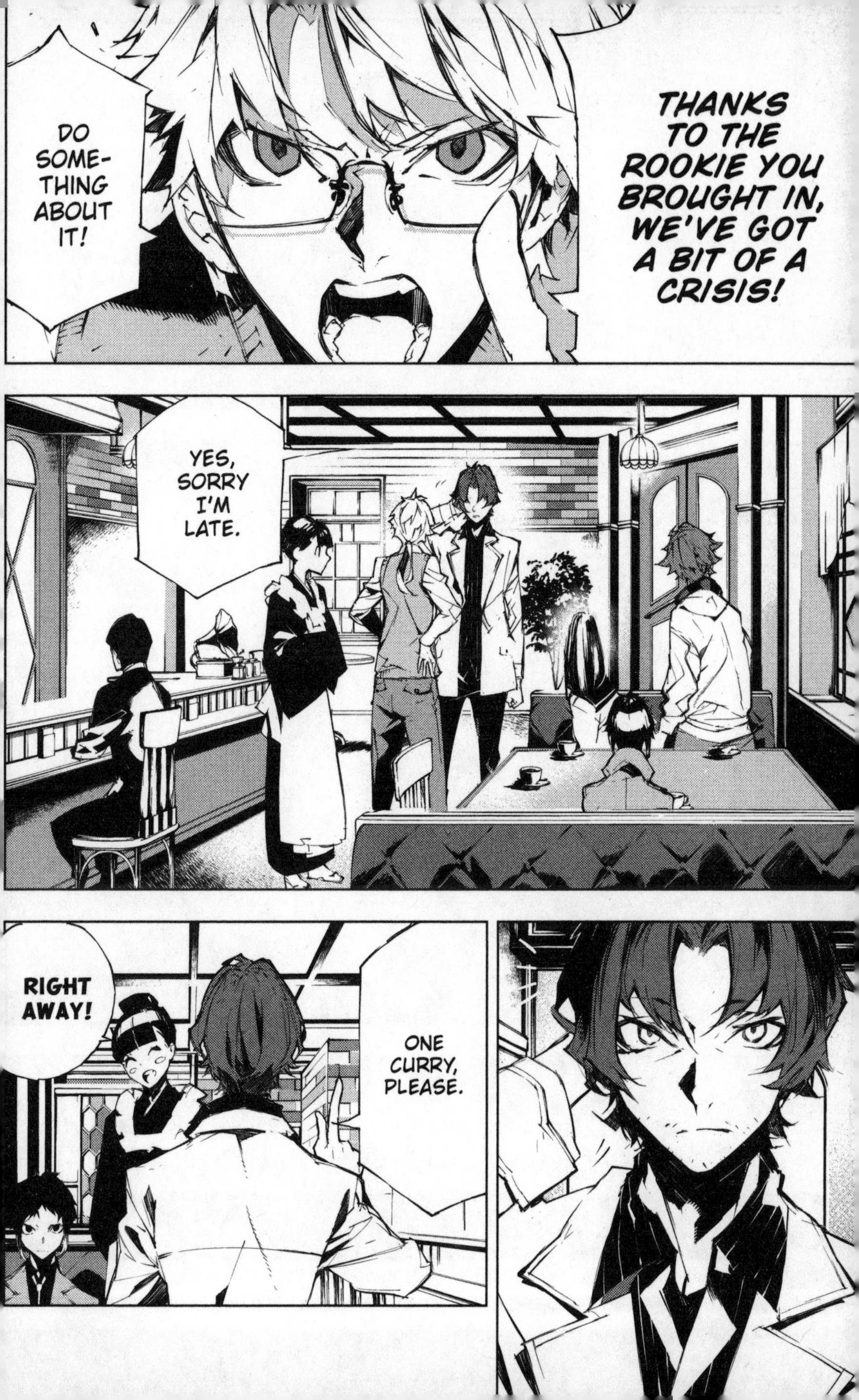
THANKS TO THE ROOKIE YOU BROUGHT IN, WE'VE GOT A BIT OF A CRISIS!
DO SOME-THING ABOUT IT!
YES, SORRY I'M LATE.
ONE CURRY, PLEASE.
RIGHT AWAY!

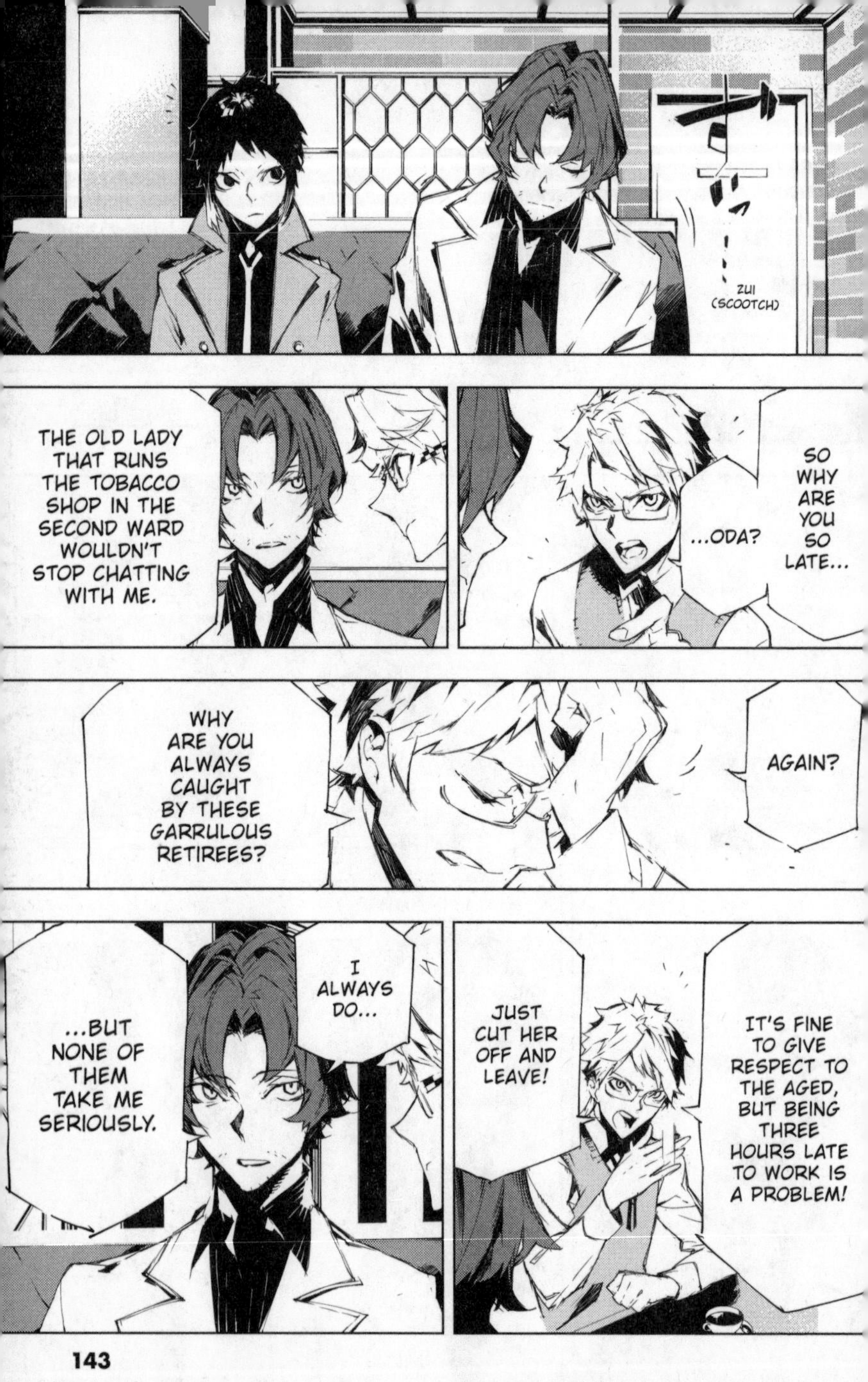
ZUI (SCOOTCH)
SO WHY ARE YOU SO LATE...
...ODA?
THE OLD LADY THAT RUNS THE TOBACCO SHOP IN THE SECOND WARD WOULDN'T STOP CHATTING WITH ME.
AGAIN?
WHY ARE YOU ALWAYS CAUGHT BY THESE GARRULOUS RETIREES?
IT'S FINE TO GIVE RESPECT TO THE AGED, BUT BEING THREE HOURS LATE TO WORK IS A PROBLEM!
JUST CUT HER OFF AND LEAVE!
I ALWAYS DO...
...BUT NONE OF THEM TAKE ME SERIOUSLY.

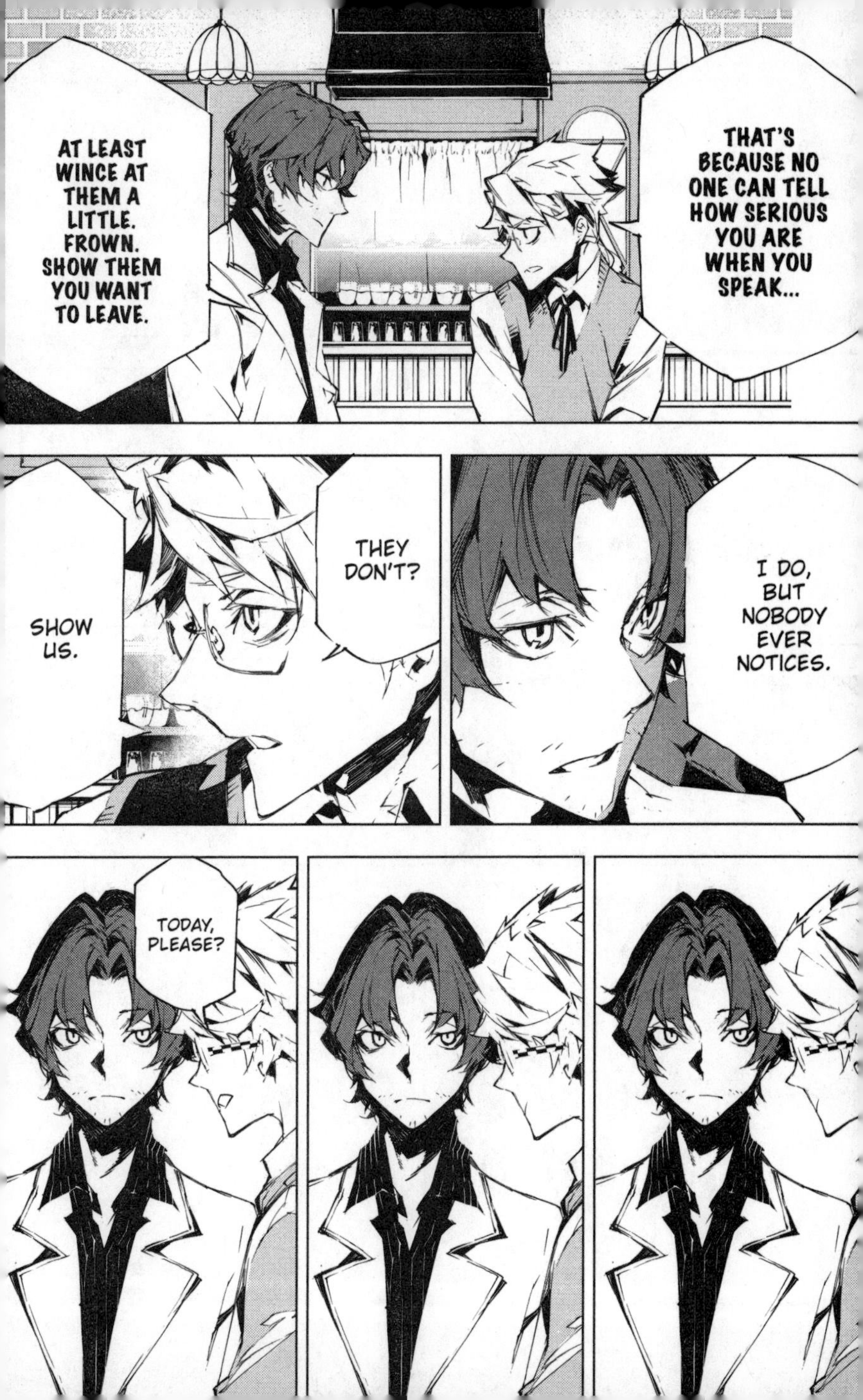
THAT'S BECAUSE NO ONE CAN TELL HOW SERIOUS YOU ARE WHEN YOU SPEAK...
AT LEAST WINCE AT THEM A LITTLE. FROWN. SHOW THEM YOU WANT TO LEAVE.
I DO, BUT NOBODY EVER NOTICES.
THEY DON'T?
SHOW US.
TODAY, PLEASE?

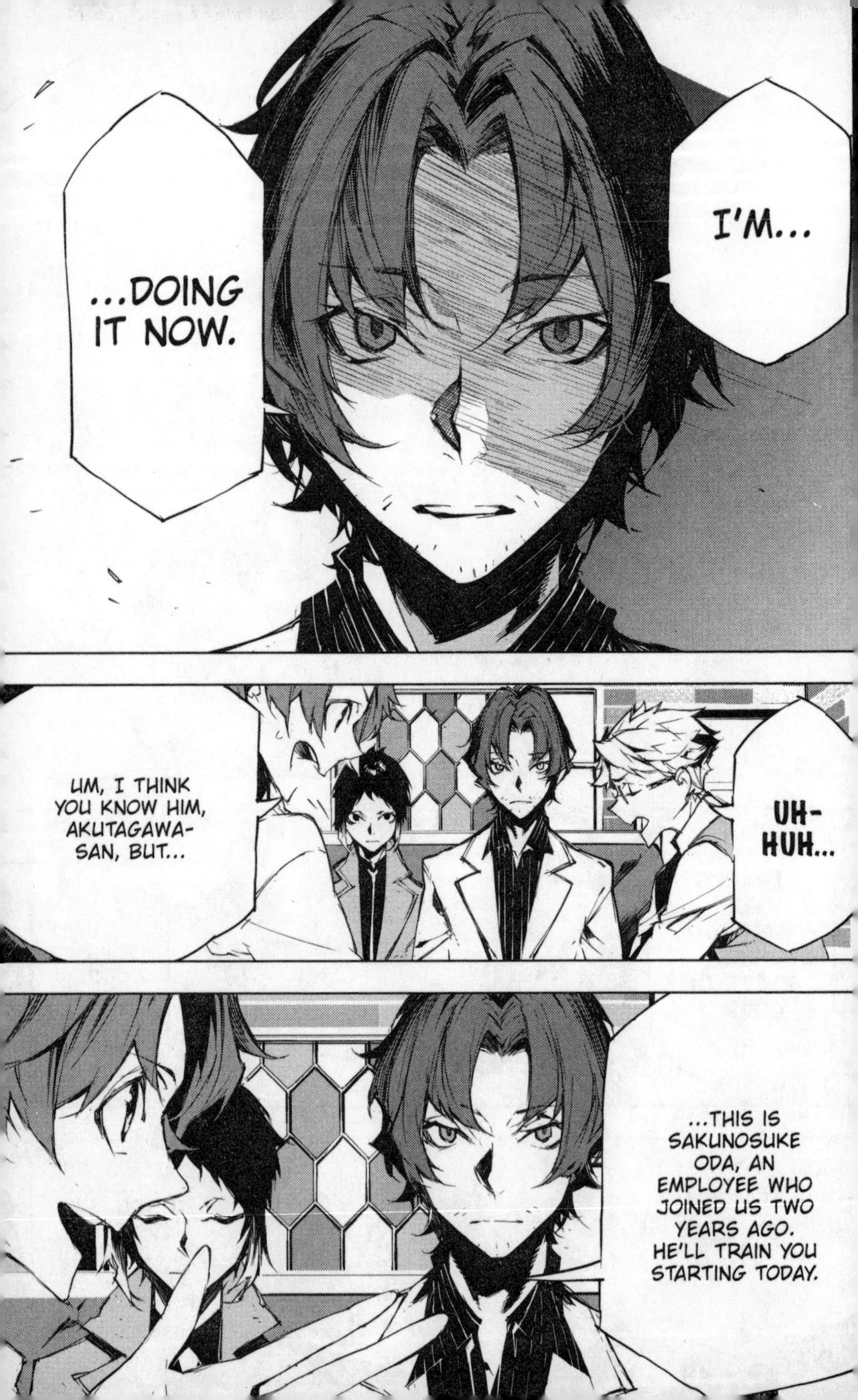
I'M...
...DOING IT NOW.
UH-HUH...
UM, I THINK YOU KNOW HIM, AKUTAGAWA-SAN, BUT...
...THIS IS SAKUNOSUKE ODA, AN EMPLOYEE WHO JOINED US TWO YEARS AGO. HE'LL TRAIN YOU STARTING TODAY.

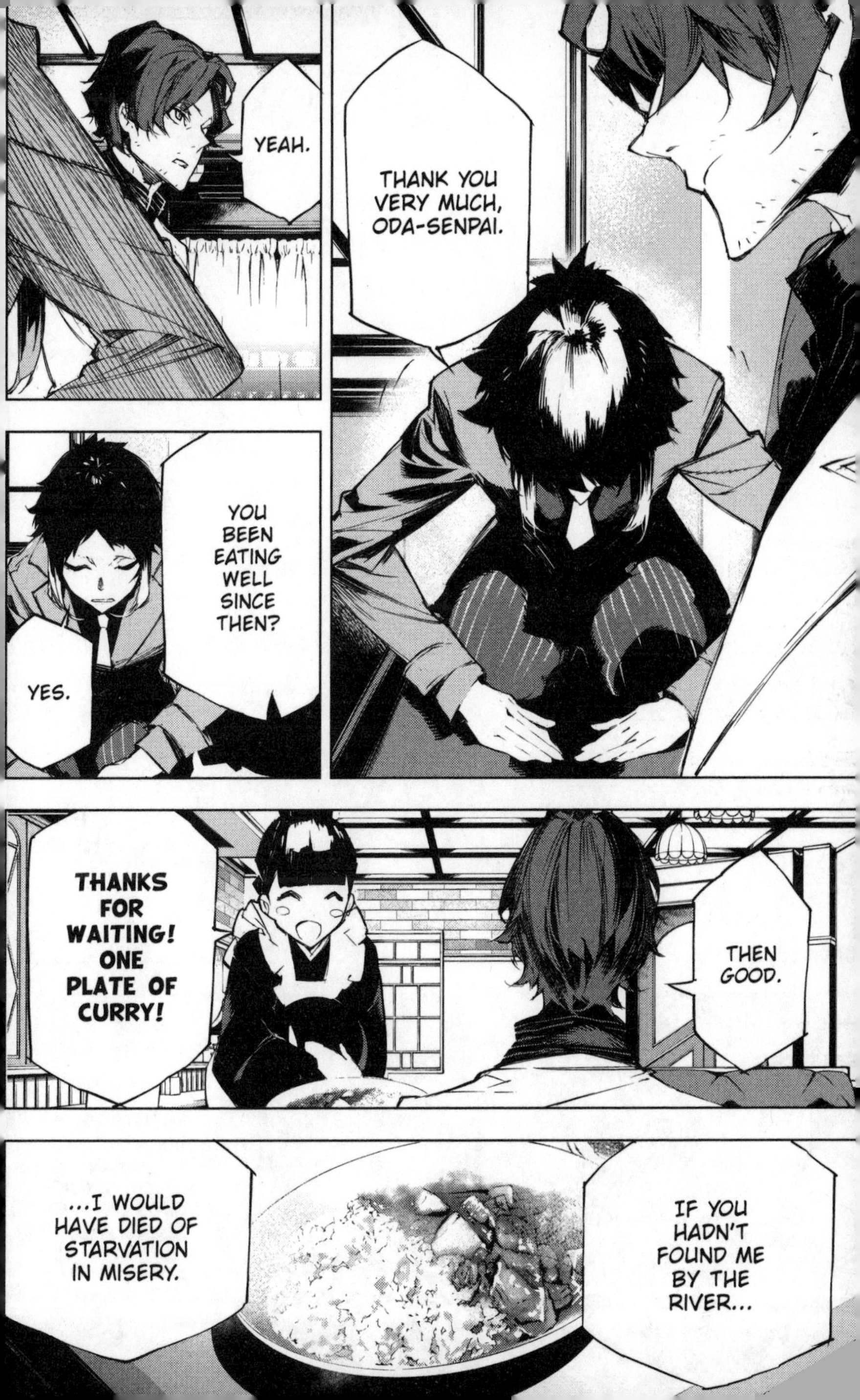
THANK YOU VERY MUCH, ODA-SENPAI.
YEAH.
YOU BEEN EATING WELL SINCE THEN?
YES.
THEN GOOD.
THANKS FOR WAITING! ONE PLATE OF CURRY!
IF YOU HADN'T FOUND ME BY THE RIVER...
...I WOULD HAVE DIED OF STARVATION IN MISERY.

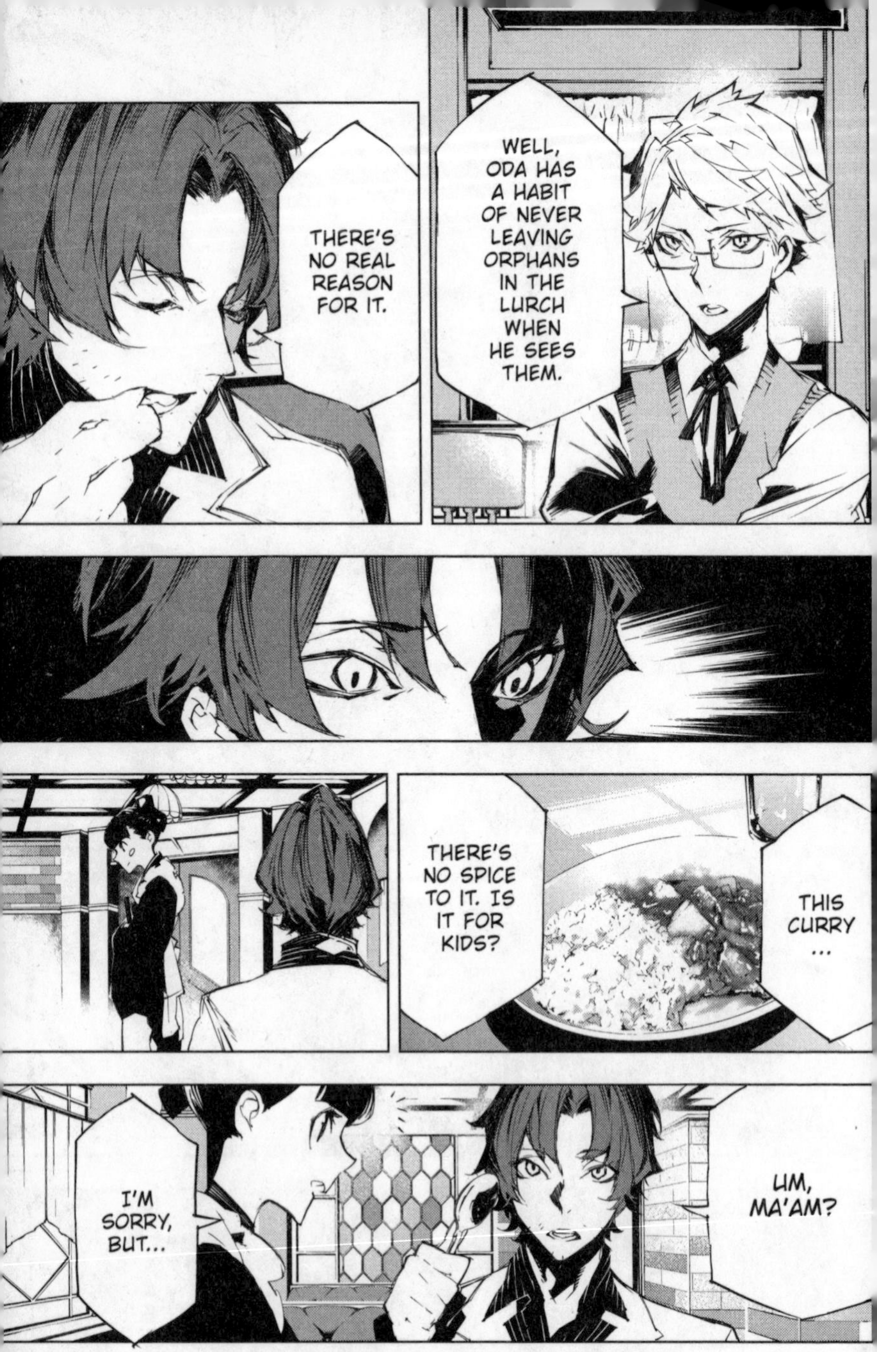
WELL, ODA HAS A HABIT OF NEVER LEAVING ORPHANS IN THE LURCH WHEN HE SEES THEM.
THERE'S NO REAL REASON FOR IT.
THIS CURRY...
THERE'S NO SPICE TO IT. IS IT FOR KIDS?
UM, MA'AM?
I'M SORRY, BUT...

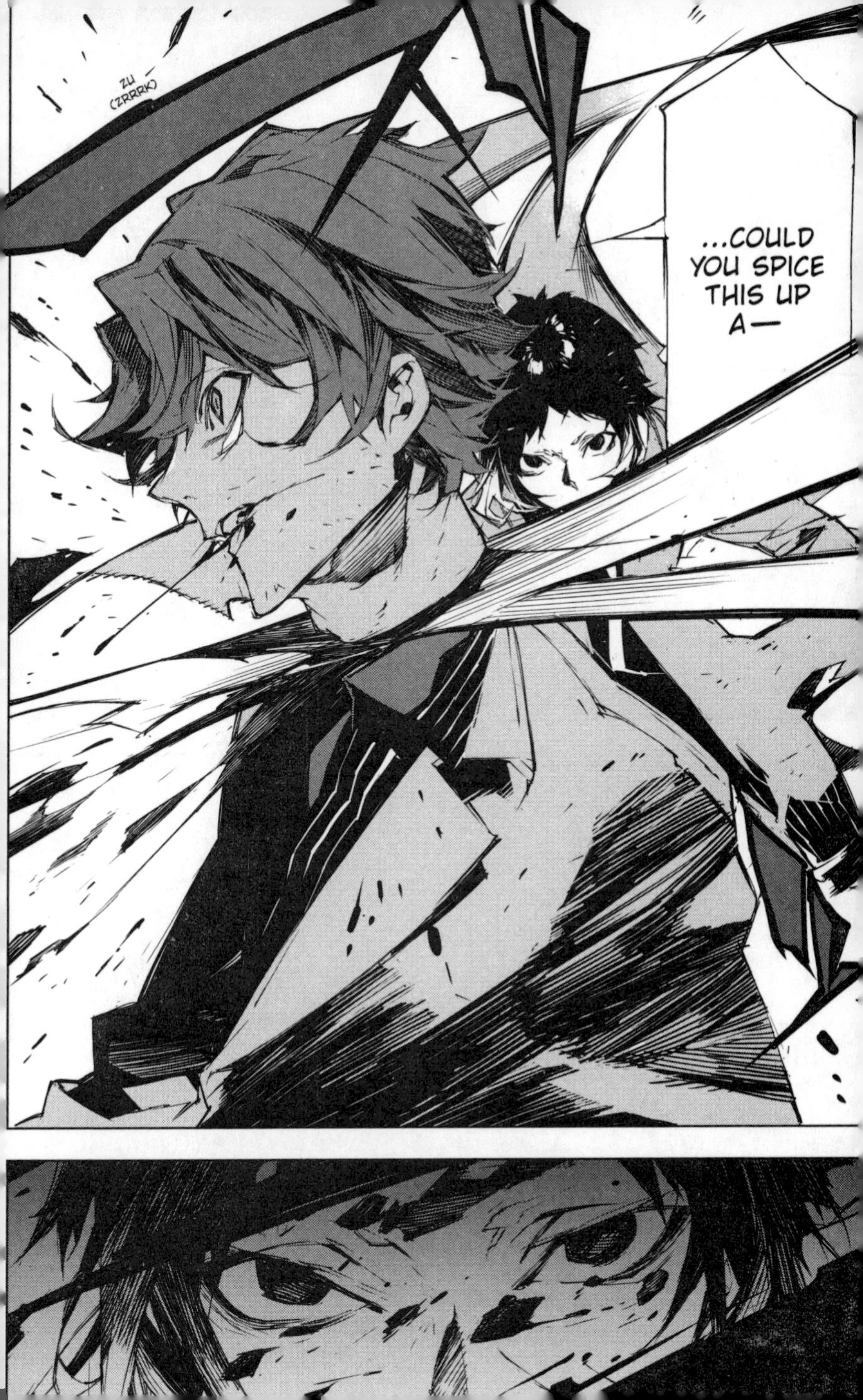
...COULD YOU SPICE THIS UP A—
ZU (ZRRRK)

Bungo Stray Dogs

BEAST

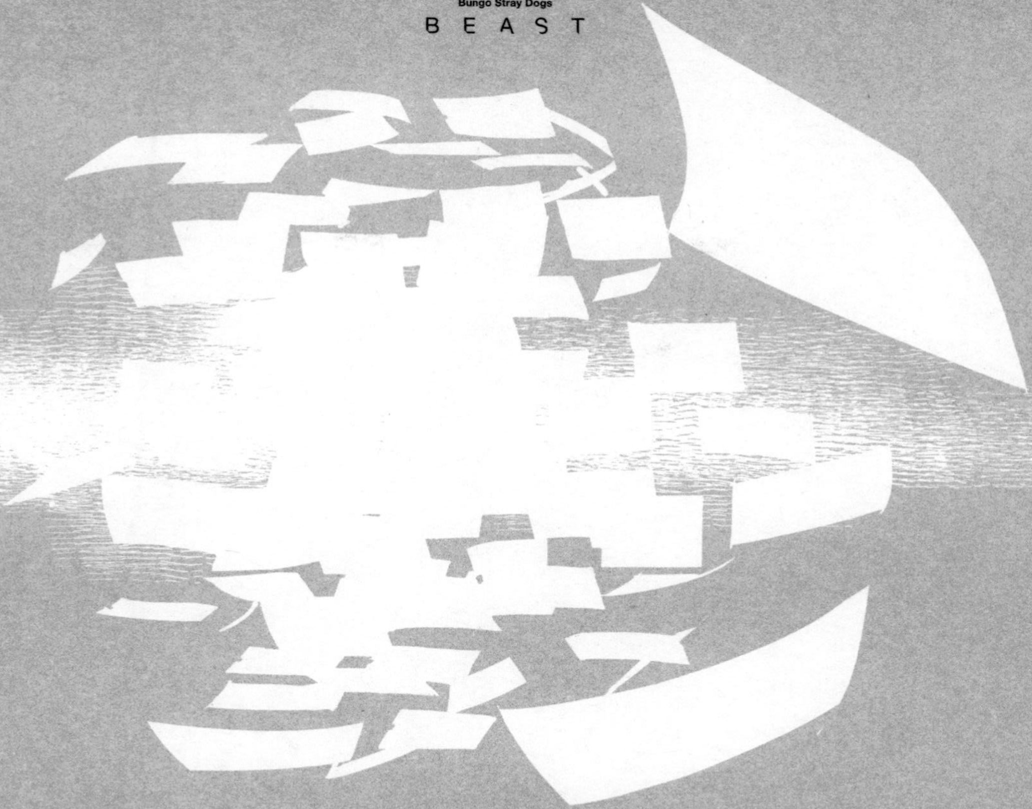

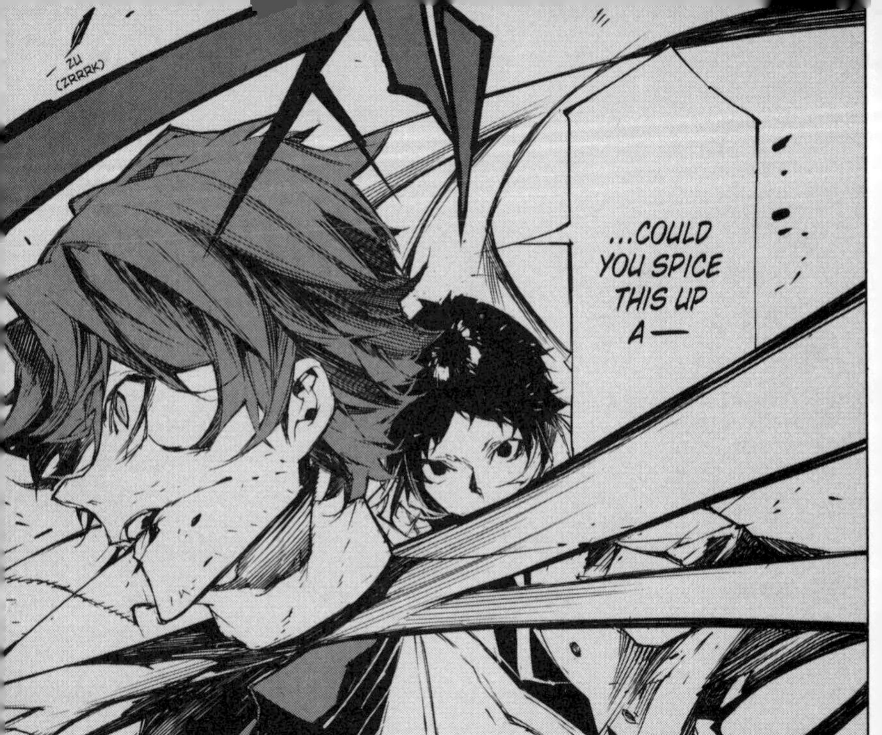
...COULD YOU SPICE THIS UP A—
ZU (ZRRRK)
00:01
#4: THE TARGET

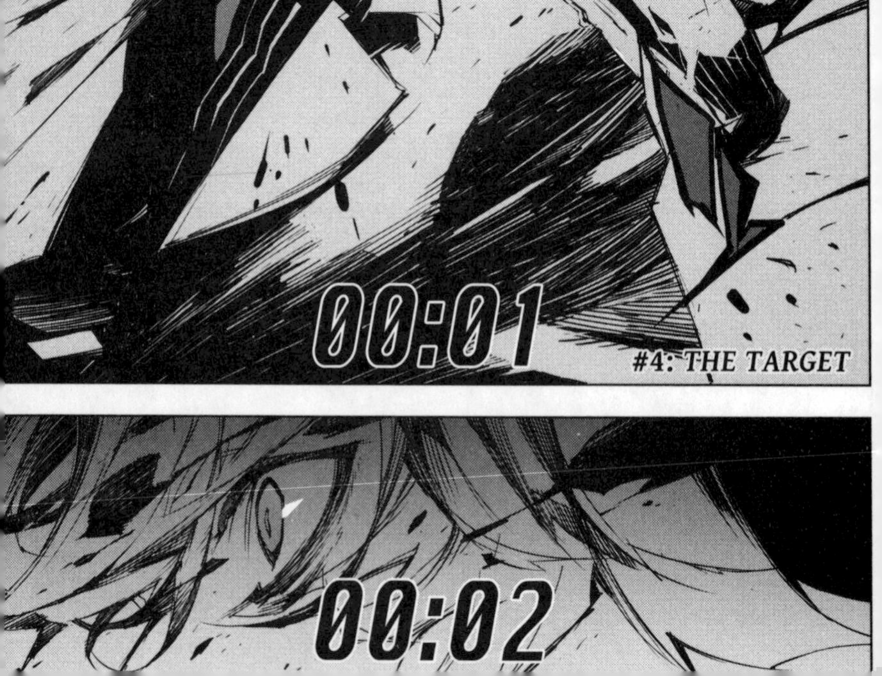
00:02

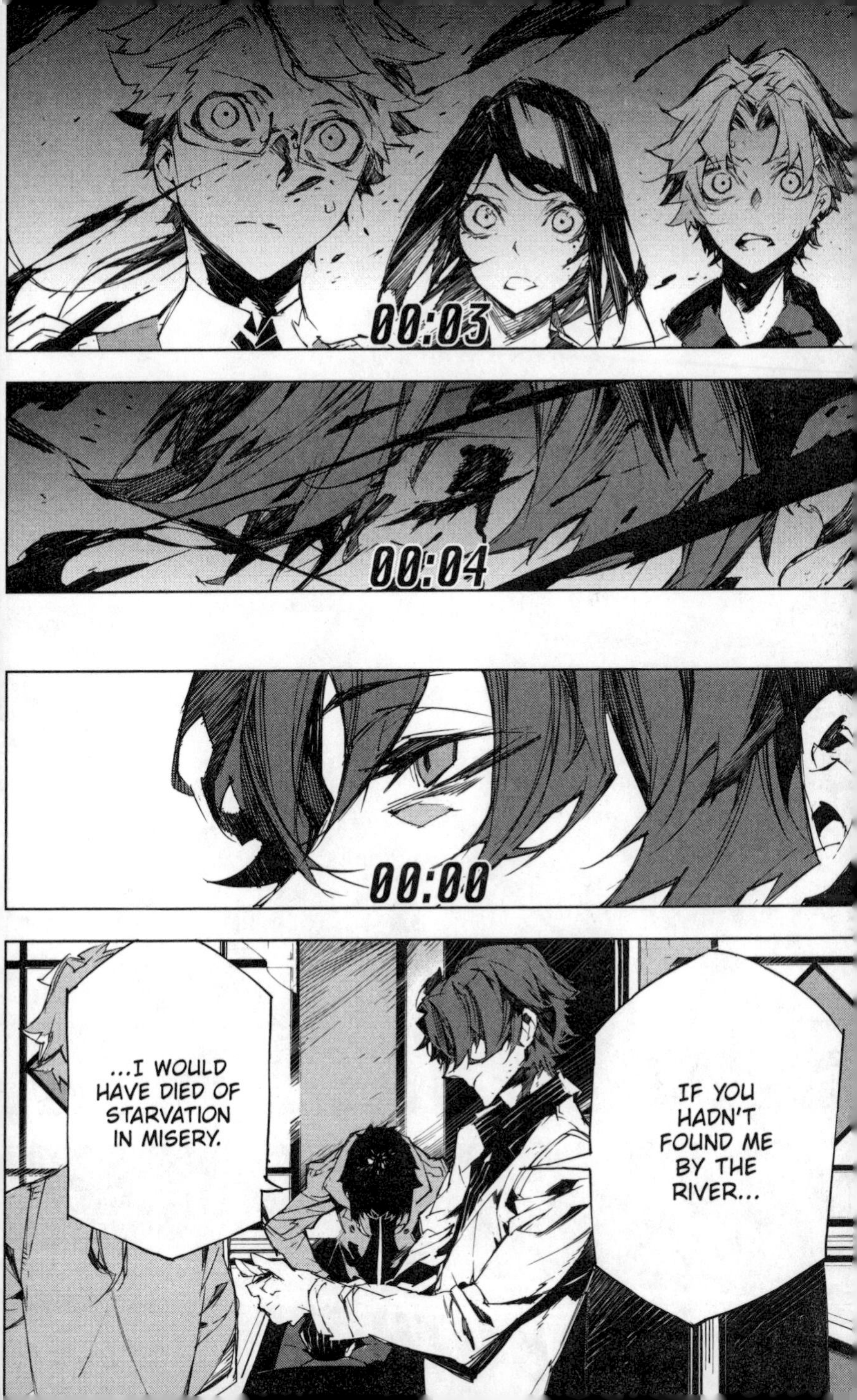
00:03
00:04
00:00
IF YOU HADN'T FOUND ME BY THE RIVER...
...I WOULD HAVE DIED OF STARVATION IN MISERY.

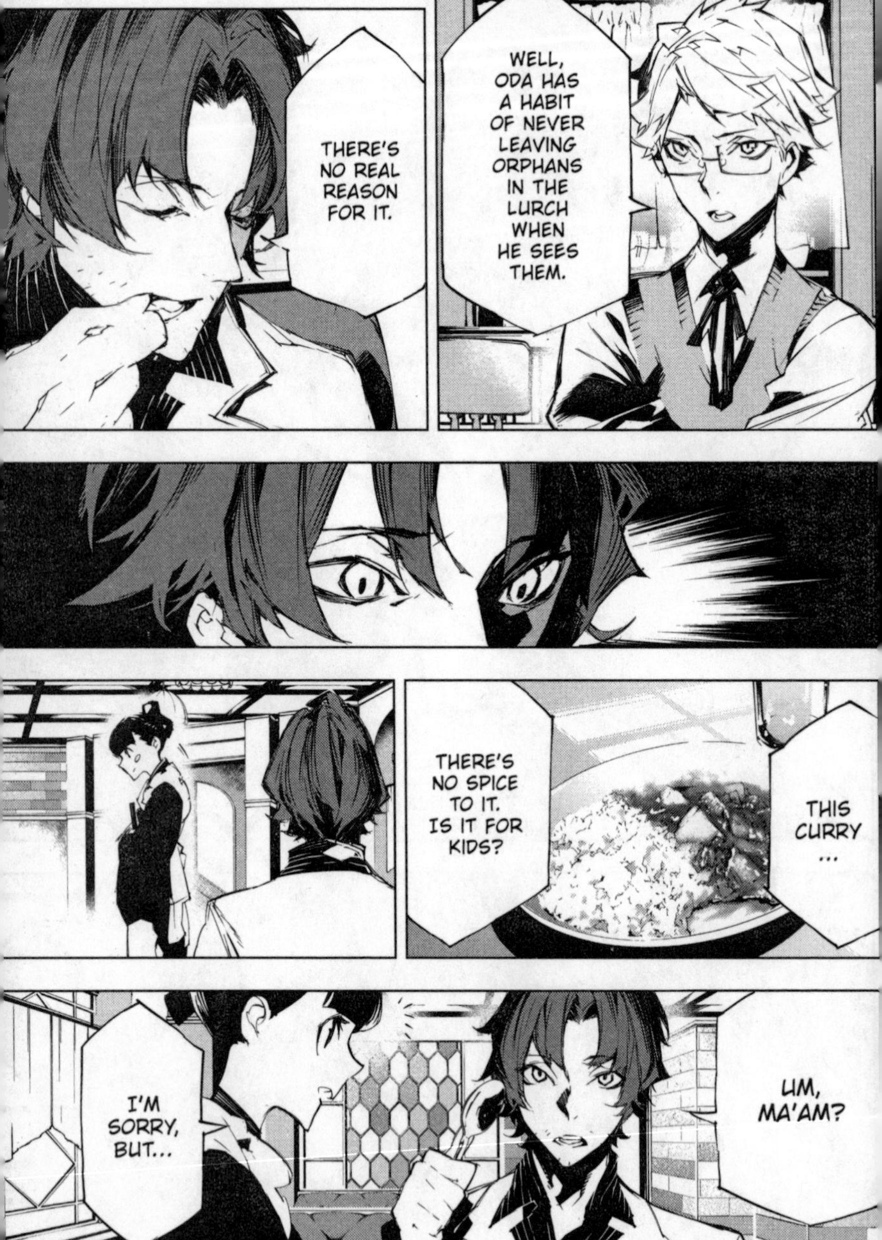
WELL, ODA HAS A HABIT OF NEVER LEAVING ORPHANS IN THE LURCH WHEN HE SEES THEM.
THERE'S NO REAL REASON FOR IT.
THIS CURRY ...
THERE'S NO SPICE TO IT. IS IT FOR KIDS?
UM, MA'AM?
I'M SORRY, BUT...

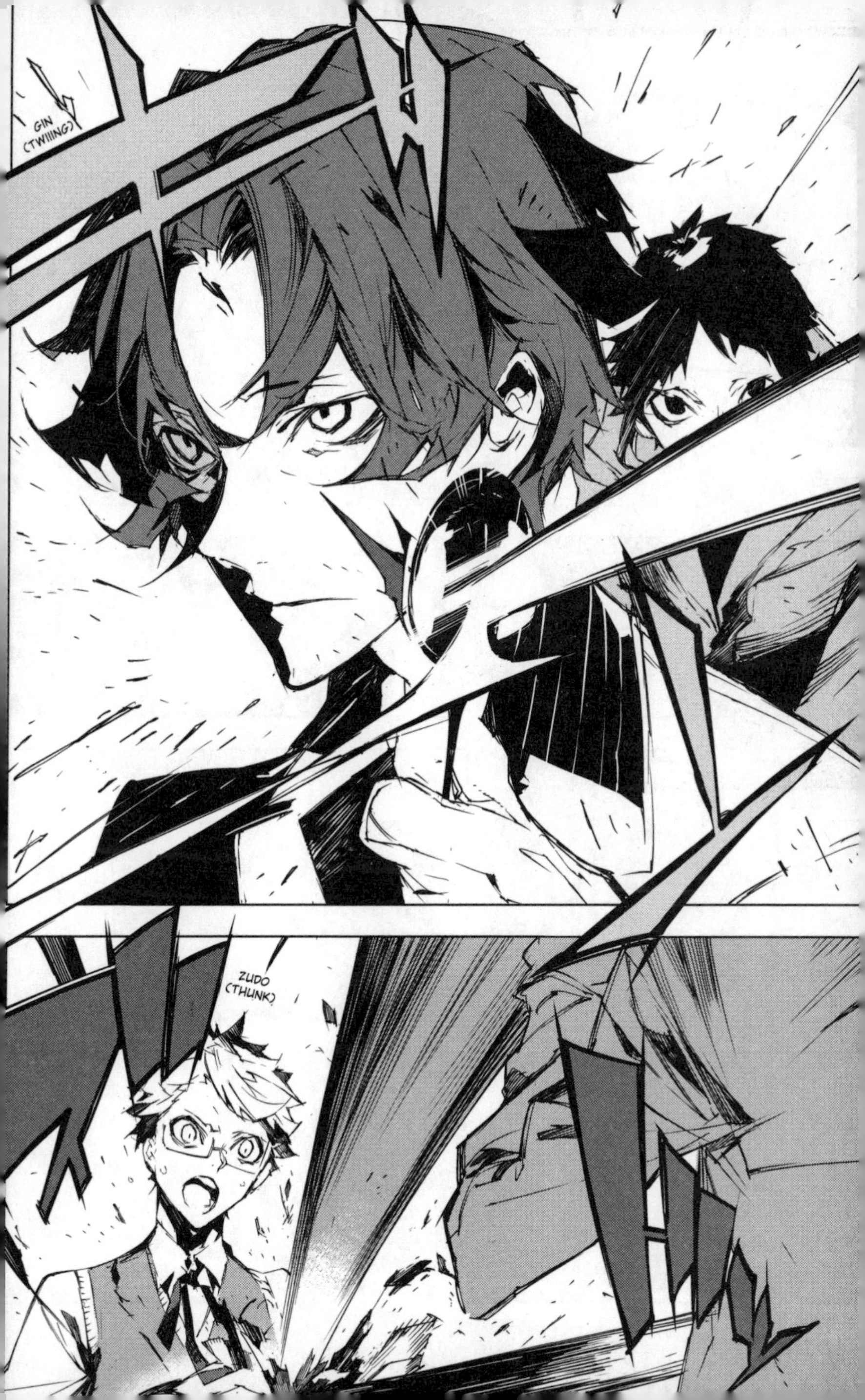
GIN
(TWIIING)
ZUDO
(THUNK)

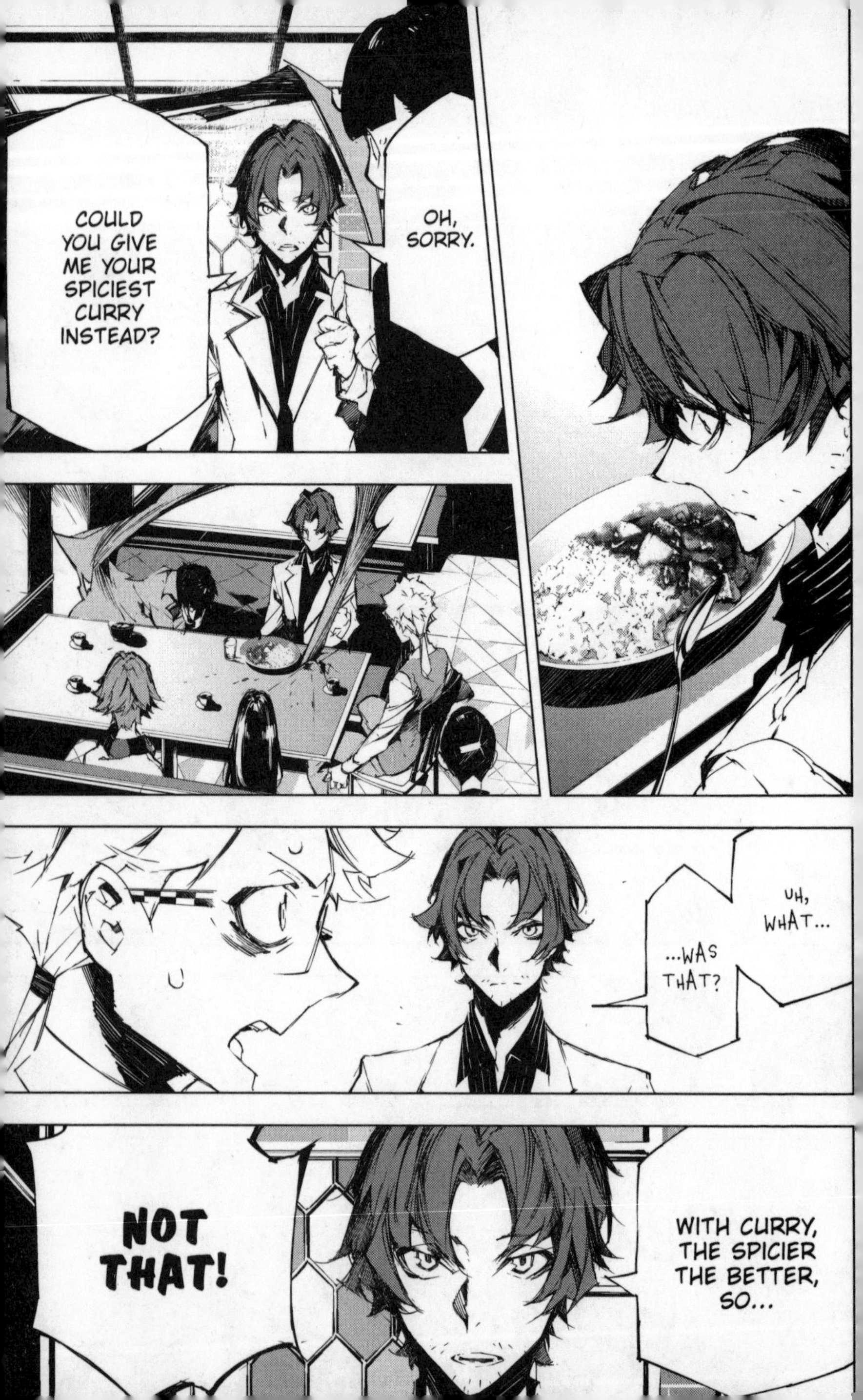
OH, SORRY.
COULD YOU GIVE ME YOUR SPICIEST CURRY INSTEAD?
UH, WHAT...
...WAS THAT?
WITH CURRY, THE SPICIER THE BETTER, SO...
NOT THAT!

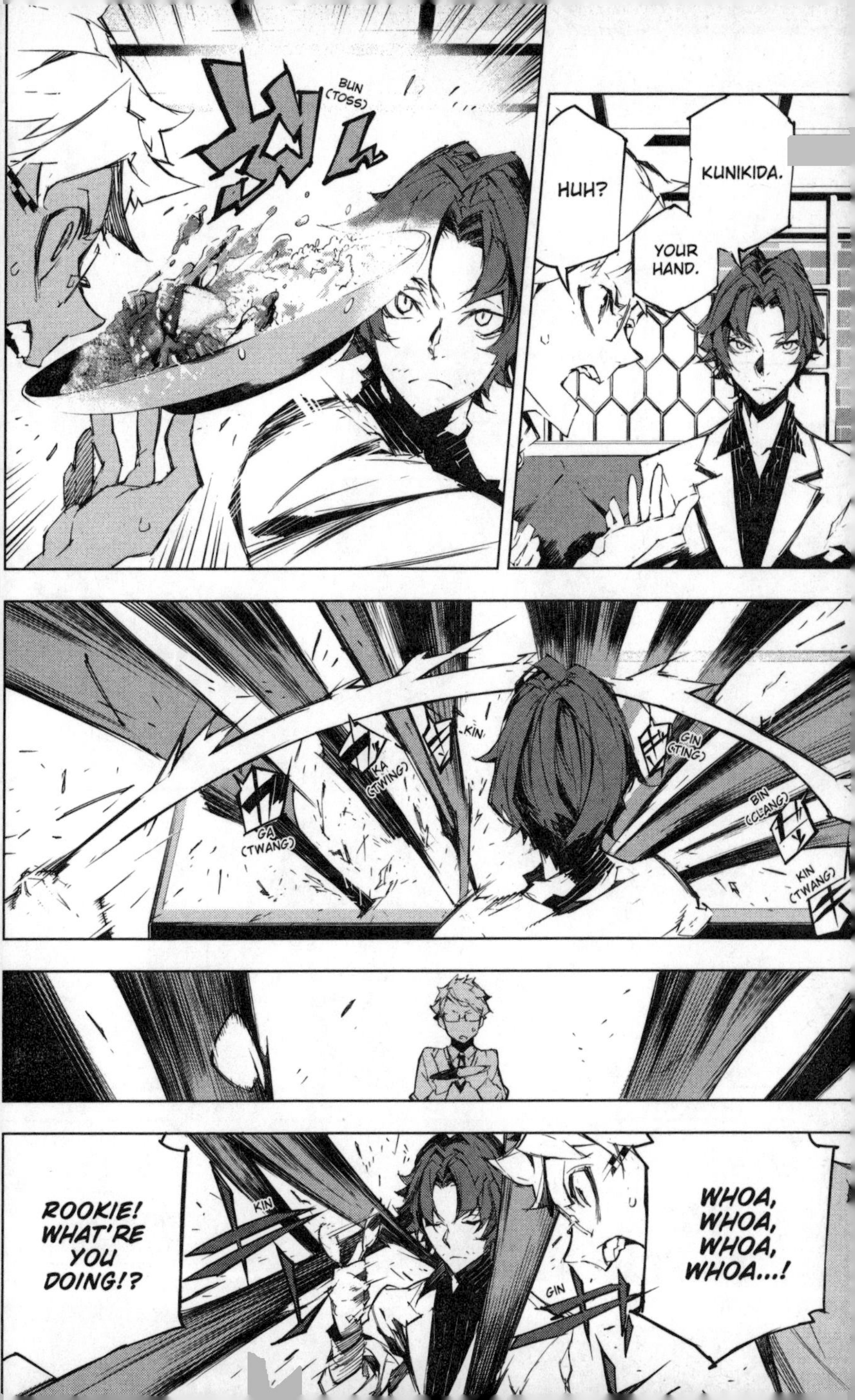

KUNIKIDA.
HUH?
YOUR HAND.
BUN (TOSS)
GIN (TING)
BIN (CLANG)
KIN (TWANG)
KIN
KA (TWING)
GA (TWANG)
WHOA, WHOA, WHOA, WHOA...!
GIN
KIN
ROOKIE! WHAT'RE YOU DOING!?

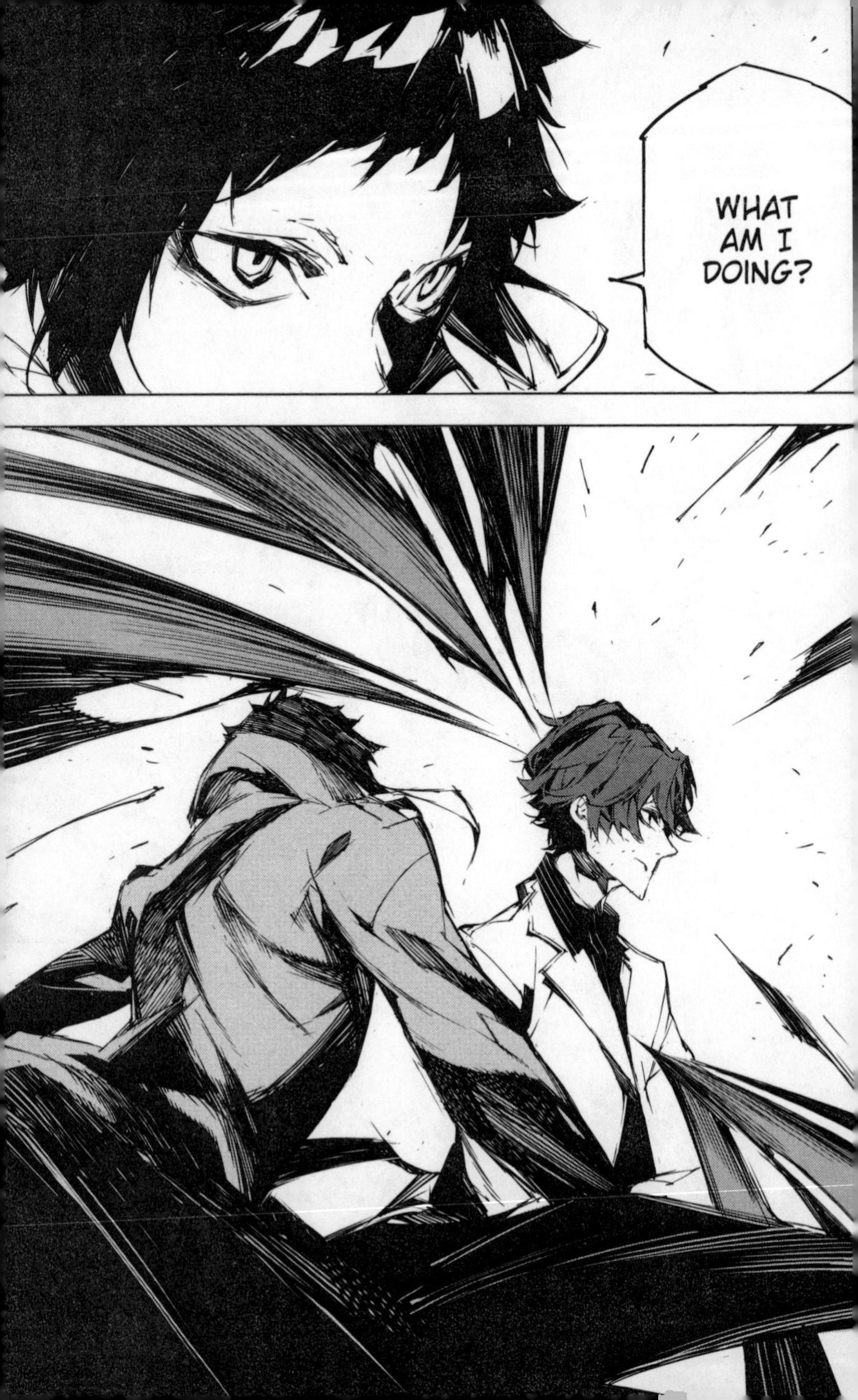
WHAT AM I DOING?

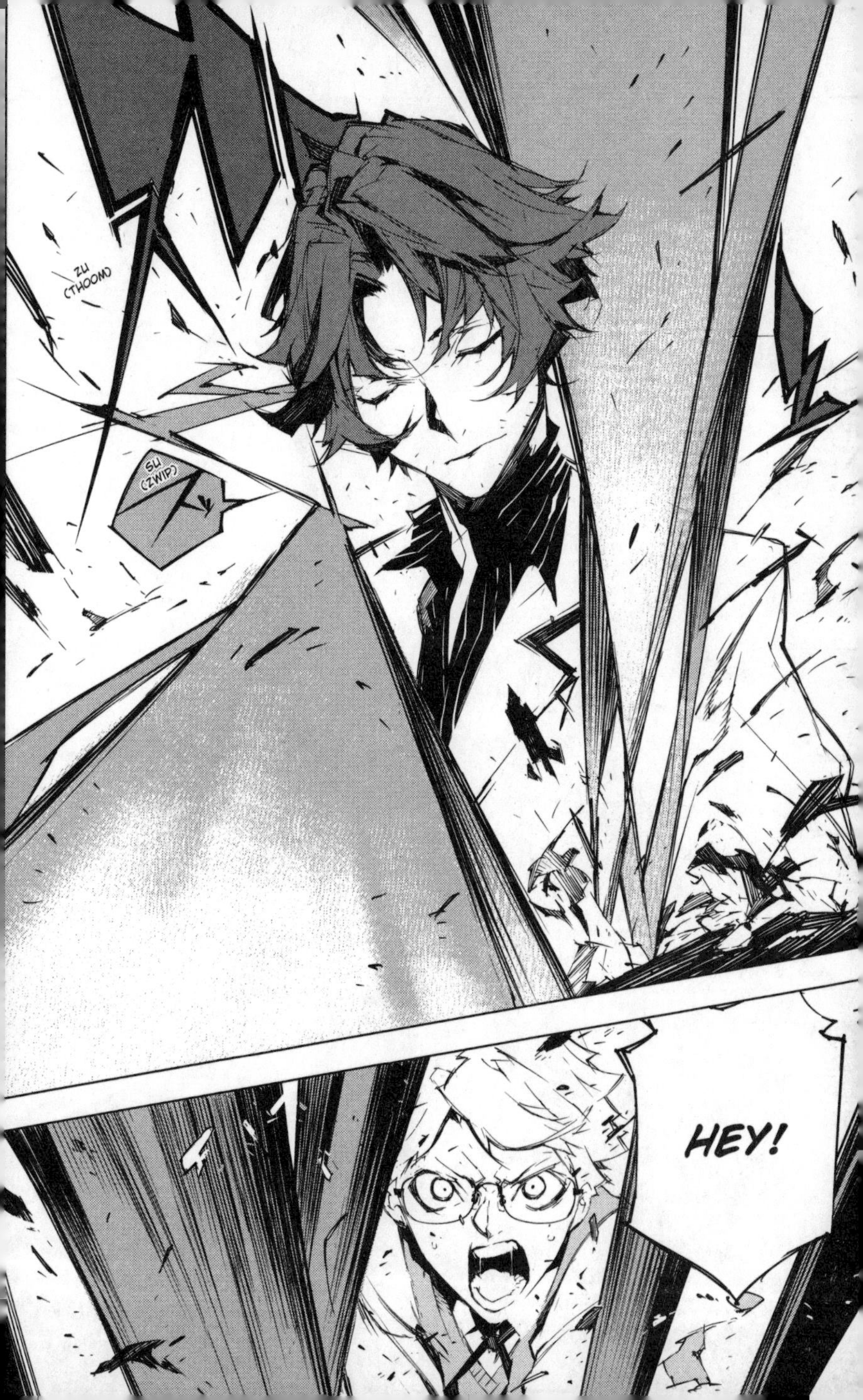
ZU (THOOM)
SU (ZWIP)
HEY!

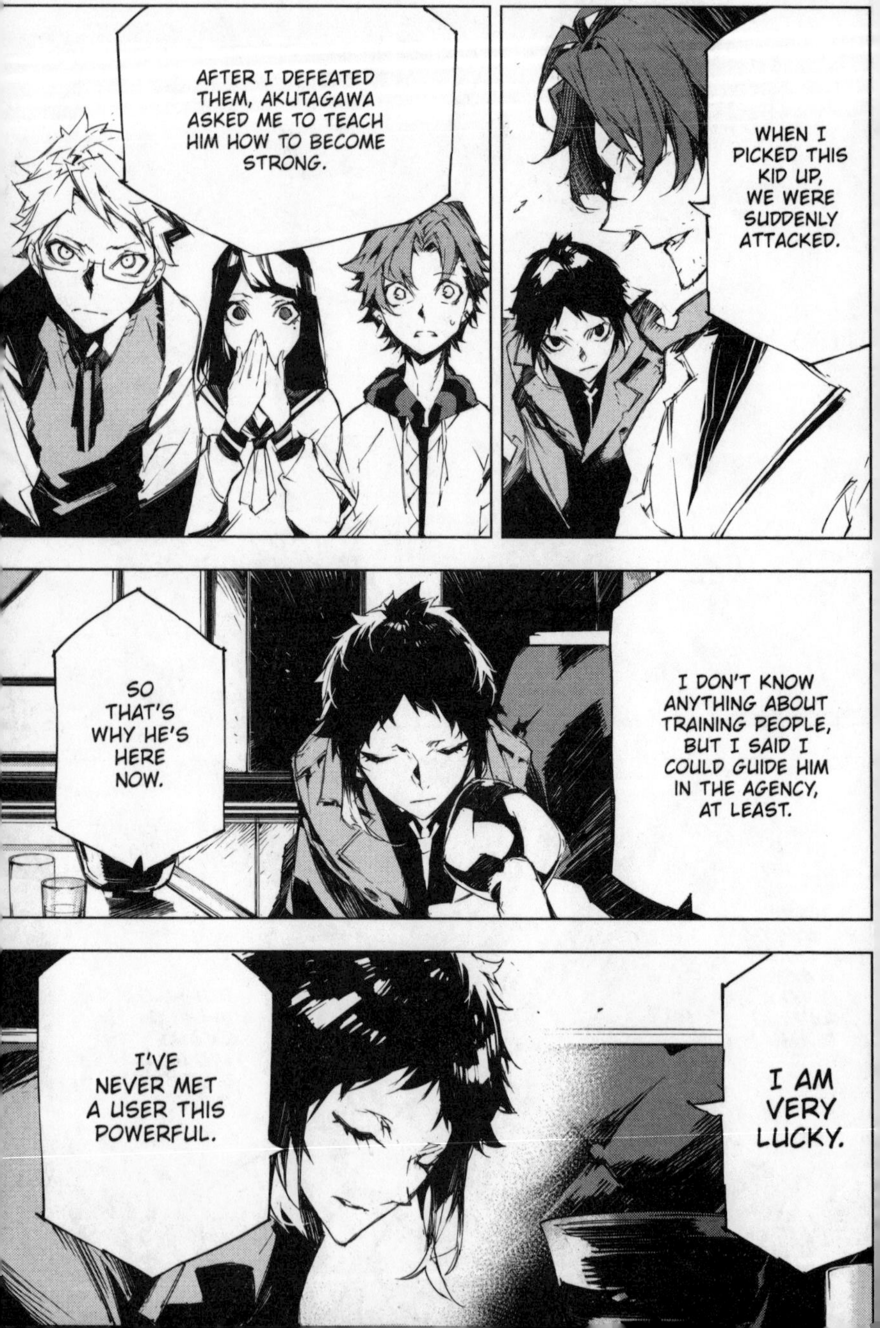
WHEN I PICKED THIS KID UP, WE WERE SUDDENLY ATTACKED.
AFTER I DEFEATED THEM, AKUTAGAWA ASKED ME TO TEACH HIM HOW TO BECOME STRONG.
I DON'T KNOW ANYTHING ABOUT TRAINING PEOPLE, BUT I SAID I COULD GUIDE HIM IN THE AGENCY, AT LEAST.
SO THAT'S WHY HE'S HERE NOW.
I AM VERY LUCKY.
I'VE NEVER MET A USER THIS POWERFUL.

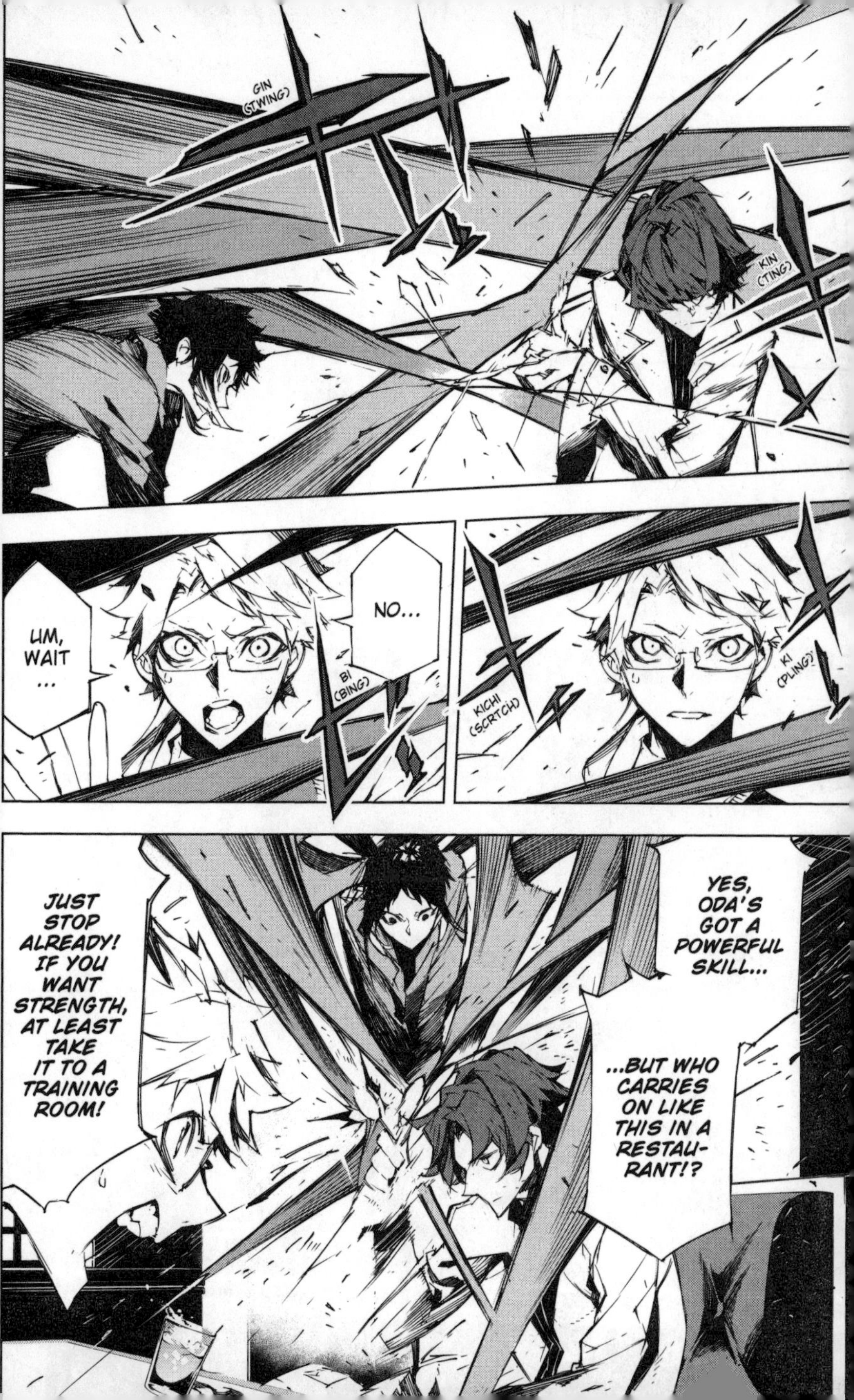
KIN (TING)
GIN (STWING)
KI (PLING)
KICHI (SCRTCH)
NO...
BI (BING)
UM, WAIT ...
YES, ODA'S GOT A POWERFUL SKILL...
...BUT WHO CARRIES ON LIKE THIS IN A RESTAU-RANT!?
JUST STOP ALREADY! IF YOU WANT STRENGTH, AT LEAST TAKE IT TO A TRAINING ROOM!

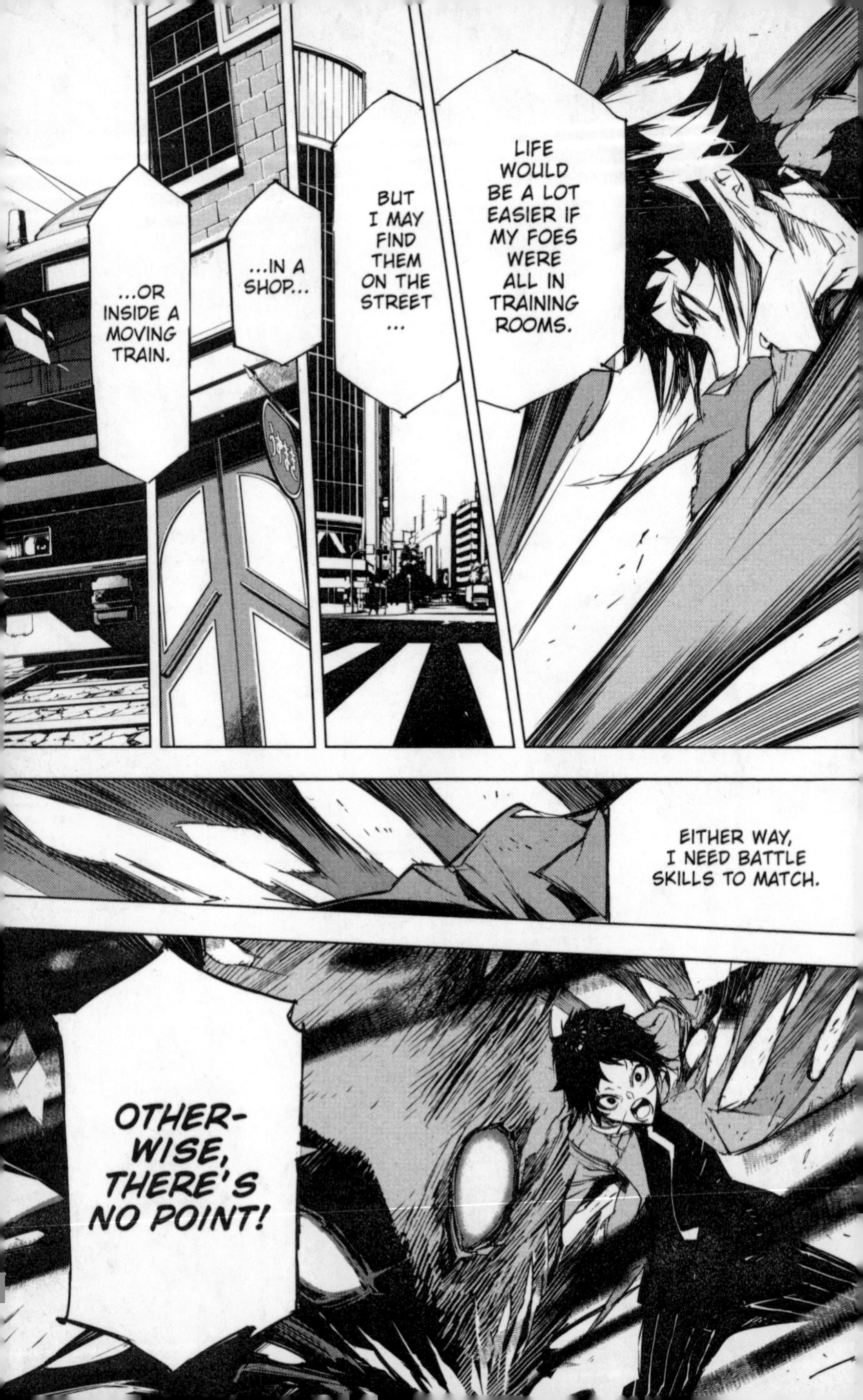
LIFE WOULD BE A LOT EASIER IF MY FOES WERE ALL IN TRAINING ROOMS.
BUT I MAY FIND THEM ON THE STREET ...
...IN A SHOP...
...OR INSIDE A MOVING TRAIN.
EITHER WAY, I NEED BATTLE SKILLS TO MATCH.
OTHER-WISE, THERE'S NO POINT!

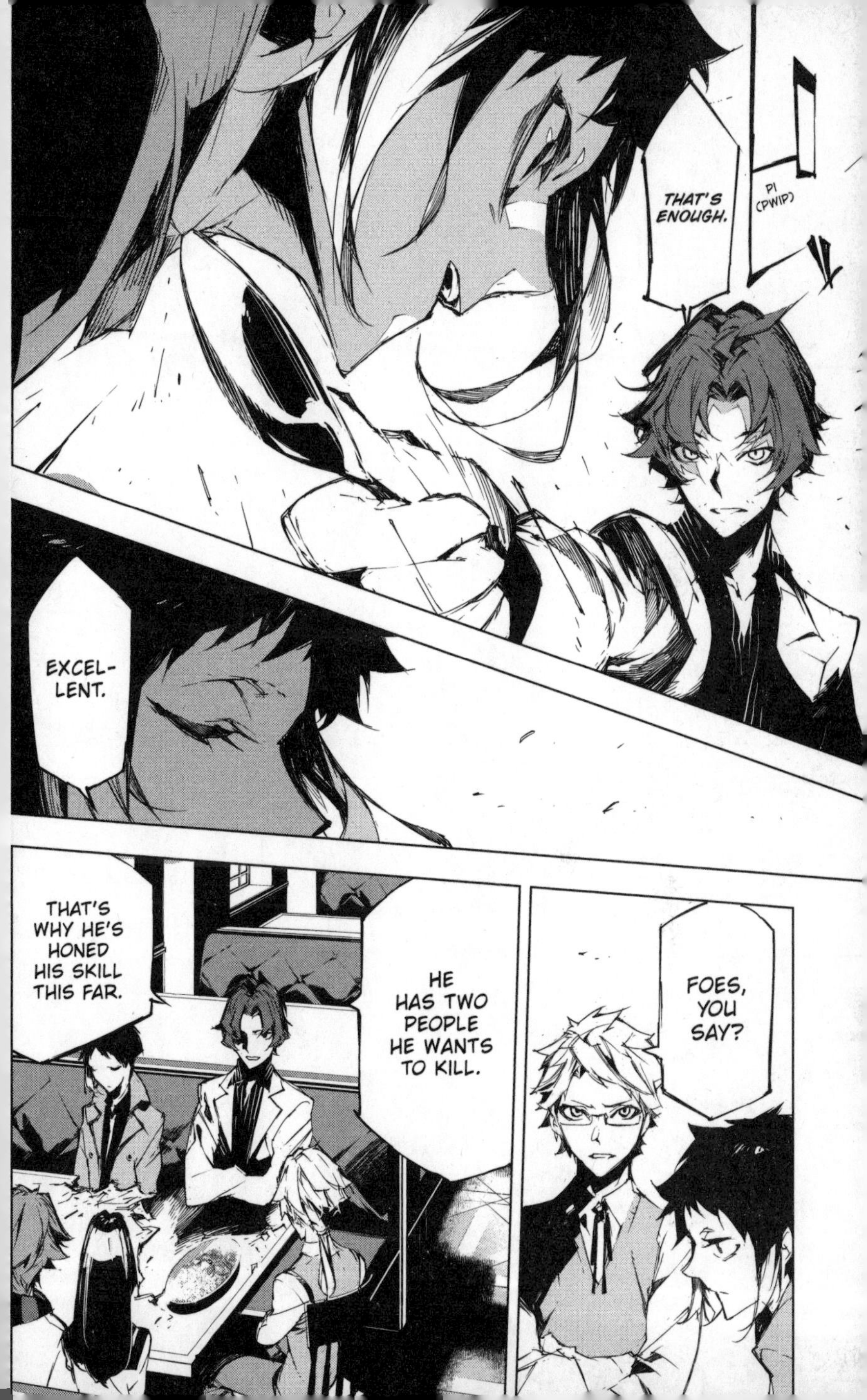
PI (PWIP)
THAT'S ENOUGH.
EXCEL-LENT.
FOES, YOU SAY?
HE HAS TWO PEOPLE HE WANTS TO KILL.
THAT'S WHY HE'S HONED HIS SKILL THIS FAR.

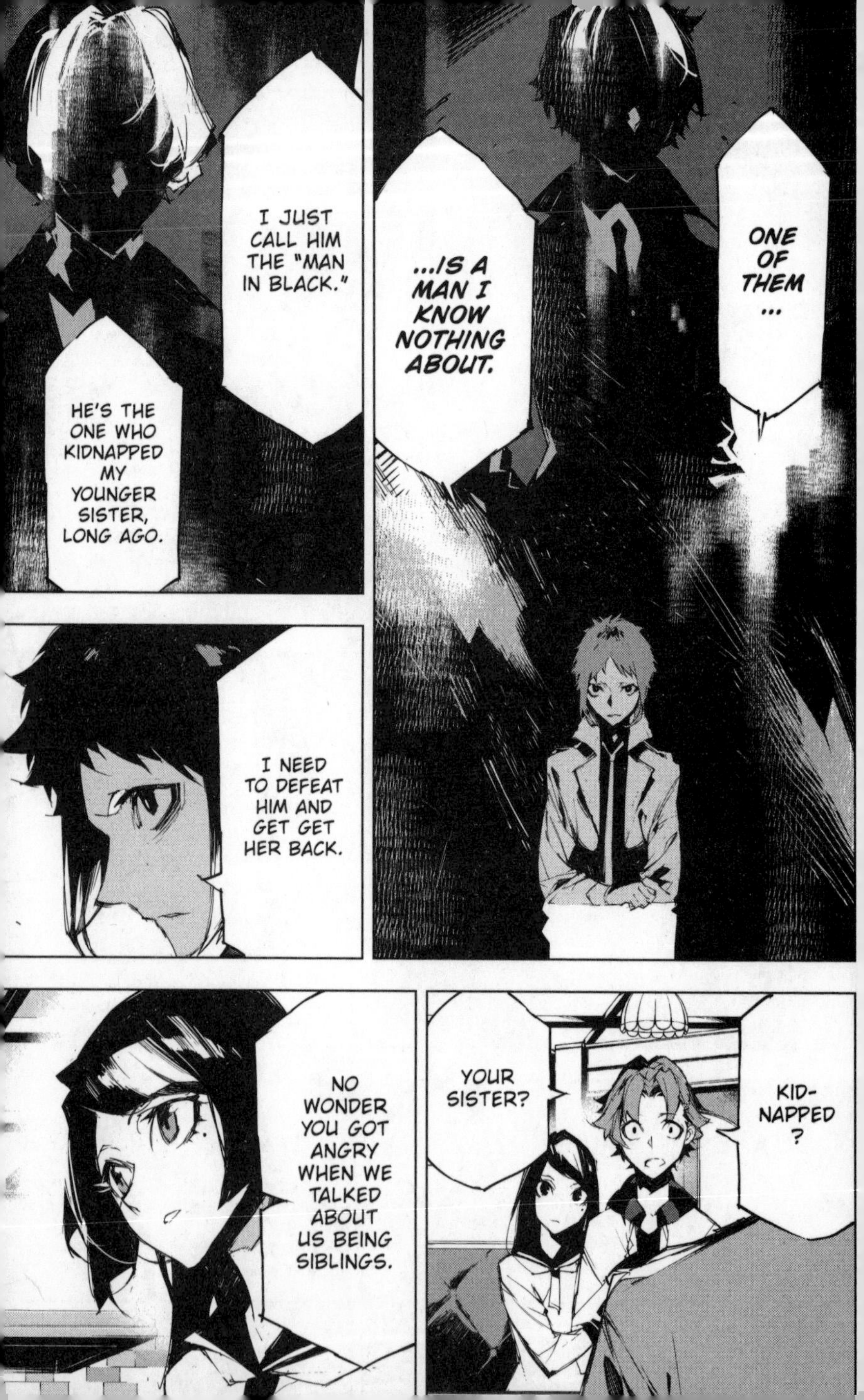
ONE OF THEM...
...IS A MAN I KNOW NOTHING ABOUT.
I JUST CALL HIM THE "MAN IN BLACK."
HE'S THE ONE WHO KIDNAPPED MY YOUNGER SISTER, LONG AGO.
I NEED TO DEFEAT HIM AND GET GET HER BACK.
YOUR SISTER?
KID-NAPPED?
NO WONDER YOU GOT ANGRY WHEN WE TALKED ABOUT US BEING SIBLINGS.

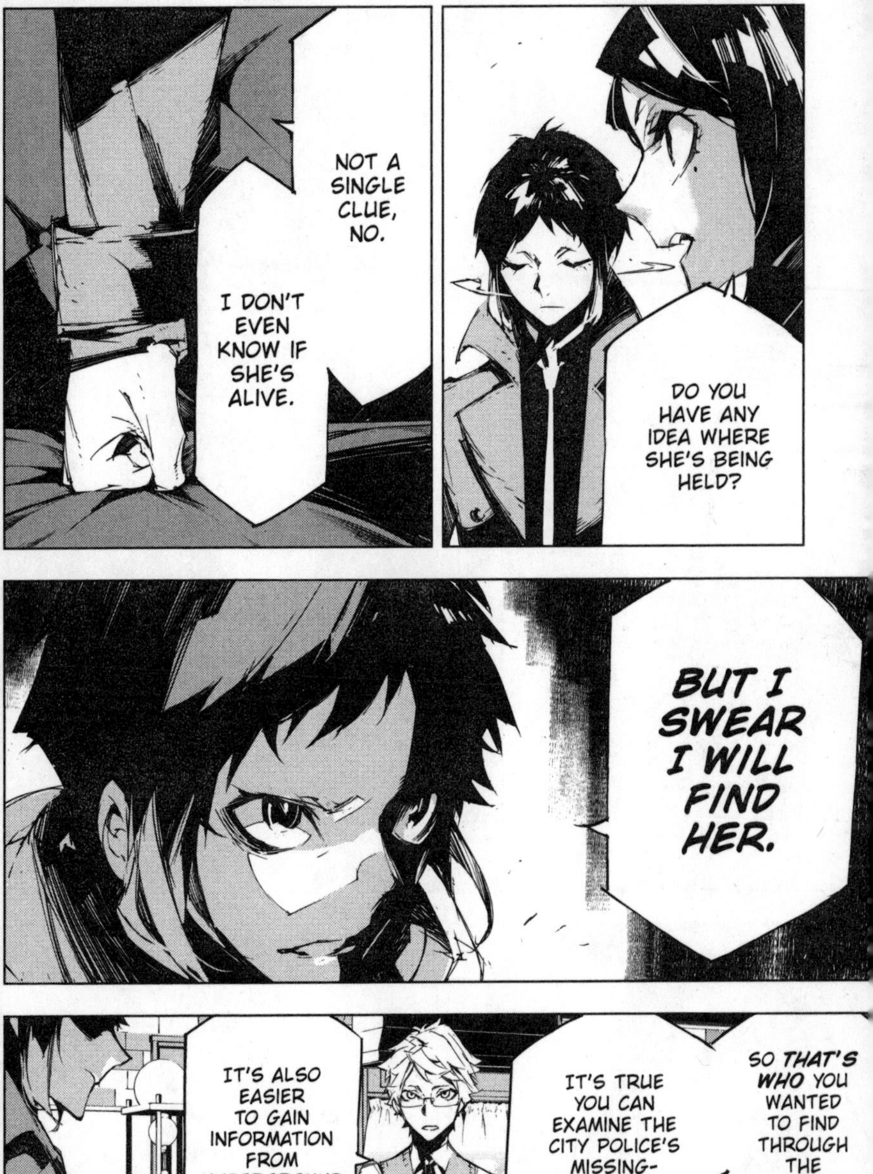
DO YOU HAVE ANY IDEA WHERE SHE'S BEING HELD?
NOT A SINGLE CLUE, NO.
I DON'T EVEN KNOW IF SHE'S ALIVE.
BUT I SWEAR I WILL FIND HER.
SO THAT'S WHO YOU WANTED TO FIND THROUGH THE AGENCY, EH?
IT'S TRUE YOU CAN EXAMINE THE CITY POLICE'S MISSING-PERSON FILES THROUGH US.
IT'S ALSO EASIER TO GAIN INFORMATION FROM UNDERGROUND SOURCES...

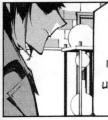

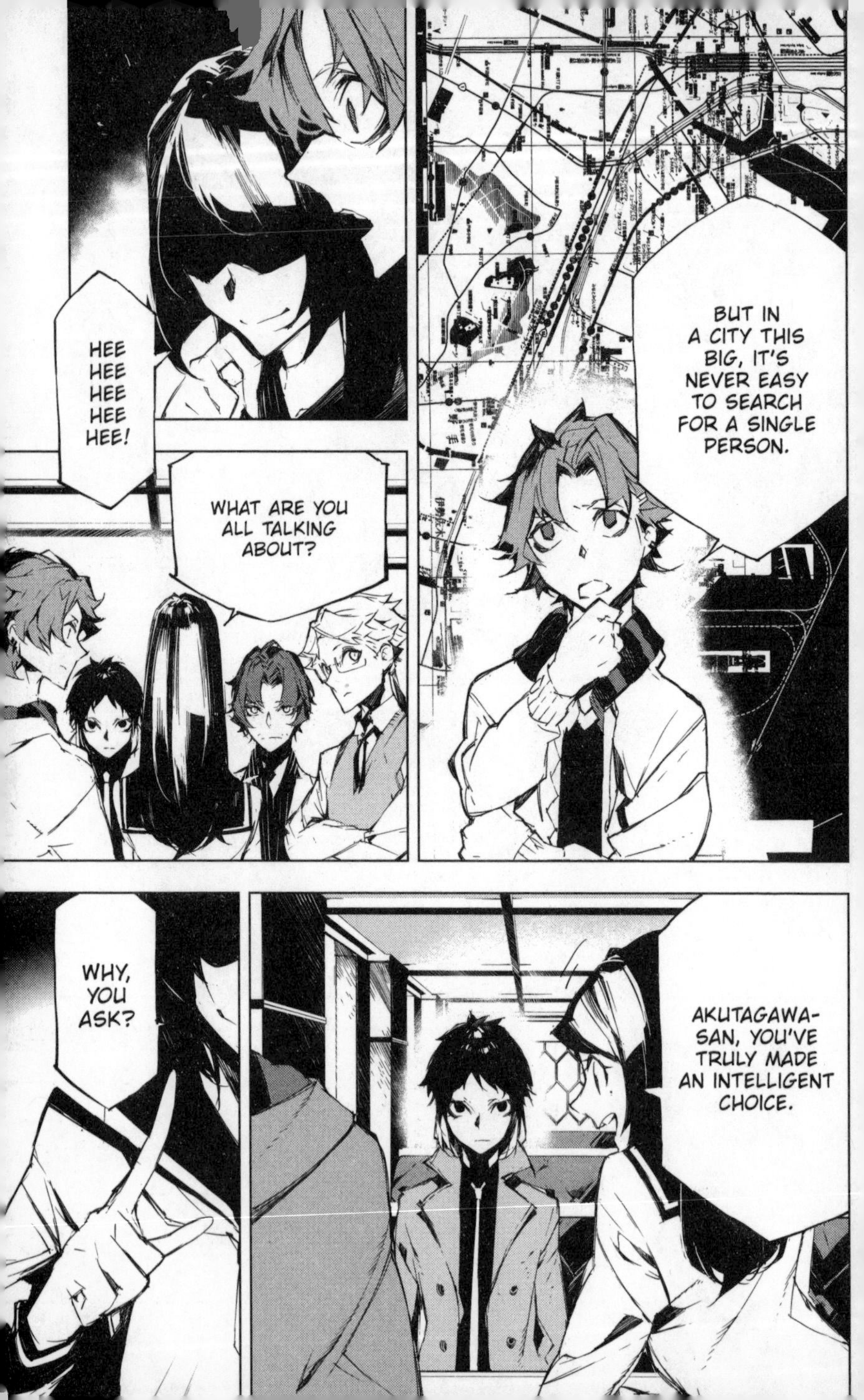
BUT IN A CITY THIS BIG, IT'S NEVER EASY TO SEARCH FOR A SINGLE PERSON.
HEE HEE HEE HEE HEE!
WHAT ARE YOU ALL TALKING ABOUT?
AKUTAGAWA-SAN, YOU'VE TRULY MADE AN INTELLIGENT CHOICE.
WHY, YOU ASK?

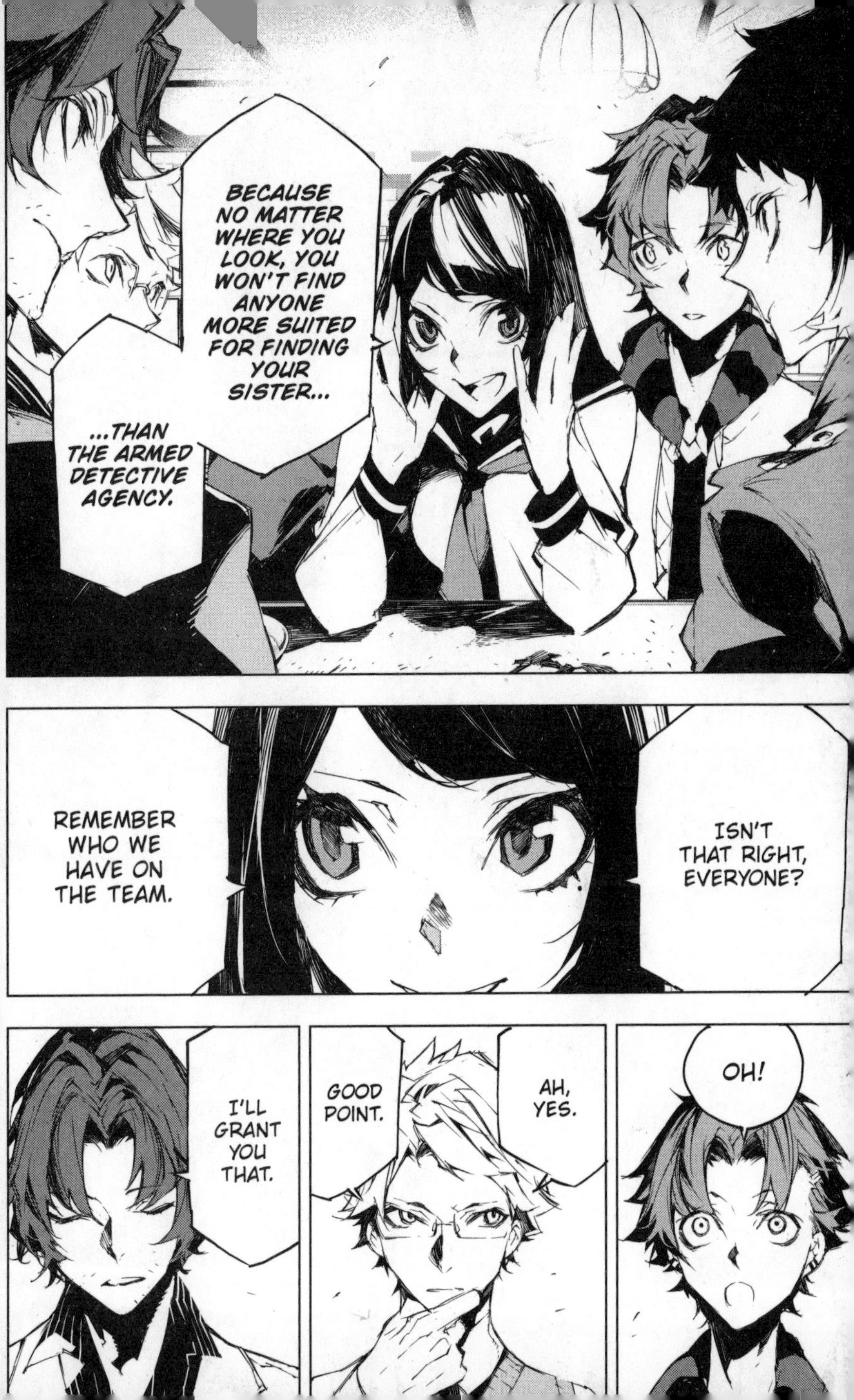
BECAUSE NO MATTER WHERE YOU LOOK, YOU WON'T FIND ANYONE MORE SUITED FOR FINDING YOUR SISTER...
...THAN THE ARMED DETECTIVE AGENCY.
ISN'T THAT RIGHT, EVERYONE?
REMEMBER WHO WE HAVE ON THE TEAM.
OH!
AH, YES.
GOOD POINT.
I'LL GRANT YOU THAT.

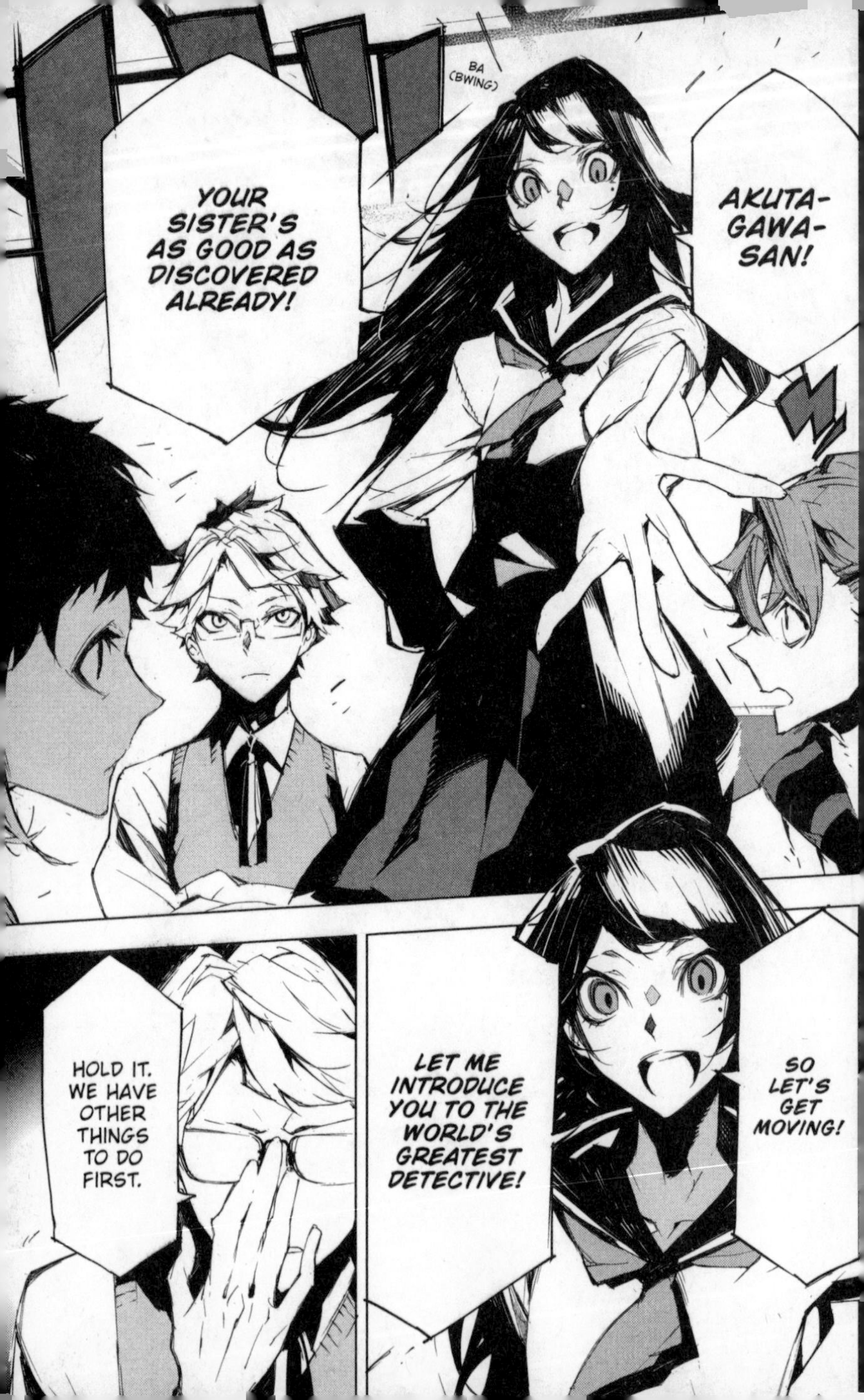
AKUTA-GAWA-SAN!
BA (BWING)
YOUR SISTER'S AS GOOD AS DISCOVERED ALREADY!
SO LET'S GET MOVING!
LET ME INTRODUCE YOU TO THE WORLD'S GREATEST DETECTIVE!
HOLD IT. WE HAVE OTHER THINGS TO DO FIRST.

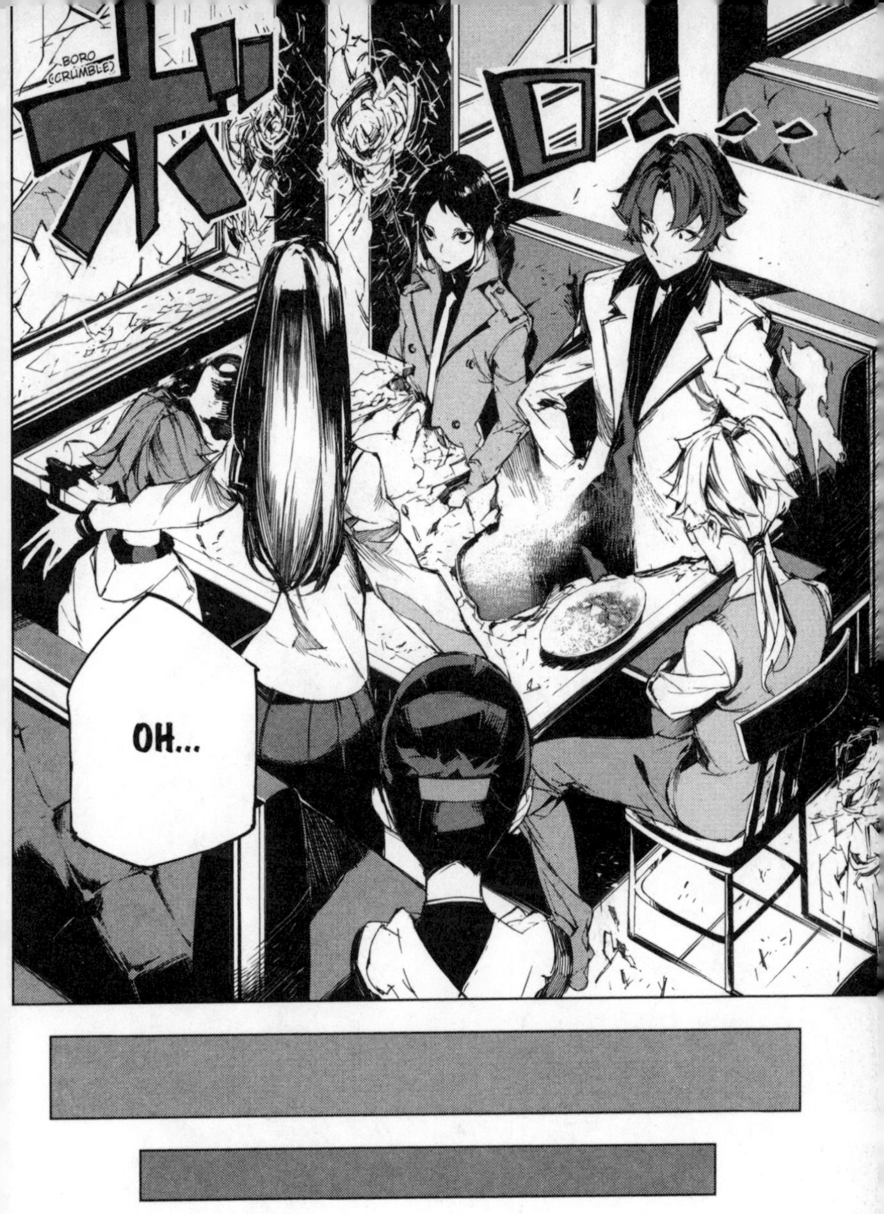
BORO
(CRUMBLE)
OH...

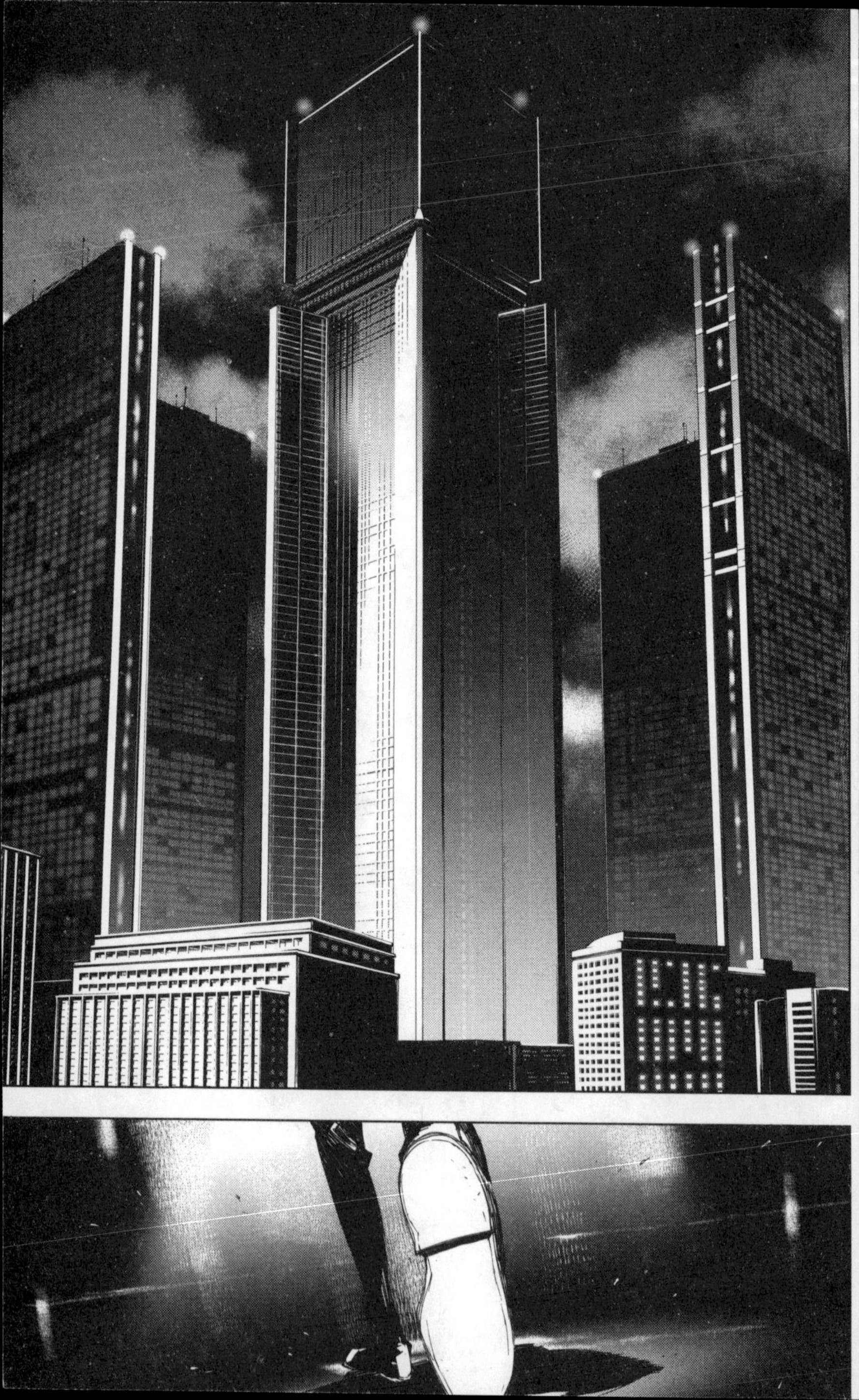

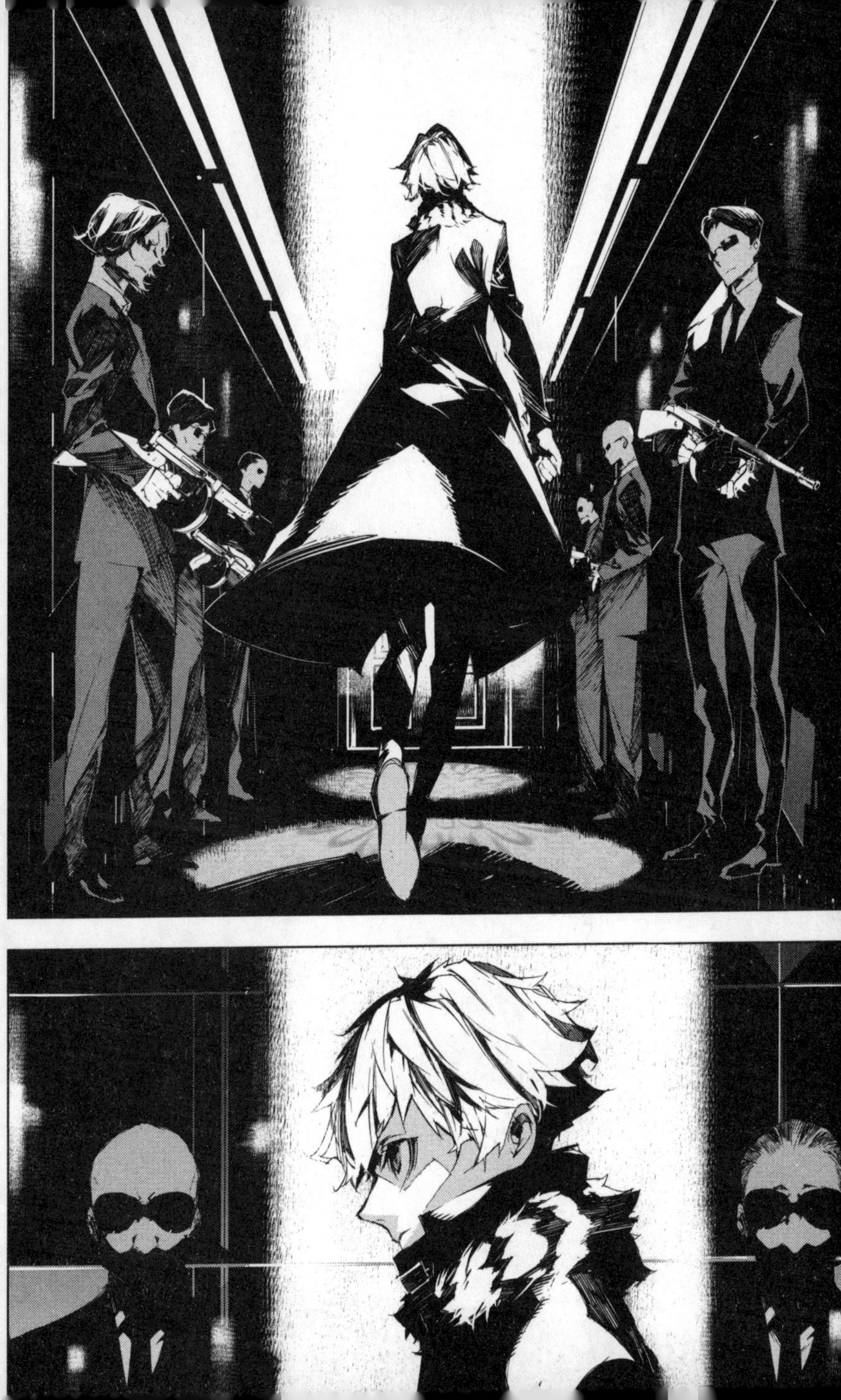

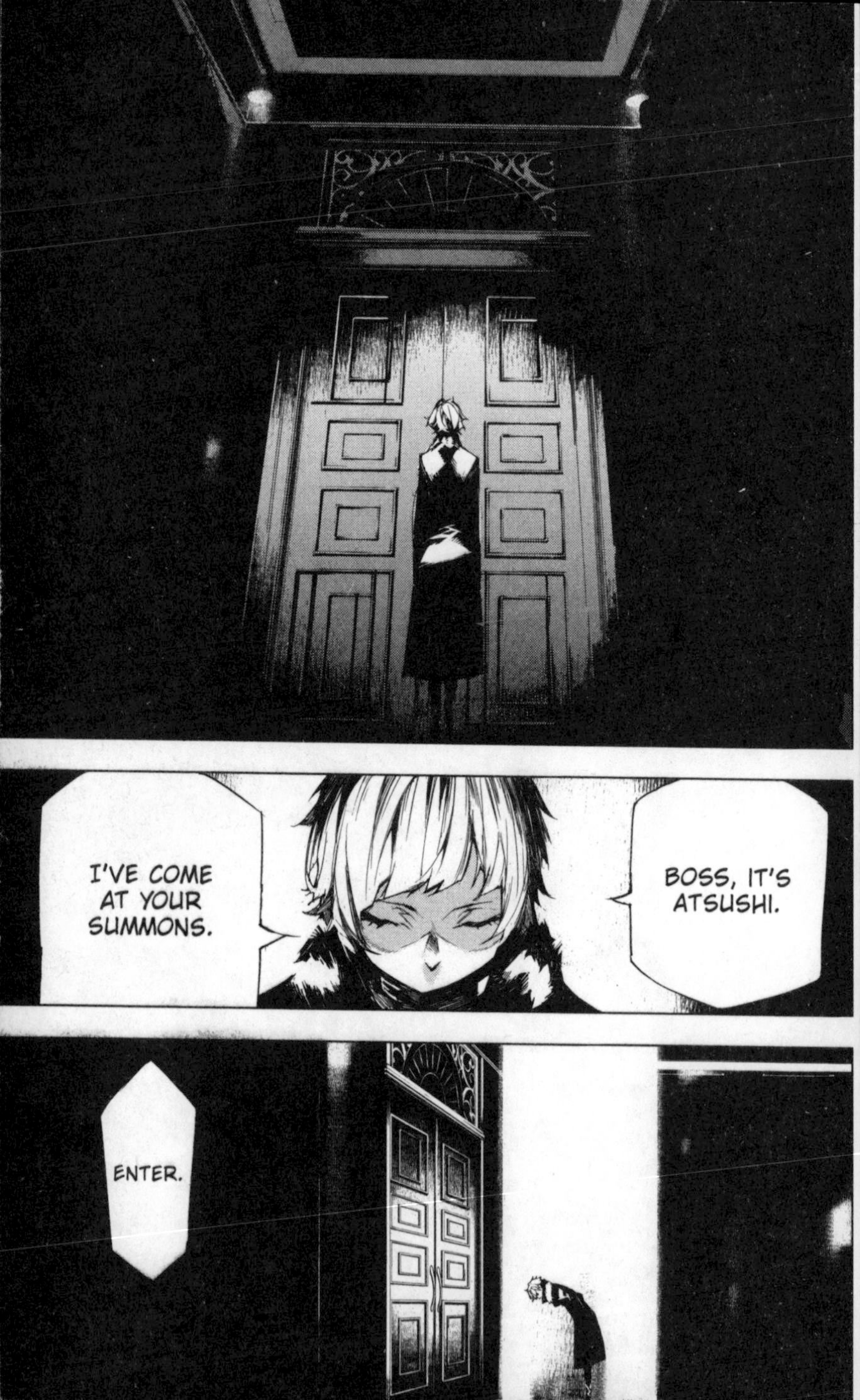
BOSS, IT'S ATSUSHI.
I'VE COME AT YOUR SUMMONS.
ENTER.

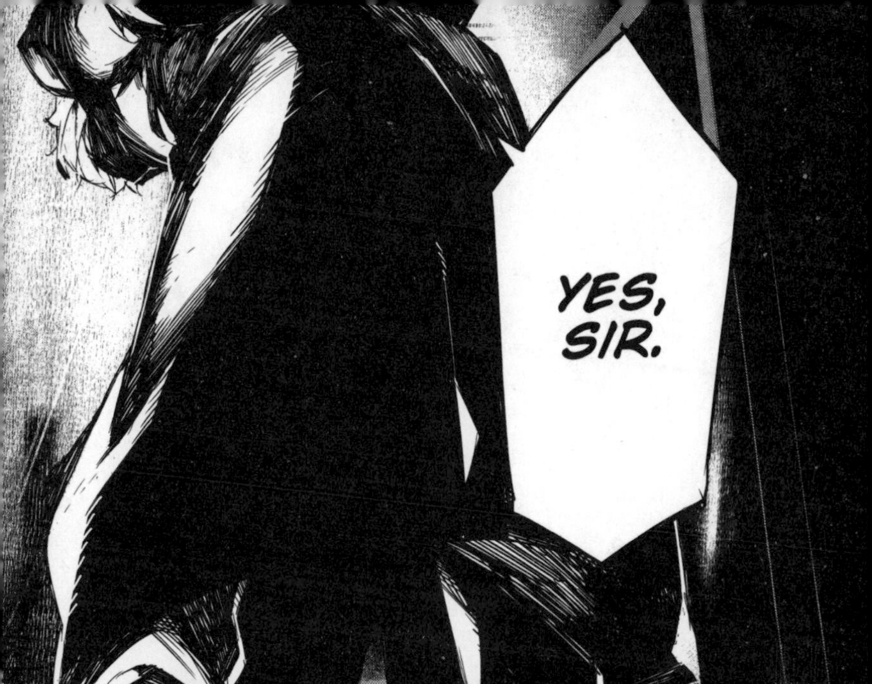
YES, SIR.
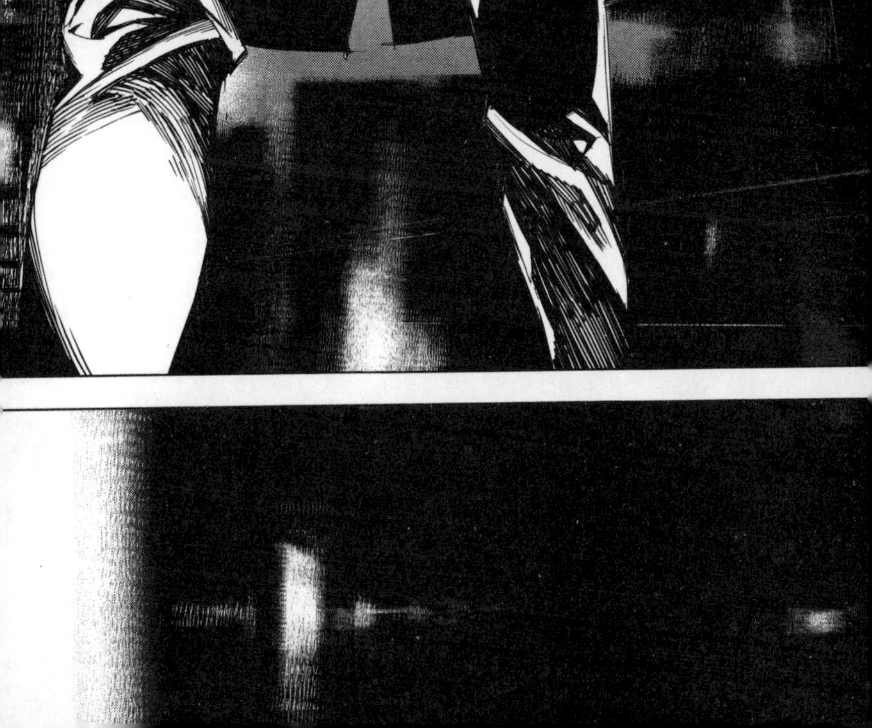

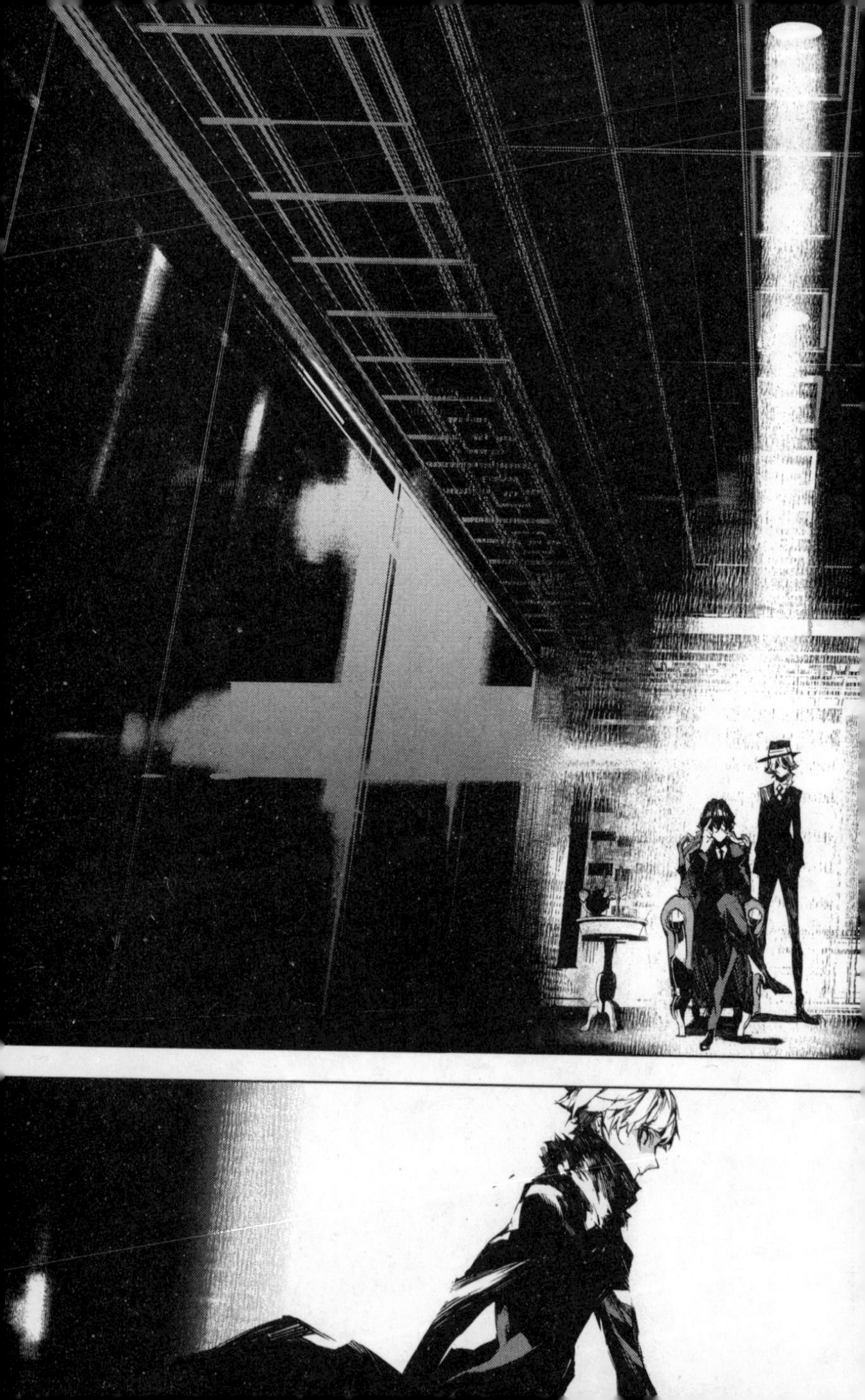

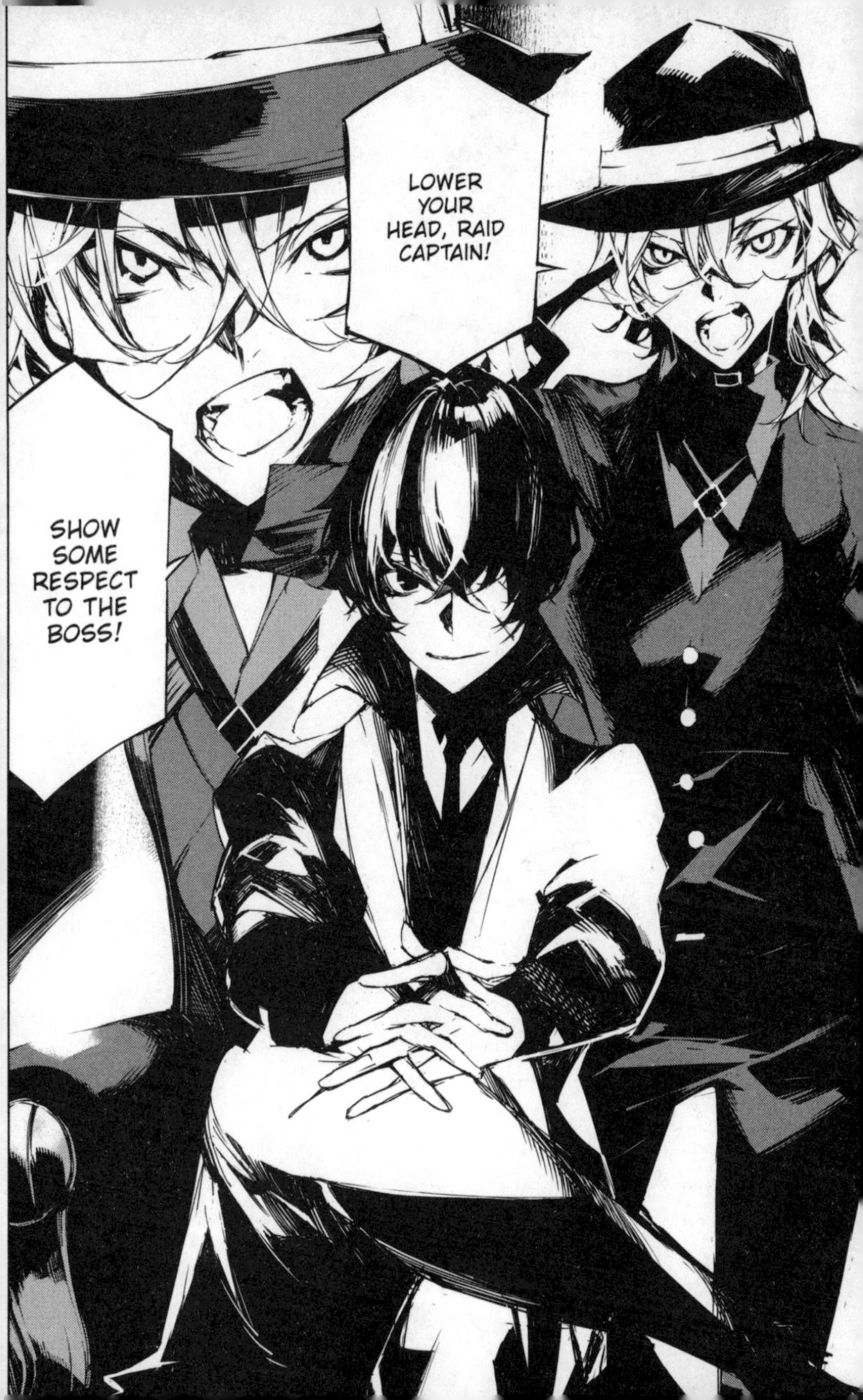
LOWER YOUR HEAD, RAID CAPTAIN!
SHOW SOME RESPECT TO THE BOSS!

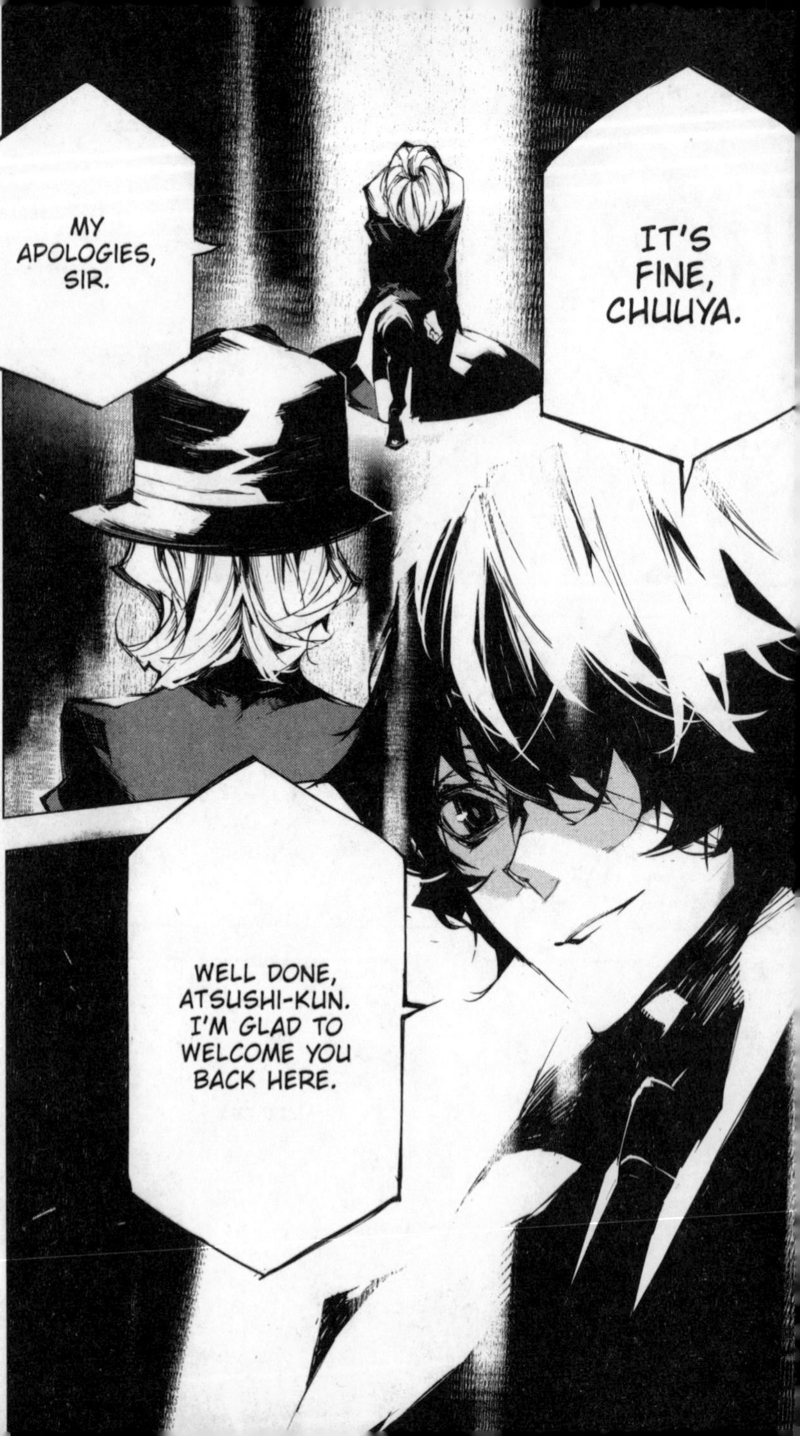
IT'S FINE, CHUUYA.
MY APOLOGIES, SIR.
WELL DONE, ATSUSHI-KUN. I'M GLAD TO WELCOME YOU BACK HERE.

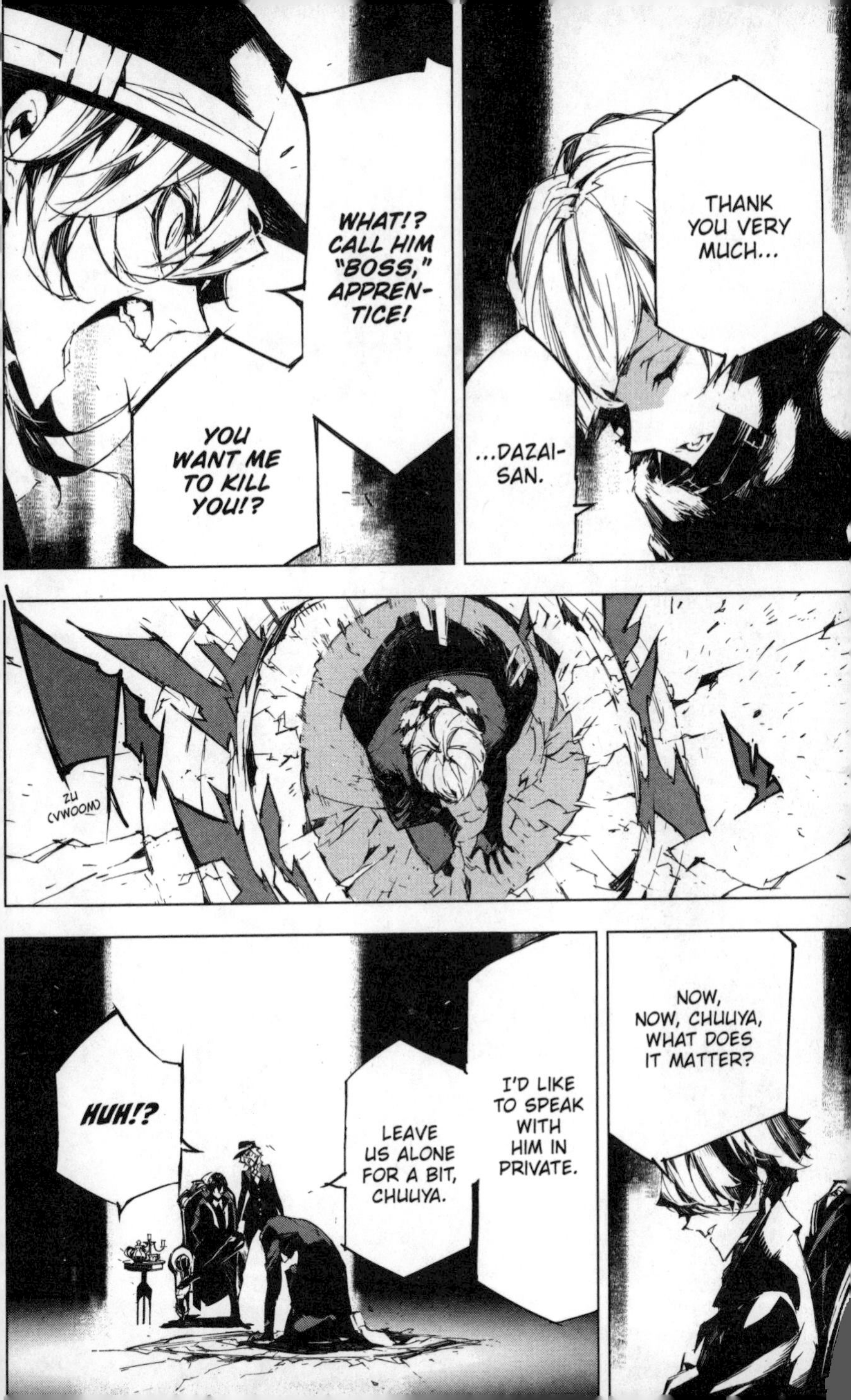
THANK YOU VERY MUCH...
...DAZAI-SAN.
WHAT!? CALL HIM "BOSS," APPRENTICE!
YOU WANT ME TO KILL YOU!?
ZU (VWOOM)
NOW, NOW, CHUUYA, WHAT DOES IT MATTER?
I'D LIKE TO SPEAK WITH HIM IN PRIVATE.
LEAVE US ALONE FOR A BIT, CHUUYA.
HUH!?

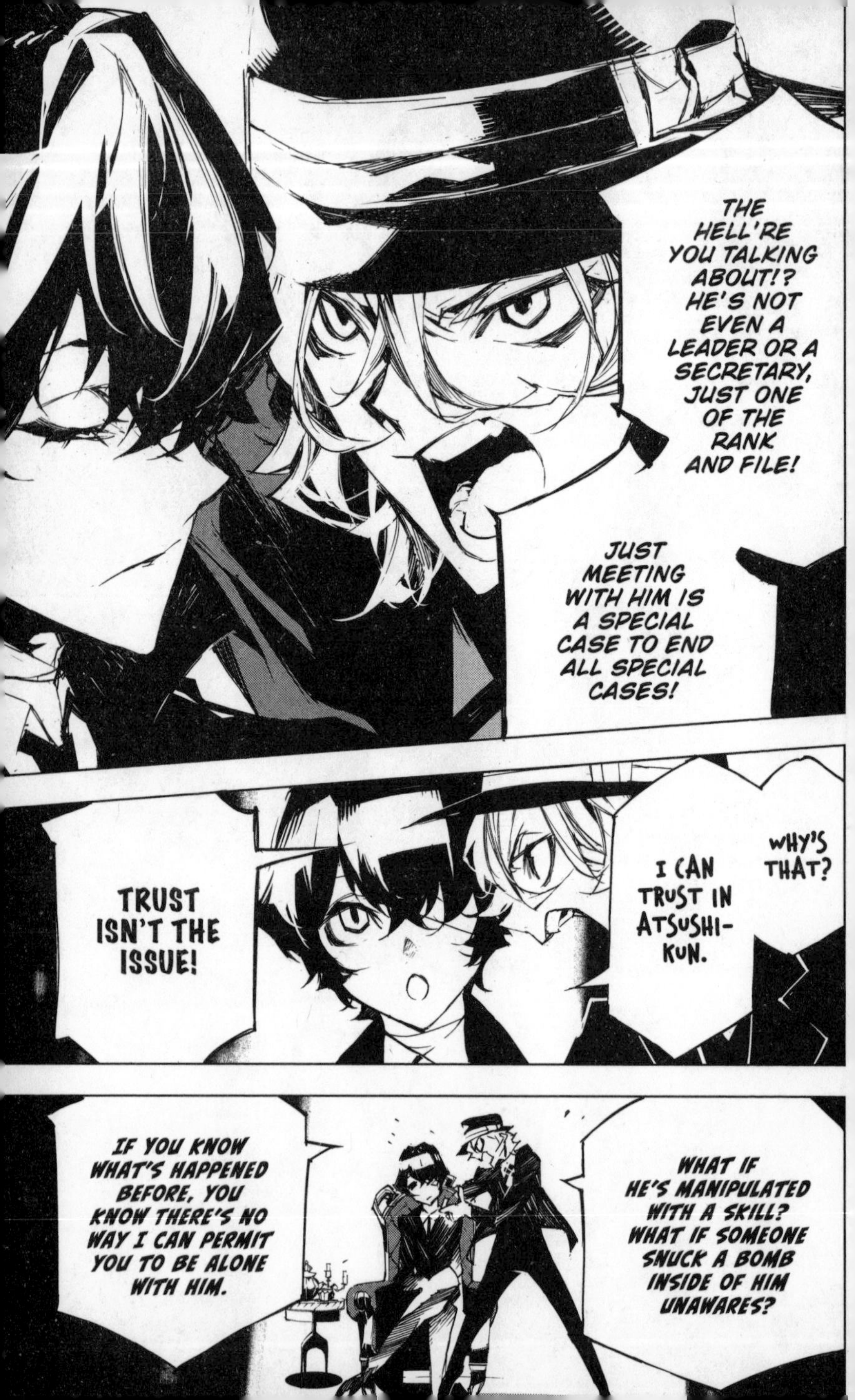
THE HELL'RE YOU TALKING ABOUT!? HE'S NOT EVEN A LEADER OR A SECRETARY, JUST ONE OF THE RANK AND FILE!
JUST MEETING WITH HIM IS A SPECIAL CASE TO END ALL SPECIAL CASES!
WHY'S THAT?
I CAN TRUST IN ATSUSHI-KUN.
TRUST ISN'T THE ISSUE!
WHAT IF HE'S MANIPULATED WITH A SKILL? WHAT IF SOMEONE SNUCK A BOMB INSIDE OF HIM UNAWARES?
IF YOU KNOW WHAT'S HAPPENED BEFORE, YOU KNOW THERE'S NO WAY I CAN PERMIT YOU TO BE ALONE WITH HIM.

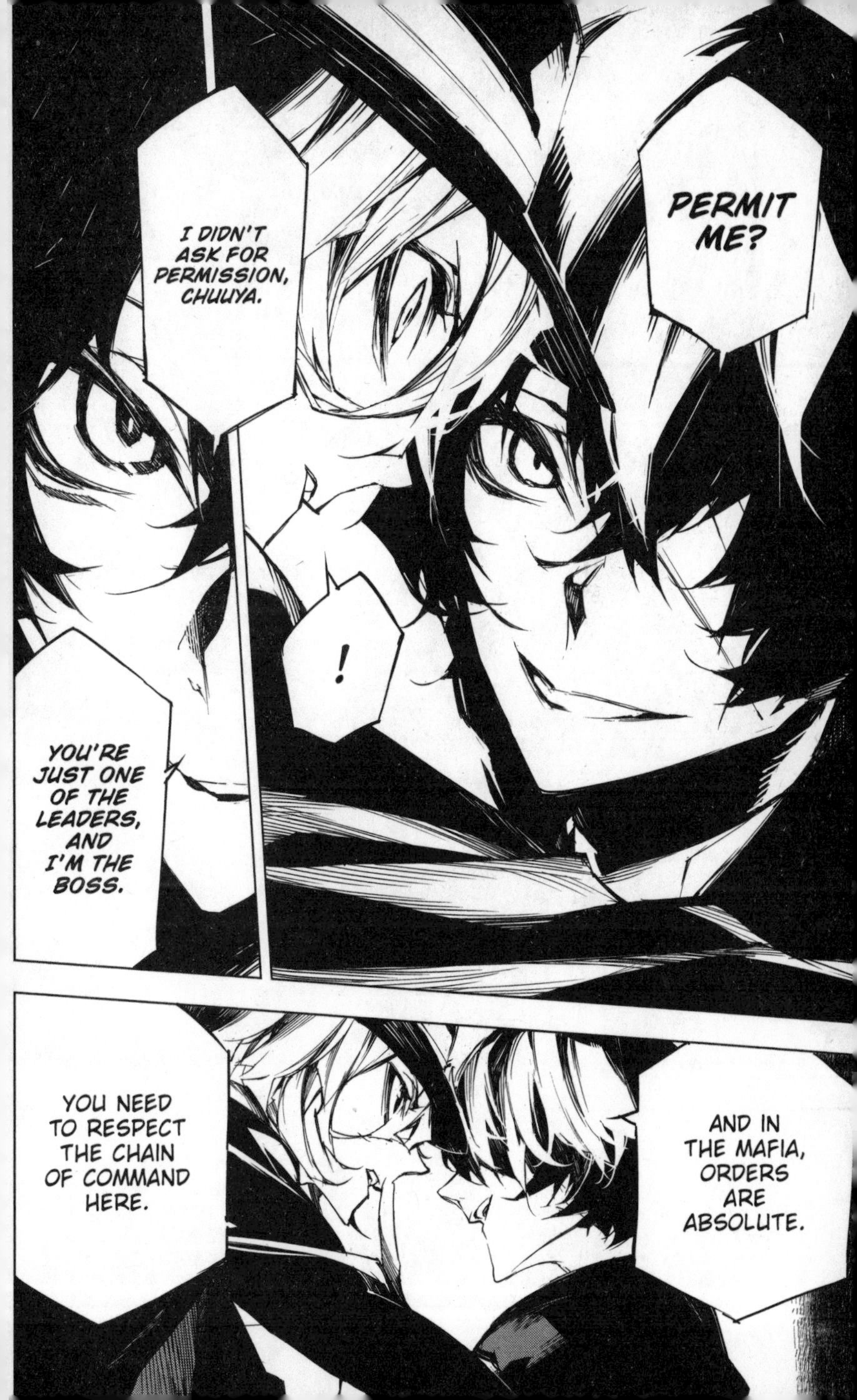
PERMIT ME?
I DIDN'T ASK FOR PERMISSION, CHUUYA.
!
YOU'RE JUST ONE OF THE LEADERS, AND I'M THE BOSS.
AND IN THE MAFIA, ORDERS ARE ABSOLUTE.
YOU NEED TO RESPECT THE CHAIN OF COMMAND HERE.

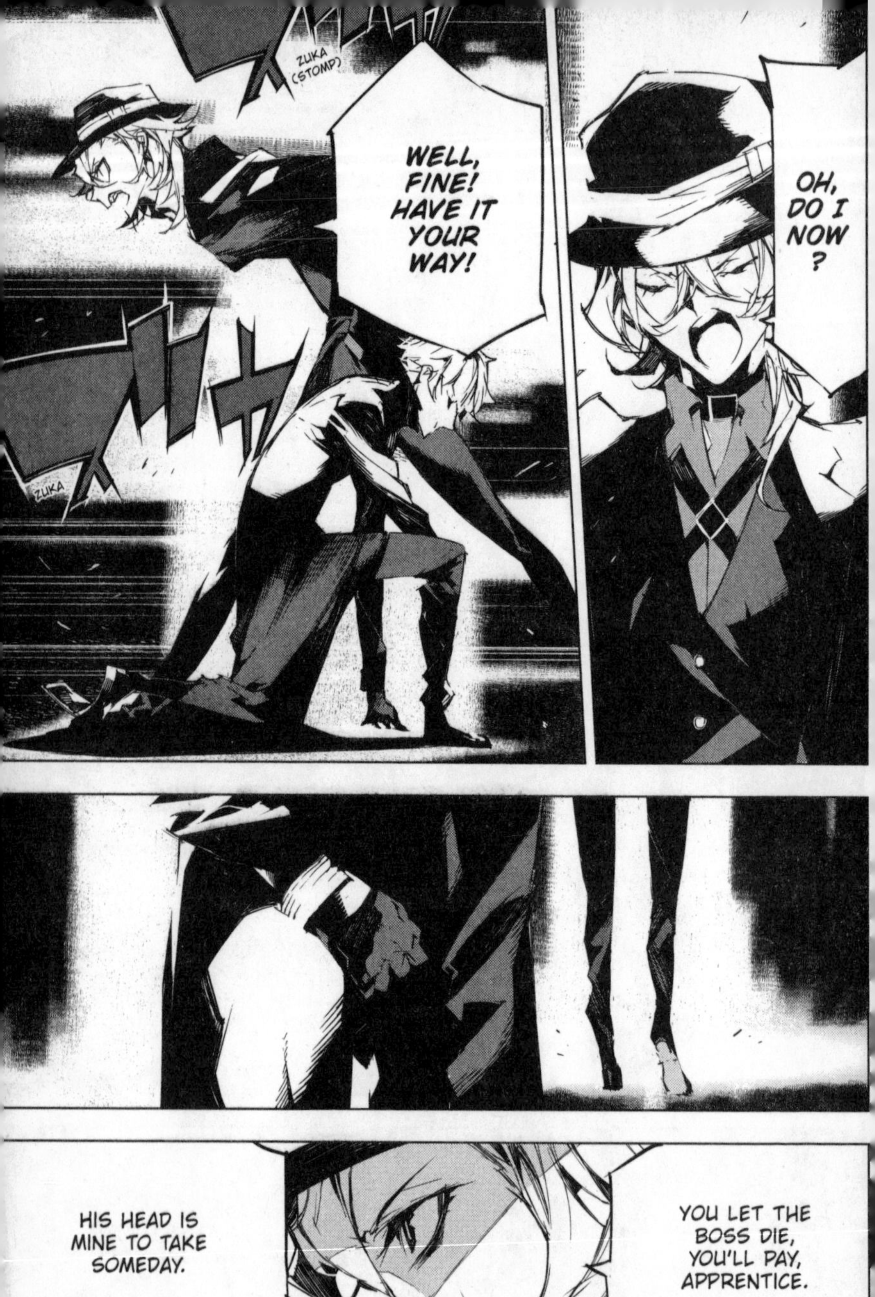
OH, DO I NOW?
WELL, FINE! HAVE IT YOUR WAY!
ZUKA (STOMP)
ZUKA
YOU LET THE BOSS DIE, YOU'LL PAY, APPRENTICE.
HIS HEAD IS MINE TO TAKE SOMEDAY.

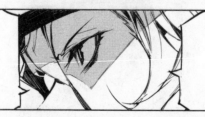

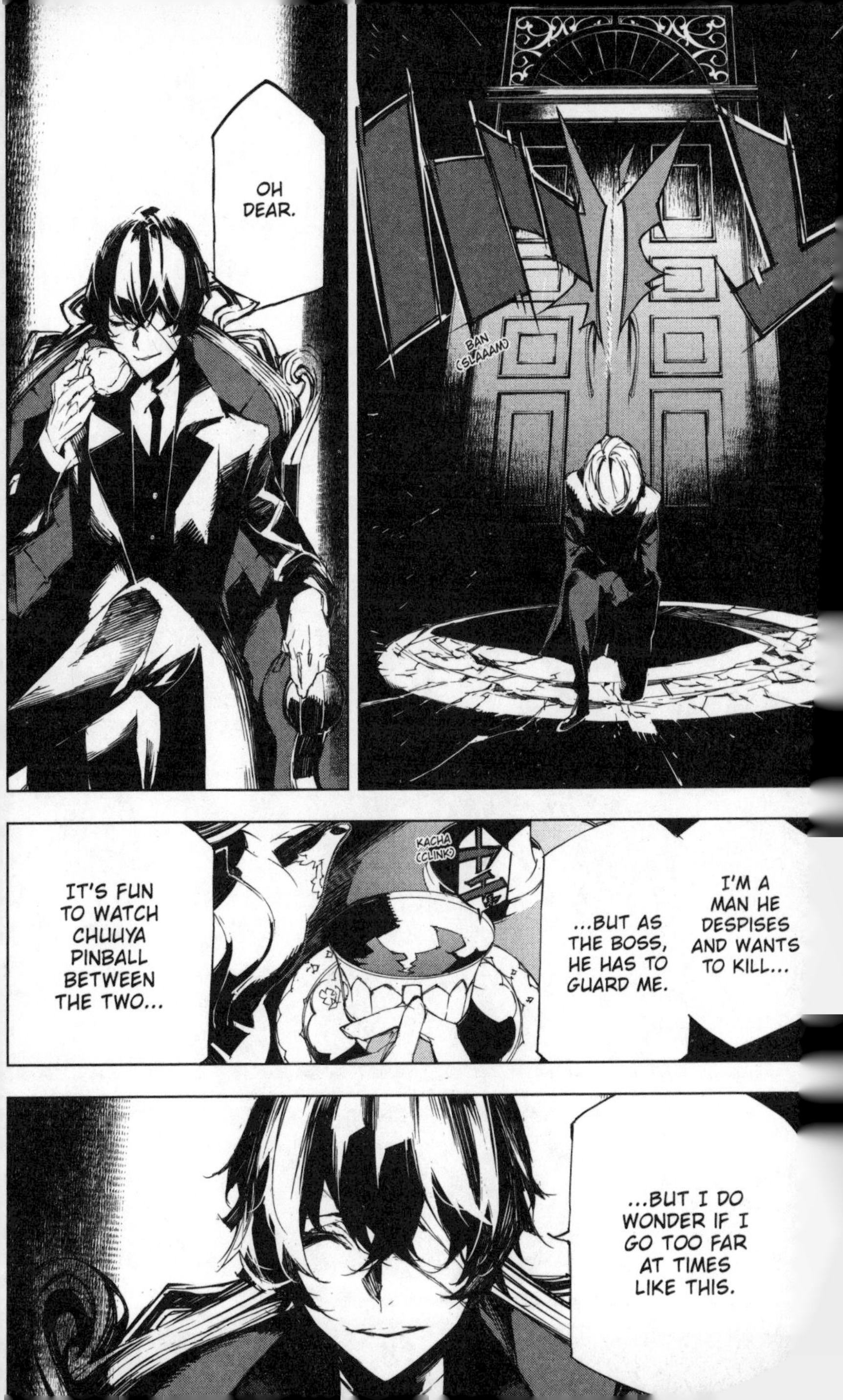
BAN (SLAAAM)
OH DEAR.
I'M A MAN HE DESPISES AND WANTS TO KILL...
...BUT AS THE BOSS, HE HAS TO GUARD ME.
KACHA (CLINK)
IT'S FUN TO WATCH CHUUYA PINBALL BETWEEN THE TWO...
...BUT I DO WONDER IF I GO TOO FAR AT TIMES LIKE THIS.

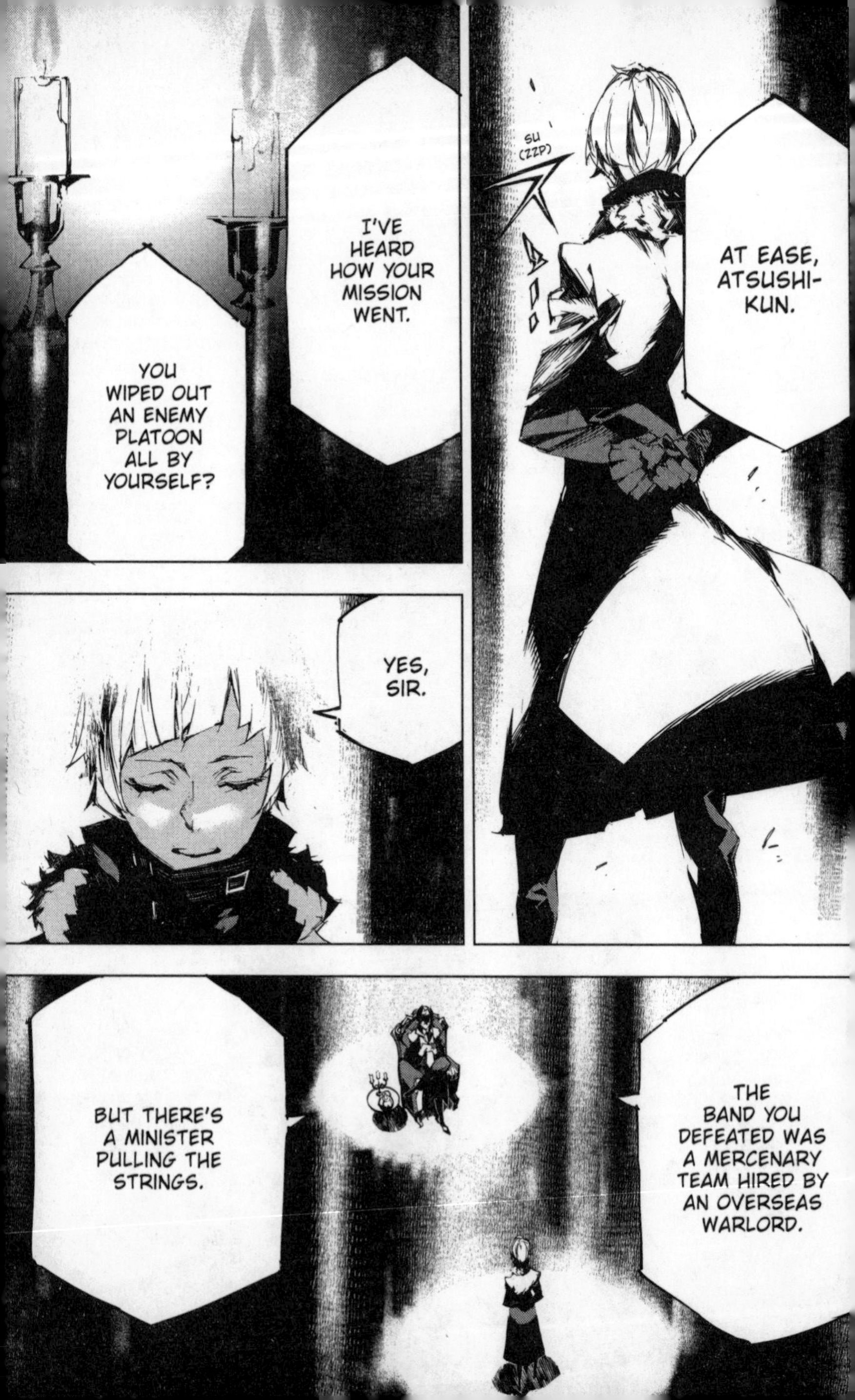
AT EASE, ATSUSHI-KUN.
SU (ZZP)
I'VE HEARD HOW YOUR MISSION WENT.
YOU WIPED OUT AN ENEMY PLATOON ALL BY YOURSELF?
YES, SIR.
THE BAND YOU DEFEATED WAS A MERCENARY TEAM HIRED BY AN OVERSEAS WARLORD.
BUT THERE'S A MINISTER PULLING THE STRINGS.

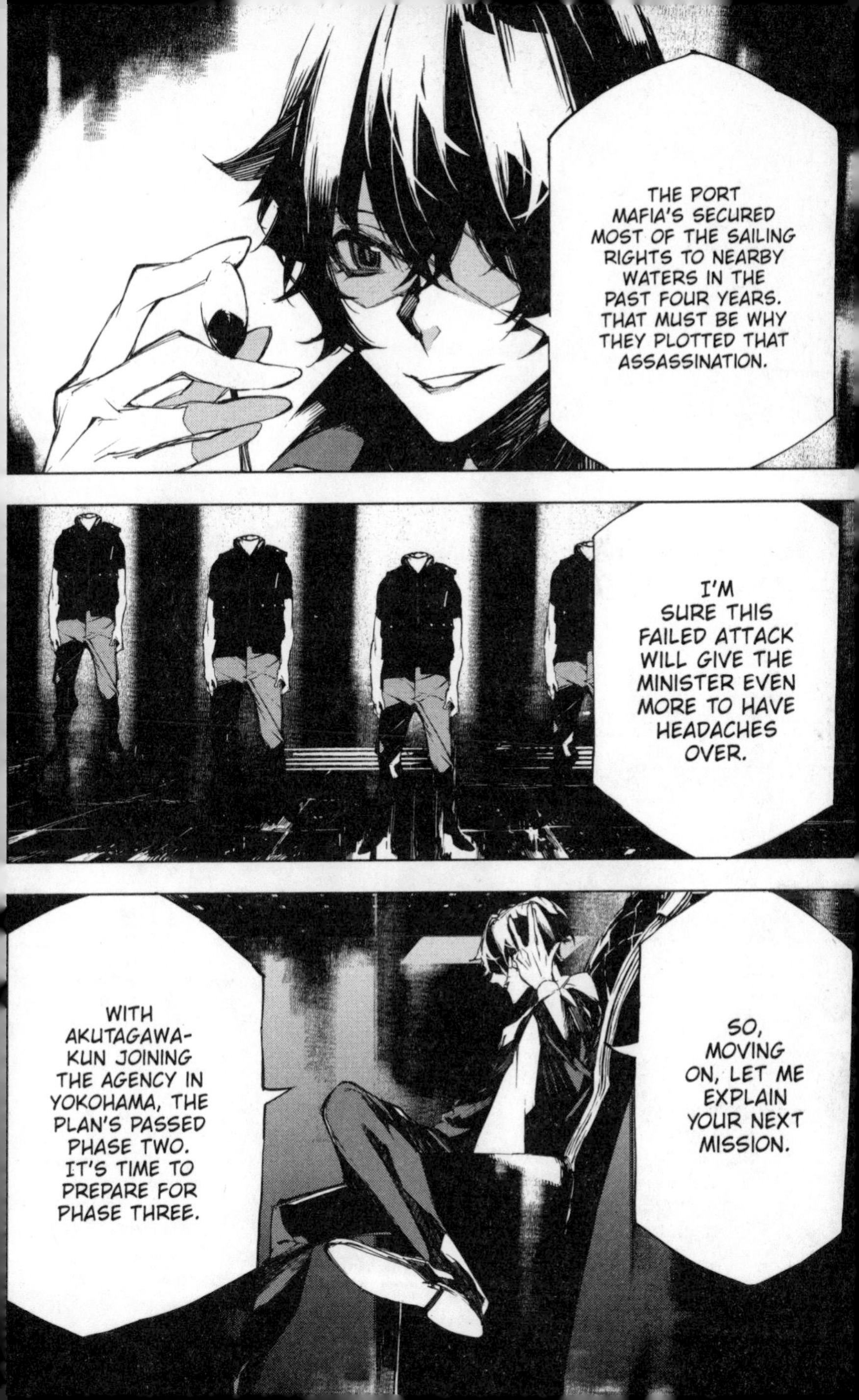
THE PORT MAFIA'S SECURED MOST OF THE SAILING RIGHTS TO NEARBY WATERS IN THE PAST FOUR YEARS. THAT MUST BE WHY THEY PLOTTED THAT ASSASSINATION.
I'M SURE THIS FAILED ATTACK WILL GIVE THE MINISTER EVEN MORE TO HAVE HEADACHES OVER.
SO, MOVING ON, LET ME EXPLAIN YOUR NEXT MISSION.
WITH AKUTAGAWA-KUN JOINING THE AGENCY IN YOKOHAMA, THE PLAN'S PASSED PHASE TWO. IT'S TIME TO PREPARE FOR PHASE THREE.

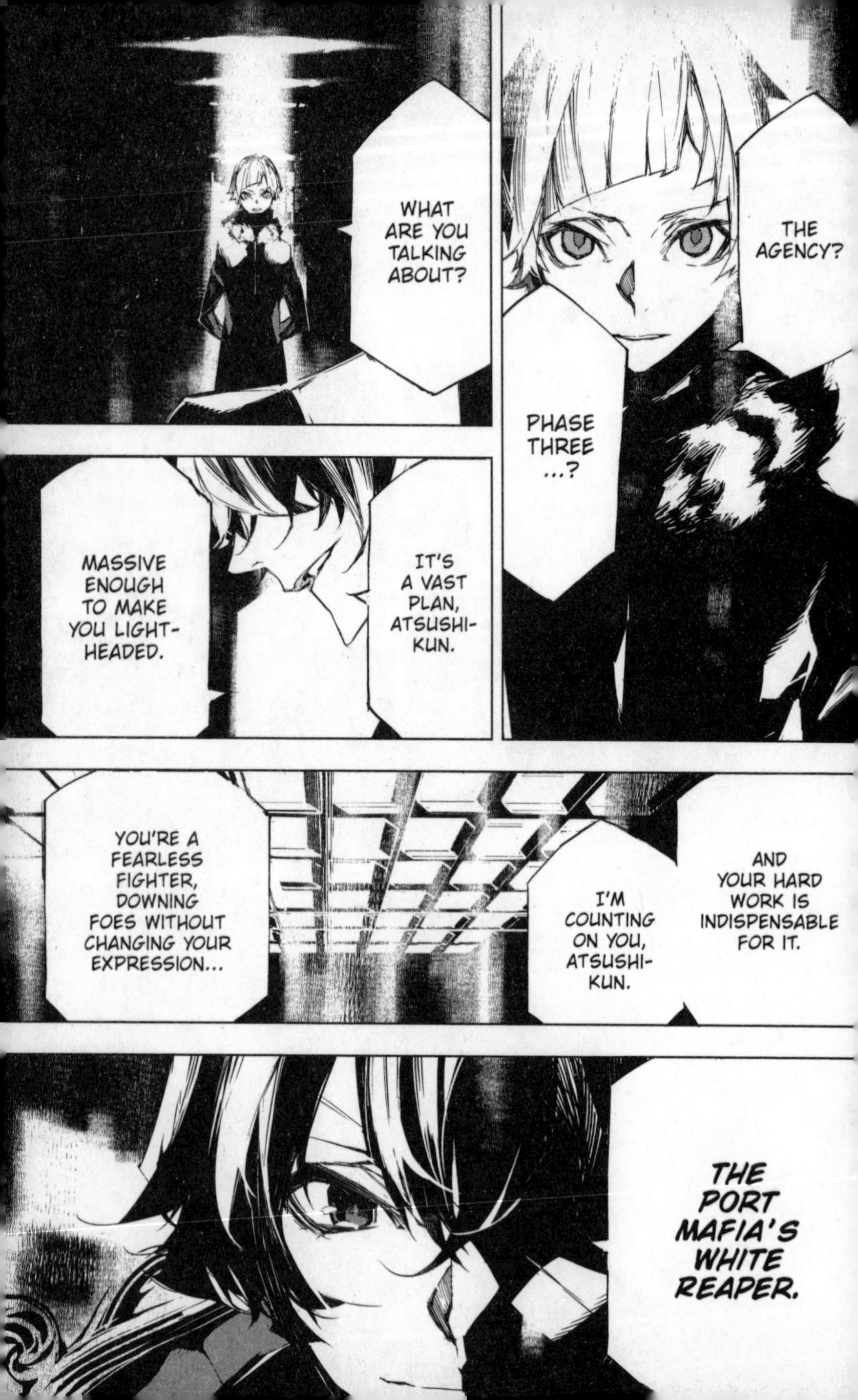
THE AGENCY?
PHASE THREE ...?
WHAT ARE YOU TALKING ABOUT?
IT'S A VAST PLAN, ATSUSHI-KUN.
MASSIVE ENOUGH TO MAKE YOU LIGHT-HEADED.
AND YOUR HARD WORK IS INDISPENSABLE FOR IT.
I'M COUNTING ON YOU, ATSUSHI-KUN.
YOU'RE A FEARLESS FIGHTER, DOWNING FOES WITHOUT CHANGING YOUR EXPRESSION...
THE PORT MAFIA'S WHITE REAPER.

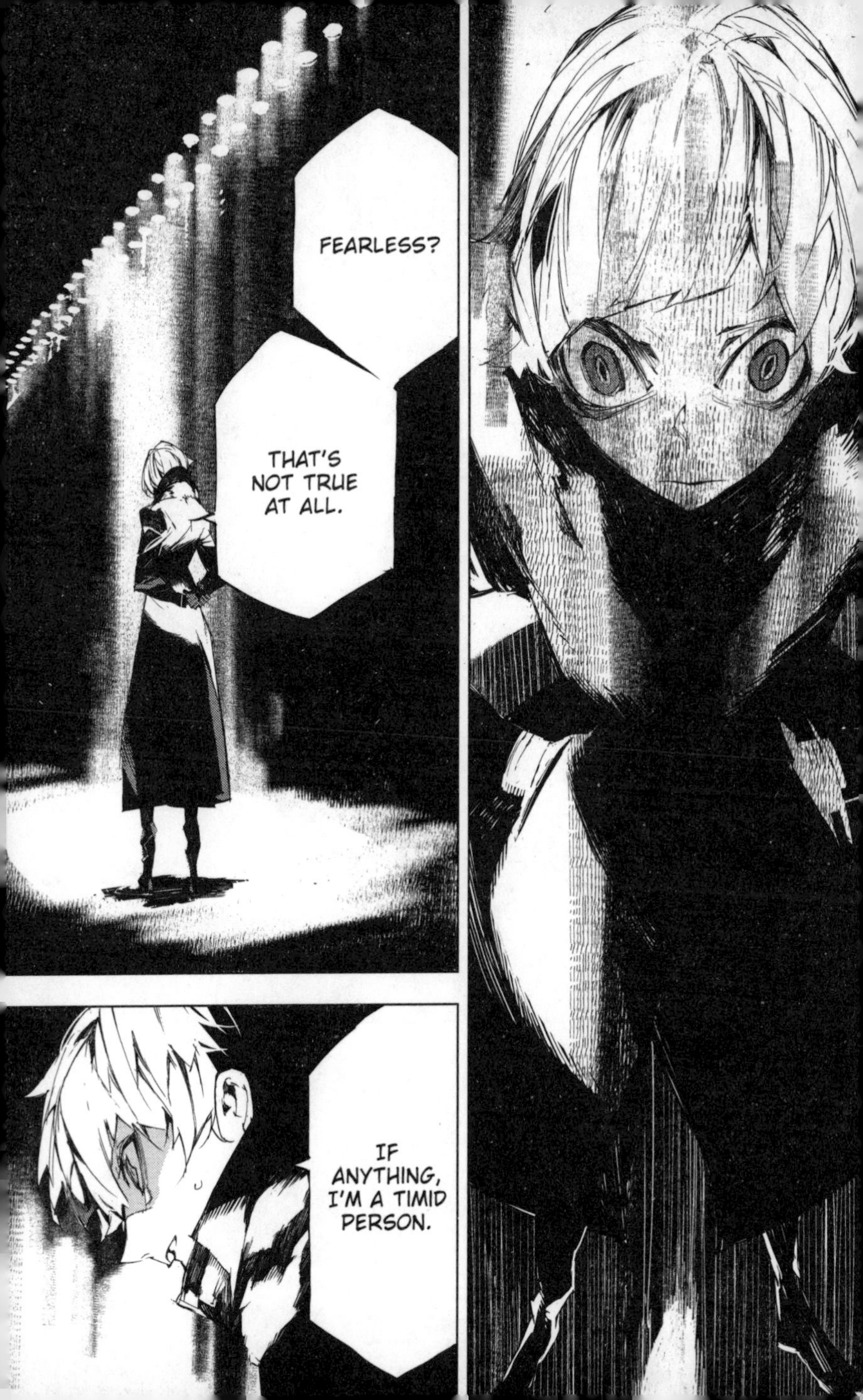
FEARLESS?
THAT'S NOT TRUE AT ALL.
IF ANYTHING, I'M A TIMID PERSON.

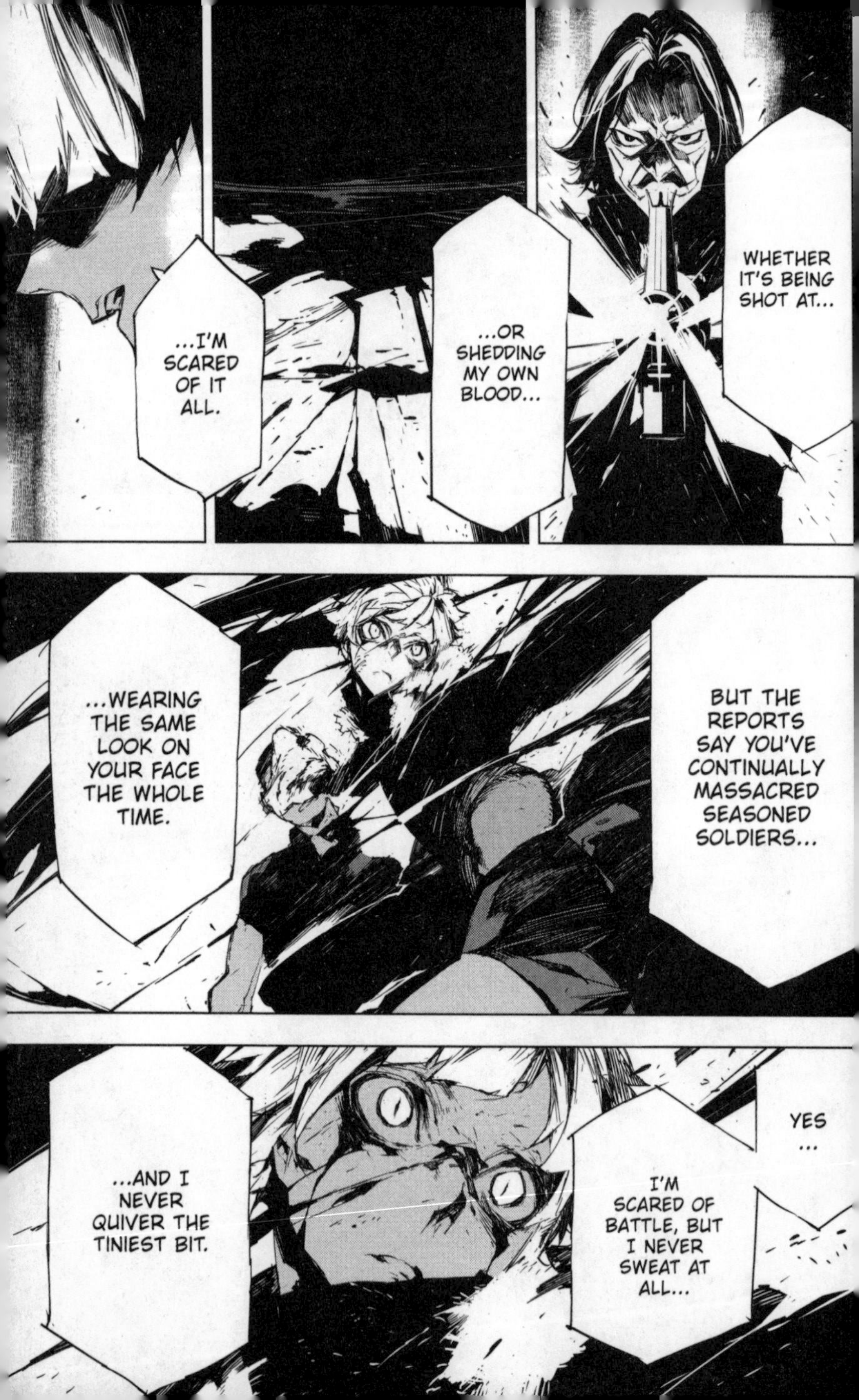
WHETHER IT'S BEING SHOT AT...
...OR SHEDDING MY OWN BLOOD...
...I'M SCARED OF IT ALL.
BUT THE REPORTS SAY YOU'VE CONTINUALLY MASSACRED SEASONED SOLDIERS...
...WEARING THE SAME LOOK ON YOUR FACE THE WHOLE TIME.
YES...
I'M SCARED OF BATTLE, BUT I NEVER SWEAT AT ALL...
...AND I NEVER QUIVER THE TINIEST BIT.

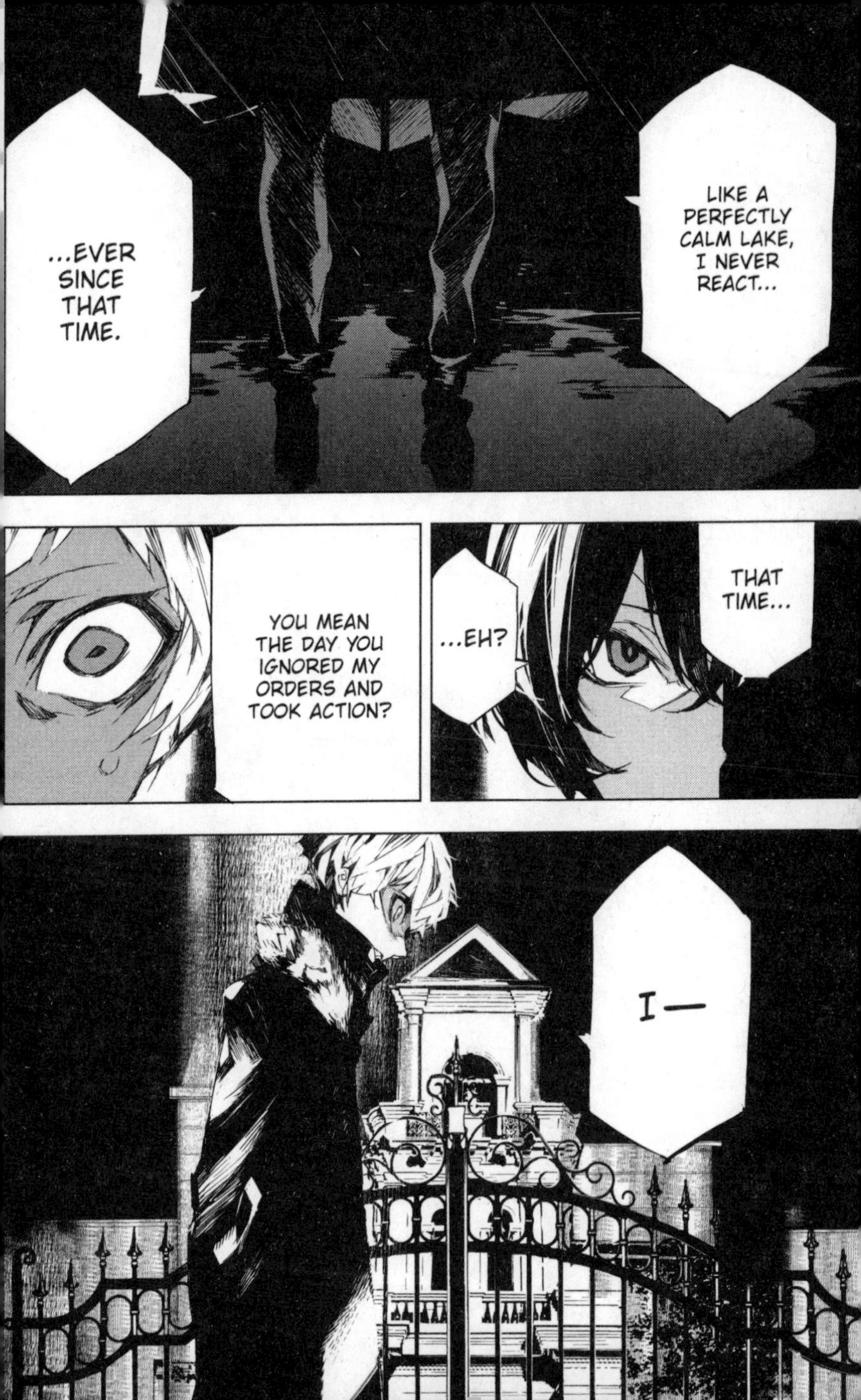
LIKE A PERFECTLY CALM LAKE, I NEVER REACT...
...EVER SINCE THAT TIME.
THAT TIME...
...EH?
YOU MEAN THE DAY YOU IGNORED MY ORDERS AND TOOK ACTION?
I—

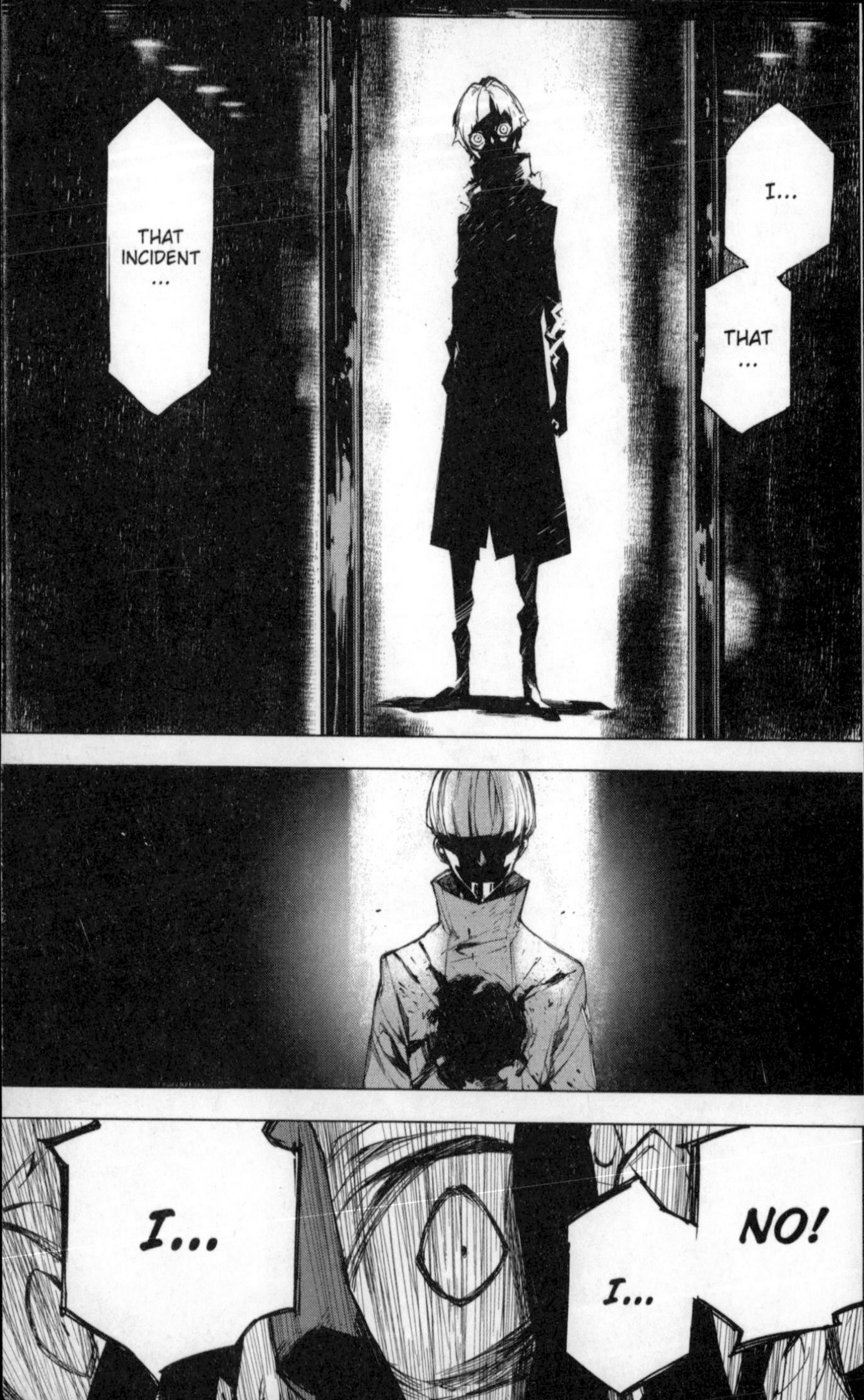

I...
THAT...
THAT INCIDENT...
NO!
I...
I...

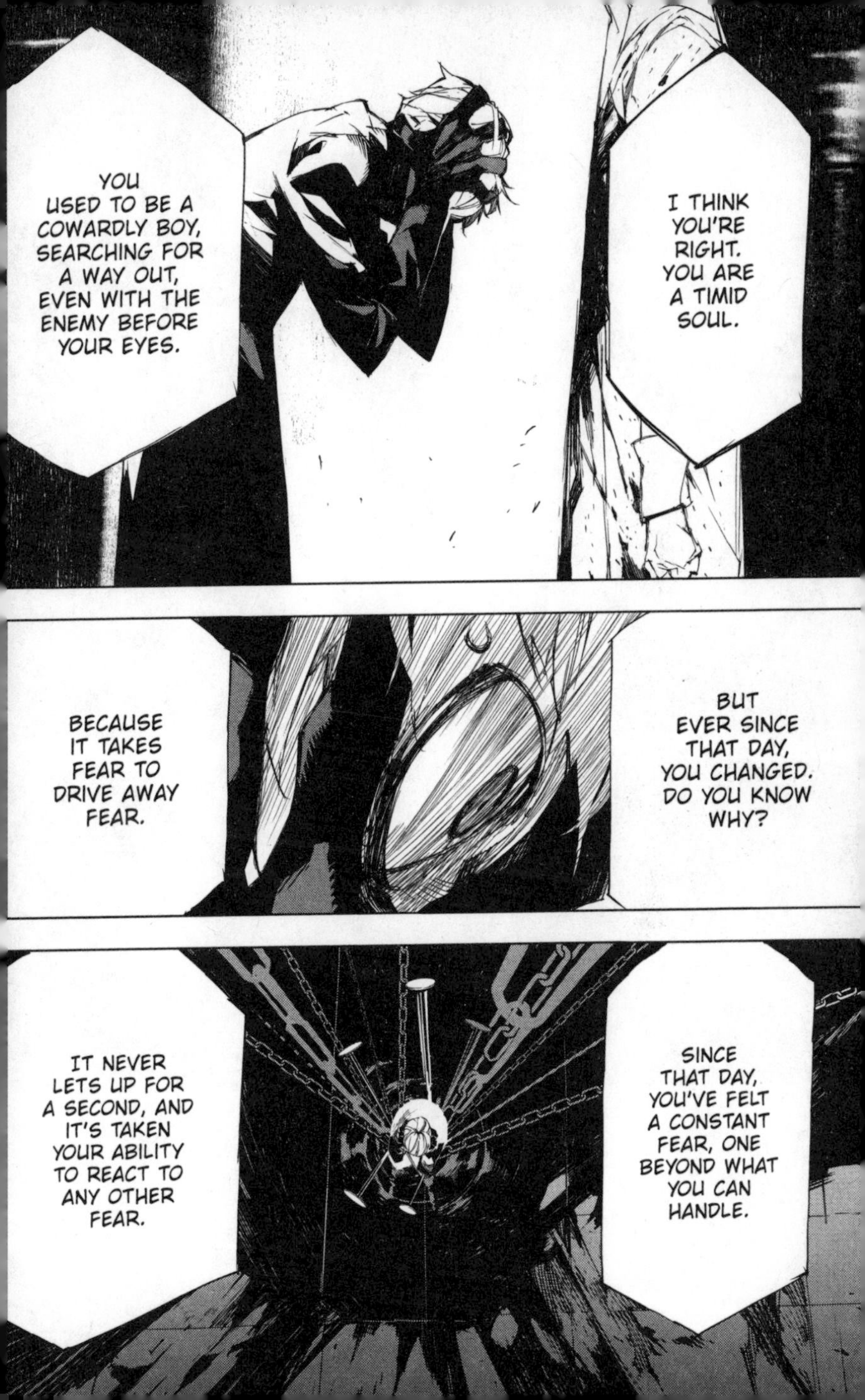
I THINK YOU'RE RIGHT. YOU ARE A TIMID SOUL.
YOU USED TO BE A COWARDLY BOY, SEARCHING FOR A WAY OUT, EVEN WITH THE ENEMY BEFORE YOUR EYES.
BUT EVER SINCE THAT DAY, YOU CHANGED. DO YOU KNOW WHY?
BECAUSE IT TAKES FEAR TO DRIVE AWAY FEAR.
SINCE THAT DAY, YOU'VE FELT A CONSTANT FEAR, ONE BEYOND WHAT YOU CAN HANDLE.
IT NEVER LETS UP FOR A SECOND, AND IT'S TAKEN YOUR ABILITY TO REACT TO ANY OTHER FEAR.

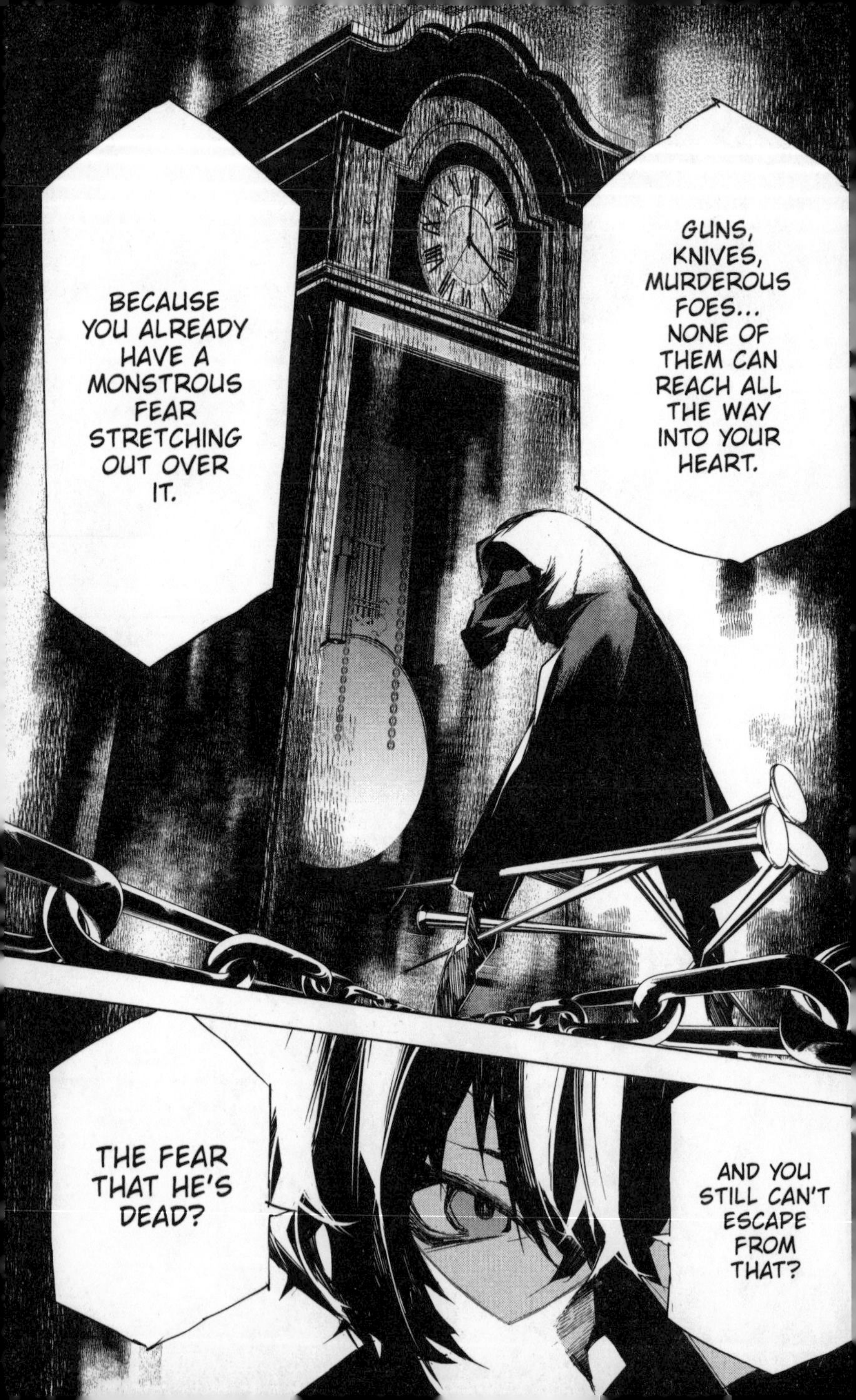
GUNS, KNIVES, MURDEROUS FOES... NONE OF THEM CAN REACH ALL THE WAY INTO YOUR HEART.
BECAUSE YOU ALREADY HAVE A MONSTROUS FEAR STRETCHING OUT OVER IT.
AND YOU STILL CAN'T ESCAPE FROM THAT?
THE FEAR THAT HE'S DEAD?

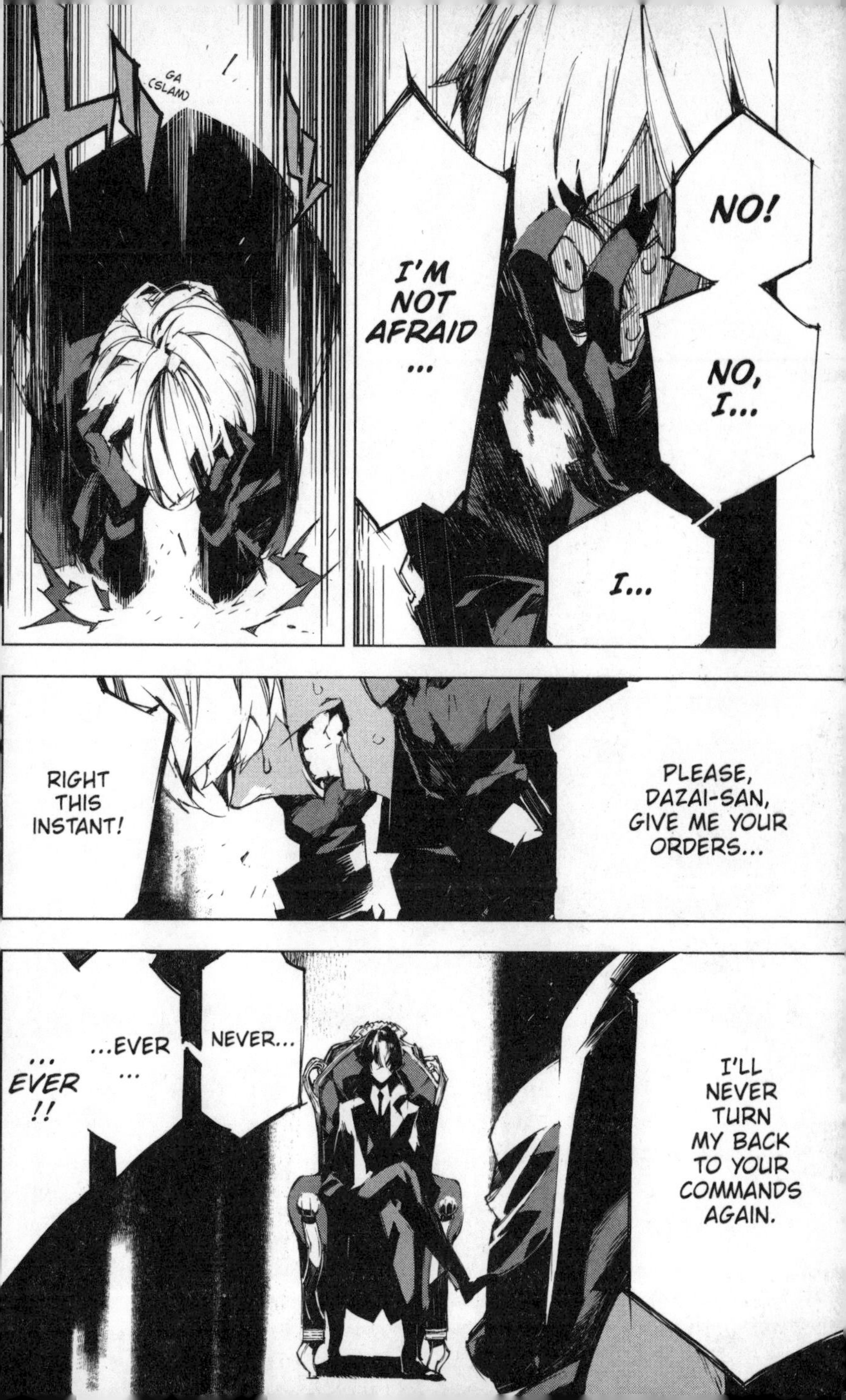
NO!
NO, I...
I'M NOT AFRAID ...
I...
GA (SLAM)
PLEASE, DAZAI-SAN, GIVE ME YOUR ORDERS...
RIGHT THIS INSTANT!
I'LL NEVER TURN MY BACK TO YOUR COMMANDS AGAIN.
NEVER...
...EVER ...
... EVER !!

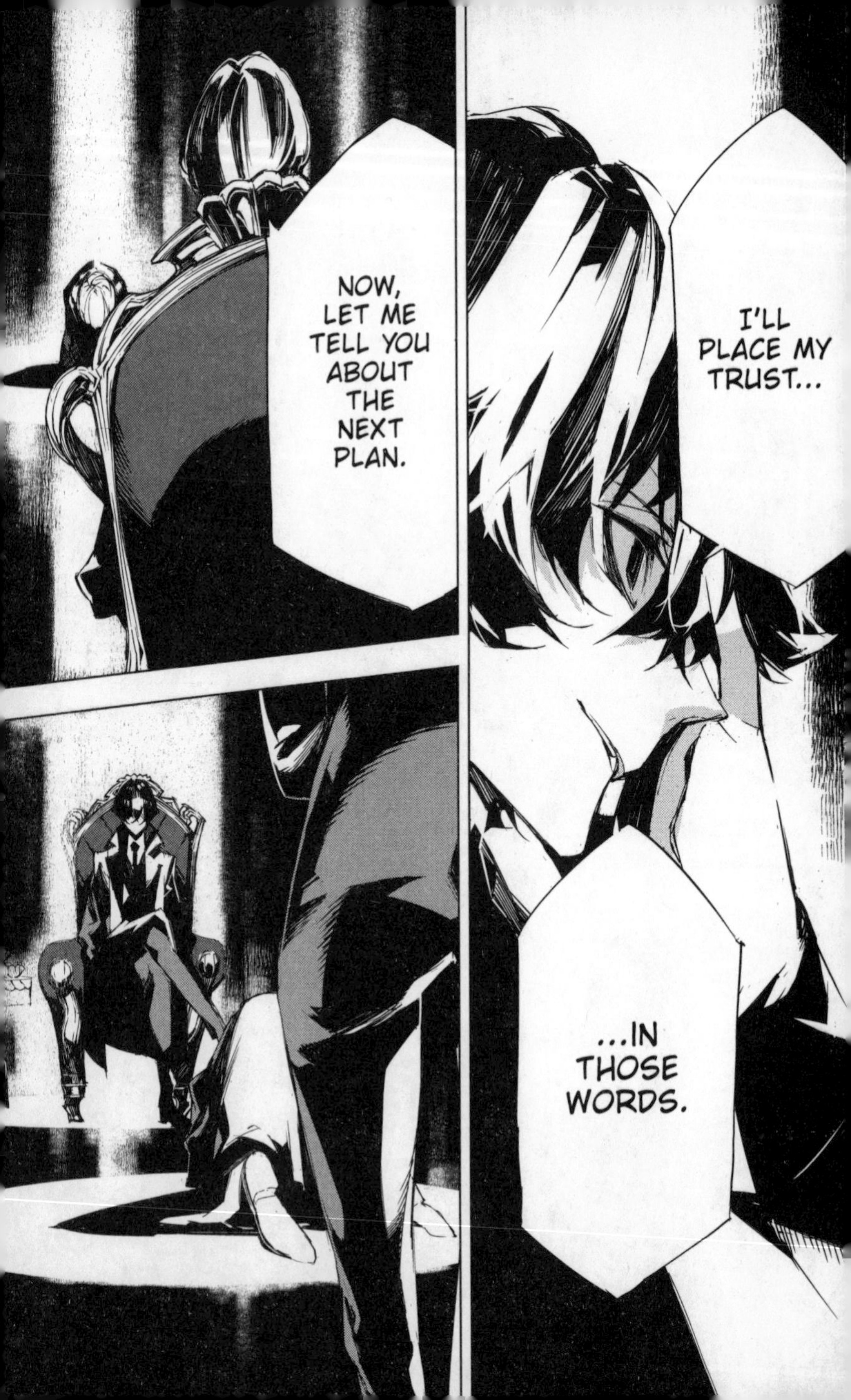
I'LL PLACE MY TRUST...
...IN THOSE WORDS.
NOW, LET ME TELL YOU ABOUT THE NEXT PLAN.

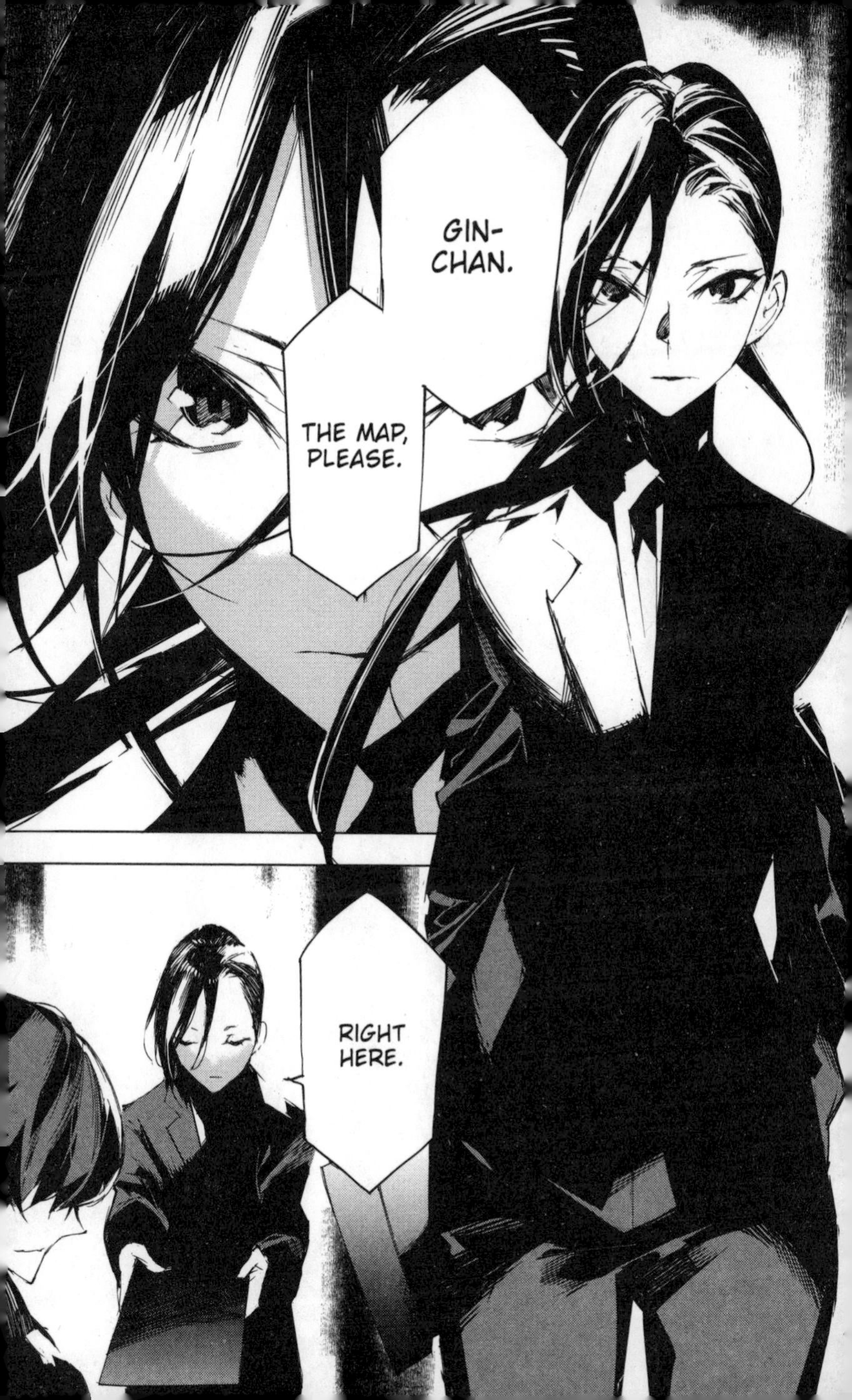
GIN-CHAN.
THE MAP, PLEASE.
RIGHT HERE.

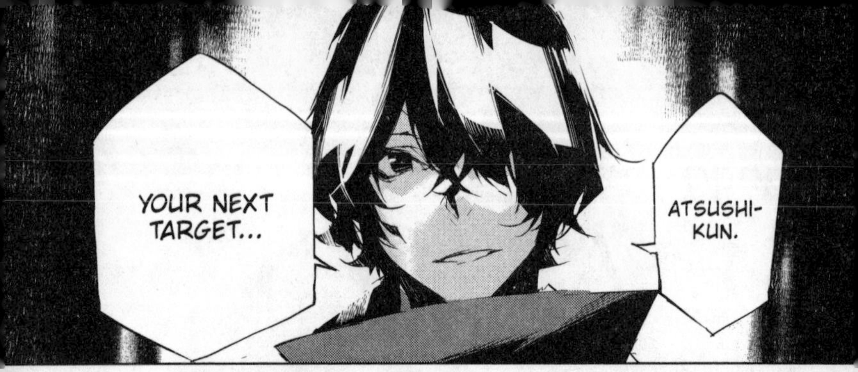
YOUR NEXT TARGET...
ATSUSHI-KUN.

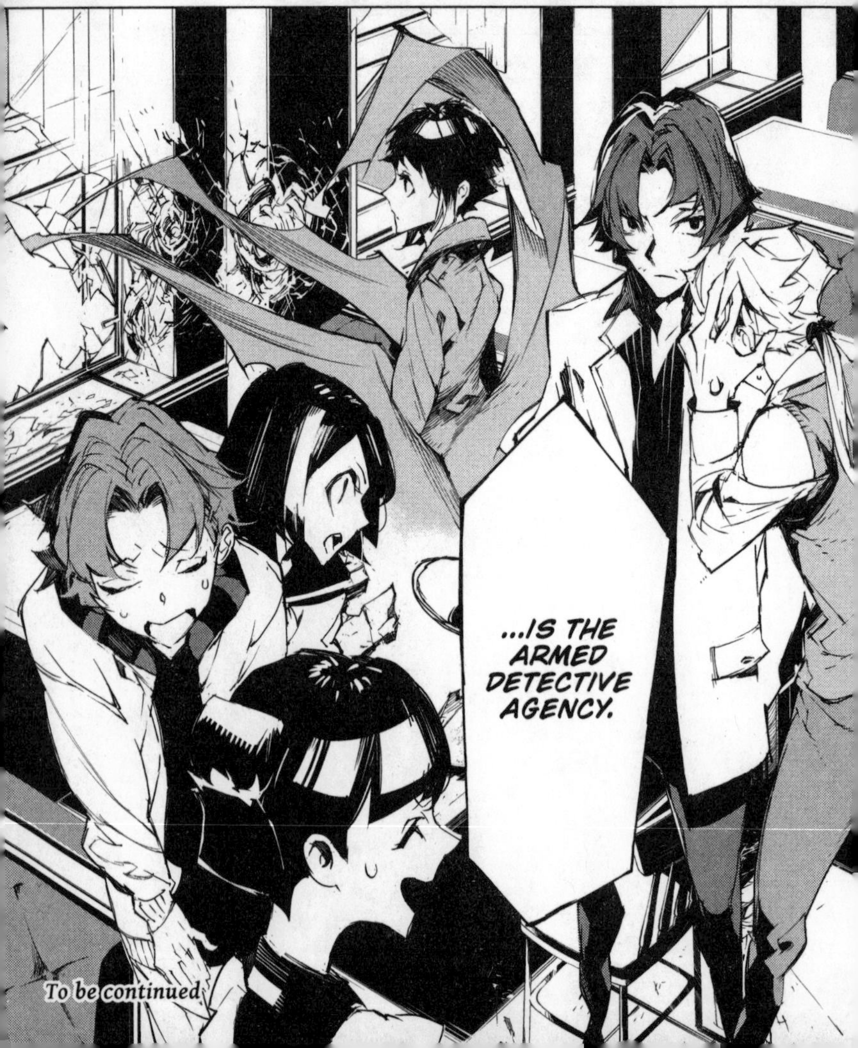
...IS THE ARMED DETECTIVE AGENCY.
To be continued

Bungo Stray Dogs

BEAST

THANK YOU VERY
MUCH FOR BUYING
VOLUME 1!! ♪

I HOPE YOU HAD A LOT
OF FUN WITH IT.

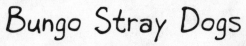

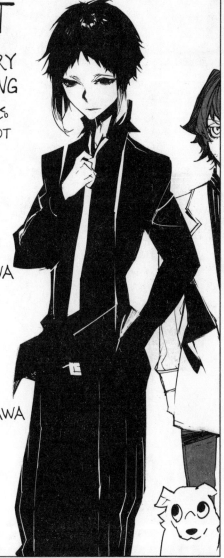

ORIGINAL STORY
KAFKA ASAGIRI

CHARACTER DESIGN
SANGO HARUKAWA

EDITOR
K-NAGA

ART
SHIWASU HOSHIKAWA

ART ASSISTANCE
ODA

Translation Notes

Page 56

Houjicha is a type of Japanese green tea. Unlike most other types of tea, it's roasted after steaming, removing much of the bitterness, turning the leaves reddish-brown, and giving it a distinct earthy aroma.

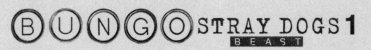

BUNGO STRAY DOGS 1 BEAST

Story: KAFKA ASAGIRI   Art: SHIWASU HOSHIKAWA
Character Design: SANGO HARUKAWA

Translation: Kevin Gifford   †   Lettering: Bianca Pistillo

BUNGO STRAY DOGS: BEAST Volume 1
©Kafka Asagiri 2020
©Shiwasu Hoshikawa 2020
©Sango Harukawa 2020
First published in Japan in 2020 by KADOKAWA CORPORATION, Tokyo.
English translation rights arranged with KADOKAWA CORPORATION, Tokyo through Tuttle-Mori Agency, Inc., Tokyo.

English translation © 2021 by Yen Press, LLC

Yen Press
150 West 30th Street, 19th Floor
New York, NY 10001

Visit us at yenpress.com
facebook.com/yenpress
twitter.com/yenpress
yenpress.tumblr.com
instagram.com/yenpress

D0920741

First Yen Press Edition: August 2021

Yen Press is an imprint of Yen Press, LLC.
The Yen Press name and logo are trademarks of Yen Press, LLC.

The publisher is not responsible for websites (or their content) that are not owned by the publisher.

Library of Congress Control Number: 2021941159

ISBNs: 978-1-9753-2567-1 (paperback)
       978-1-9753-2568-8 (ebook)

10 9 8 7 6 5 4 3 2 1

WOR

Printed in the United States of America